Discover The Hidden Secrets and The Main Conspiracy Theories. Destroy The New World Order and Take The Millennial Kingdom By Force

Simon Smith

The information herein is provided for educational purposes exclusively and is universal. The presentation of the data is without contractual agreement or any kind of warranty assurance.

All trademarks inside this book are for clarifying purposes only and are possessed by the owners themselves, not allied with this document.

Disclaimer

All erudition supplied in this book is specified for educational and academic purposes only. The author is not in any way responsible for any outcomes that emerge from utilizing this book. Constructive efforts have been made to render information that is both precise and effective. Still, the author is not to be held answerable for the accuracy or use/misuse of this information.

Foreword

I will like to thank you for taking the very first step of trusting me and deciding to purchase/read this life-transforming book. Thanks for investing your time and resources on this product.

I can assure you of precise outcomes if you will diligently follow the specific blueprint I lay bare in the information handbook you are currently checking out. It has transformed lives, and I firmly believe it will equally change your own life too.

All the information I provided in this Do It Yourself piece is easy to absorb and practice.

CHAPTER ONE

Understanding The Meaning Of Qanon

QAnon is a far-right conspiracy concept asserting that a cabal of Satan-worshiping pedophiles running international sex-trafficking acting against President Donald Trump. He is battling them, leading to mass apprehension of reporters and also political leaders. None of this theory part is based upon truth.

In October 2017, a blog post stated the theory on the anonymous imageboard 4chan by "Q," who was likely an American person, which has turned out to be a group of people. Q proclaimed to have access to categorized info, including the Trump administration and also its opposition in the United States. NBC News uncovered that three individuals took the original Q message and broadened it throughout several media systems to construct internet followings for earnings. Q has accused a lot of liberal Hollywood actors, Democratic political leaders, and also upper-level authorities of being participants of the cabal. Q also declared that Trump feigned collusion with Russians to get Robert Mueller to join him in revealing the ring and avoiding a successful stroked'état by Barack Obama, Hillary Clinton, and George Soros. QAnon followers usually mark their social media networks posts with the hashtag #WWG 1WGA, signifying the motto "Where We Go One, We Go All."

QAnon followers began showing up at Trump reelection project rallies in August 2018. In the August 2019 rally, a guy hailing the crowd before Trump spoke used the QAnon adage "where we go one, we go all," later on, rejecting that it was a QAnon reference. This happened hours after the publication of news that the FBI had determined QAnon to be a possible resource of domestic terrorism, the very first time the company had so rated an edge conspiracy theory. According to a research carried out by Media Matters, as of August 2020, Trump had multiplied QAnon messaging at least 216 times by retweeting or talking about 129 QAnon-affiliated Twitter accounts, in some situations multiple times a day. Into 2020, the selection of QAnon followers was unclear; nonetheless, they had a massive existence on social networks, especially Twitter. Twitter banned thousands of QAnon-affiliated accounts and also modified its formulas to lower the theory's spread in June 2020. A Facebook analyst reported in August how he discovered numerous followers throughout countless pages and groups; Facebook acted to restrict and get rid of the QAnon task later on that month. Fans had also migrated to dedicated message boards such as EndChan as well as 8kun, where they gather to wage information warfare to affect the 2020 elections.

On October 30, 2016, a Twitter account posting white supremacist product which stated a New York lawful agent ran it improperly asserted that the New York City Police Department (NYPD) had uncovered a pedophilia ring linked to members of the Democratic Party while discovering Anthony Weiner's e-mails. Proponents of the concept had a look at the e-mails and declared they contained code words for pedophilia and also human trafficking. Advocates additionally proclaimed that Comet Ping Pong was a conference ground for Satanic routine misuse. The tale was later published on bogus news web sites, starting with Your News Wire, which mentioned a 4chan blog post earlier that year. The Your News Wire write-up was ultimately expanded by pro-Trump websites, including SubjectPolitics.com, which added the case that the NYPD had burglarized Hillary Clinton's residential property. The Conservative Daily Post declared that the Federal Bureau of Investigation had verified the concept.

Anons.

The majority believes an "anon" describes any type of unidentified or pseudonymous website poster. The concept of anons is proclaiming to divulge classified information, while a vital component of the QAnon conspiracy concept is never a part of it. Before Q, a lot of so-called anons also declared to have unique government accessibility.

An individual recognizing as "Q Clearance Patriot" originally appeared on the/ pol/ board of 4chan on October 28, 2017, posted in a thread entitled "Calm Before the Storm," a reference to Trump's puzzling summary of an occasion of United States army leaders he took part in as "the calm before the storm." "The Storm" is QAnon parlance for a brewing occasion when thousands of supposed suspects will be jailed and executed. The poster's username indicated that they hold Q clearance, a United States Department of Energy safety and security clearance needed to gain access to Top Secret information on nuclear tools and materials. An NBC News examination uncovered that in November 2017, two moderators of the board, "BaruchtheScribe" and also "Pamphlet Anon," connected to YouTuber Tracy Diaz to promote Qanon. The three after that produced a Reddit community (subreddit) "CBTS_Stream," which was necessary for spreading the theory. In March 2018, the subreddit, which had 20,000 members, was banned for "motivating or inciting violence and posting private and personal details." "Pamphlet Anon" after that introduced "Patriots' Soapbox," a YouTube live stream devoted to the theory. One archived live stream shows up to reveal him seeing to "Q"'s 8chan account before the feed swiftly removes.

False Claims And Beliefs

QAnon's very first message on the/ pol/ message board of 4chan, on October 28, 2017, Q's uploading project has a background of false, unwarranted, and unproven claims. Beginning with the first blog posts poorly predicting Hillary Clinton's impending arrest and complied with by more false claims, such as declaring that North Korean Supreme Leader Kim Jong-un is a creature leader mounted by the CIA. Q's messages have been more ambiguous by allowing fans to map out there own ideas in it. By generating a keyboard heatmap of Q's coded messages, information safety, and security. Scientist Mark Burnett ended that they "are not actual codes, just arbitrary typing by someone who may play an instrument and makes use of a QWERTY key-board" adding that "almost all the characters" in the codes alternative in between the left and right hands, or the keys are close to each other on the keyboard.

A few of Q's other allegations include their February 16, 2018, false claim that U.S. Representative and previous Democratic National Committee chairwoman Debbie Wasserman Schultz employed Salvadoran gang MS-13 to murder DNC staffer Seth Rich. A July 7, 2018, article in The Daily Beast likewise maintained in mind that Q incorrectly proclaimed that "each mass shooting is a false-flag strike organized by the cabal." Different other ideas held by QAnon followers include that Obama, Hillary Clinton, George Soros, and others are intending a stroke of genius while at the very same time entailed as participants of an international child sex trafficking ring. According to this concept, the Mueller investigation is a counter-coup led by Trump that made believe in conspiring with Russia to hire Mueller to examine the Democrats secretly.

Another false belief is that some particular Hollywood stars are pedophiles, which the Rothschild family members lead a hellish cult. By interpreting the info Q feeds them, QAnon supporters conclude on these conclusions. On many parties, Q has rejected their false claims and incorrect forecasts as willful false information, declaring that "disinformation is necessary." This has led Australian psychologist Stephan Lewandowsky to emphasize the "self-sealing" quality of the conspiracy theory, highlighting its anonymous purveyor's use of feasible deniability and keeping in mind that evidence against the theory "can come to be proof of credibility in the minds of believers." Writer Walter Kirn has explained Q as an innovator among conspiracy philosophers by engaging viewers with "clues" rather than stating claims directly: "The internet evaluators do not want read, but just to write. It does not want answers supplied; rather, they desire to look for them."

By 2020, some fans began using the Twitter hashtag #SaveTheChildren, coopting a trademarked name for the youngster wellness organization "Save the Children," creating an August 7 statement by Save the Children on the unauthorized use of its name in campaigns. Data from the National Center for Missing & Exploited Children reveal that the frustrating huge number of missing youngsters are runaways; the second-largest reason is kidnapping by a family member, with less than 1% being nonfamily kidnappings.

Identity of "Q."

There has been much conjecture regarding the intent and also the identification of the poster, with theories ranging from an army intelligent officer to Trump himself, to an alternating game by Cicada 3301. Anybody might originally have used the handle to post anything as 4chan is confidential, and it does not enable registration by individuals. The Italian leftist Wu Ming framework has guessed that QAnon is encouraged by the Luther Blissett personality, which anarchists and also leftists used to arrange tricks, media stunts, and also scams in the 1990s. "Blissett" launched the one-of-a-kind Q in 1999. As Q relies on a tripcode to verify themself, and the tripcode is confirmed by 8chan's server and not reproducible on other imageboards, Q was incapable of posting when the website shut down adhering to the 2019 El Paso capturing. Some have guessed that Jim Watkins himself is Q; both Jim and also Ron Watkins deny recognizing Q's identity.

Analysis.

QAnon might best be comprehended as an instance of what historian Richard Hofstadter in 1964 called "The Paranoid Style in American Politics," associated with spiritual millenarianism and apocalypticism. The vocabulary of QAnon mirrors Christian tropes--" The Storm" (the Genesis flooding narrative or Judgement Day) and "The Great Awakening," which evokes the historic spiritual Great Awakenings from the very early 18th century to the late 20th century. According to one QAnon video, the fight between Trump and also "the cabal" is of "scriptural percents," a "fight for the planet, of wicked versus outstanding." The forthcoming numeration is stated by some QAnon supports to be a "reverse rapture," which is not merely the end of the world as it is currently understood, yet a clean slate also, with redemption and a paradise on earth for the survivors. Within less than a year of existence, QAnon came to be significantly identified by the whole populace. According to an August 2018 Qualtrics survey for The Washington Post, 58% of Floridians recognize QAnon to have a viewpoint regarding it. Of those who had a point of view, many were unwanted. Positive feelings towards QAnon were uncovered to be significantly associated with being at risk of conspiracy theory thinking. According to a March 2020 Pew study, 76% of Americans claimed they had never heard of QAnon, 20% had listened to "a little concerning it," and 3% stated they had heard "a great a lot."

Some QAnon followers have inevitably begun to acknowledge that they have actually been divided from family and also liked ones, and experience isolation as a result of it. For some, this is a path to beginning the process of divesting themselves of their cultish ideas. In contrast, for others, the isolation reinforces the advantages they obtain from originating from the cult.

People in the QAnon community usually mention alienation from pals and family members. Though they usually speak regarding just how Q tore their connections on personal Facebook groups. Yet they think these problems are temporary and also primarily the mistake of others. They frequently comfort themselves by visualizing that there will be a min of retribution at some factor in the future, which will show their beliefs. They think of that after this occurs, not just will their relationships be brought back; however, individuals will depend on them as leaders who understand what's taking place better than the remaining of us.

Disillusionment can also originate from the failure of the theories' projections. Q anticipated Republican success in the 2018 United States midterm political elections and asserted that Attorney General Jeff Sessions was related to secret benefit Trump, with obvious tension in between them a cover. When Democrats made substantial gains, and also Trump terminated

Sessions, there was disillusionment among whole lots of in the Q neighborhood.

Much more disillusionment came when a forecasted mass arrest and jail time in the Guantanamo Bay apprehension camp of Trump's challengers did not happen, neither did the discontinuation of charges versus Trump's previous National Security Advisor, Michael Flynn. For some, these failings started the treatment of separation from the QAnon cult, while others recommended direct action in the form of an insurrection against the federal government. Such a reaction to a stopped working forecast is not unusual: apocalyptic cults such as Heaven's Gate, individuals' Temple, the Manson Family, and Aum Shinrikyo considered mass self-destruction or mass murder when their assumptions for explorations or the gratification of their predictions did not arise. Psychotherapist Robert Lifton calls it "requiring completion." This sensation is being seen among some QAnon believers. Some frustrated QAnon believers may take matters into their own hands as Pizzagate follower Edgar Maddison Welch done in 2016, Matthew Phillip Wright did at Hoover Dam in 2018, and Anthony Comello accomplished in 2019, when he killed Mafia manager Frank Cali, thinking himself to be under Trump's safety and security.

Popular QAnon fan Liz Crokin, who in 2018 asserted that John F. Kennedy Jr. forged his fatality and also is now Q, mentioned in February 2019 that she was shedding perseverance in Trump to apprehend the anticipated members of the youngster sex ring, suggesting that the time was coming close to for "vigilante justice." Different other QAnon followers have taken on the Kennedy theory, asserting that a Pittsburgh man named Vincent Fusca is Kennedy in camouflage and also would certainly be Trump's 2020 running mate. Some took part in 2019 Independence Day events in Washington, anticipating Kennedy to appear.

CHAPTER TWO

Issues Surrounding Qanon

Who is Q-Anon?

We have no definitive response. Is Q a person? Probably not. There is a concept gaining appeal that John Kennedy Jr. faked his death as well as is Q? I check out Q is intrigue within the NSA, armed forces, FBI, Assange's team, the present management's board, or the President himself. If I were to suggest an enlightened guess, I would think Q is a collective of modern patriots jointly understood as the 'White Hats.' Where did Q originate from? Q-Anon initially showed up on internet boards in the fall of 2017, became famous with word of mouth, went viral, and now is being buffooned on tv.

Q has web links to videos, short articles, photos, and information on website boards. Q developed code names and also phrases for people and companies. In 2018 a sophisticated, and complex message system developed. Followers use time and date stamps, and various other clues within a blog post, to plug into a cipher of kinds and get understanding or a message.

Q usually uses the army motto, "Where We Go One We Go All." Q often advises readers, "Trust the plan and take delight in the show."

Where is Q attempting to take us? What show and what is the plan?

If you wonder, you can comply with the white rabbit. Since the white rabbit typically takes you to another globe. Not only is it different than the world you understand; however, it is a place that forces you to peel the blinders from your eyes and also peer behind the looking glass. It resembles the famous culture stage about taking the red pill. Once your eyes are opened up, you can never return to the globe you knew. The White Rabbit Express is a one-way ticket to a new level of your presence.

Under normal scenarios, I would certainly advise you to comply with the white rabbit only if you attempt. Nonetheless, these are desperate times in which we live. Since he's running after you, there is no need to chase after the rabbit. He is jumping at warp rate in our direction, and he's bringing his world, our parallel globe, with him. A fact is entering into the light, and also the structures will move. Hold on, be daring and strong, do not hesitate or discouraged. United we will stand, divided we will fall. United, we will certainly emerge triumphantly.

Enemies Operating Behind The Scenes (Glinda)

Several enemies exist in this world. Most times, we are our own worst enemy. I'm going to discuss the enemies operating behind the scenes. We typically accept the stories they use to spoon-fed to us. In some cases, I feel we usually act like Dorothy, the Munchkins, and the citizen of Oz. We blindly adhere to Glinda's plan to acquire what we want most from life, but is she truly on our side?

Glinda is constantly around viewing and spying.

The land of Oz is where the massive political machinery of this world live. Oz is the new world they want to take us to where they will rule and reign without opposition. A lot of Glinda wannabes are working behind the drape to create all the smoke and mirrors used to hide what is taking place in the shadows.

The witches of the east and the west are the two-party systems highjacked to hold our governments for ransom with their inaction. I purposely make use of government in the plural type since practically all nations around the world appear to be ruled by a two-party system jointly called liberal and conservative. Particularly, in the United States, they take down the Constitution and chip away our sovereignty. Glinda did have one thing. The Witch of the West is even worse than the Witch of the East. One party is extra wicked than the other. In reality, they are nothing more than contrary sides of the same coin. Both sold us out on to the large organization, costly powerbrokers, and work tirelessly to push the program Glinda has been preparing for decades. They just have a different vision on how to complete it.

The Wizard is the media and entertainment firm. They use the positive, grinning face to market Glinda's publicity to the masses. They make use of the Tokyo Rose approach to persuade us there is an opponent we need to be terrified of. To be safe, we must sacrifice our liberties, kids, and freedom. They consistently advertise numerous boogie guys who do not exist and begin disputes that lead to war in other to push their agenda. This group are the sacrificial pawns in an elaborate video game of three-dimensional breast. They are the sirens on the rocks that tempt us into battles abroad and home. They all help Glinda, a type of darkness government and antichrist.

Wars abroad bring huge cash and bring several materials into their coffers. Battles at home produce turmoil. Glinda's slogan is "Order Out of Chaos." What's the trick? Divide and conquer. Glinda strives to divide us and also put us at each other's throats and promotes hate.

It's now done openly. You can see on the internet ads working with protesters. A number of these protestor teams are moneyed by affluent entities or individuals; they give power to a team that feels powerless. It can likewise make the opposition quest their position.

Glinda works relentlessly to persuade us the reason why things are fallen apart is that a political party is out to damage all of us. A large group of people refuse to fall for this scam, so then it must be as a result of unreasonable benefits in between the sexes. You don't desire to munch on that particular lure? Maybe you'll bite down on the little socioeconomic worm. Glinda attempts to split us due to what component of the nation we are from, our academic level, spiritual battles, revenue degree, unlawful versus legal immigration, blue-collar against white-collar, young versus old, healthy versus unhealthy, heterosexual against homosexual, and also the shade of our skin.

This is among the problems Q-Anon is bringing to the leading edge. Q is like Toto getting hold of the curtain with his teeth, and drawing it back to reveal the wizard is nothing more than simple mortals hiding behind the scenes playing a game. The game is dangerous and real. People's lives are at stake during the time of wars. When the individuals awaken and realize the truth, it is a mathematical assurance they can overthrow the warmongers; they always do as Q has been revealing us, with incredible information going down to the public at large, more than warmongering going on.

The paradise of Oz is a facade. It hides the scary acts of the witches and wizards behind the scenes as they try to make our lives a living heck while gratifying their lusts for power, money, and ascendancy. What is Glinda's end game? What is her plan for Dorothy today? What does she desire from us? She maintains Dorothy, the people of Oz, and the Munchkins combating among themselves regarding crafted charges and acquisitions. The wizard fuels the fires while the witch of the East and the West remove our freedom to confine us. Some are currently oppressed and are used for clinical testing, biowarfare, and the sex slave industry. They collect individuals' parts for organ substitutes, hair expansions for usage. A lot are used as employees to generate the products and services they want while keeping us in poverty and illness. They pound us to sell things we do not need, sicken us with Franken-food and pollute our air and water to drain us even more through financial bills.

What is Glinda's end game? By all looks, it seems to be corporate communism on a global scale while at the same time introducing an age in the world where evil reigns without rights or freedoms for the individuals. We have a chance to rise if Q is official. The wizards and witches require to pass away.

Politicians, Celebrities, And Rulers!

When a word like a criminal is mentioned, several things come to mind. A lot of people think about thieves, murderers, smugglers, and rapists. There is a more significant number of crooks in this world, and they tend to go unpunished. How do several celebrities and political leaders get away with a crime over and over again? Sometimes the court provides them with a slap on the wrist to appease the dissatisfied masses. It is a show! When we knock on the door of justice and demand solutions, the wizard just tells us we need to vanish.

Yes, renowned people and good political leaders exist, but they are few in numbers. We identify most celebs are spoiled brats that live an indulgent lifestyle with no breaks.

A lot of them have sold their soul for popularity and love of money. They simply inform you just how they funnel different beings, or entities, while they do their craft. Why are they getting paid? If they need to surrender their body to a spiritual entity to do their task for them, because I wouldn't call it a skill. They offer interviews where they explain how this entity does with them. Essentially, they are describing to us how they engage in sorcery act. We lose hours of our lives watching their television programs. Why? Since we are being programmed to do so. We've been conditioned from birth to see tv for recreation and enjoyment. The wizard regurgitates the lie that these people are unique, far better than us. They are absolutely nothing greater than a dog-and-pony program for the witches of Oz, and also they cast their spells through lyrics and dialogue as entertainment.

Political leaders metamorphize right into much the same. They relate with celebrities to solidify their relevance and also validity with the everyday Joe. They team up for galas, banquets, and fundraising occasions. They make use of celebrities to get appeal, which will certainly turn up their placement within the elite gentility. Why do we remain to vote them when they habitually overlook the will of the people they assert to serve? Why do we not hold their feet to the fire on their campaign promises?

We shrug our shoulders and also move on with life and take the condition quo. This is among the lies they press twenty-four seven. The truth is we are neither inapt nor powerless. We can alter things.

Both politicians and stars are amateurs compared to imperial family members throughout the world. In my opinion, this archaic power structure ought to be eliminated. There is no such thing as a unique bloodline. That decided that the Munchkins needs a wizard to subjugate them? What makes him so great and also powerful? Why should a family be allocated the capability to rule over people due to their birthright? Study your history books and see the number of royal leaders was scientifically outrageous, mostly as a result of interbreeding that created deformities and uncommon conditions. This is the only point unique about their bloodlines.

These criminal families live a way of life that is unbelievable. They take pleasure in first-class every time. They delight in the most expensive food, apparel, safety and security, gems, buildings, businesses, holidays, and so on. The best part of them is their luxurious way of living. An added benefit is the reality that is usually tax-free. They fooled individuals, right!

Progressively we see detraction after scandals coming out about these three groups. Where there much smoke, you better believe a raging fire is the reason. This is one of the things Q addresses, and we can see these traits in these people. They played us for a fool.

CHAPTER THREE

The Plans to Save the World

Have you at any point in time wondered why people go to war or why individuals never appear to have the ability to avoid financial obligation? Why is there division, crime, and poverty?

What if I draw your attention to the fact that there is a reason for everything?

What if I let you know it was done on purpose?

What if I informed you that those corrupting the world, poisoning our food, and igniting conflict were themselves about to be removed entirely from the earth?

We acknowledge that criminals exist. They steal your phone; they rob your house, they can even murder you as well if they think they can get away with it.

We do have knowledgeable criminals in one way or another. Criminals, as we understand, are those who pick individual gain over the rights of others without any regard for laws.

But here's where you need to broaden your thinking. Criminals can also prosper in politics and business and can be chosen as our leaders.

If a criminal becomes the president, imagine what they could accomplish. They might use the full weight of their executive power to commit much more significant crimes and ensure they and their good friends were supported to the fullest extent possible.

A criminal president might create alliances with other criminal presidents and then work together on more global criminal activities, including; human trafficking, drug-running, or whatever makes the big bucks.

The 20th Century was unstable with war, economic scarcities, catastrophe, and displacement.

We have always accepted these as simply human nature and merely the way the world works, i.e., something inevitable to the weak points of human nature that lead us to such actions.

This is where we are all tragically wrong. I am not a criminal. You are not a criminal.

How should we just believe or assume that all this discomfort and suffering are driven by human nature?

What if it wasn't human at all, and as a result of something more intentional?

We were taught. Capitalism was the reason for an enormous rich/poor divide and the primary reason for poverty, which in turn is the reason for war, starvation, and criminal activities.

Others have been taught that Communism, the system of equal wealth among all people, was truly responsible for the mess.

None of the above-mentioned factors is exactly true. It is not in any way our nature to fight and be racist; it is not in our usual nature to steal or rob from others.

You should have known that it was the CRIMINALS the whole time!

Yes. They got power. More power than a criminal must ever have.

They somehow rose to the top of the media business that manages our news and home entertainment.

They rose to the top of the banking system.

To the Oval Office.

To Brussels.

To the Vatican

To the Crown.

They sneaked in silently.

They ended up being leaders of agricultural companies who have control over food supply and big pharmaceutical businesses, the ones we rely on to help us when we are sick.

No-one stopped them, and they simply recruited more bad guys to assist them. They accumulated the wealth of the world.

They invented a money system called Central Banking, which provides cash to governments with interest, positioning countries into everlasting financial obligations.

While individuals' wealth got less, their wealth got more. Much more.

When a criminal is currently as rich as they can get, then securing their ill-gotten gains becomes the top priority.

Unhappy citizens, tired of being poor, are a significant challenge and can revolt if they suffer enough. The criminals need to avoid this. So they end up diverting attention to their remaining competitors- the people of the world: You and me.

We are not happy being ruled by bad guys and need to execute tasks simply to survive. They know we will not accept it. Therefore, they make use of their control of the media to set black versus white, young versus old, man versus woman, or Muslim versus Christian.

Such people try to make us believe we are the problem so that we end up battling and destroying ourselves. To get it done much faster, they assault all elements of humanity that make us strong, like family.

Making use of their impact over culture, they popularize ways of life that cause a surge in broken homes, lost youth, and drug abuse.

We ware merely trying to get on with living. Where are all the right people?

Good people simply want to get married, have kids, earn a living and enjoy their liberty.

Well, there were lots of heroes.

One ended up being the president of the United States in January 1961. He learned about these crooks and wanted them gone. He knew their objectives for us all, and he wished to fight them. Regretfully, he had no idea how effective they had become.

Reagan likewise had good objectives for the American people. He knew this criminal mafia managed almost everything by this phase, consisting of the significant criminal intelligence agencies.

His financial policies were promising, but the criminals needed a weak America to keep their power in place.

Reagan was therefore shown with a bullet that a growing United States economy and flourishing people were not what the criminals desired.

Each time someone wished to stand up and do the ideal thing, they get stopped.

Were we ever to be released?

The bad guys are also considered as the cabal or deep state because of how they control things behind the scenes.

Every president after Reagan was one of these Deep State terrible guys, and their empire grew even more powerful.

With every bad president came new depths America and the world would sink.

The world collapsed into darkness.

Do you want me to tell you how?

Damaged industries, declining employment rate, sicker people, destroyed Iraq, Syria, and Yemen with pointless war, displacement of individuals into Europe, ISIS, terrorism, collapsed governments, genocide, and poverty.

TOTAL MISERY.

Do you think that was inevitable? Not at all!

Well, here is where things start to take a new turn.

When the complete picture comes to be understood, it will forever be regarded as the biggest story ever told.

Some amazing people still held some positions of power. Such persons valued humanity as well as the rule of law.

While the bad guys discussed their tactical plan at the annual Bilderberg conferences, the great guys were making plans of their own.

The Information age has altered history permanently.

As the Internet became accessible in every home, and home appliances became smarter. People began carrying tracking devices, an excellent opportunity to stop criminal control over the world was emerging.

We became well connected, surveilled, and trackable. However, SO DID THEY. They ended up being dependent on email, SMS, and instant communication, just like we did.

It made crime a lot easier, but it likewise put them on a grid that, if accessed by the best individuals, would expose their crimes to the general public.

In this new age of information, it was thought that the military needs also to have its own intelligence company to focus on cybercrime and espionage. They called this the NSA, the National Security Agency.

The importance of the NSA in the story can not be understated. Here we had every phone call, e-mail, and text from every device saved and processed.

Whether it be somebody making a physician's consultation or the Deep State, establishing a massive heroin buy from the Taliban. In the best hands, it would suffice info to point out the whole sinister criminal plot to rob us..

The heroes were designing a PLAN to reclaim the world from the cabal and return it to individuals. It would include alliances with several countries, since the criminals had global trade and other facilities in place that would require their cooperation.

It boiled down to two options for America; Introduce a military coup to seize the government from whichever cabal puppet remained in the White House Or winning legitimately, taking control of the NSA, expose the criminals for what they are, and apprehend them all.

The very first alternative would be very uncomfortable for the general public.

With a lot of people still significantly preoccupied with some cabal-engineered social issues, they would likely revolt and injure themselves as well as others.

No, it would have to be the latter. They needed a prospect who might win and who might win big.

Several states like California had been so heavily flooded with criminals that even the ballot machines were electronically established to swing votes. It would need to be a decisive victory.

Good patriots in the United States military, together with their global partners, asked Donald Trump to run for president so that they might take back control of America legally without stressing the public.

Trump was an excellent option, certainly, since he conquered the citizen scams and won. He was a patriot, and the public admired him.

He was not interested in being part of the cabal, primarily because they disliked America, and he did not concur with them on that point.

As soon as he showed interest in taking power, they activated their media properties to turn on him viciously. That's when we saw the abrupt hatred developed.

Even when he won, the cabal still had no form of idea what he was part of, and the advanced plan that was about to unfold against them.

Shocked at their loss, they mobilized their complete arsenal of intelligence, media, money, and innovation to take back the lost power.

Their people at the top of the D.O.J and FBI then created a strategy to frame Trump up and have him impeached. This is where we come back to the NSA once again. All messages were kept and could be used to expose this plot and avoid Trump's overthrow.

Here is the point. The world is presently experiencing a great covert war of scriptural percentages between the forces of evil and good.

The cabal had complete control over North Korea. They pirated the Kim Dynasty, took them captive, and developed a nuclear toolbox to threaten the world.

We are all beginning to see the pattern now that enough time has passed, that our most significant worldwide concerns are beginning to recede, and peace is returning.

It is all proof that the heroes are winning the war. But we are still in the middle. While a lot is happening, it still puzzles many people that the majority of these known bad guys are always complimentary.

Specifically, higher-ups like Hillary Clinton, the Bushes, and. Obama.

That can be found in the next chapter of the story.

That's why we have Q.

The good people, with control over the NSA, began the Q intelligence.

Dissemination program to conjure up an online grassroots motion called "The Great Awakening.".

It began on underground Internet channels and then moved to the mainstream.

Q has been a fun interruption for those who follow world occasions and desire reality. Still, it will begin a much more crucial and necessary phase-keeping the public informed when the Deep State war breaks out onto the surface. By this, I am referring to high-profile arrests.

Yes folks. The criminals being referred to are famous actors, political leaders, singers, CEOs, and celebrities; individuals who have earned our admiration, regard, and trust.

They have done terrible things that are all known and documented, and they will be severely punished.

Those people who have followed Q since the start will help you make sense of upcoming events.

We are part of the first few to realize that our partisan divisions are simply minor distractions, and we are all oppressed by a hidden enemy.

We understand that the issue was never Socialism or Capitalism, Republican or Democrat, black or white, Christian or Muslim.

We do know it was mighty criminals who had excessive power.

Fellow slaves, this is the time to buckle your seatbelt, acknowledge your real enemy, and accept a new future that we all owe to our brave patriots who so much risked their lives to attain victory against the biggest force of evil the world has ever known.

CHAPTER FOUR

History Of New World Order

QAnon's mandates and language are closely related to the spiritual idea of millenarianism and apocalypticism, leading it to emerge as a spiritual movement. It has been commonly defined as "baseless," "unhitched," and "evidence-free."

Its proponents have been called "a psychopathic conspiracy cult" and "a few of the Internet's outré Trump fans." Travis stated the essence of the theory is that: there is all over the world cabal of Satan-worshiping pedophiles who rule the globe, basically, and also they manage whatever. They control politicians, and they regulate the media. They manage Hollywood, and they cover their presence, essentially.

"Q" is a poster on 4chan, who later on moved to 8chan, that discloses details about this secret behind the scene fight, and additionally methods concerning what the cabal is doing.

Supporters of QAnon equally believe a brewing event called "The Storm" in which countless people, participants of the cabal, will be incarcerated, potentially sent to Guantanamo Bay jail, or to encounter military tribunals, and the U.S. military will take control of the country. The outcome of The Storm will be salvation and paradise in the world.

New World Order (conspiracy theory).

The Latin expression "Novus ordo seclorum," showing up on the reverse side of the Great Seal since 1782 and on the back of the U.S. one-dollar since 1935, translates to "New Order of the Ages." It started in the time where the United States of America is an independent nation-state; conspiracy philosophers claim this is an intimation to the "New World Order." The New World Order (NWO) in conspiracy concepts is the hypothesis of a secretly arising totalitarian global government.

The regular motif in conspiracy theories concerning a New World Order is that a deceptive authority with a globalist program is conspiring to eventually rule the world through an authoritarian government, which will change sovereign nation-states and publicity ideology.

Countless famous historical and contemporary figures have been declared to be part of the cabal that runs countless business to take care of the substantial political and financial events, by creating systemic crisis to pushing through questionable policies, at both national and global levels steps to achieve world dominations.

During the early period of the 1990s, New World Order conspiracism was restricted to two American countercultures, the militantly anti-government right as the primary and component of fundamentalist Christianity about the end-time of the Antichrist as the secondary. Doubters, such as Michael Barkun and also Chip Berlet, observed that traditional democratic conspiracy theory concepts relating to New World Order had not been welcomed by many seekers of stigmatized knowledge but leaked right into prominent society. Inaugurating into a period during the late 20th and also early 21st centuries in the United States where individuals are proactively preparing for apocalyptic millenarian scenarios. Those political scientists are concerned that mass hysteria over New World Order conspiracy theory concepts could ultimately have devastating effects on American political life, varying from heightening lone-wolf terrorism to the rise to authoritarian ultranationalist demagogues.

History of the Pre-Cold War.

Throughout the 20th century, political figures such as Woodrow Wilson and Winston Churchill made use of the term " new world order" to describe a new period of history characterized by a significant alteration in world political thoughts and the worldwide balance of power after World War I and also World War II.

The interwar and post-World War II period were deemed opportunities to implement hopeful proposals for global administration by collective efforts to take care of worldwide issues beyond the capability nation-states to resolve, appreciating the right of countries to self-determination. Such cumulative efforts showed up in the formation of intergovernmental organizations such as the League of Nations in 1920, the United Nations (UN) in 1945, and the North Atlantic Treaty Organization (NATO) in 1949, together with worldwide regimes such as the Bretton Woods system and the General Agreement on Tariffs and also Trade (GATT), executed to keep a harmonious balance of power and also help with reconciliation in between countries to avoid the global dispute. These cosmopolitan efforts to convey liberal internationalism were regularly pounded and opposed by American paleoconservative service nationalists from the 1930s.

British writer and also futurist H. G. Wells went better than progressives in the 1940s by redefining the term "new world order" as a basic synonym for the establishment of a technocratic world state and also of a prepared economic, gathering popularity in state socialist circles.

Cold War period.

Throughout the Second Red Scare, both Christian and nonreligious right American agitators, primarily influenced by Canadian conspiracy theorist William Guy Carr, gradually invited and spread out suspicious fears of Freemasons, Illuminati, and Jews as the proclaimed driving forces behind a "global communist conspiracy." The threat of "Godless communism" in an atheistic, bureaucratic collectivist government was demonized as the "Red Menace," is the focus of apocalyptic millenarian conspiracism. The Red Scare came to form one of the core aspects of the political right in the United States, which are progressives and liberals, with their welfare-state policies and international cooperation programs such as foreign aid, apparently contribute to a gradual process of global collectivism that will result in nations being changed with a communistic/collectivist one-world government. James Warburg, showing up before the United States Senate Committee on Foreign Relations in 1950, famously discussed: "We will have world government, whether we like it or not. The question is just whether the world government will be attained by consent or by conquest."

After the autumn of communism in the early 1990s, the de facto subject of New World Order conspiracism moved from crypto-communists, viewed to be outlining to creating an atheistic world communist government, to globalists, perceived to be plotting to bring out a collectivist, unified world government ultimately handled by an untouchable oligarchy of international lenders, corrupt political leaders, and corporatists, or the United Nations itself. The change in perception was motivated by growing resistance to corporate internationalism on the American right in the 1990s.

President George H. W. Bush clarified his objectives for post-Cold War global governance in participation with post-Soviet states in a speech toward New World Order on 11 September 1990.

He stated that the world had been divided, a world of barbed wire and concrete block, conflict and cold war. Now, we can see a new world appearing—a world in which there is a genuine possibility of a new world order. A world where the United Nations, launched cold war stalemate, is poised to satisfy the historic vision of its founders. A world in which freedom and respect for human civil liberties find a residence among all countries.

Chip Berlet, an American investigative press reporter, specializing in the study of right-wing movements in the U.S., state that the Christian and secular far-right were frightened by Bush's speech. Fundamentalist Christian groups equated Bush's words as signaling the end times. At the same time, much more nonreligious theorists approached it from an anti-communist and anti-collectivist viewpoint and also feared for supremacy over all nations by the United Nations.

Post-Cold War

American televangelist Rub Robertson wrote the 1991 most rated and selling book, "The New World Order." With his 1991 famous, wound up being one of the most preferred Christian disseminator of conspiracy theories concept regarding present American history. He describes a situation regulating the flow of events from behind the scenes, nudging people constantly and secretly towards the direction of the world government for the Antichrist.

The militia movement's anti-government ideology was spread through speeches at rallies, books, meetings, and video programs. There was an argument that AM radio shows a propagandistic viral content online that has enormously added to more extremist actions to the threat of the New World Order. This caused the considerable development of New World Order conspiracism, with it retroactively locating its way right into the formerly apolitical literature of numerous Kennedy assassin biologists, ufologists, and partly influenced by fears surrounding the Satanic panic occultists. From the mid-1990s onward, the amorphous appeal of those subcultures moved New World Order conspiracism to a bigger target market of fans of stigmatized knowledge, with the typical characteristics of the disillusionment of political efficiency.

From the mid-1990s to the very early 2000s, Hollywood conspiracy-thriller television shows and also flicks also contributed in offering an essential target market to the various fringe and mystical concepts connected with New World Order conspiracism, which had developed to include black helicopters, FEMA "prisoner-of-war camp," and so on. Complying with the beginning of the 21st century, and especially during the late-2000s economic dilemma, numerous politicians and professionals, such as Gordon Brown and also Henry Kissinger, made use of the term "new world order" in their advocacy for a detailed reform of the global economic system and their calls for a "New Bretton Woods" taking into consideration arising markets such as China as well as India. These public declarations rejuvenated New World Order conspiracism, culminating in a talk-show host by Sean Hannity stating on his Fox News program Hannity saying that the "conspiracy philosophers were right."

In 2009, American movie supervisors Luke Meyer and Andrew Neel released New World Order. This incredibly well-known docudrama movie explores the world of conspiracy theorists, such as American radio host Alex Jones, that intensely oppose what they regard as an emerging New World Order. The expanding circulation and popularity of conspiracy theory concepts have additionally established a partnership between conservative agitators and songs' artists (such as KRS-One, Professor Griff of Villain, and also Immortal Strategy), revealing just how anti-elitist conspiracism can produce not likely political allies in initiatives to oppose a political system.

CHAPTER FIVE

Conspiracy theories

There are many systemic conspiracy theories where the concept of a New World Order is seen. The following is a checklist of the major ones in roughly sequential order:

End time

In the 19th century, a lot of apocalyptic millennial Christian eschatologists, starting with John Nelson Darby, have forecasted a globalist conspiracy to impose a tyrannical New World Order, controlling structure as the fulfillment of prophecies concerning the "end time" in the Bible, specifically in the Book of Ezekiel, Daniel, the Olivet discovered in the Synoptic Gospels and the Book of Revelation. They claim that individuals who have dealt with the Devil to obtain riches and also power have become pawns in a supernatural chess game have moved humanity right into approving a utopian globe government that hinges on the spiritual frameworks of syncretic-messianic world faiths, which will in the future subject itself to be a dystopian globe empire that imposes the imperial cult of an "Unholy Trinity" of Satan, the Antichrist and also the False Prophet.

Dynamic Christians, such as preacher-theologian Peter J. Gomes, caution Christian fundamentalists that a "spirit of fear" can batter scripture and history with precariously incorporating

47

scriptural literalism, apocalyptic timetables, demonization, and overbearing bias. In contrast, Camp cautions the danger that Christians could pick up some added spiritual baggage" by credulously accepting conspiracy concepts. They seek Christians that enjoy conspiracism to repent.

Freemasonry Masonic conspiracy concepts

Freemasonry is just one of the globe's earliest nonreligious fraternal business and also developed during the late 16th and very early 17th century Britain. Over the years, several cases and conspiracy theories have been routed towards Freemasonry, including the claims that Freemasons have a concealed political agenda and are conspiring to cause a New World Order, a world government organized according to Masonic concepts or governed just by Freemasons. The mystical nature of Masonic importance and ceremonies resulted in Freemasons initially implicated in secretly practicing Satanism in the late 18th century. The original claims of a conspiracy theory within Freemasonry to overturn religion and governments to take control of the world traces back to Scottish writer John Robison, whose reactionary conspiracy theory concepts went across the Atlantic and influenced breakouts of Protestant anti-Masonry in the United States throughout the 19th century. In the 1890s, French writer Léo Taxil composed a series of pamphlets and books disparaging Freemasonry and also billing their lodges with venerating Lucifer as the Supreme Being and Great

Architect of the universe. Even with the fact that Taxil confessed that his claims were all a rip-off, they were and still are believed and also repeated by many conspiracy theory philosophers and had a significant effect on succeeding anti-Masonic claims regarding Freemasonry.

Some conspiracy theory philosophers eventually assumed that some Founding Fathers of the United States, such as George Washington and Benjamin Franklin, were having Masonic spiritual geometric layouts interwoven right into American culture, particularly in the Great Seal of the United States, the United States one-dollar bill, the design of National Mall sites and the roads and highways of Washington, D.C., as a component of a master method to create the first "Masonic federal government" as a design for the coming New World Order.

A Masonic Lodge area

Freemasons rebut these claims of a Masonic conspiracy theory. Freemasonry, which advertises rationalism, places no power in occult symbols. It is not a part of its principle to see the illustration of symbols, regardless of how large, as an act of managing or consolidating power. Additionally, no published details are establishing the Masonic membership of the men accountable for the design of the Great Seal. While conspiracy philosophers assert that there are aspects of Masonic impact on the Great Seal of the United States, these components were purposefully or accidentally used, considering that the developers knew the symbols. The many Grand Lodges are independent and sovereign, recommending they act independently and do not have a common agenda. The points of belief of the numerous lodges regularly differ.

Illuminati

The Order of the Illuminati was an Enlightenment-age secret society established by Adam Weishaupt on 1 May 1776, a university professor, in Upper Bavaria, Germany. The movement include advocates of freethought, secularism, sex, liberalism, and also republicanism equal rights, hired from the German Masonic Lodges, that looked for to educate rationalism through enigma schools. In 1785, the order was penetrated, separated, and reduced by the government reps of Charles Theodore, Elector of Bavaria, in his preemptive campaign to neutralize the risk of secret societies before winding up being dens of conspiracies to topple the Bavarian monarchy and its state religious beliefs, Roman Catholicism. There is no evidence that the Bavarian Illuminati survived its reductions in 1785. In the late 18th century, reactionary conspiracy philosophers, such as Scottish physicist John Robison and also French Jesuit clergyman Augustin Barruel, started hypothesizing that the Illuminati had withstood their reductions and has come to be the masterminds behind the French Revolution and the Reign of Terror. Throughout the 19th century, fear of an Illuminati conspiracy was a real concern of the European gentility. Their oppressive reactions to this unproven fear provoked in 1848 the changes they sought to prevent.

The Protocols of the Elders of Zion

The Protocols of the Elders of Zion is an antisemitic canard, at first released in Russian in 1903, proclaiming a Judeo-Masonic conspiracy theory to obtain globe prominence. The message claims to be the minutes of the secret meetings of a cabal of Jewish masterminds, which has co-opted Freemasonry and also is plotting to rule the world on the part of all Jews because they think themselves to be the chosen people of God. The Protocols integrate many of the core conspiracist themes outlined in the Robison and Barruel assaults on the Freemasons and overlay them with antisemitic allegations about anti-Tsarist movements in Russia.

Round Table

During the second half of Britain's "royal century" between 1815 and 1914, English-born South African businessman, mining mogul, and politician Cecil Rhodes promoted the British Empire reannexing the United States of America and also changing itself right into an "Imperial Federation" to generate a hyperpower and also enduring world tranquility. In his initially will, written in 1877 at the age of 23, he revealed his dream to fund a secret cub (described as the Society of the Elect) that would advance this objective: To establish and grow a Secret Society, the real aim will undoubtedly be for the expansion of British guideline throughout the world, the perfecting of a system of emigration from the United Kingdom, and colonization by British subjects of all lands where the means of revenue are attainable by energy, labor and specifically the occupation by British inhabitants of the entire.

The Open Conspiracy

The Open Conspiracy British author and futurist H. G. Wells promoted cosmopolitanism and prepare blueprints for a world to establish a technocratic world state and also ready economic situation. Wells warned, nonetheless, in his 1940 book The New World Order that: when the battle seems drifting in the direction of a world social democracy, there might still be great delays and disappointments before it winds up being an efficient and beneficent world system.

Countless individuals will indeed despise the brand-new world order, be rendered disgruntled by the frustration of their enthusiasm and aspirations with its growth, and will die protesting against it. When we attempt to assess its promise, we have to bear in mind the distress of a generation or more of malcontents, countless of them graceful-looking and mostly gallant individuals. Wells's books were significant in offering the 2nd meaning to the term "new world order," which would just be used by state socialist supporters and anti-communist oppositions for generations to come.

Despite the appeal and also prestige of his ideas, Wells failed to work deeper because he was not able to concentrate his energies on a direct appeal to intelligentsias who would, inevitably, have to collaborate the Wellsian brand-new world order.

New Age

Allies Bailey, a political and spiritual occultist, saw a government world as the final thought of Wells' Open Conspiracy but positively suggested that it would certainly be synarchist because it was routed by the Masters of the Ancient Wisdom, intent on preparing humanity for the magical 2nd coming of Christ, and also the dawning of the Age of Aquarius. According to Bailey, a team of ascended masters called the Great White Brotherhood works with the "inner planes" to monitor and oversee the New World Order;; however, the participants of this Spiritual Hierarchy are just understood to a couple of occult researchers, with whom they interact telepathically.

Christian appropriate conspiracy theorists have condemned new Age author Alice Bailey's jobs.

Bailey's works, in addition to American writer Marilyn Ferguson's 1980 book The Aquarian Conspiracy, added to conspiracy theory philosophers of the Christian right watching the New Age motion as the "false religious beliefs" that would certainly supersede Christianity in a New World Order. Skeptics say that the term "New Age movement" is a misnomer, typically used by conspiracy theory philosophers as a catch-all rubric for any brand-new religious movement that is not fundamentalist Christian. For That Reason, New Age conspiracy philosophers, such as the manufacturers of documentary film like Esoteric Agenda, assert that globalists who outline in support of the New World Order are simply misusing occultism for Machiavellian ends, such as accepting 21 December 2012 as the specific day for the establishment of the New World Order for the feature of taking benefit of the growing 2012 sensation, which has its origins in the fringe Mayanist theories of New Age authors José Argüelles, Terence McKenna, and Daniel Pinchbeck.

Alien invasion

Since the late 1970s, extraterrestrials from other habitable worlds or parallel dimensions (such as "Greys") and intraterrestrials from Hollow Earth (such as "Reptilians") have been included in the New World Order conspiracy theory.

British writer David Icke declares that shapeshifting aliens called Reptilians regulate the Earth.

The usual theme in these conspiracy theories is that aliens have been amongst us for centuries, years, or centuries. Still, a government cover-up carried out by "Men in Black" has shielded the public from understanding the unusual secret intrusion. Inspired by speciesism and imperialism, these aliens have been and are independently manipulating developments and changes in human society. In some concepts, alien moles have shapeshifted right into human form and freely move throughout human society, even to the point of taking control of positions in governmental, business, and spiritual institutions, and also are currently in the last phases of their plan to take control of the world. A mythical covert government business of the United States code-named Majestic 12 is often visualized being the darkness federal government which collaborates with the alien profession and allows unusual abduction in exchange for assistance in the development and testing of the army "flying saucers" at Area 51, for United States militaries to achieve full-spectrum supremacy.

Unbelievers, who comply with the psychosocial hypothesis for unknown flying things, suggest that the merging of New World Order conspiracy theory and UFO conspiracy concept is a result of not only the period's prevalent suspicion of governments and the popularity of the extraterrestrial hypothesis for UFOs but the joining forces.

Brave New World

Antiscience and also neo-Luddite conspiracy philosophers emphasize on modern technology forecasting in the New World Order conspiracy concepts. They speculate that the global power elite is reactionary modernists going after a transhumanist agenda to establish and make use of human improvement technologies to become a "posthuman ruling caste." Conspiracy theory philosophers fear the result will either be developing a Brave New World-like dystopia, a "Brave New World Order" or the extinction of the human kinds.

Merely as there are many overlapping or clashing concepts among conspiracists concerning the nature of the New World Order, so exist several ideas about exactly how its architects and coordinators will execute it:

• Gradualism

Conspiracy theorists generally guess that the New World Order is being carried out gradually, discussing the development of the U.S. Federal Reserve System in 1913; the League of Nations in 1919; the International Monetary Fund in 1944; the United Nations in 1945; the World Bank in 1945; the World Health Organization in 1948; the European Union as well as the euro money in 1993; the World Trade Organization in 1998; the African Union in 2002; as well as the Union of South American

Nations in 2008 as considerable milestones. The concept holds that a group of mainly anonymous and shadowy global elites are planning to change the federal government of the United States with a multinational federal government. Consequently, conspiracy theory theorists think the boundaries between Mexico, Canada, and the United States are in the procedure of being gotten rid of, discreetly, by a team of globalists whose supreme goal is to change across the country government governments in Washington, D.C., Ottawa and also Mexico City with a European-style political union and even a puffed up E.U.-style administration.

- Coup d'état

American populist conspiracy theory theorists, especially those who joined the militia movement in the United States, assume that the New World Order will be executed via a dramatic coup d'état by a "secret team" using black helicopters in the U.S. and also other nation-states to create a totalitarian globe federal government handled by the United Nations as well as implemented by soldiers of foreign U.N. peacekeepers. Adhering to the Rex 84 and Operation Garden Plot plans, this armed forces stroke of genius would certainly include the suspension of the Constitution, the imposition of martial law, and the check out of military commanders to head state capture objectors.

Before 2000, some survivalists wrongly thought this process would be set in motion by the forecasted Y2K problem creating social collapse. Taking into consideration that countless left-wing and also conservative conspiracy philosophers believe that the 11 September attacks were a wrong flag operation done by the United States intelligence community, as part of a method to validate political suppression in your house and also preemptive battle abroad, they have ended up being encouraged that a much more tragic terrorist event will certainly be responsible for causing Executive Directive to complete the change to the transition state.

• Mass tracking

Conspiracy theorists thinking about surveillance abuse believe that the New World Order is being executed by the cult of knowledge at the core of the surveillance-industrial complex through mass monitoring and using Social Security numbers, the bar-coding of retail items with Universal Product Code markings, and most recently, RFID tagging by integrated circuit implants. Declaring that corporations and the federal government are intending to track every relocation of customers and citizens with RFID as the most current step in the direction of a 1984-like safety state, consumer privacy advocates, such as Katherine Albrecht and Liz McIntyre, have ended up being Christian conspiracy theory philosophers that believe spy chips need to be withstood because they argue that modern data source and communications innovations, combined with progressed ID and also authentication systems, now make it possible to require a biometrically associated number or mark to make purchases.

• Occultism

Conspiracy theorists of the Christian right, beginning with British revisionist chronicler Nesta Helen Webster, assume there is an ancient occult conspiracy theory, begun by the initial mystagogues of Gnosticism and continued by their proclaimed mystical successors, such as the Kabbalists, Cathars, Knights Templar, Hermeticists, Rosicrucians, Freemasons, and also, inevitably, the Illuminati, which tries to overturn the Judeo-Christian foundations of the Western globe and carry out the New World Order via a one-world religion that prepare the masses to accept the imperial cult of the Antichrist. More generally, they hypothesize that occult agencies of some sort guide globalists that lay out on behalf of a New World Order: unidentified superiors, spiritual hierarchies, satanic forces, fallen angels, or Lucifer. They believe that these accomplices make use of the power of occult sciences (numerology), symbols (Eye of Providence), rituals (Masonic levels), pillars (National Mall spots), buildings (Manitoba Legislative Building and centers (Denver International Airport) to progress their story to rule the world.

Skeptics argue that the demonization of Western esotericism by conspiracy theorists is rooted in religious intolerance nevertheless also in the same honest panics that have fuel witch tests in the Early Modern period and satanic abuse allegations in the United States.

• Population control

Conspiracy theory philosophers assume that the New World Order will similarly be implemented through making use of human populace control to monitor the movement quickly and control the people. The means vary from stopping the development of human societies through reproductive health and family planning programs, which advertise birth abortion, abstaining and control, or actively decreasing the mass of the world populace with genocides by mongering unwanted wars, via plagues by engineering emergent virus and tainting vaccines and through ecological catastrophes by regulating the weather (HAARP, chemtrails).

Conspiracy theorists say that globalists plotting on behalf of a New World Order are neo-Malthusians who take part in overpopulation and environment change alarmism to develop public assistance for forceful populace control and also inevitably, world government.

- Mind control

The worst concern of some conspiracy theorists, nevertheless, is that the New World Order will certainly be implemented through making use of mind control, a broad selection of strategies able to rescind a person's control of his or her very own thinking, habits, feelings, or preferences.

Doubters say that the fear behind a conspiracy theory philosopher's attraction with mind control, population control, occultism, safety misuse, Big Business, Big Government, and also globalization creates from a combination of 2 aspects, when she or he: 1) holds strong independent value and 2) lacks power.

The first attribute describes people that care profoundly concerning an individual's right to make their very own selections and also guide their very own lives without disruption or responsibilities to a more extensive system (like the government), yet combine this with a feeling of powerlessness in one's very own life. One obtains what some psychotherapists call "agency panic." When enthusiastic lone wolves feel that they can not exercise their independence, they experience a situation and also assume that more immense forces are at fault for appropriating this freedom.

Criticism

Skeptics of New World Order conspiracy theories accuse its advocates of delighting in the furtive misconception, an idea that significant truths of history are always threatening; conspiracism, a globe sight that centrally places conspiracy theories in the unfolding of history, instead of social and financial forces; and combined fear. Domhoff, a researcher in psychology and sociology who study concepts of power, wrote in 2005 an essay, "There Are No Conspiracies." He says that for this concept to be true, it needed several "wealthy and extremely enlightened individuals" to do things that do not "fit with what we comprehend about power structure." Claims that this will take place in previous decades and have been proved wrong.

Although some social doubters see super conspiracy theories about a New World Order as "postmodern metanarratives" that could be politically equipping, a way of giving normal individuals a narrative structure with which to doubt what they see around them, doubters suggest that conspiracism leads people right into cynicism, convoluted reasoning, and also a tendency to feel it is hopeless.

Criticisms of New World Order conspiracy theory philosophers also originate from within their environment. Several conventional democratic conspiracy theory philosophers hold sights that are inappropriate with their proclaimed libertarianism, such as dominionism, white supremacism, and even eliminationism

CHAPTER SIX

Nothing Will Stop What Is Coming

We are at the edge of a precipice, and the dominoes might start dropping at any day now. Once that cascade begins, there's truly no stopping it.

Has President Trump addressed "the question yet"?

" What question?" you might be asking yourself.

The question with regards to whether or not the figure recognized as "QAnon" is real. Possibly you've listened to the name now. Probably you have never heard it discussed whatsoever-- which, if that holds, that's not unexpected either. Do not worry; you will learn even more than you most likely ever wanted to know concerning this mysterious figure, in a short time.

However, researchers probably know that the answer President Trump will offer when the time comes is most likely:

" Where we go one, we go all."

The expression was pulled by Q himself from the 1996 Ridley Scott film named White Squall, where Jeff Bridges' character joins a rowdy number of boys and transforms them into practical sailors to travel worldwide. However, before they are surpassed by a sudden and extreme tornado, a storm known to experienced seafarers as the titular "white squall." The tornado would be so big, so terrible; it would put their willpower, their skills, and their capability to function as a group to the supreme test.

" Where we go one, we go all."

That's been the rallying cry for Anons because Q presented the expression to our collective consciousness. The only difference is, as opposed to trying to save a ship, we're trying to save America, and undoubtedly, the whole world. Q has been helping over a year now to educate us, to whip us in, to form and provide us the skills essential to sustain what we know is undoubtedly coming.

As well as if Trump has responded to the question Anons already know ... The Storm is currently upon us.

It's no exaggeration to say that we've been kept in the dark our whole lives. It's like Plato and the Allegory of The Cave attributed to him.

That allegory propounds that we have all been trapped, sent to prison in a cave, only permitted to see the passing of change and twisting shadows dancing across a cavern wall surface. It's so dark, we can not see anyone else, nor can we see the chains binding us, but we can feel them, and we can listen to as well as bump right into various other unfortunate hearts entrapped in the cave alongside us. We try to bear in mind exactly how we got here, but the basic truth is that all of us were born here, in this prison, and as soon as we could understand our position, we then found ourselves bound and lacking the ability to leave.

In our version of the tale, a few of our fellow prisoners, with brilliance, toughness of personality, and resourcefulness have figured out how to run away from this infernal cavern and have since come back, bringing information of a wide world; a world of great wonders that can hardly be defined to those who have been somehow kept in the dark all their lives. It's a world hidden from us by others who desired to keep us bound, oppressed, and methodically manipulated our entire lives. Basically: it's a peculiar world that needs to be well seen to be believed.

That is precisely why these brave warriors have decided to return and attempt to help free everybody caught in this infernal cave. This isn't mere wishful reasoning or optimistic deception. Still, the very reality we could understand within our lifetimes if only we would arise, and together, break off the chains that have kept us bound for long.

You would have assumed that every person would leap at the opportunity, but the truth is, many aren't too eager to leave the cave. Some have gotten accustomed to the mashed cockroach gruel provided by the caretakers every morning. And besides, haven't you heard the saying?... The "outside world" is just a "Far-Right Conspiracy" peddled by crackpots!

That implies that some will require more convincing than others. They require access to the truth and real knowledge.

How would you begin to explain something like color to somebody who has only seen shadows their entire life? Just how would you describe a tree to a person that has no precise idea of what a tree is? How would you set someone free that has determined he "prefers" his chains?

The relevant answer is, in fact, surprisingly straightforward.

You would have to bring a little of that outdoors light right into the cavern.

Q has commonly explained what will occur as a "Great Awakening;" a minute when the reality will radiate forth so clearly as to be indisputable, and motivate a nearly spiritual fervor among the people. There will be no form of debate because you can't effectively debate against the truth. You can't also negotiate terms with the truth. The truth will occur so powerfully as if to say, "I am right here! Behold me!" And also, there will be no argument with it at that phase in the game.

People will eventually see the liars as our prison gatekeepers, and the truth will become so distressing, so disturbing, that a lot of people will intend to reject it outrightly.

That's what happens when the cave gets filled with enough light.

Anons have been planned for this minute for more than a year; possibly two or more by the time all this starts to fall. We know far better than most people what to expect and for a good reason.

The general public?

Not much of that. So it's somehow difficult to guess or assume what the collective reactions of people will be.

Those on the Conservative side of things might welcome this; those well accustomed to these particular individual's past criminal activities, who refused to turn a blind eye to their oppressions and injustices over all the years.

Those on the Left?

They're having a much more difficult time processing what's going on today, seeing as lots of people do not even understand the first point concerning, for instance, the path of bodies that have been left in the wake of the Clintons over the previous few years. So typical has this incident been, it's even obtained its name now: Arkancide (that's Arkansas murder, for those playing along in the house).

There will probably be efforts by the media and different "grassroots" groups to manipulate this discrepancy and get people who have long considered themselves Democrats, or politically Left to riot. However, that type of message could only be relayed periodically, as much of those who would typically stir up such step will have possibly additionally been apprehended as soon as all these decreases.

Not to point out the mass arrests of those in the media that are themselves guilty of joining this treason.

Indeed, what they desire from the Left when this all drops is for them to be their good foot-soldiers, to create as much civil agitation as feasible while they attempt to leave the justice that is coming for them. To those that consider themselves "liberal" or "left-of-center" that might read this, I would certainly say this:

Do not be somebody else's useful idiot. Don't be another person's cannon straw, a mere pawn to be given up by elites on the altar of their list. Most Americans desire the truth and not a mere list. It's just a matter of having a clear understanding of the actual reality of the situation now.

Make no mistake; what I'm most likely to clarify to you throughout this book is not merely listening. However, it's going to be needed. And as it has been stated by Q, the farther we drop the bunny opening, the more "unrealistic everything ends up being."

Whether you decide to get on board with Q, or join some armed Anti-Trump resistance group roaming the drains of DC, planning paramilitary strikes on critical targets ... You must understand the truth first before you act. It's just in the light of reality that you can act appropriately.

If Q holds, the events you'll see unfolding around you will be the result of years of work by good women and men embedded across the different strata of government and society; a kind of underground team of good men, collaborating, often in secret, to ensure the safety of the residents of the United States. As of this writing, there are over one hundred thousand sealed charges or indictments waiting to be unsealed at short notice. When that takes place, a cascade of arrests will start, the sort of which the world has never experienced before. Many individuals will be caught up in such operation, which happens to be a result of police authorities working inside the Department of Justice along with Military Intelligence (MILINT), at the behest of President Trump. This has been organized or planned with army precision, and no details about the specifics of this particular have been released to the general public.

The people scheduled for arrest are spread across our society. Some are from the government. Others are from the private sector. Others are TV personalities and chatting heads, people whose faces we have seen in our living rooms countless times. Some are moguls, while others are criminals. Still, others are judges, who will be removed from the court system and called into judgment. Despite where they come from, all these individuals will be tried in a series of military tribunals. Because of this, several, if not most, will be punished with serious jail time.

For the worst, such people will be sentenced to death, and it will be a death well deserved, for if exposed and the government did not execute such a sentence, the people would most likely do it.

For centuries, our world has been ruled by a secret ancient death cult. From research and experience, this cult is simply known as the Cabal. The said Cabal is a hierarchical organization that, at its core, is Satanic in origin. They are an occult group that leverages institutions like media, governments, banking, as well as blackmail, human sacrifice, pedophilia, and even cannibalism to attain their goals. Absolutely nothing is off the table, so long as it accumulates power for themselves. They have effectively embedded themselves in the halls of power all over the world and make use of whatever means they have to keep that power.

The depths of wickedness in which they want to involve expose their essential depravity. And the dangerous thing about them is that just like serpents in the yard, they are experts at hiding in plain sight.

Many, if not most of the individuals to be arrested as well as tried, are all members of the Cabal.

This is not as strange as it appears. What number of household names have been exposed in public now for their past transgressions? There was a certain time when Bill Cosby was regarded as the ultimate TV father figure. And then Harvey Weinstein-- but Hollywood would have you believe he's just the exception to the general rule, correct? Oh, what about Kevin Spacey? And Bryan Singer? And ...

They all seem so normal or regular for the absence of a much better term. Barack Obama was the "trendy" president, right? Hillary? Well, isn't it so praiseworthy just how she forgave Bill all those years ago? And also she was, as the media line went, one of the most knowledgeable people to ever run for such office! It was her turn, and Trump stole that election by conspiring with those Russians! ... Right?

These are all finely-crafted impressions given to you by their media lapdogs, who are members of the Cabal themselves. These women and men have been charged with the specific mission of promoting Cabal candidates and ensuring public point of view moved in whatever direction the Cabal deemed fit. The mainstream media is primarily a tool of the Cabal, leveraged to sway public perceptions and also accumulate power by configuring the individuals with, well, their "programming.".

In my opinion, the real fact, which the talking heads deliberately hide from you, is that the likes of Hillary and Obama had only the devastation of the United States as their goal. And no, I'm not speaking about simple economic wreck or problems due to mass migration. Those were facets of it, yes, but I'm discussing nuclear catastrophe and the initiation of World War III. The sheer range of evil here is so enormous; it's virtually astounding. It was called "The 16 Year Plan".

The scary component? The truly terrifying component.? ... It is exactly how close they got fulfilling their plans.

The money had changed hands. Deals were created on the uranium, and the Cabal-affiliated possessions planted in secret bases worldwide were at work making the bombs that they intended to one day rain down upon our heads, to transform our loved ones right into bit greater than loads of ash and eliminating our way of life from the face of the earth.

Information asymmetry...

That is the fundamental imbalance you need to understand if we're to succeed in this endeavor.

Information asymmetry is how they keep their power. The old Greek word gnosis, meaning "expertise," (and where we acquire the term "Gnostic," as in Gnostic secrets) is usually made use of to indicate secret knowledge; things which are reserved only for some people. Why is this done? The answer is simple. You have a distinct benefit over them when you understand what others don't. You can maneuver and place yourself better, always aligning yourself in one of the most useful methods, while the hapless rubes scramble for cover listed below. A discrepancy in understanding enables you to exploit other weaknesses and failures. Information asymmetry grants the Cabal power over others. This has been the main benefit The Cabal has leveraged over these several centuries.

I do desire to excite upon you the importance of what I'm saying, precisely since I already know-- many thanks to Q-- what kinds of challenges the world is going to be encountering quickly, and how lots of people will react to the events unfolding before their very eyes. I wish that in creating this, people will find convenience in these words, that they will undoubtedly bring solace and some degree of understanding to those that require it, and that it will certainly assist in charting a new course ahead for all patriots.

To make a shift in the balance of power, things that have been concealed should now come to light. To accomplish that, it is crucial that we now have to capture a few of that light and bring it to our level, so all can see. This is the time to get out of the dark and move into the light.

CHAPTER SEVEN

The "Q" War

The earth is littered with wars

- Hardship increases

- Economic crashes appear to turn on a nonstop cycle

- Scarcity

- Genocide

- Weather control

- Man-made disasters

- Population displacement

- Incorrect flag occasions

They openly talk about controlling the population and reducing our numbers. There are many mechanisms in place to ensure they remain in power. They push a broken education system to dumb down upcoming generations so they can not resist intellectually. They bombard us with a hazardous pharmaceutical industry that markets a wide range of drugs with terrible adverse effects. They lace vaccines with mercury and other neurotoxins that alter who we are, so we are less likely to resist. They promote and champ single mothers, fatherless children, lawlessness, and glorify the drug culture. They encourage a fractured family to hurt our souls in the hopes that we will be too screwed up to resist.

Our yellow sun is typically a white sun that is much hotter. The trees and plants are passing away. The seasons are increasingly out of order. The heavenly bodies are all moving in the sky to places they never were in the past. The magnetic poles are moving. Their mines in the Arctic are triggering many of the glacier meltings that requires the sea levels to increase. They manipulate the weather condition. They spray the sky with heavy metals that are not just killing us but the planet.

They work all the time to create the worldwide global warming or global cooling, or climate change they accuse us of doing. They come to us with carbon taxes and other tricks to collect the money to fix the problem they are developing daily. They even douse our food with chemicals that fill the soil. They push a toxic agriculture system upon us to sicken our bodies, so we are too week to resist.

They remain in the position of ruining countries worldwide by liquifying their sovereignty and stripping them of their power. They relentlessly work on shuffling masses of people from one part of the world to another through illegal migration. They never send the best in these migrant caravans throughout Europe and the Americas. They send the impoverished, ill-educated, trained terrorists and gang members. They use these migrants to drain pipes, resources, and finances of the countries they enter the privilege programs. Yes, criminal activity and rape certainly go up in areas they unlawfully inhabit.|

They push a world without borders, which is another expression for the world in chaos. Borders and laws are needed in this fallen world. They guarantee some type of stability and security. Frames also enable different cultures to flourish. While we are all one humankind, we are broken into various cultural groups that share collective beliefs, traditions, and ideas. Multiculturalism is a good idea. America is a distinct culture kind from the homogenization of numerous cultures from around the globe.

They craft addicting electronic devices that sidetrack us, so we do not have time to resist. They promote sports like a god and encourage you to put your money and time watching them on television. They want you to acquire tickets to the regional service for your sport's group every week.

CHAPTER EIGHT

President Trump and The "Q"

Many non-Americans often asked why Donald Trump was chosen? Many of these people come from socialist centered countries, and they have a problem comprehending the American mindset. Throughout the years, the United States transitioned from a Republic to a democracy. In 1989 it began a new transition towards socialism and starting around 2008, progressive socialism—the majority of Americans contempt socialism in all its forms. The majority of the country adjusted to the reality that we run a democracy; however, the mindset amongst the majority is still that of a Republic.

Guideline by law and the Constitution reigns supreme.

Americans like regimes and have little persistence for monarchies. They like the liberties, rights, and advantages that the Constitution guarantees. Many Americans own a weapon for support and defense. Many Americans support the Second Amendment. The battle cry of the liberals has been that weapons promote violence. They encourage the belief that they only desire to eliminate the Second Amendment to clear the population of guns. However, that's not the whole reality.

The Second Amendment is not only about the right to own and bear arms. The Declaration of Independence states that governments derive their powers from the consent of the governed. Just powers are entrusted to a government by the individuals to establish, as the Declaration of Independence states, "security and happiness." The Declaration of Independence is quite clear on this matter of power for the government. It likewise mentions that "whenever any Form of Government becomes destructive of these ends, it is the right of the individuals to modify or to eliminate it, and to set up new Government.".

Many anti-gun liberals will cite the militia act of 1792. This act was passed a couple of years after the Constitution was ratified. It did not modify the Constitution. They use this activity to convince individuals that the militia comes under the control of the government, and today is referred to as the National Guard.

The Second Amendment of the Constitution does certainly grant Americans the right to revolt, and the Declaration of Independence backs it up as a witness. It approves Americans the right to form militias that are armed to the teeth, can practice on public land, and gives to compose tyrannical, unconstitutional government that abuses the powers given to them by the individuals if they need to.

Some Americans are upset that Trump is the President, while others are pleased. His fame continues to grow. Why not? Joblessness has struck a forty-nine-year low. Pro-American deals are being made and executed all over the world. Peace is on the horizon in numerous places, and the citizenry is having its power brought back, not just in the United States, but in lots of other nations. Consumer confidence is high, and the stock exchange is climbing up at jaw-dropping speed. Whatever seems to be showing up roses. Unless, of course, you're in the continuously shrinking group that dislikes President Trump increasingly more every day where they only see the thorns.

Why was he elected?

Throughout the last numerous previous administrations, things were heading south at a quick rate. We were constantly being told that the jobs lost would never return. A growing number of those tasks went overseas. Energy sources were being closed. We provided our cash to countries all around the world for no reason. I appear to recall it was 2009 that we offered sixty billion dollars to Poland to construct a museum. If Poland wants a museum, they ought to foot their bill. That's my opinion. Foreign companies bought American companies. The new company owner from China eliminated all the American employees. We would've lost a lot of tasks to the East if President Trump had not stopped the transpacific collaboration.

Trillions of dollars were lost every year through unjust and bad means with other nations. It was bankrupting America, but that was the strategy. There are many cases where a foreign country purchased American companies for the sole purpose to mine and export our natural deposits. The United Nations charged carbon tax fees to the United States, yet China and India paid absolutely nothing while continuing as the top polluters in the world. China exported much of our innovation and trade secrets through bad deals with our companies dealing with, or in, their country.

The United States paid a big portion of the military workforce and security expenditures to protect Europe. Over the last couple of years, we have lost our tasks, earnings, credit rating, the value of the dollar, natural resources, trade tricks, technology, and economy to the elite (or whatever you wish to call them; because they go by many names) playing their world rule games.

I understand if someone who once had a high-security clearance. He was informed by a good friend, still in those circles, something that chilled me to the bone. It had to do with a year before September 11, 2001. A conference took place someplace over in England with the little pawns that work with the elite. One of the Englishmen presents made a statement that practically everything was in place. In place for what? You might ask. In business for the new world order, one-world government, world courts, an imprisoned world, and they were all set to take over the world.

That man allegedly leaned over to Americans face and stated, "There is just one thing standing in their way. That's America's self-reliance, and it has got to go." I do not understand if that holds. I can not validate that event took place, but I think the individual who told me.

What was the outcome of 9/11?

The Patriot Act. An act that daily strips Americans of their constitutional rights and freedoms for some sort of security blanket. Security from what? Lots of answers are floating around for that question.

Q claims that Trump, his administration, and excellent individuals who still hold positions within the government and military are on our side playing a quantum-level chess video game for freedom.

Q guarantees us that there is a strategy in place to knock this evil elite group out of power and restore it to individuals. Q insinuates that this plan remained in place years before Trump ever ran for office. I do not understand if this is all real; however, I'll inform you what I know. Americans have been whispering in corners for over a year about reclaiming control. In the years leading up to the 2016 presidential election, people no longer whispered. They talked loud enough for everyone to hear. They spoke of revolution to bring back the Constitution. These same people saw Trump as a tranquil transformation.

These same individuals are all set to help their fellow Americans recover the control all of us lost. The majority of Q followers are all set to march together with all Americans and assist other countries in accomplishing this goal.

Lots of people do not like President Trump. An equal amount of individuals who do like him. I understand both sides. There are numerous qualities and associates to like and dislike. He's a very wise man, and I can ascertain that he has a very high IQ. By all looks, he appears extremely patriotic and pro-American. He's anti-drug and alcohol, anti-sex trafficking. These are all excellent and extremely positive. Lots of "Never Trumpers" are frightened he will bring about the death and destruction of America. In contrast, lots of Trump advocates put him in a godsend position. Individuals in the middle of these two camps are treading with both care and optimism.

Nevertheless, I'm a realist. Despite his less than saintly past, I don't believe Trump is the devil incarnate. Neither will I attempt to raise him to anything near the position of an American savior. I understand the fact. Trump is nothing more than a man. He is not going to conserve the Constitution, the nation, or the world from this elite group of occultic people pressing their Satanic agenda upon all of us. However, God can use Trump to hold up the clock and provide us more time, or to obliterate them.

Make no mistake.

Any intelligence, ideas, tactical plan, strategies, or successes that Trump, the administration, or military impose against this evil group of individuals will be because of God. Since God allowed him to win the presidency, he's in the workplace. If he's working on a strategy to get rid of these wicked groups and restore the Constitution, freedom, and power to the people, it will be God using him to do it. Maybe God wishes to provide us with another chance of space. If anybody's going to conserve our nation and our world from these people, it will be God, and God alone. God can use whomever He pleases to accomplish His will, even Donald Trump.

Why Donald Trump? Because there was nobody else. Since all the rest appear to be members of the same group, Americans wished to remove from power. Hillary, even by Democrats, is typically referred to as the most resented female in America. There are a lot of reasons many have offered her that title. Trump didn't imitate a political leader. He did use the well-rehearsed responses that political leaders provide. When he spoke, he seemed to shoot directly from the hip, and he said lots of Americans were thinking. Many people believed that he would do and try what he stated, and if he pulled half of it off, they would enjoy it. It was a great starting point and a serene choice. He provided himself as an American who wished to roll up his sleeves, work with others, and conserve our country from the destruction the globalists/deep state were planning. All this is why Trump was chosen.

CHAPTER NINE

Martial Law

The possibility of martial law being imposed in the United States has been circulating for decades. It began when people became aware of the US Worker Camps that started construction under the Clinton administration, finished under the Bush administration, and unimportant that they needed to be relabelled US Reeducation Centers under the Obama administration. Americans jointly refer to them as FEMA Camps. Reports of run amok the every one of the administrations pointed out above were going to enact martial law for whatever factor. It is no different with the Trump administration.

Nevertheless, what if the information coming from the Q post is correct? What would happen if a lot of high-ranking people are jailed and pursued crimes and treason? There could be civil discontent. It could be in localized pockets, or might be widespread. Under those scenarios, martial law may be possible. It must be momentary and loose under the circumstances. I don't like to entertain the idea; however, I will not rule it out as a possibility.

Will martial law be declared?

That is always a possibility with any administration. I think the response to that question depends on if there are significant arrests and how the population manages it? The majority of people following the Q post anticipate arrests and will likely pop a cork on a champagne bottle instead of taking to the streets. Extremely political liberals, once the shock diminishes, will not be pleased campers. Depending upon the criminal offenses for which they are jailed, and to what degree their advocates believe the allegations, I think will depend upon the amount of civility exercised throughout such a tribulation within the nation.

I want to believe no American would take to the streets, which they would let the legal system play out to find guilt or innocence. Nevertheless, over the last several years, I saw groups going to the streets, riot, ruin property, and participate in other types of civil disobedience over much ado about absolutely nothing. I know the fact, because it has been effectively recorded, that much of these groups that take part in such actions are hired by entities and individuals with a plan.

If this whole Q/Trump list is legit, then I must take my hint from what I've seen so far. What I have experienced is an administration that appears to be taking excellent strides to avoid civil unrest. I'll cite two examples:

1. The overwhelming majority of the Q community thinks that John McCain was detained, attempted by military court, and

executed. The governor of Ohio that said throughout an interview on national television,

" It's like 24 hours because John McCain was put to death." I comprehend when people were talking, they often slip up and say a word that does not make any sense or jumble their words. All of us do it, but that is an uncommon choice of words for somebody who died of brain cancer.

2. A vast number of the Q community believes that HW Bush was detained in September and was condemned by a military court. They also think he did not pass away of natural causes but was carried out. Some share alleged varieties of the sealed indictment used to make the arrest, some site post on the Q boards, and others claim an inside source who confirmed it.

I do not know if the two examples above hold. However, for the sake of argument, let's say that they are. Unless you follow the Q posts and the Q community who deciphers encrypted messages within the base in tweets to discover hidden messages, you are oblivious to what's going on behind the scenes. It is an extremely wise move if this is indeed what is going on. Then justice should be served if there are lots of high-ranking people that are guilty of criminal activities, trafficking, or treason. If it can be served in stealth mode, this is helpful in lots of levels. It allows for justice, cleaning up the house, eliminating corruption, and the connection of government and services as the nation continues to run without interruption.

This is probably the very best circumstance for the nation. It would keep martial law at bay. People want to see the wicked penalized, and most Q fans want vindication for individuals who do not think the Q posts. They desire to scream from the rooftops, "See, I told you so!"

If a stealth operation is going on, it's a much better choice for the nation. Parading the guilty through the streets may cause civil unrest and martial law. If the Q movement is legitimate, and these culprits are being jailed and brought to justice behind the scenes, Q followers must approach it from a different angle. Instead of dancing on the streets, think about yourself as part of an elite unique ops group. For whatever reason, God chose you to be awakened to see corruption and scams. You have been privy to arguably, one of the most significant declassified information drops of perpetuity. You've been delegated with delicate info. You were called upon to be persistent, proactive, and to wish the success of this objective. The catch is, it's a secret mission. Only those involved and informed will know the level of what took place.

Your reward is the satisfaction of knowing that the mission was a success, and the nation will progress in a better, and safer, position them before the objective began

Much Better Safe Than Sorry

There is massive civil discontent, and martial law is declared. What do you need to do to be prepared? This is a scenario that could happen. Many people highlight the emphasis President Trump put on national preparedness when he resolved the nation in September 2017. They indicate Q motivating people to get ready for such an occasion. The new President Text Alert System used to communicate with all Americans using the cell phone quickly. The Emergency Text System trial run in October 2018 succeeded. Hence, numerous claim these are the signs that martial law is coming. Others declare the system was used to access your cam and take a photo of the person who addressed the text for a national database, I deem the person operating the phone.

Many Q followers are on a countdown to January 1 when the Presidential Executive Order 13818. There is an assumption that military tribunals, on a massive scale, will start happening in 2019. Numerous presume it will result in martial law, and martial law brings uncertain fear of what might occur. Less deal with the circumstance that martial law is stated. There's no requirement to overdo it. You don't need to offer everything and move out in the middle of nowhere, construct a home out of shipping containers, and go off-grid. Neither do I think you need to have a bug out bag all ready to go. Most likely, in civil unrest that arises from military tribunals will be included in localized pockets throughout the nation.

One can only assume this would be most likely in big cities; pacifically liberal areas. If there is a disturbance in services and goods, then the country could be impacted. Realistically a martial law event under the circumstances, and this administration, would more than likely last a few days or not more than three months.

Every home ought to have one month's worth of supplies for any such disaster that might happen. Regarding martial law under the scenarios that Q followers are thinking, it would be a good idea to have a three-month supply if you wish to err on the side of care, stock up for six months. I will store up more than that. Be will be prepared if martial law comes to fulfillment. You can always use the items throughout the year if nothing takes place. So what must the average person need to be gotten ready for one month of sustainability should a disaster strike? Below is a standard list of products you must needed:

1. Enough food to sustain one individual for 30 days. This food needs to be nonperishable foods based upon 2000 calories daily.

2. One gallon of water per individual per day. You can save gallons of water; you could thoroughly clean the bathtub and fill it with water (this will keep for numerous days), or using a gravity water purification system to filter any kind of water for usage.

3. Expenditures. It's always best to attempt to have whatever paid for. The majority of working individuals have loans for their houses and autos. It's an excellent general rule to have 3-6 month's worth of your income kept in case of an emergency or job loss. The very same would use here.

4. Cash. You require a couple of hundred dollars, in small costs, on hand. You may need to use hard cash in case the computers decrease. You can not depend on swiping a credit card to pay with your phone.

5. A month's worth of medication and toiletries. This list would consist of: prescriptions, vitamins, herbs, toilet paper, soap, shampoo, meal washing liquid, toothpaste, etc.

6. A one-month supply of food for your animals or livestock on. This would likewise consist of a one-month water supply for your animals.

7. If you are a weapon owner, an adequate supply of ammo for defense is hunting.

Just increase the contents of the list of items above by the number of people in your house, and then by the number of months you wish to stock up. Allow me to restate the reality that you do not require to overdo it. You need not end up being a prepper and learn to live off the land. If the nation gets hit by an EMP, then you will need the skills. According to the world preppers, catastrophe is a couple of days away. Do not flip out if you have absolutely nothing ready for you and your household.

Cash: Bailout, Reset, Or Reallocation?

Fiat currency is a catastrophe and a headache waiting to take place. The world works on fiat currency and digital cash that isn't there. The only thing that permits the paper currency you carry in your wallet, no matter what country's currency you bring is the idea that it's worth something of value. The person using the currency and the one receiving the currency in exchange for an excellent or service put their trust in the fact that the paper has value. It does not; the US dollar deserves about three and a half cents. There is absolutely nothing to support it up. The dollar is not backed by gold any longer, nor is it backed by silver, palladium, platinum, or any commodity.

A basic and short summary of what took place to the United States dollar began when President Woodrow Wilson permitted the Federal Reserve to take control of the printing of the US dollar. He signed the Federal Reserve Act on Christmas Eve in 1913 when the Congress and Senate were a house for the holidays. Among the duties of the U.S. Congress, who manage the handbag strings, is to print and coin money for the United States. The Federal Reserve has been doing this task because, in 1913. The Federal Reserve is not a federal company or bank; it is never proven on any ledger to have reserves.

The US-backed, proportionately, the United States dollar with a specific portion of gold. In 1971, that percentage was around 35%. That is until President Nixon, on August 15, 1971, got rid of the United States dollar from the gold requirement and switch to a petrodollar. The United States dollar is not backed by gold, rare-earth element, or product. The Federal

Reserve is never proven to back the currency with anything. This is why they can continue to print cash that does not exist. This is how banks can lend some money that does not exist. They simply produce brand-new digital cash in the ledger that wasn't there before. It runs through a cycle of loaning, offering, borrowing, and rate of interest that makes fiat cash that is based upon absolutely nothing of value from digital cash that never existed. Fiat currency is a home of cards. It is a lie, a scam, and a rip-off.

Fiat currencies worldwide will collapse. Lots of currencies have collapsed; however, they are typically saved through a bailout. They tell you banks, and specific corporations, are too huge to stop working. If the federal government does not bail these organizations out, they use scare tactics to encourage individuals that catastrophe will strike in the world will drop into chaos. Naturally, they do not bail these banks and businesses out, but the individuals do through taxes.

The government will let you file and fail insolvency and lose everything you out; however, banks and major corporations are too big to stop working. Why? Since it makes excessive money. Individuals are awakening and starting to comprehend more about the fiat system currently running the world, and numerous want to return to a metal base system.

There are three choices: another bailout, reset, or reallocation.

We all know what happens with the bailout. All the big banks and corporations who lost, mismanaged, or inadequately invested their money get more. All indications indicate the citizenry of most countries declining to enable another bailout. Is Q followers, and Trump supporters, are bidding on reset. There is no clear image of what reset may look like. The Federal Reserve might be deserted, and the United States start printing a brand-new currency. There needs to be some sort of physical exchange of Federal Reserve for the brand-new notes. The Federal Reserve note can be guaranteed by a certain percentage backed by gold or another rare-earth element. There are multiple alternatives when it comes to resetting, however, the money should be revalued. For example, a brand-new note is issued, and it carries a worth that is 40% lower than the current value of the Federal Reserve note. Regardless if you have one hundred dollars or five hundred million dollars, the wealth distribution stays the same. Nobody went up or down the economic ladder.

Some people are hoping for reallocation. The fiat currency begins to crash due to another failure in the banking system, derivatives, and losses within the marketplace. Instead of a bailout or reset, the cash is reallocated based on a pre-formulated criterion. What are those requirements? You must be on inside to know that at this point. It might be based upon holdings, investments, Social Security balances, or anything. How would the cash be reallocated? Will it be in Federal Reserve notes, a gold-based dollar, a silver-based dollar, or a digital dollar based on cryptocurrency? If reallocation is being prepared, there's just a handful of people who understand how it will be implemented.

What can you do? Try to get your real property, and hard possessions settled. The US dollar is presently compared to the worth of silver; however, they might use palladium or platinum.

CHAPTER TEN

No One Can Be Against Us

Why do we require Q? The Internet boards that Q runs is an open platform used to inform the people about the back screen that's running behind the front program that they allow people to see. Q is our proverbial Toto pulling back the curtain to reveal to us what's going on behind the scenes and exposing the wizard to be a fraud, exposing the witches of the east and the west for who they are, and Glinda for the devil that she is.

A lot of our people remain blind to the evil matrix that has been built around us. About a 3rd of can't bear to look, so they conceal in electronic devices, sports, entertainment, and any other diversion that will take their mind off what they fear they are incapable of managing. Each of us knows it's dark out there. We can all see the violence and the raging storm. The plug needed to be pulled because we were all going to drown. It was drawn in November 2016, and the predators in the angry waters are not going to reduce without a fight. They are throwing whatever they have in the world. They are defending their lives, wealth, power, and, more significantly, their agenda.

What is their agenda?

Is it power? Is it wealth? Is it manage? Is it the freedom to do what they desire despite how sick, perverted or evil it maybe? The response to all these questions appears to be a definite yes. The above aforementioned are just the advantages and perks they make while serving the primary program. It appears they wish to introduce the guideline of their god on this earth. That may appear stunning since many of the claim to be atheist. They promote atheism as sound logic and reason. These individuals are not atheists. Far from it.

They serve their god with extraordinary commitment. Essentially, they are witches, wizards, sorcerers, occultists, Luciferians, and Satanists. You can call them what you want; however, I believe their practices are dark and inhuman. They dislike the God that produced all people in His image. Their god is the one who rebelled. They wanted all the power, wealth, and control for himself. They like their father, and they serve him tirelessly. They imitate him, and they want him here reigning and ruling. However, the point they neglect is the reality. He is using them as they use us. When in power, he will step on them like an ant. They stop working to acknowledge that he failed; therefore, will they.

They don't care about us. These kinds of individuals use others to increase their power, and perhaps for periodic home entertainment. They will compromise you, your kids, your nation, and your freedom to live to keep their ability. They are the definition of tyranny. They strive to persuade you that you are an animal. They desire you to act like an animal and manage you like an animal. They want to evaluate their pseudoscience, biowarfare, chemtrails, and chemically altered food and water on you like an animal in a lab. They desire to train you to be loyal like an animal. They want to confine and rent you like an animal. They desire to train you like animals to attack each other over sex, race, political celebrations, and any other social program they produce to keep their pet fights running. They are entertained when we battle each other, they bank on which pet will win, and they use it as an excuse to take more control and tighten up the choker they positioned around our necks.

You are not an animal. You are a person. You were produced in the image of God Himself, and God is not an animal. You were not divinely designed by God to act and act like an animal. We were all developed to desire the same things: God, peace, kinship, and love. Satan only longs to kill, damage, and take. Those are his fingerprints, and they are all over this wicked plan to take over the world and our lives.

They eliminate us every day; they steal and rob people of their family, their livelihood, their self-respect, their peace, their hope, their finances, their security, their health, and even their humanity. They ruin individuals, their faith, their countries, their cities, their lives, and their kids. They kill, steal and destroy similar to their dad, the devil.

And I desire to see us unify as one country under God. One individual. One America. I wish to see other nations stand together under God and his security for their country. I desire to see us united under the blanket of defenses and flexibilities this country-- the Republic-- was established. I desire all of us to take pleasure in the fruits of the land God provided us. Since some manufactured war began by a group of Satanists, I want our people to motivate each other and not tear each other down.

There are no special bloodlines born to rule. No sex is superior. No color of skin reigns supreme. There is, however, one race, which is the humankind. God did not create animals in His image.

Nevertheless, every person was created in the image of God. When we assault each other, it's nearly like we attack God. This is not who He created us to be. This is not how He created us to act and behave.

For you are all kids of God through faith in Christ Jesus. And all who have been unified with Christ in baptism have placed on Christ, like putting on new clothes. There is no longer Jew or Gentile, servant or son, male and female. For you are all one in Christ Jesus."

The wizard, nor the witches, can pull the wool over your eyes. They can't motivate you to combat an opponent that isn't there. Glinda's us versus them propaganda falls on deaf ears. Because when a real Christian sees the adjustment and hears the lies, they escape from that trap quicker than the Witch of the West from a water park.

When it comes to Q-Anon and Trump, I think it's all legitimate. I hope it is. I could be wrong and showed a fool. At this moment in time, I still rely on the strategy. I haven't read anything from Q, or even Trump's tweets, that shocked me. I just discover confirmation for what I currently thought. I figured out my federal government had been hijacked. I understand the fact evil continues to be promoted in more areas of life. I've seen families torn apart, and friendships ripped asunder over propaganda wars intended at dividing and conquering us.

I've seen the family broken and the damage and destruction it leaves behind. I've lost a member of the family to the drug culture they press. I've witnessed the anger and disappointment spill out onto the streets. I watch frightened as the murder rates increase. Increasingly I'm the victim of some fellow countryman who does not like me because of my skin color, my sex, my political convictions, or my Christian beliefs because they all think Glinda's propaganda.

They sell Oz as the answer to all our issues, but Oz does not exist. There is no land over the rainbow. They have all of us going after something that does not exist. We've all been deceived. Do not feel embarrassed. Your eyes are now opened to the truth, and you are empowered to break devoid of their matrix. The big-headed emperor has no clothes, so the embarrassment falls entirely upon them.

If Q-Anon and Trump are a scam, it won't be long until the evil elite has their day at our expenditure. Nevertheless, if this thing is legitimate, then we should unify and support each other. We need to reinforce one another to stand during the uncomfortable hour that is coming. It will be hard to see. It will most likely embarrass the nation. It will be a lot to comprehend. The same opts for other countries out there.

To my Americans, it will be hard to stand but stand we must. Stand, we will. Not just will we stand through the storm, we will emerge out the opposite joined and embrace the destiny that we were all born to meet as Americans. This is our home. This is not how we go down. We will defend our God-given freedoms, our lives, and our kids. We will unify. We will battle, and I believe we will win. To my fellow Americans who will enlist in Operation Restoration, my satisfaction is to serve by your side.

Where we go one, we go all. If God be for us, who can be versus us? The response is: NO ONE.

CHAPTER ELEVEN

Defusing The Qanon Cabal

Following Q, even after all this time, can be described as quite compelling. Indeed, it's still hard to even start approaching the subject of Q, precisely because the operation is referred to as QAnon is still ongoing as at the time of writing this book; however that does not make it less compelling in any way.

Writing about Q as the plan is still ongoing every day, is like attempting to construct a submarine at two-hundred fathoms below the sea level, while sliding along to some undisclosed secret location. The task is quite daunting, with dizzying conditions and a completely alien landscape - however, Q reassures us that we are headed towards a perfect place. It is, however, no surprise that following Q often leaves one feeling like she or he needs to come up for air at regular periods.

This is an attempt to describe QAnon to an audience that maybe finding out about him for the very first time; an audience who may, in truth, be opposed to the ideas existing as they struggle so much to accept the events that have either already happened, or are occurring around them.

Many individuals love President Trump and the GOP; a lot more than the Legacy Media would prefer the world to believe. They will be happy to learn for the first time about the systematic and highly imaginative disclosure of long-suppressed intel by the Trump administration. They will be amazed as they find out about the military accuracy of this operation, carried out for their advantage. For them, the information about to be provided will unquestionably feel more like a missing puzzle piece eventually discovered after years of searching; a crucial foundation in their mental framework, and one which empowers them to build a more precise and meaningful worldview-- something that is going to have a profound effect on society when done en masse. And you'll note here that this is my hope: that after reading this book, both the people at first hostile to Q and those who willingly embrace Q from the beginning will end up at the very same spot- with a significantly increased understanding of reality, and that they will have the ability to come together as people or citizens of the same Republic, and develop a stunning future together. I hope that this increased understanding will assist people on both sides of the aisle to shake off the mass deception committed against everyone for so long and finally realize that this isn't a Right versus Left battle any longer. It never was.

What occurs when you check out Q is that you find out that what we are experiencing is a fight between Darkness and Light. That's why Q typically refers to this particular movement as a Great Awakening, and he's right. We are discussing Truth versus Lies as well as Good versus Evil. Some simply require a bit more assistance than others in breaking off the psychological shackles placed there in secret by the agents of Darkness.

No matter your reaction, the problem faced in attempting to discuss Q is more intensified by the inherent complexity of Q- from the numerous encoding methods he utilizes to the broad series of topics covered, to the key list of players involved. Even the misinformation intentionally positioned in the drops by Q himself, to mislead any evil person following along, to press them into making errors, tipping their hands too early, and using up important resources at a time when they really can't afford to lose anything. This is even further intensified by the sheer amount of Q's posts. Since this writing, Q has been posting for over a year and a half now, and has collected over 3,300 posts throughout this time. Who understands the number of posts there will be in the end, or for how long this operation will go on! Distilling that amount of information-- information that's been spread out over the course of these numerous months and heavily supplemented by a research study from Anons throughout that whole time, is no small task.

The work of understanding and sharing Q's drops as a full-time job for the entire duration Q has remained active.

Once again, this is not about Right versus left or Liberal versus Conservative. Once the Cabal's evils have been exposed to the whole world for all to see clearly, it will end up being apparent to all that this is about Light versus Darkness, Good versus Evil, Truth versus Falsehood, -- and who doesn't desire Light, Goodness and Truth to follow them all of their days?

Of course, all of us want that! It may take some work to get everybody there, since ... well ... I think you'll quickly see the immensity of the evil that has become ingrained in our society over many years, and the work many patriots have devoted to help excise that evil from our world.

As with any discussion, it's best to initially specify our terms, academic though that may prevent any unnecessary confusion. Contrary to all you may have heard in the Legacy Media (which is what I call anything transmitted one-way, through traditional mediums such as TV, radio, and print, where there is no genuine opportunity for response, feedback, or user interaction), QAnon is not a simple "conspiracy theory.".

It's worth noting here that the term "conspiracy theory," though extant from at least the late 1890s, was promoted by the CIA in the wake of the Warren Commission. For the more youthful audience, that was the commission developed by Lyndon B. Johnson (LBJ) to investigate the assassination of JFK (which is a joke in and of itself ... considering LBJ was probably the one who had him eliminated in the very first location, so he might increase to power and introduce a host of disastrous reforms that would end up producing things like the well-being state, among other cultural quagmires).

Regardless, the term was weaponized by the CIA (or Clowns in America, as Q likes to call them) to cordon off specific areas of inquiry in the general public consciousness. The maximum chilling effect of all this was to get the people at large to stop asking concerns, questions that were rather inconvenient to those in power. Before this, enterprising Americans would provide hypotheses and test them carefully, doggedly looking for the reality. After this report? "Conspiracy theories" became the area of insane folk with questionable taste in metal headgear, and the news itself grew increasingly homogenized.

One such troublesome concern at the time of the JFK assassination disputed the main conclusion delivered by the Warren Commission in 1964 that Lee Harvey Oswald had acted alone. Well, when President Trump just recently declassified over 3,100 supersecret documents relating to the JFK investigation, never before seen by the public, it turned out that this had been a thoroughly crafted lie! There were, in fact, a minimum of 2 shooters involved in this conspiracy to murder the president, and much more included in the general conspiracy.

And it's here that we must keep in mind the extensive distinction between "conspiracy" and "conspiracy theories." Is it not human nature for people to collude and conspire together? The root of the word indicates "to breathe together," and in that sense, individuals "conspire" every day. The word "conspiracy" has gotten a bit of luggage over the years, not least due to the CIA's efforts. However, in reality, any group of individuals, meeting anywhere, discussing whatever, are "conspiring" together. The subject may be fun and unimportant. It may be basic chatter about the everyday drama of our lives, but conspiring is what we, as social animals do. People conspire all the time, and is it so unexpected to discover that those in power and influence would conspire to make sure they retain their power and effect.

It's ominous, isn't it? Not only were there several gunmen involved in this "conspiracy," but those who proposed anything contrary to the main narrative set forth by the Warren Commission were demonized by government intelligence companies and the media to keep these "bothersome concerns" at bay. This can not be downplayed: real individuals were vilified for several years for seeing truth properly and pressing for more information. The question then ends up being; why keep the details of this assassination hidden?

Furthermore, who would desire to keep such info hidden, and what tools do they have at their disposal to keep such information concealed?

Who is QAnon that the Legacy Media should malign him so? Why has his movement taken the world by storm, in which other "conspiracy theories" before him haven't? Is it merely the grand mack daddy of them all, rolling bits and pieces of all theories into one big tin foil mish-mash? Is the QAnon movement just conspiracy theory on "bath salts," as one reporter put it?

We need to step back and set the stage a little at this point, because a great deal of events were unfolding so quickly during this time that to understand QAnon genuinely, you have to understand everything that came before QAnon. You need to get a real feel for the landscape at the time, the real context of these events, and not the Mockingbird Media's retelling of such events, but the true version they helped conceal from you, because that's the setting into which QAnon emerged. If you desire to understand QAnon, you need to first become an Anon by seeing the world and the events leading up to it, as an Anon would see them. This formidable look at history will not be very easy, but it will be needed if you wish to stand any chance of understanding what's taking place now, about Trump, Q, and the Great Awakening. It's time to strap on your Nightmare Vision safety glasses and see the world through the eyes of an Anon.

So, on June 16, 2015, Donald Trump formally announced his presidential campaign in Trump Tower. Many took it as a joke and dismissed it outrightly initially, but the man quickly gained the needed traction. By 2016, the Trump Train outshined the competition, beating out eleven other prospects.

Within weeks, on June 27, Anons created /r/The _ Donald on Reddit as a "/ pol/ colony," to help facilitate this effort by bringing in the "normies." The site became the single largest source of Trump's online support, and triggered a multitude of continuous memes, which just served to drive his popularity and his message home to numerous people by directly bypassing the Legacy Media, much to the shame of Leftists all over

The campaign continued to grow, and quite quickly, the raucous fun was spreading like wildfire across social networks. Centipedes (that is, the label provided to Trump advocates on /r/The _ Donald- which was a reference to the tune "Centipede" by the drum and bass band, Knife Party) took over Reddit so efficiently, the Reddit admins quickly decided to censor the subreddit and pull it from the front page-- a relocation that had never been done before in the history of Reddit and which has considering that never been duplicated. The movement is a sensational one for those acquainted with the site, which had formerly prided itself on operating with FOSS principles in mind-- liberty, openness, totally free speech, democratic sharing, etc. The admins would then obfuscate the real customer count, initially capping it around 600,000 (when in reality, the marketer tools on the web site's back end showed the count to be closer to six million users-- a far more precise count, considering the company would be devoting scams if they ever messed with those numbers).

Far too huge to delete straight-out (the users would revolt and ruin the site if they did), the Reddit admins (consisting of Steve Huffman, who is believed to be the mediator of/ r/Cannibals, where he discusses his very first time eating human flesh using a sockpuppet account) effectively turn/ r/The _ Donald into a "containment" subreddit, guaranteeing Trump's message and his supporters are cut off from the more comprehensive website, with the paid-off admins of other subs like/ r/Politics routinely censoring pro-Trump content at the "ground level."

On February 13, 2016, Supreme Court Justice Antonin Scalia would be discovered dead at Cibolo Creek Ranch Vineyard in Texas, leaving a vacancy on the most significant court in the land throughout the last year of Obama's presidency. Obama would nominate Merrick Garland as his replacement, but Republicans would block the verification by invoking, ironically, "the Biden guideline," named after the then vice president Joe Biden, which mentioned that the Senate was under no responsibility to validate the Supreme Court choice of an outbound administration.

During the campaign, Trump dealt with a troubling quantity of disruption from the extreme left. On March 11, he would be forced to cancel a rally in Chicago as countless violent protesters came down upon the University of Illinois place, where brawls would break out on the rally floor. At least five arrests would be made, and two law enforcement officers injured due to the violent mob. In March, George Papadopoulos would sign up with the Trump project as a foreign policy adviser, after leaving the Ben Carson project.

Complete disclosure: I'm undecided as to what Papadopoulos' larger role in all this was. Part of me thinks he's Mossad-- and a specific blog writer I respect has stated multiple times now that his partner is a Russian spy, though she rejects that herself-- but I'm withholding judgment till this element of the story becomes more apparent. However, without jumping too far ahead, Q himself would highlight Papadopoulos among his more current drops, and imply that much more was going on than what we could currently see on the surface area:

On March 12, Thomas Dimassimo would hop a barricade and attempt to deal with Citizen Trump at a rally, before being dealt with by Secret Service and apprehended.

On March 14, while in Italy, Papadopoulos would meet a Maltese professor by Joseph Mifsud. The latter claimed to have ties to the Russian federal government, and likewise claimed to have a lot of e-mail dirt on Hillary Clinton. In reality, Mifsud would have ties to the Saudis, UK intelligence, Australian intelligence, and would later go missing out on before revealing up again, very recently, holed up in the United States Embassy in Rome.

The public would later be told that it was this conference in between Mifsud and Papadopoulos that would trigger the "Russian Collusion" examination and the production of the

Steele dossier. It would also end up being a subject of intense analysis in the later Mueller investigation, but in 2018, Mifsud's lawyer would come out and claim that Mifsud had been working for the FBI the whole time; that is, at the wish of James Comey to entrap Papadopoulos (who may or may not have been a double agent himself and whose other half, a minimum of according to that blogger who you'll satisfy later, was likewise a Russian spy). More information continues to emerge daily about all these gamers, but it's looking a growing number of like this was a worldwide entrapment operation staged by multiple global intelligence firms, coordinating to frame Donald Trump for collusion with the Russians, successfully staging a coup for the Cabal.

On March 21, Trump would announce Carter Page as another diplomacy advisor for his campaign. Page had previously worked with the FBI in 2013 as an undercover worker, assisting in building a case versus Evgeny Buryakov, who would later plead guilty to charges of conspiracy against the United States, previously impersonating a trade representative and gathering secret information about the US energy sector. Q would, later on, notify us that Page was, in truth, an undercover FBI plant into Trump's campaign and that his contact with Russia would later on function as a basis for the FBI opening an investigation into Trump and his staff.

On March 29, Paul Manafort would sign up with the Trump campaign as his project supervisor. Unbeknownst to Trump at the time, Manafort was yet another plant took into the Trump campaign by the Podesta Group, a lobbying firm run by Tony Podesta, the sibling of Hillary's campaign supervisor, John Podesta. As this was going on, it would, later on, be revealed that a Democratic National Committee (DNC) lawyer by the name of Alexandra Chalupa was examining Manafort since at least 2014 and producing a lot of "opposition research study" on him as someone colluding with the Russians. Long story short, this "research study" would work its way through Ukraine, of all locations, to Steele, into the hands of the previous director of public prosecutions for the Crown Prosecution Service in the UK, Alison Saunders, who would then fly to the United States to have supper with Bruce and Nellie Ohr. Bruce was deputy attorney general of the United States at the time, and Nellie was working for the CIA front referred to as Fusion GPS ... which was the exact very same business the Hillary project had hired to produce the Steele Dossier in the first place. If you're confused now, I won't blame you at all. The coup is highly convoluted.

This would soon function as the whole set up for the eventual "Russian collusion" story, as Manafort would purposefully set up a meeting between Donald Trump Jr. and some Russians: one being Natalia Veselnitskaya, a Russian attorney and Magnitsky act lobbyist who worked under one Saak Albertovich

Karapetyan, a Russian attorney general (who would, later on, pass away in a "strange" helicopter crash, in October of 2018). See, according to Q, Veselnitskaya had been given special access to the US by none aside from the Obama administration's attorney general of the United States Loretta Lynch. Previously, she had been barred from the country due to obstruction of justice charges, and hence, had to be given unique entry.

To put it simply, a plant in the Trump campaign was secretly working for the bro of Clinton's campaign supervisor, and collaborating with the Obama administration's attorney general of the United States, to establish an incriminating looking conference, which would then be used to justify obtaining a FISA warrant, for a sitting administration to take part in illegal bulk, "umbrella" FISA spying on all Trump project interactions, to dig and attempt up dirt on behalf of their preferred prospect, Hillary Clinton. What I indicate by that is since of this meeting, Obama might "lawfully" get a warrant to spy on Donald Trump Jr. and Jared Kushner. And because of the way FISA warrants work, you generally get to surveil everybody they enter into contact with. By putting these warrants in location, Obama now had "legal" access to spy on, successfully, the entire Trump campaign.

Oh, he was spying in advance, but the FISA warrant made it "legal." In reality, Obama would get British intelligence, part of the "Five Eyes" alliance, to do his dirty work for him, when Government Communications Headquarters (GCHQ) director Robert Hannigan was permitted to wiretap Trump and his associate from Fort Meade. Hannigan would later on, in the summertime of 2016, fly to consult with the then director of the CIA John Brennan ... which was odd, considering his American equivalent was Admiral Michael Rogers, director of the NSA. You see, the CIA is officially expected to use its power against foreign states and actors. Simply put, it's not allowed to spy on US people. To skirt around this legal issue, the Obama administration turned to foreign allies and their intelligence firms, because nothing is preventing them from spying on United States people, legally speaking. And then these foreign intelligence companies can turn around and honestly share what they found out with our intelligence firms. See how that works? I believe we may appropriately label this following the letter, but not the spirit of the law.

Three days after Trump took office, Hannigan would resign from his post as head of the GCHQ. Perhaps you see a preponderance of British names involved in this whole Spygate scandal. You've got Christopher Steele, the former MI6 operative employed by Fusion GPS to develop the Steele Dossier, Alison Saunders, the previous director of public prosecutions who ate with the Ohrs, Robert Hannigan of the GCHQ, and others I haven't mentioned yet, such as Arvinder Sambei, who introduced Mifsud to

Papadopoulos, and Saunders to the Ohrs. How do they loop in all this? Rather just, through the Queen's Privy Council, upon which sits Steel's previous MI6 boss and existing chairman and founder of Cambridge Analytica (previously referred to as SCL), Richard Dearlove, alongside Saunders, and a variety of Soros-affiliated individuals, consisting of Lord Mark-Malloch Brown, who, as we'll see later, is the chairman of among the largest ballot maker companies in the world, Smartmatic.

It must be kept in mind here that Tony Podesta would close his whole lobbying operation the very day Mueller prosecuted Manafort and Rick Gates for stopping working from signing up as FARA representatives-- activities which would inextricably lead back to the Podesta Group.

It also needs to be noted that, only weeks before Manafort joining the Trump project, the then director of the CIA, John Brennan, had made a secret visit to Moscow to consult with Deputy Foreign Minister Oleg Syromolotov. I'm sure that had "definitely nothing" to do with any of the occasions that followed.

Since this writing, it's uncertain when exactly Trump found out that Manafort was a plant, but discover he did. There has been massive speculation that eventually, Trump could get Manafort to flip and could leverage him in a plan to counter all this subversion (though, since right now, nobody but those in the intelligence neighborhood, those straight involved, and Trump himself understands for sure).

However, back to our timeline, for the time being:

On May 3, 2016, Trump would officially end up being the Republican candidate, defeating all his competition. Despite all this censorship and resistance, it proves too little, too late, and Trump would now go on to take on versus the Democratic candidate.

In May 2016, Inspector General Steve Linick would provide a report condemning Clinton's usage of private e-mail servers. She had not looked for or gotten governmental approval or authorization. The story about Clinton's private e-mail servers was initially broken in the wake of the Benghazi panel and was reported by the New York Times in March of 2015. To cover her criminal activities, she used a program called "Bleachbit" to eliminate over 30,000 incriminating emails and ruined a variety of mobile phones with hammers.

Now, this is of particular note, since Bleachbit isn't just your routine recycling bin program. See, when a file is written to a disk drive, all those nos and ones are composed onto a magnetic disk, and they are not overwritten until the computer says they can be. When most computer systems "delete" a file, it's merely marking that space as safe to overwrite with new data, new ones, and nos. This implies forensic experts can usually obtain files or parts of files, even if they've been erased-- because the initial ones and zeroes are still there, a minimum of up until they're overwritten.

Bleachbit, on the other hand, is the equivalent of a digital file shredder. It overwrites whatever files you desire with null data; generally a long string of nos-- and it does this many times over, making sure there is no residual, leftover data on the drive, entirely obfuscating whatever was written there previously, making it difficult to resurrect the deleted data. When she was questioned about it was a total farce, her pretending like she didn't know what Bleachbit did. When she was asked if she had wiped her servers, she couldn't have been more transparent when she said: "What, like with a fabric or something?" No, she had first to buy that program, then set up that program, then set it to overwrite her information with a string of zeroes seven times over. It would later come out that Paul Combetta, who went by the username "Stonetear" on Reddit, had gone to Reddit to request for help in erasing all way of information.

On May 10, George Papadopoulos would have a conference with the Australian diplomat, Alexander Downer, at the Kensington Wine Room. In London, after among Downer's associates made the ask for the set to meet. While Papadopoulos did refer to what Mifsud had previously told him, Downer would report the details of the discussion back to the Australian federal government in the next day or two. So by July 22, the details of that conversation were divulged back to the FBI, though no intelligence was reported as being traveled through "main" Five Eyes channels. How did the FBI find out of this discussion, which was, again, entirely legal?

Once again, the response is that this was all a set-up by our Five Eyes allies, operating at the request of the Obama Administration, to help set up the "Russian Collusion" story and frame the Trump campaign as treasonous traitors. Those in power viewed Trump as an existential risk to their sovereignty, even in those early days of the project, and understood he had actually to be stopped no matter what. Hiring a few favors from abroad allowed the Obama administration to surreptitiously side-step any legal defenses- consisting of the Fourth Amendment protections afforded to all United States citizens by the US Constitution-- by efficiently "outsourcing" the job of spying to foreign intelligence.

Oh, and by the method, this specific conversation between Papadopoulos and Downer would later be mentioned by the FBI as the sole reason they opened a counter-intelligence examination into the Trump project. Want another connection?

Former MI6 employer Richard Dearlove knew the CIA/MI6 asset (and pal of the Bushes) Stefan Halper through the Cambridge Intelligence Seminar. Halper met Papadopoulos, tried to have another representative seduce him, and likewise works for personal intelligence firm Hakluyt. Downer formerly worked for Hakluyt and stayed in an advisory board. Downer also formerly helped organize the single most significant foreign contribution to the Clinton Foundation that they ever received, some twenty-five million dollars. The rest of Hakluyt is composed of spooks, a number of whom are listed as having contributed to Hillary's governmental project.

On May 19, former congressman Anthony Weiner (and partner to Hillary Clinton's favorite, long-time aide Huma Abedin) would plead guilty to sexting with an underage teen, get sentenced to 21 months in jail, and made to register as a sex culprit. As part of the examination into Weiner, his laptop computer was seized, which included a wide variety of "insurance" files. Contained inside were several e-mails, supported from Hillary's e-mail server as well as files which, according to reports, made grown NYPD officers break down in tears. What sort of files could produce such an effect on seasoned NYPD officers?

Later, the OIG report provided in June of 2018 would validate what many already correctly inferred:

" Crimes Against Children." Let that sink in for a minute. Folks, I'm not lying when I say the Clintons, operating through the Clinton Foundation, are a few of the worst criminals of human trafficking in the history of humanity. We'll talk more about that in a later chapter, but understand that for now, according to Q, two NYPD officers would pass away as a result of what they had seen on that laptop computer, their deaths marked as random murders, but in truth, they were assassinated; two more victims of Arkancide.

On May 19, Trump would promote Paul Manafort to project chairman. It would later be exposed in a congressional interview with former FBI director, James Comey. The FBI had opened four different investigations into four individual Trump advisers that extremely same day. The four in question were: Michael Flynn, Paul Manafort, Carter Page, and George Papadopoulos. These investigations, together with information from Five Eyes allies, would form the basis of the FBI's investigation into "Russian collusion" within the Trump campaign, called with the code word "Crossfire Hurricane."

On June 3, a female would be backed versus a wall and showered with eggs, bottles and spat upon for supporting

Trump. Numerous other Trump advocates would be beaten, assailed, and daunted by increasingly violent infantrymen of the Left, like Antifa and La Raza.

On June 6, Hillary would end up being the Democratic Party nominee. She accomplished this by stealing the Democratic election from Bernie Sanders utilizing "Super-delegates," enraging numerous on the Left by efficiently invalidating their votes. One of these who worked throughout the super-delegate coup would be Democratic National Committee staff member (and Bernie Sanders Supporter) 27-year-old Seth Rich.

On June 9th, the trap was set, and all set to spring. Paul Manafort, Jared Kushner, and Donald Trump Jr. would meet Natalia Veselnitskaya, that Russian attorney. The latter, again, was allowed into the US after being supplied unique entry by none besides Attorney General Lynch. As part of this setup, the Russian lawyer guaranteed dirt on Clinton: 1) never provided, and 2) not a criminal activity for anyone there to hear. She wished to pressure Jr. about the Magnitsky Act-- which makes sense because she, as a legal representative, focused on this location.

On June 18, a British citizen called Michael Sanford would try to assassinate Trump when he would attempt to steal a cops officer's gun. He would fail, end up apprehended, serve some time in prison, and later be deported back to the UK.

On June 27, 2016, Bill Clinton and Attorney General Loretta Lynch would meet at Phoenix airport, on Lynch's jet. Critics instantly called out the "Tarmac Meeting" as a terrible dispute of interest, coming at a time when Bill's partner Hillary was still under investigation by the Justice Department for her usage of a personal, unauthorized e-mail server, and because somebody in Lynch's position has an ethical duty to, at the minimum, keep up the pretense of impartiality. Even lots of Democrats would go on to talk about the evil "optics" of the meeting. And while Lynch herself would go on to say the conference was primarily social, and that she and Bill had simply talked about "grandkids" and "golf," we would quickly learn an extremely various (and scary) variation of the story from Q. In reality, what had happened was something much more ominous, and even treasonous. You'll hear more about that soon.

In June, the Obama administration would have the intelligence community make its first official FISA warrant request to spy on the Trump campaign. It would be rejected. (They would return a while later on, in October, after acquiring the Steele Dossier, and succeed in obtaining a warrant.).

It's essential to keep in mind that this is the first "authorities" instance of spying. Trump had already been under prohibited monitoring for some time at this point, with no courts involved, no warrants provided, and absolutely nothing even resembling due procedure-- let alone an evidentiary basis to justify this spying. (And he wasn't the only one, either. Q would later notify us that the Ted Cruz project was also being spied upon at the same time.)

It's crucial to understand, moving forward, that the NSA had scooped up quite much every electronic communication, every bit, and package sent out throughout the internet (yes, whatever, from everyone), and it was basic practice to share that intelligence amongst all different American intelligence companies. For circumstances, a CIA agent could query the NSA database to discover all sorts of things, at any point in time. Because of regular auditing practices, the NSA can find out if this gain access is being abused in any way. And in fact, that's exactly what happened.

The CIA was abusing their access to such an extent when it concerned illegal Trump project surveillance (again, at the wish of the Obama administration, for the advantage of the Hillary Clinton project), that at one point, they expected they would be captured if they kept this up, and simply copied the whole database over to their cloud, hosted by none other than Amazon.com's S3 cloud services.

See, Amazon isn't just an online merchant. The most crucial segment of their service has traditionally been their web services, and they had a whopping contract with the CIA, valued at six-hundred million dollars alone. S3 web services run significant portions of the web, with a few of the biggest companies leveraging Amazon's server farms to run their businesses and host all their information.

And, if you're clever here, you'll keep in mind that Amazon is owned by Jeff Bezos, the same Jeff Bezos that owns the Washington Post. That would be the very same Washington Post that has been ruthless, leading the attack in post after post against Trump, and also against QAnon. As Q likes to say, there are "No Coincidences." And though the Washington Post was not alone in its attacks against Trump by any step, many have given that started to hypothesize that part of the reason for the strength of these media attacks has been because a lot of this very same media business took money from foreign governments to change their diminishing subscribership and decreasing advertisement dollars, and failed to register as foreign representatives at the same time. To put it simply, this could indicate enormous quantities of arrests at media business for FARA violations-- the very same thing Manafort, and more recently, long-time Clinton lackey Greg Craig was indicted for.

On July 10, 2016, Seth Rich would be shot two times and left to die outside one of his favorite bars less than two miles from his DC apartment. Reports would call it a "break-in" even though nothing was drawn from Rich. We would, later on, find out (through Q) that Seth Rich was accountable for leaking gigabytes of emails to Wikileaks, to expose scams and corruption within the Democratic Party, and that Democratic Party authorities were the ones responsible for buying the assassination. Since this writing, we are still either awaiting Wikileaks' creator, Julian Assange (who has simply been evicted from the Ecuadorian Embassy and arrested by British authorities), to testify in court about this fact, or for the US Government to in some way produce Wikileaks' server at some time. As Q has informed us time and time again, they have "the source.".

As a result of his wounds, Seth Rich would be hurried to MedStar Washington Hospital Center after he was found bleeding, but still alive. He would catch his injuries.

Almost a year later, in 2017, an Anon claiming to be a surgical homeowner at that healthcare facility would step forward and declare that Rich had been successfully supported and had, in reality, begun to recuperate before expiring under suspicious circumstances.

Anons would, later on, discover that the director of surgery at that healthcare facility, and hence, the man in charge of Rich's care, was one, Dr. Jack Sava. Sava's partner is one Lisa Kountoupes, a previous Department of Energy worker (with ties to Uranium One), and a top DC lobbyist who had previously been hired by the Clintons. Kountoupes would likewise go to the White House twenty-three times during the Obama administration. In 2008, Sava himself would go to the Bohemian Grove, that "summer camp" for the elites, out in California, where rumors of wild orgies with minor prostitutes, and odd, esoteric rituals abound. The Bohemian Grove is perhaps most famous among Alex Jones fans, that seasonal figure of the conspiratorial world who runs Infowars.com (and who, as Q has told us, has several ties to many intelligence firms, consisting of the CIA, Stratfor, and Mossad-- which would make him not the "info warrior" he claims to be, but rather, controlled opposition). Still, in 2000, Alex Jones would slip on to the 2,700+ acres owned by the Grove and covertly film a ritual there referred to as the "Cremation of Care," wherein what looked like an effigy was burned in front of a massive owl statue, sustaining speculation that this was all one element of ancient Molech praise, reanimated, and restored into the modern. And while the Grove is a center of Cabal activity, it is a typical belief amongst the Q community that the real disclosures delivered by Bill Cooper, author of Behold, a Pale Horse, frightened the Cabal so severely that they propped up Jones to detract and sidetrack from Cooper's claims, therefore making his documentary on the Grove some sort of odd, regulated disclosure operation;

something to keep the "conspiracy" crowd satisfied, even as their strategies and activities continued. Do not check out that bit as a recommendation of Cooper.

While Q has referenced him on a minimum of one celebration, there's much that he writes that I, personally, find it very challenging to think at this point. But regardless of what one believes of Cooper himself, there's no denying that he was shot dead by Apache County sheriffs, in 2001, after correctly forecasting the 9/11 attacks.

As for Dr Sava, he would also soon manage the care of Rep. Steve Scalise, following a stopped working assassination attempt by Leftist James Hodgkinson at the annual congressional baseball game. Trump would go to Scalise in the health center, but would also bring his doctor, Dr. Ronny Jackson, along for the trip.

On July 2, 2016, "FBIAnon" would appear on/ pol/ for the very first time, declaring to have an intimate understanding as a "high-level analyst" dealing with the Clinton e-mail examination, while consistently encouraging Anons to take a look at the Clinton Foundation, saying things like:

The real point of interest is the Clinton Foundation, not the e-mail server. We got the server from Benghazi; then, from the server, we found data on the CF. Then we realized the scenario is much worse than previously believed.

And,..

Eliminating HRC would not cause this problem to go away. The issue is with the Clinton Foundation, as I mentioned, which you should simply think of as a massive spider web of connections and money laundering implicating hundreds of top-level individuals. I do not have a high opinion of Hillary; she is simply a piece - albeit a considerable selection-- of this enormous shitstorm.

And,.

The D.O.J probably wants to save itself. Discover everyone associated with the Clinton Foundation, from its donors to its Board of Directors, and the picture they are all implicated.

And,.

We have our hands tied. My message to you and everybody on this board do not get sidetracked by Clinton's emails. Concentrate on the.

Foundation. All of the nightmarish truth exists. The emails will pale in contrast.

Similar to Q, FBIAnon would come on and drop "breadcrumbs" for Anons to follow across several threads, mostly concerning the Clinton Foundation and associated corruption, and typically in a question-answer format. While I generally believe most of what FBIAnon has posted, in reality, he can't declare one hundred percent precision-- which, in an unusual method, actually boosts the case for legitimacy, because when you consider he claims to be an expert making informed guesses about things, it makes sense that he should misjudge sometimes.

The feeling I get when checking out FBIAnon is that he's part of the rank and file, an expert, as he declares (there has been some speculation amongst Anons that previous FBI director James Comey is FBIAnon, although I find that highly not likely). Much of what FBIAnon would eventually state would line up with what Q would later on say himself.

And it's also significant that FBIAnon wasn't the only one adopting this "breadcrumb" method. Another would be

WhiteHouseAnon; that is, this particular Anon claiming to be somebody who worked in the White House:

WhiteHouseAnon would go on to explain things like the "Slingshot theory" and the "Ring of Fire Theory" to Anons; the primary being the method Trump used to keep the media perpetually off-balance, and the latter being the technique the Clintons used to cover their criminal offenses, by making them so heinous, they might just be a part of a wild and unhinged "conspiracy theory."

Other noteworthy accounts would turn up in time. These include High-Level Insider Anon, DNC Hatchetman, and the Knowledge Bomber. However, all these drops illustrate an issue/ pol/ had at the time, with confirmation and imitators. It's easy enough to recognize somebody by their ID number (a unique set of digits offered to each confidential function that only exists within that thread). Still, once you move into a new line (particularly on a new day), it can be challenging to identify who they claim to be. This would frequently attract copy cats (Live Action Role Players), who take pleasure in pretending to be somebody like FBIAnon. Take, for instance, this post by "WhiteHouseAnon" in which almost whatever he says here is false:

Undoubtedly, all his "predictions" here failed. However, this is necessary since you're now seeing just a little bit about how different factions, groups, and companies were waging a detailed war on the Chans before, throughout, and after Trump's election. And all that's on top of attempting to figure out whether what they were saying was honest (to the best of their knowledge) at the time. I wasn't exaggerating before when I called this "information warfare" and described Anons as soldiers, fighting in the trenches. Arranging through all the noise and lies requires a high level of cumulative intelligence and a vital eye (even to fear). Luckily, this issue of LARPers hopping on your ID and pretending to be you is fixed using tripcode verification (which is what Q would later on use) during his shift to 8ch.

However, back to our timeline for the moment, we've still got a lot to make it through:

On July 5, 2016, FBI Director James Comey would recommend "No charges" for Hillary Clinton for her mishandling of categorized e-mails throughout her period as secretary of state, calling her, in the end, "exceptionally reckless." Once again, we would quickly gain from Q the treasonous thinking behind this recommendation. In the meantime, it seemed that when again, Hillary Clinton had wriggled her method out of a seemingly impossible circumstance, the sort of scenario that would get others secured for a really, long time.

And we can't forget the information about the three Muslim siblings, Abid, Imran, and Jamal Awan, in all of this. All three were born in Pakistan; all three were members of the Muslim Brotherhood. All three handled the IT for the House Permanent Select Committee on Intelligence and other legislators as "shared workers." And yes, all three were prohibited from accessing your house network back in February of 2016 for believed theft and data breaches. Despite this, Imran Awan was kept on by DNC chief Debbie Wasserman-Schultz throughout this time. The Awan story is mainly involved and winding. Consists of various criminal activities that vary from the theft of devices, money laundering (through a shell business referred to as Cars International A-- yes, abbreviated CIA), and equipment theft, to the formerly pointed out data breaches. We would, later on, find out from Q that these males, acting upon behalf of the Muslim Brotherhood, were using incriminating communications and e-mails to blackmail members of Congress-- which Obama knew at the time, who is himself Muslim Brotherhood. Yes, all that media spin about him being a "Christian" is yet another Mockingbird lie.

On July 16, Stefan Halper, an "ex" FBI and CIA operative with double citizenship in the US and Great Britain (and with lots of contacts throughout western intelligence companies), would have a meeting with Carter Page at Cambridge. Halper had been teaching as a professor at the Centre for International Studies at Cambridge when the Obama administration made some unusual deposits to his bank account.

Later, Carter Page would affirm before a House Intelligence Committee that he had indeed spoken with a few Russian authorities in July while checking out Moscow to speak at two financial and foreign policy events going on there. But Carter Page was working undercover for the FBI at the time and had done so at least given that 2013. So here again, you have the FBI and the CIA colluding with each other to set up the pretense of a Trump-Russian collusion narrative; even wanting to toss their possessions under the bus to accomplish this, it appears.

Julian Assange had an ax to grind with one Lady Clinton. A devoted white hat and perpetual fly in Hillary's lotion, Hillary had formerly tried all manner of tactics to eliminate Assange, consisting of proposing to State Department staffers that they send in a drone to assassinate him, and later, according to Q, accuse him with all way of rape and sexual assault accusations (a preferred method of the Deep State, as all of us, saw during the Kavanaugh verification hearing. Yes, the Deep State has properties all over; suggestible people who have undergone Monarch mind control programs, including routine abuse. We'll cover that more in-depth in a later chapter). So you can see why Assange would jump at the possibility to strike back at her finally. And strike he did.

On July 22, Wikileaks would blindside the Democratic party by releasing near 20,000 DNC e-mails (with numerous more en route). Debbie Wasserman-Schultz would resign as DNC chairwoman in the wake of this enormous scandal. To counter and include any of the damage that would originate from those asking "troublesome" concerns resulting from this leakage, the Deep State had to respond rapidly. They needed to drop some chaff to throw individuals off the path and keep this from spiraling out of their control. And so, they prepared up a false identity, a "hacker" calling themselves "Guccifer 2.0" claimed obligation for hacking the DNC servers and leaking the e-mails to Wikileaks. Guccifer likewise declared he dripped details to former Trump consultant Roger Stone, also-- once again, trying to set up a Trump-Russia narrative.

The Guccifer 2.0 story would begin the ball rolling and form the basis of the "Russian Hacker/Russian Collusion" story (and the later Special Counsel investigation, run by Robert Mueller) as outlets like Buzzfeed and the Daily Beast (upon whose board of directors sits one Chelsea Clinton) began to report that Guccifer

2.0 had "screwed up" 7 and mistakenly exposed he belonged to the Russian Intelligence Agency, the GRU.

How convenient for the DNC.

Julian Assange, creator and editor of Wikileaks, would, later on, reject any involvement with Russian intelligence and these leakages.

However, after this, control of the Wikileaks Twitter account would be wrested from Assange and taken possession of by the Deep State. The date when this transpired isn't clear, but in the wake of these drops, Assange remained in for a world of hurt, holed up in the Ecuadorian Embassy. Later on, in November of 2016, Russia Today would publish an "interview" in-between Assange and John Pilger. Still, several weird artifacts in the video, including what can best be explained as digital morphs (such as the kind used in Hollywood extraordinary impacts to change one subject into another, as in the movie Willow), were seen by Anons. At particular points in the video, his collar would snap in an unorthodox method. He would have his eyeball shift position on his head, mixing into another picture of his eye, but focused in a completely various direction. It's something somebody needs to see in motion to genuinely value. The footage has been controlled in some startling methods.

On July 31, the FBI would formally open its "Crossfire Hurricane" counterintelligence examination into the Trump campaign, led by FBI representative Peter Strzok.

On August 1, Strzok and others would fly to England to meet numerous members of the intelligence community there and to interview one Alexander Downer, the same Alexander Downer who had spoken with George Papadopoulos back in May. The existence of this examination would not be divulged to Congress until March of the list below year. Peter Strzok would state in a text, rather actually in all caps, like some kind of rowdy teen:

OMG, I CAN NOT BELIEVE WE ARE SERIOUSLY LOOKING AT THESE ALLEGATIONS AND THE PERVASIVE CONNECTIONS.

Days later on, on August 15, Strzok would message Department of Justice legal representative Lisa Page, talking about their "insurance coverage" in case of a Trump win in November:

I wish to believe the course you threw away for factor to consider in Andy's office-- that there's no other way he gets chosen-- however, I'm scared we can't take that danger. It's like an insurance policy in the not likely event you die before you're 40

...

The story Strzok and Page had been given is that they were secret fans, admirers, but I do not believe that this is the case. The "enthusiasts" story is, in truth, one of the earliest cover stories the Deep State has at its disposal. I don't think they were ever enthusiasts. I believe they had actually both been tasked by the most significant levels of the Obama administration to assist spy on and take down Trump, a civilian. I do not have evidence of this assertion right now, but Q has told us that Lisa Page is working together witness now so that the fact will come out in time.

Q would later release a series of monitoring photos drawn from traffic webcams in London, tracking Strzok, Page, and several others as they worked their way through the city to the CIA field office ... One Gina Haspel (who Trump would designate as CIA director after the election) just occurred to be operating at the time.

On August 16, in the wake of the Seth Rich murder, the Washington, DC, chief of cops, Cathy Lanier, would step down to work as head of security for the NFL.

On August 19, Manafort would resign from the Trump campaign, amidst questions about his ties to Russian operatives.

On September 9, Hillary would stumble with her now-notorious "Basket of Deplorables" speech, which we discussed in the previous chapter.

And then, on September 11, Hillary would be shot collapsing outside of a 9/11 memorial occasion in lower Manhattan, losing not only her awareness, but a shoe while doing so. This, and several other episodes throughout the year (such as her duplicated coughing fits and the time when she spat up mucous plugs into a glass of water while giving a speech in front of cams and a crowd) would give rise to a variety of questions about the state of her health (and thus, her physical fitness for the workplace of the presidency). She would later begin Jimmy Kimmel and prove her vigor by ... opening a jar of pickles.

Sidenote: Kimmel would be explained as an "Activist" by Barack Hussein Obama in a promotion video he helped cut to support U2s straw man Bono with his RED initiative. Obama would go on in the same video to label Bono, a "Ringmaster." Q would clue us in that both were concealed titles/roles provided and acknowledged within the Cabal hierarchy, which Obama was sending out a message, hidden in plain sight, to interested parties who were focusing

In reality, Q would confirm that the surprise message Obama was sending at the time was, in fact, a response to this concern, sent out by Bono (or his handlers), through his RED website:

Obama was ready to meet whoever was asking the question, and Kimmel was intentionally assisting in transmitting the message. And that's simply a little a foretaste for the sort of mind-bending stuff the Cabal finishes with consistency, to keep their efforts hidden from the rest people. We'll be looking at a lot more of that example in the coming chapters.

On September 13, Halper would meet with George Papadopoulos in London, where his female "assistant," alias Azra Turk, would be designated by the FBI to accompany Halper and target Papadopoulos. Turk would try to seduce Papadopoulos, with Papadopoulos later calling her a honeypot, to extract more details from him relating to Russian Collusion within the Trump campaign.

On October 7, 2016, Wikileaks would start posting what they would entitle "The Podesta E-mails." John Podesta, you may remember, was Hillary's campaign supervisor at the time. Discussions consisted of within the archive would cause discoveries about "Spirit Cooking" and "performance artist" Marina Abramovic, along with a "Pizza Code," all of which would form the basis of "Pizzagate;" a hypothesis that dark, even Satanic practices were commonplace amongst elites, and that human trafficking and pedophilia was happening with frightening regularity, right under typical individuals's noses. Searching for "Spirit Cooking" online would cause a video on YouTube which featured a routine where Abramovic would blend blood, semen, and breast milk in a vat, and then use that mix to compose inscriptions on the walls of the structure she was carrying out the ritual in, before putting the clotted sludge over child-sized effigies (such as the one pictured on the bottom right corner in the photo listed below, which is taken directly from that video):.

John Podesta would eagerly welcome his sibling (and one of the largest lobbyists in Washington, DC, at the time, Tony Podesta) to the "supper."

The revelation that Washington elites were going to bloody routines would set the web on fire, which was simply the start. When the "Pizza code" was found, all bets were off. The hypothesis here was that the code itself referred to kids and women and specific sexual show thinly-veiled food referrals, the most notorious example probably being this e-mail, here:

" Do you believe I'll do better playing dominos on cheese than on pasta?" Not precisely standard English phraseology, is it?

And that is far from the only example. Others would include descriptions of a "walnut sauce" in a back and forth with Democrat mega-donor, financing, and billionaire source behind the continuous "Need to Impeach" project against Trump, Tom Steyer, in addition to an e-mail explaining the discovery of a "pizza-related" handkerchief, leading some to question if that was, in and of itself, a recommendation to the handkerchief code frequently employed within the homosexual neighborhood. Horrified by their initial findings, Anons, in dogged pursuit of the truth, combed through all of the e-mails and quickly found a striking relationship between the Hillary Clinton project and James Alefantis' DC-based pizza store, Comet Ping Pong.

The first thing that was right away obvious about Alefantis himself is that he was noticeably well-connected, being the ex-homosexuals partner of David Brock, creator of Media Matters for America and friend of the.

Rothschilds. (Full disclosure, Media Matters for America would, on their website in 2018, attack me as a "right-wing amplifier" of Q. It's likewise believed that the Deep State attempted to assassinate David Brock at one point, causing a cardiovascular disease that put him in the hospital, but which eventually failed to kill him). GQ would even name Alefantis among the fifty most influential people in Washington, DC, which is very odd for a little restaurateur. It was heavily speculated at the time that Alefantis was a Rothschild himself, though no definitive proof of this was ever discovered one method or the other (at least to my understanding-- however, I find some of the theories out there rather engaging).

Anons instantly started scouring his social media accounts, which exposed, well ... lots of, lots of unfortunate images similar to the one you see here:

As you can picture, that didn't precisely assist Alefantis' case in the eyes of Anons. And it should be kept in mind that this was far from the only example, and not even the worst image exposed. It also needs to be kept in mind that Alefantis' avatar on Instagram at the time was a statue of Antinous, the boy-lover of Roman Emperor Hadrian, even more fueling wild web speculation.

At any rate, the point I want to convey here is that the Cabal was so desperate for you not to take note of the Wikileaks, they needed to hunt up some secret recording from a year before and blast it out for weeks to incense the quickly manipulated, and distract them from the real scandal being discovered by volunteer researchers every day.

Another significant discovery consisted of among the Wikileaks was a record of a personal speech Hillary had offered to the National Multi-Family Housing Council in 2013, where she explained how you needed both a "public and private position" when it concerned the similarity Wall Street reform in essence, advocating lying and pandering to whoever occurred to be in the room at the time to gain impact and votes, while always understanding to whom you owed your allegiances. She would, later on, dismiss objections to this by referencing, of all things, the Spielberg film Lincoln, at a later governmental debate.

On October 20, Trump would offer his now-famous speech at the Al Smith charity dinner (what I've because taken to calling "The Red Dinner"), hurling some of his most vicious criticism of Clinton to date, to her face, with her cackling along with distinctly required laughter the entire time. To say it was savage would be an enormous understatement. It was clear from Trump's tone (and by the shocked expressions of the guests, who were by now profusely sweating in their seats and dying to get out of that space) that there was much more truth to these "jokes" than many in the room cared to acknowledge.

Parallel to the Pizzagate investigations, there was also a chain of query triggered by yet another Wikileaks email contained within the Podesta Archives, where a thinly veiled plot to assassinate Supreme Court Justice Scalia was discovered.

In essence, a "screenwriter" had pitched John Podesta a motion picture concept, complete with characters, plot, setting, and cost. Why is practically looked like he was trying to get approval for an agreement? One big issue: John Podesta isn't a movie manufacturer. Add that to a few of the inconsistencies observed in Scalia's death: that he was initially reported to have been discovered with a pillow over his head, and then, all of a sudden, there was no pillow. There was likewise the reality that no autopsy was ever performed, which Scalia was cremated, regardless of being a devout traditionalist Catholic, who even rejected the rulings of Vatican II, and thus, would have rejected cremation on profoundly spiritual grounds. Things just didn't build up when it comes to Scalia's death, and Anons took notice.

On November 6, Donald Trump would lastly win the presidency, to the shock of many around the nation. And the shock was for a good reason. For weeks, the people had been becoming aware of how Trump had practically no chance of winning. A day before the election, the Princeton Election Consortium had offered Hillary a ninety-nine percent possibility of winning. The Huffington Post, a ninety-eight percent opportunity.

Daily Kos, ninety-two percent. CNN, ninety-one percent. The New York Times, eighty-five percent. FiveThirtyEight, seventy-two percent. All the polls were tilted in her favor, and yet, in a stunning upset, Trump had flown in from behind and trounced her like some kind of maniac dark horse.

Hillary would refuse to concede at first, instead, sending out her campaign manager, John Podesta, around 2:00 a.m. to speak with the crowd collected for her "crowning" as the presumptive winner. He would inform everyone to come back tomorrow after discovering more, leaving several Hillary's upset and weeping fans mystified regarding what had simply occurred, unwilling to accept reality. And as a side-note, there's a famous story out there that Trump won the electoral college, while Hillary won the popular vote (therefore, we must do away with the electoral college; that old guideline that was developed by all those founders who happened to be "white males," and subsequently utilized each election to keep "white guys" in power-- when in reality the explicit function of this is to keep a balance of power between populated regions and, for instance, less populated areas where all the FOOD is grown). Lunatic Leftists-- particularly the kind that congregate in cities-- tend to forget that there's a whole world outside their metropolitan bubble. If the electoral college were gone, all somebody would have to do to rule as a despot from here on out is convince these population focuses on keeping choosing them; frequently by promising all sorts of "advantages" they have no intention of ever genuinely delivering. But this misconception about Hillary winning the popular vote isn't genuine either, at least, not when you understand the full extent of the voter fraud that took place that night ... and who owns the ballot machines ... and the efforts patriots and White Hats went through to strategically secure the election

The country is FAR more Red and far more Conservative than anybody has been led to believe by the Legacy Media. You could even call it overwhelmingly conservative, but again, the extent and duration of the established citizen scams that have occurred every year have distorted our perceptions. And as of this writing, the Department of Homeland Security (DHS) has till the end of December 2018 to launch a report on the scope of election fraud throughout the 2018 midterm elections. We're visiting that come back around and bite lots of "chosen" officials in short order.

We would, later on, discover from Q that White Hats (that is, heroes included in intelligence, working to hinder the efforts of Black Hats) had tactically placed sufficient pressure on locations where scams were generally widespread and had guaranteed enough election stability to counteract and reduce all the citizen scams going on elsewhere. It sufficed to tip the electoral scales, however not the popular scales. It belonged to the factor why none of the networks would call the election till really, too late (because, again, the media works with the Mono-party, and the election wasn't expected to have this outcome because it was rigged in Hillary's favor). This is likewise why all the polling outlets could offer us such exceptionally inaccurate ballot data right up until the day of the election. Even the surveys were deceptive, leveraged to establish an established narrative. As Q likes to advise us, "They never believed she would lose," and thus, didn't have a plan for that scenario when it finally happened.

Hillary would, however, be required to yield the next day eventually. And practically immediately, the motion that would become referred to as "The Resistance" got underway. Conjuring up all sorts of fiction, from Harry Potter to Star Wars, to A Handmaiden's Tale, the motion's acolytes saw themselves as some sort of brave army, rebelling versus a Darth Vader or a Voldemort (when in truth, they were unsuspectingly serving the most evil character of them all). It was merely an amalgamation of anti-Trump rage without any real instructions, no unifying concepts, however a great deal of financing (thanks to George Soros) and lots of stars backing it.

On November 9, David Wilcox would be pulled from his car in Chicago by anti-Trump protesters and badly beaten by numerous foes while bystanders looked on and motivated the violence, yelling out expressions like, "He voted Trump! Beat his ass!"

On November 10, 2016, Besta Pizza would alter its logo design, getting rid of the interior decoration, distancing itself from the boy-lover symbol association.

On November 17, 2016, NSA director, Admiral Mike Rogers, unbeknownst to other members of the intelligence neighborhood, would privately travel to Trump Tower and, in an excellent act of heroism, divulge to Trump the presence of the unlawful spying operation against him and his campaign. The Deep State had actually jeopardized Trump Tower itself. However, instead of leaving then and there the day Admiral Rogers came to visit, Trump would have his individuals wait a day before lastly relocating the campaign headquarters the following day to Bedminster, New Jersey. And there was an excellent reason for this ...

Q would later disclose that the Trump project, upon knowing of the unlawful spying, would reverse and almost instantly utilize this to their advantage by utilizing it to feed bad intel to the Obama administration and Clinton project. In one particularly hilarious exchange, Q would verify that Trump had used a Twitter post to bait the Obama administration into spying in on all their "upcoming" project plans:

On November 23, Reddit would unexpectedly ban the/ r/Pizzagate investigative neighborhood on incorrect pretenses, stating they were in offense of Reddit's anti-doping policy. This was, obviously, a broad farce. As an active investigator at the time, I can state I never as soon as I saw personal info displayed publicly there for doing anyone. The sub's mediators were vocally against any attempts at doing or calls for violence. If any info had been published to the sub, it was by a bad operator who was trying to provide the Reddit admins a reason to get rid of the sub.

In the wake of the sub's removal, dozens of clones turned up overnight (since anybody can make a sub on Reddit), and most were gotten rid of within a couple of days (despite these users never breaking the rules, either). Among my subs was eliminated, regardless of the truth that it was personal and set to

Invite-only, and had constantly followed all the site-wide guidelines. It was clear to the community that the Reddit admins just wished to censor all Pizzagate-related examination once it was obvious that it wasn't going to disappear or wane by itself. Lots of "Reddit-refugees" would soon settle over at Voat and continue investigating for the next two years, churning out volumes of thorough research study, all individually validating that, yes, the elites in this country and all over the world participate in ritual pedophilia, human trafficking, and even worse-- and that this was all intentionally concealed from the typical male.

However, with the censorship implemented on Reddit, the Pizzagate crowd-sourced investigation would suffer a significant blow to its reliability on December 4, 2016, after Edgar Welch would walk into Comet Ping Pong and fire off three shots from an AR-styled weapon. To be sure, this has constantly been considered a "false-flag" attack by the Pizzagate community (that is, an attack by the Deep State, carried out to make an opposition celebration look bad by framing them in a criminal act), as nobody from the community knew who this person was. The neighborhood had constantly been vocally versus all vigilantism. However, the damage had been done. In between the circular reporting by the media, knocking Pizzagate as a "debunked conspiracy," and the continuous refrain of Pizzagaters being "gun-wielding maniacs," the repair was in. Pizzagate was all but effectively memory-holed by Deep State stars looking to secure their pedophilic masters.

Things cooled off for a bit as the vacation season passed, and people proceeded with their lives. Still, they quickly picked back up again in January, as Trump was formally sworn in on January 20, 2017, and many on the Left relatively lost any last staying vestiges of their peace of mind. Nowhere has this been immortalized (and turned into numerous memes) than in this specific image, lovingly dubbed by Trump fans, "The Scream Heard Round the World."

While it was temporarily fun for Anons viewing many on the "Salt Left" lose their minds for a time, it soon grew troubling to see how violent and unhinged the Left had become in such a short time. It was bad enough throughout the election itself, and now it seemed to get ramped up to brand-new heights with each passing day. It was right away clear that, while Trump had won the election, the war was far from over.

For on January 3, 2017, a mentally disabled male would be kidnapped by 4 Black Lives Matter supporters from the Chicago area, seemingly for being a Trump fan. They would go on to connect the man up, gag him, beat him, burn him with cigarettes, and force him to consume foul toilet water out of a revolting, putrid toilet bowl-- throughout a live-streamed video on Facebook-- all while screaming "F *** Donald Trump!" Authorities believed the unique requirements man had been held for at least two days, and would require several days in the medical facility to recuperate completely.

Trump would take office, and within days, on January 21, the so-called Resistance movement was on full display screen, with millions of males and women coming down upon DC, dressed up as vaginal areas, putting on pink "pussy" hats, and opposing in the streets. A more ludicrous screen had never been seen in America, and riots would break out in some areas with, at the end of the day, over 200 individuals being jailed (though this was far from the first anti-Trump riot, with dozens being apprehended in Portland months before).

The Resistance motion would quickly show as outrageous as it was misdirected, for Trump had actually hardly taken office and had not even done anything yet when they were in full swing. This left many questioning what it was that this motion was opposing, precisely. In the end, it would prove only to be a sort of vague outrage that Trump had actually in some way "taken" this election. From the way the media experts were wailing, you may not be faulted for thinking that Trump was "literally Hitler," and was all, however, set to set up a Fascist program and steamroll the opposition before putting women, gays, Muslims, minorities, and, heck, furries for good measure, in prisoner-of-war camp by the trainload-- or so the narrative went. And hence, came the "ethical" validation for the Resistance. If Trump was Mecha-Hitler on steroids, his followers were little more than American Brownshirts, and who could be blamed for thinking that punching them was their only recourse?

And how had Mecha-Hitler on steroids achieved all this? Why, he cheated, naturally! He must have cheated! (Or so the "thinking" went.) Impeach! Impeach!

The Democrats had an issue, and they knew it.

That problem was Seth Rich.

Go back with me to 2016 for just a moment:

Q tells us that Rich had been assassinated in July in retaliation for dripping those emails, and initially, the Dems thought they had gotten away with everything. But then they recognized where the emails he had taken had wound up: in the hands of

Julian Assange and Wikileaks. The race was on. It was just a matter of time before those emails would end up being public understanding. That would be a disaster for the Democratic Party, and they understood it. Assange and his group were working to arrange and distribute the e-mails as quickly as they could. Hillary, Obama, and the Democrats required a cover story, ideally one which would revile Assange and Wikileaks and Trump at the same time.

In July, the same month Rich passed away, the DNC approached their legal team at Perkins Coie (specifically Michael Sussman, a partner at Perkins Coie) and laid out their case. Sussman, in turn, approached Shawn Henry at Crowdstrike to carry out "forensic analysis" on the DNC's servers. Working with the FBI (which was headed by James Comey), the "Russian collusion" narrative was formally crafted. Crowdstrike would state that undoubtedly, the DNC's servers had been hacked by Russian IP addresses (all the while, denying FBI detectives access to the actual servers). After that, the emails had been turned over to Wikileaks. You'll recall that by July 5, Comey had currently let Hillary off the hook for her "mishandling" of her private e-mail server (which is much bigger than the public examination ever let on-- once again ... more on that in a bit).

The Washington Free Beacon had actually "approached" Glenn Simpson of personal intelligence company Fusion GPS to carry out an opposition research study on Trump during the governmental primaries. The problem with this story? Simpson is wed to Mary Jacoby, and Jacoby worked for Rose Law firm. You understand, the one down in ... Little Rock, Arkansas. That name must recognize to you because it's the very same company at which Hillary Clinton worked throughout the Whitewater years. When I say that the Washington Free Beacon had "approached" Fusion GPS for this ... well, it's not hard to read between the lines and see what took place. And also recall the

"error" Guccifer 2.0 had made, "inadvertently," letting on that he worked for the GRU.

The crafting of the public narrative had begun.

Oh, however, it becomes worse. One of the individuals associated with the opposition research was none aside from Nellie Ohr, spouse of the Obama administration's associate deputy chief law officer Bruce Ohr. For the less critical souls out there, that ought to check out: MAJOR dispute of interest. (We would later on gain from Q that Nellie Ohr had been trained on "the farm"-- that is, CIA's Camp Peary-- and to avert security of her communications by White Hats like the NSA and MILINT, Ohr tried even to use ham radio to interact with her co-conspirators at one point).

It didn't work. Her comms were still intercepted.

Furthermore, it would later come out throughout Bruce Ohr's congressional testimony that he had fulfilled with Glenn Simpson as far back as August 2016, back when they were still attempting to spin the Steele dossier as reliable.

To produce what would ultimately be called the "Russian Dossier," Fusion GPS looked abroad to foreign intelligence services, and specifically, to previous MI6 spy, Christoper Steele. Using "his" reports, which were most likely composed by an underling. (It's been a point of speculation that Steele didn't compose the file, however simply loaned it his credibility as an informant by slapping his name on the last item.) Combination GPS would prepare up what would become referred to as the "Trump-Russia Dossier." This would describe all the different behind-the-scenes criminal acts of subversion being used by Trump and the Russians to topple American sovereignty, including the ludicrous and dubious part about "golden showers," where Trump was supposedly recorded in a Russian hotel encouraging prostitutes, who he had allegedly worked with, to urinate on each other (a rumor which, if you dig back deep enough in arcane Chan history, might have been started by an Anon as an over-the-top joke, and oblique jab at the child of a reporter loathed by lots of Anons, Rick Wilson).

Welcome to the Red Scare, 2.0, restarted for the twenty-first century, with Putin cast as a scheming, mastermind dictator/puppet master, and Trump, his pussy-grabbing' crony and capitalist henchman.

And how did "Steele" (again, in all possibility, Baumgartner) source all this information? Why, by speaking with none besides "ex" FBI and CIA informant, Stefan Halper! Yes, the same one who not just served as an

FBI and CIA informant in the past, but who had been paid right after his meeting with Carter Page at Cambridge, and who had set up the conferences with Papadopoulos and Mifsud; the conference Papadopoulos would then convey to Alexander Downer ... who would likewise run back and tattle to the FBI?

And don't forget the UK's and Ukraine's contributions to all of this: Saunders, Dearlove, Hannigan, and Chalupa-- all forming a nexus within this elaborate conspiracy, laundering information to frame an innocent guy.

To even more compound the cover-up, Perkins Coie would connect to Fusion GPS to continue their "research study," putting the last discuss the Trump-Russia Dossier, before handing it off to Chuck Schumer, who then commended John McCain, who then handed it ... back to the FBI, who then utilized it as grounds for obtaining FISA warrants.

But it may be essential here to describe what the FISA court is, exactly, so people have a whole point of view of the kind of treason that went on here. Essentially, the Foreign Intelligence Surveillance Court is a personal court utilized by intelligence companies and the like to obtain warrants for security against spies from foreign nations operating in the United States. Or, a minimum of, that was its designated purpose. See, in the United States, we have this pesky thing called the Fourth Amendment, which suggests we're safe from unreasonable searches and seizures by the United States government. It actually puts a hinder on the type of work some of the more jackbooted types may like to attempt and get away with, but there it is, enshrined in our gorgeous Constitution. The FISA court? That's targeting non-citizens, so the Fourth Amendment does not safeguard them, right?

Sort of. See, simply because they might be a spy, they may be in contact with somebody here who is not a spy, and in spying on both of them, you may be, in fact, incidentally breaching a US person's Fourth Amendment rights. That's kind of standard practice. Nevertheless, with a FISA warrant, this goes even more. Because of "umbrella surveillance" strategies, that second person is now a target that you can "legally" spy on. And after that, you can also follow who they're talking to

Put differently; even if you don't think Trump was established in all this, he speaks with his daughter Ivanka. The Deep State can now spy on everything Ivanka says and does. So Ivanka goes and talks to her spouse, Jared. The Deep State can now spy on Jared. It goes on like that until the "warrant" to.

Spy on a single person extends to such a degree that, at a particular point, it's a carte blanche to spy on whomever, whether they're a criminal or not.

And when you consider that the FISA warrant was obtained since the FBI inserted its spies into the Trump project, and then sent intel to spies overseas, to foreign intelligence companies, well ... Simply put, this is "info laundering" at its absolute dirtiest. And that's all presuming this was the only spying being done on the Trump campaign. Once again, according to Q, this is just the legal face put on the prohibited spying operations that had currently been underway for some time.

In essence, an examination was started on incorrect pretenses. A sitting administration engaged in cooperation with foreign, federal governments to produce proof. A complicit media covered for them the whole time, despite knowing the reality (which we'll get to in a bit). And why? To trap Trump with phony treason charges so he might either be locked away for life, or possibly even performed-- because such is the sentence for treason. Believe about that for a moment: Obama and Hillary wanted Trump dead.

From Strzok, to Comey, to Lynch, to Wasserman-Schultz, to Obama, to Hillary, therefore a lot more ... this isn't a "conspiracy theory." This is a genuine criminal conspiracy at the highest levels of federal government.

But again, we have to ask ourselves why? Why would a sitting president collude with a governmental candidate to stop a fair electoral process and allure a personal person? Was Trump that much of a threat to them? Why run the risk of devoting treason yourself to frame another person for treason?

The fact is, a lot more was at stake for Obama, Hillary, and this around the world Cabal. If Trump won, they knew that they would lose everything, which is why they did everything to try and stop him.

Back to January 2017.

On January 6, like one last Parthian shot from the outbound Obama administration, the Office of the Director of National Intelligence, headed by James Clapper, would issue an assessment9 alleging Russian disturbance in the 2016 governmental election Russia tipping the scales in favor of Donald Trump. Numerous intelligence firms were now investigating this supposed collusion, including the FBI and the CIA.

Before the male is even sworn in, on January 10, Buzzfeed would release the Steele file in its entirety. We would later gain from Q that

Buzzfeed had received this document from none aside from Senator John McCain, who had also dripped it to the former director of security for the Senate Select Committee on Intelligence, James A. Wolfe, who, in turn, dripped it to Buzzfeed reporter Allie Watkins. See, Wolfe and Watkins had been having an affair because 2013. He was fifty-three at the time, and she was twenty-two. He had previously dripped all sorts of intel to her, consisting of the Senate Intelligence Committee's report on CIA abuse that almost won her a Pulitzer. This wasn't the only reporter Wolfe was leaking to; no, there were at least three others involved. Wolfe ultimately would be charged with dripping classified intel on June 7, 2018, almost a whole year-and-a-half after Buzzfeed initially released the report on January 10, 2017.

The very next day, on January 11, Trump would take to Twitter, and he would not mince words, calling the file "nonsense" and a "total fabrication."

On January 17, Putin, too, would call the file false.

January 20 would finally arrive. Trump would be inaugurated in Washington DC, and throughout his speech, he would utter words which would chill the Cabal to the bone:

Today's event, however, has really unique significance. Since today we are not simply transferring power from one Administration to another, or from one party to another-- but we are moving power from Washington, DC, and giving it back to you, the American People. For too long, a little group in our nation's Capital has gained the benefits of government while individuals have paid.

Washington thrived-- however, the individuals did not share in its wealth.

Politicians flourished-- however, the jobs left, and the factories closed.

The establishment protected itself, however, not the citizens of our nation.

Their triumphs have not been your victories; their achievements have not been your victories, and while they celebrated in our country's capital, there was little to celebrate for struggling households throughout our land.

That all modifications-- starting right here, and today, since this moment is your moment: it belongs to you.

It comes from everyone collected here today and everyone viewing throughout America.

This is your day. This is your event.

And this, the United States of America, is your nation.

What matters is not which celebration manages our federal government but whether the individuals manage our government.

January 20th, 2017, will be remembered as the day the people became the rulers of this country again.

The forgotten men and women of our nation will be forgotten no longer.

Everybody is listening to you now.

You came by the 10s of millions to become part of a historic movement the similarity which the world has never seen before.

At the center of this movement is a crucial conviction: that a country exists to serve its people.

But the fix was currently in.

And even as Obama left the workplace, he didn't select to go house to Chicago. No, he did something no other US president has ever done before, and that was to stay in DC, taking up home a short ignore the White House. Much more strangely, Valerie Jarrett, his senior adviser (and someone who has long been associated with the lives of the Obamas) would relocate with Barack and Michelle, where they would right away get to work setting up what the media would describe as an anti-Trump "switchboard" with a particular objective in mind: to either require the resignation or impeachment of Donald J. Trump as president.

Once again (and we'll get into this in-depth in the following chapters), I want you to ask yourself, "Why?" What might perhaps have encouraged Obama not just to have his people plant spies in the Trump campaign, not only have the intelligence device of the United States federal government spy on the Trump project, not just utilize foreign intelligence agencies and media business against the man, but then on top of all that, set up a central office close by to work and attempt to weaken him at every step? What kind of existential hazard did Trump represent to the established order that inspired such impassioned opposition?

Here's one thing Q had to state about the lengths Obama and the Cabal went to stop Trump.

What do you call a former president who tries not just to undermine, however physically hurt a standing president? Oh, and there were assassination efforts, also. Lots of numerous assassination efforts, but the scale of those incidents is frequently so substantial. It's difficult for the average reader to comprehend just On February 8, the Senate would validate Jeff Sessions for United States Attorney General, with a 52-- 47 vote.

On February 13, General Flynn would resign as a national security consultant, as rumors swirled about a conversation he had with Sergey Kislyak. Flynn served previously as director of the Defense Intelligence Agency (DIA) from 2012 until 2014, and Obama disliked him. In reality, during Trump's shift, one of the crucial things Obama explicitly asked for was that he did not employ Flynn. It turns out that Obama had been strategically gutting the military for many years, eliminating patriots from their offices, and installing Cabal loyalists in their stead. Flynn was an individual and understood numerous "troublesome truths," which could irreparably harm Obama politically. Eventually, on December 1, 2017, Flynn would plead guilty to "lying" to the FBI concerning his telephone call with Kislyak, but this would, later on, turn out to be him perjuring himself. Why would Flynn perjure himself?

In brief, Flynn knew where all the bodies were buried. After leaving the DIA, Flynn ran the Flynn Intelligence Group (FIG), which would go on to work with Turkish customers, in specific. What is now theorized is that, as an expert spook, Flynn was running a counter-intelligence operation with FIG, a counter-intelligence operation developed to catch these Turkish spies.

These spies had direct connections to the Clintons and Obama. It's likewise theorized that Flynn himself underwent a FISA warrant and was hence being utilized to spy on the Trump administration. Remove Flynn from the White House, which's one less vector for the Deep State to make use of.

Flynn would work with the Special Counsel on various synchronized investigations, leading some Anons to think that Mueller was genuinely working for Trump throughout this time. However, Q has repeatedly and vocally denied this. If this particular bit turns out to be intentional disinformation on Q's part, it will be a stunning discovery when the time comes, though I would not be amazed.

Despite Session's current verification, on March 1, the Washington Post would publish a story claiming that Attorney General Sessions had met the Russians during the 2016 project, to remove him from office. Many in Congress called for Sessions to resign right away, however. In the end, what Sessions did wasn't illegal, and therefore, didn't need his resignation. Under normal situations, it's completely legal for an inbound administration to begin to speak with representatives of other world powers. Instead, Sessions would recuse himself from any investigations into Russian collusion, successfully delegating all power over any potential examinations to his subordinates, which in this case would be the deputy attorney general. One wasn't quite in place, nevertheless, given that, in January 2017,

Trump had fired the then deputy lawyer general Sally Yates for declining to institute his travel ban.

You see, Yates had formerly accepted some of the FISA warrants versus the Trump campaign, and was an all-around bad star, so she had to go.

Discovering a replacement became a leading priority. On April 26, the Senate would confirm Rod Rosenstein for deputy attorney general.

As the Trump presidency got underway, things moved briskly. He withdrew the United States from the Trans-Pacific Partnership, okayed to the Dakota Access and Keystone pipelines, nominated Neil Gorsuch to the Supreme Court, implemented his cabinet, eliminated reams of policies and bureaucracy, and much, much more. And again, I understand many approaching this book might not see why a few of these things are great; however, that's because these few things as they appear on the surface, and require to be seen through the lens of QAnon, that is, through the lens of Military Intelligence, to be totally appreciated. Take, for instance, Trump pulling us out of the Paris Agreement. Environmentalists everywhere lost their minds when he did this, however, when you understand that the arrangement is a program designed to take and rearrange United States taxpayer funds into Soros-backed organizations, slush funds, and throughout Iran, and not to combat environment change, the relocation handles a different tenor. And even now, as I compose this, riots are breaking out all over France, and individuals are threatening to overthrow Cabal puppet Macron, precisely because their leaders forced this sort of treaty, and all the included regulatory concern, upon them with no option. And besides, the United States is currently surpassing the standards detailed in the Paris Agreement anyhow, no tax theft essential! Believe me when I state that when you dive into Q-world, you'll experience this sensation of the imbalance, nearly like the ground shifting underneath your feet, over and over and over; however, you'll eventually bring out a higher understanding of reality as an outcome. It's a fundamental paradigm shift in your thinking, and you can't genuinely appreciate it unless you force yourself to grit your teeth through any emotional distress you might be experiencing and press forward till you break through whatever psychological barriers there get and are to the real fact of the matter. And isn't that where you wish to be anyway?

Still, all was not well in DC even if Trump had taken charge. The Deep State still controlled numerous firms in the federal government and were still loyal to the previous Administration and the Cabal. Trump, in truth, had to figure out who was clean, who was unclean, and how best to tidy home while still staying above reproach. This was challenging, by any stretch of the imagination, as he had to work privately with White Hats to root out whole networks of Black Hats. This was particularly pushing because these Cabal followers were doing everything they might to subvert and attempt President Trump's efforts at every turn, typically through dripping classified or fortunate details to the press, to try and help Cabal actors prevent Trump's plans.

On May 8, previous deputy chief law officer Sally Yates, and former director of national intelligence James Clapper, would affirm before a Senate subcommittee relating to any Russian collusion throughout the 2016 election. Both would talk about the classified intel they had seen, in which Trump and those near to him had been unmasked (and keep in mind, when we discuss "unmasking," we're speaking about FISA spying). They were little on information, concealing behind the previously mentioned "classification" as their defense, while likewise declining to say who ordered the unmasking. One possible candidate for that would be none besides United Nations ambassador Samantha Power, who abused her security clearance to order unmasking a minimum of 260 times throughout the 2016 election. Power would, later on, be brought before your home Intelligence Committee and questioned as to why this had happened under her clearance. Her reaction was that it wasn't her doing; that somebody in the Obama White House had bought all those unmaskings utilizing her qualifications without her understanding.

Well, what can you state, folks? Either she's lying or the Obama administration is lying. There's truly very little room for alternative descriptions in this scenario, so place your bets while you still can!

However, there was still the concern of FBI director James Comey, or "Leakin' James Comey," as Trump liked to call him at the time. Comey, you'll remember, previously refused to prosecute Hillary Clinton for the use of her unauthorized e-mail server. Through Q, we would find out that this was because charging her would have led directly back to Obama and numerous others, as Hillary was not the only one operating a personal, unlawful e-mail server to avoid security. (But once again, more on that in a bit). Remember, for now, that Comey was in charge of the FBI when all this massive spying was going down when all these plants were being placed into the Trump campaign. Definitely, he had to understand what was going on in his own house. And if not, what was he, incompetent? That's the line the DOJ took up, that he was not able to properly lead the Bureau, because incompetence is constantly a better defense than outright malice. And so, Comey was ousted. But to call Comey rank-and-file Cabal would be an understatement. We'll dissect his particular brand name to treachery later on, but for now, I'll say this: it's even been greatly suggested by the Q drops that Comey is a family Rockefeller.

Therefore, on May 9, Comey gets fired. This causes an enormous outcry and provides the Democrats enough of an incentive to demand a Special Counsel investigation into Russian meddling in the 2016 election.

Then, on May 17, 2017, the Special Counsel investigation is born. Rod Rosenstein employs previous FBI director, Robert Mueller, to oversee the investigation. And the big problem with this, as we would first learn from Q, is that Rod Rosenstein was among the initial individuals who approved the FISA warrants to spy on POTUS' campaign in the very first place! (Actually, on FBI plant Carter Page, specifically.) Not just that, however, Rosenstein is wed to United States attorney Lisa Barsoomian, who was the protegé of both Robert Mueller and James Comey, and who formerly functioned as legal representation for Barack Obama, Bill and Hillary Clinton, and the Department of Justice. Much later, we would likewise discover of a plan in which Rosenstein would use a wire to covertly record President Trump, in the hopes of catching something incriminating, or at the extremely least, something that might be used versus him to lead and conjure up the twenty-fifth change to impeachment proceedings.

Does this mean that Rod Rosenstein and Bob Mueller are bad individuals, working for the Cabal? This has been a particular point of contention amongst the QAnon research study neighborhood for some time. However, at the least, my readers need to comprehend that the ethical ground upon which the whole Special Counsel stands has been quite unsteady right from the start. As of this writing, the only thing keeping the Special Counsel going is the fact that President Trump hasn't declassified the Office of Inspector General report documents, which would expose Rosenstein's conflict of interest. The report itself, some 568 pages long, was first released in June 2018 but not before Rosenstein could get his hands on it and edit his name, along with other keywords, guaranteeing their continuous defense because Trump has ultimate authority over declassification, he could shoot whenever he wants, and end the investigation in a heartbeat.

He didn't.

He had months to end this investigation with the stroke of his pen unilaterally. So why didn't he?

Ah, welcome to the world of Q, where things are rarely as they appear, and wherein some cases Q has to keep us Anons in the dark, so regarding likewise keep bad stars in the dark. As Q has said, "Disinfo is required," since it's not simply the hero enjoying, and we would not want the plan telegraphed ahead of time to bad actors.

However, again, back to our timeline:.

On May 20, Trump would show up in Saudi Arabia, where he would take part in a ritual called a "Sarah" or "sword dance." It's a routine one does before going to war. Before leaving Saudi Arabia, Trump would broker an offer with the Saudis to wean them off their dependence on oil exports, allow them to join the United States stock exchange, and, at the brand-new Saudi counter-terrorism center, he would place his hands, along with Saudi King Salman bin Abdulaziz and Egyptian President Abdel Fattah al-Sisi, on a radiant globe that drew lots of contrasts to a Palantir from the Lord of the Rings novels.

On May 23, 2017, "MegaAnon" would appear for the first time. Much like FBIAnon before him, and QAnon after him, MegaAnon concerned drop all sorts of intel about, a minimum of to begin, Seth Rich. Most of MegaAnon's initial claims were that because there was a lot of data that needed to be moved around safely, the likes of Julian Assange were leveraging the server power of Kim Dotcom's MegaUpload service (and later, Mega.nz) to achieve their "White Hat" goals. He would validate Rich as "Panda" (Rich always used "panda" permutations in his different screen names, with a packed panda even making a look later on in a video recorded by his moms and dads). MegaAnon would continue for numerous months, publishing into January 2018, and speaking about a variety of topics, practically all related to different facets of the Trump administration-- consisting of inside some of QAnon's own/ CBTS/ threads. In other words, Q and MegaAnon were publishing simultaneously, typically along the same lines, about the same subjects while informing Anons' point of views:

I know it sounds absurd; however, that's merely since I'm trying to convey the broadness and scope of what will be publicly disclosed. My only point is that after it's all over, nobody will have the ability to turn away from the truth. The masses will never again be able to declare with 100% certainty that 9/11 DIDN'T have within, US-sponsored and moneyed, department/agency coordination, designated resources, and help. Nobody will EVER have the ability NOT to think that our fucking firms and departments and previous admins didn't play a significant function in shit like JFK, OKC, 9/11, ISIS, Pizza, Vegas, and so on. They won't be able to turn a blind eye to what they consider "conspiracy theories," today just since the MSM told them to.

The only thing that everybody will be able to agree on when it's all stated and done is that we've all been horrifically lied to on incomprehensible levels. Absolutely nothing we've been led to perceive as our "truth" for generations because the fucking day GHB was sworn into the admin as Director of the CIA has been the entire reality and nothing. Nobody will have the ability to use lack of knowledge as a reason anymore. Do individuals think they're in charge?! Haha, well, now Trump is going to offer it to them. He's going to give us all the fucking openness we can manage, and when he does ?! That's when you'll genuinely see what "we, individuals" are made from. You'll have individuals who can't manage it, pleading to give the reality BACK to the admin. I wish to ensure I'm clear here, too ... when I use terms like "reveal," "truth," etc. I am in NO WAY IMPLYING Trump is revealing any of that things you all raise like "aliens," "Antarctica," etc. not saying I do not personally believe in some of it; however that's not the "storm" that's coming. Simply to clarify.

While I can't state that MegaAnon was always one hundred percent precise (nor, like so a number of these "insiders" can we verify if it was all the same individual), I will say archives of MegaAnon's posts make for some of the fascinating reading you can discover out there, to date.

Even as experts, we're shedding light on years of corruption, the Deep State was at work, combating back. On July 27, George Papadopoulos would be arrested for accepting cash from a foreign national while in Greece; $10,000, exactly. The pretense for this was that this was a "retainer" while Papadopoulos exercised an energy offer for Charles Tawil, an Israeli American business person. Except, Papadopoulos' "spy-der sense" was tingling. He attempted to give the cashback on one celebration. However, the man declined. Before leaving the island to return to the US, Papadopoulos left the cash in the care of a local lawyer in Greece, feeling agitated by the whole affair-- and it's an advantage he did, too, because upon landing and deplaning at Dulles Airport, he was instantly jailed by officers who went trying to find the $10,000. See, there's a guideline that you have to state quantities of cash over 10 thousand dollars when flying back into the United States (so our pal George would have been in massive difficulty if he had just packed that wad of money in his suitcase). Papadopoulos would, later on, tell federal private investigators that he believed Tawil was working for a foreign government. When the officers discovered out that Papadopoulos didn't have the money on him, that he left it in Greece, they were furious. Papadopoulos had seemingly dodged an entrapment scheme. It appeared like he was about to get away completely untouched when the Special Counsel could catch him on a "process criminal offense" " lying" to the FBI. Papadopoulos said he thought he initially spoke to Joseph Mifsud before starting work for the Trump project, when in truth, it wanted.

Papadopoulos would become sentenced to fourteen days in jail, after which point he was complimentary to do and talk as he pleased.

And as summer season was warming up, so too was the political divide in the country. The "Unite the Right" rally was slated in Charlottesville on August 11 and 12, 2017. The goal of the rally was to have anyone even remotely on the Right reserved their differences and march against the forces of Marxism that were attempting to enforce Leftist ideology on all aspects of society, through things like the policing of speech; doing opponents online; deport forming significant figures in the movement; and rioting at the similarity Jordan Peterson and Ben Shapiro rallies, on top of doing things like taking down Confederate monuments (and some not-so-Confederate monoliths; simply old monuments of historical figures who just took place to be white). The mostly-male group was made up of routine MAGA conservatives, groups like Identity Evropa, those associated with Richard Spencer's National Policy Institute, and more extreme groups like American Vanguard, the Traditionalist Worker Party, and different neo-Nazi/National Socialist groups (through intense study of the fundamental principles undergirding these latter groups would expose their ideology to be profoundly Left-wing in origin).

And state what you want about those groups, however, they were protesting peacefully—a minimum of, at the start. The rally would start with the individuals making their existence understood, marching with tiki torches in hand, much to the horror of Leftists across the country, who instantly drew parallels to the Ku Klux Klan. Then, due to several choices made by the mayor's workplace and the local authorities, decisions which went versus normal policy, these authorities decided to permit Antifa into the mix. Now, if you understand anything about Antifa, you know they're Communist foot soldiers. We're discussing the real dregs of society here—drug-using, gender-confused, violent anarchists, with a despicable nihilistic streak. Numerous like to consider themselves as "anti-fascist" revolutionaries, drawing comparisons to themselves and the D-Day soldiers of the Greatest Generation, when really, their actual ideological forebears were the ones developing the gulags in the USSR. Needless to state, when the two groups met (and were encouraged to meet, through the strategic opening and closing of streets, and redirecting of traffic by the cops, upon orders from more significant ups), dispute erupted throughout the city.

Absolutely nothing is more emblematic of that dispute than the occurrence involving James A. Fields and Heather Heyer. Fields was with American Vanguard, and Heyer with Antifa. While attempting to leave the city in his Dodge Challenger, Fields' automobile was swarmed and attacked by Antifa, who had been poorly funneled into the street by the regional police. One Antifa member first struck the back of Fields' automobile with a bat, scaring Fields. Another struck a window. Finally, another tossed a bottle of frozen urine (tossing bottles of urine-- frozen or otherwise, is a favorite Antifa) at the windshield, breaking it and lodging itself there before the mob came down around the car. One Antifa member is even caught on an electronic camera pointing a pistol at Fields' vehicle.

In a panic, Fields sped up to twenty-eight miles per hour, charging the crowd, hoping it would distribute. It didn't, and he had to knock on the brakes simple split seconds later. He managed to slow it to twenty-three miles per hour before striking another vehicle, likewise stopped by the crowd in front of him, at seventeen miles per hour.

In a considerable panic, Fields reversed out of the crowd and backed up the one-way street, driving backward as quickly as he could, desperate to leave the mob.

When the cops discover him, he can't stop asking forgiveness. When he hears someone struck by his cars and truck has died, he weeps. He is jailed and charged with very first-degree murder in the death of Heather Heyer-- a morbidly overweight female who had been marching with Antifa for hours that day. The media does its best to prevent discussing her weight, which is seen in the video as at least SEVEN guys, firefighters, and lifesaver-- carrying her to an ambulance, stomach exposed and, honestly, undulating collective action of the emergency workers. Instead, they transmit photos of her face, painting her as an unfortunate martyr, instead of one of the mob who attacked Fields' car.

And while I apologize for the image, I include it, so you realize I am not overemphasizing one iota. The coroner would state she died of a cardiac arrest. He never said it resulted from being struck by a car going about twenty-three miles per hour and decreasing.

However, the story doesn't end there. Not able to manage representation, Fields was eventually assigned an attorney by the state-- but the attorney has a good record, and wishing to make an example out of Fields, the judge combs through the lawyer's records and finds that he, too, was opposed to the removal of Confederate statues. The judge frames this as, somehow, an ethical dispute, and now gets to change Fields' representation.

He subs in a social justice warrior-type, complete with pink hair (and who, previously, was also associated with a sex scandal). However, to her credit, she makes a demand that the case is vacated Charlottesville, where the regional press would continue to rail against Fields' the entire time. The judge rejects the motion. At the end of the case, Judge Moore would say to the jury, "I do not know what intent he had aside from to eliminate. We understand what we saw."

In December 2018, Fields would get sentenced to life in jail, plus FOUR HUNDRED AND NINETEEN years, for first-degree murder, which requires intent. To call this, a miscarriage of justice is an understatement. And while I disagree with Fields' ideology, I do think the fact is essential. This was a morbidly overweight lady marching with a mob on a hot summer day-- a group that was intentionally funneled into locations where they must not have been permitted, stopping up traffic while swarming and attacking automobiles with weapons. The Leftists in charge of the government there sent in their infantryman to violently threaten and intimidate anyone they disagreed with; in this case, the Unite, the Right protesters. They wished to make an example out of Fields.

The rally had licenses to be there. Antifa did not. The rally had been serene till Antifa began attacking them. And completion result of all of it was a terrible and entirely preventable loss of life.

It would not be until a month later when an Anon would ask United States Senate Anon a concern:

If conservative death squads became genuine and start massacring Antifa advocates left and right, will Trump intervene to stop us or let us cleanse the nation for him?

Is Trump simply as happy to put down a right-wing uprising as he is a left-wing one?

Can we count on him as a pal or enemy on the Day of the Rope?

SENATE Anon would have this to state on the matter: Soros desires you to form right-wing death teams and combat Antifa, so you don't combat him. I'm unsure there's ever been a clearer photo of that reality placed on display than in the disaster that occurred in Charlottesville that summer season day. At any rate, I didn't wish to be Soros' beneficial moron. As much as I may have sympathized with a few of the ideas being upheld by a few of the groups there (I've never disliked anybody by their race, or the color of their skin, even though I do tend to be pro-Western Civ), I wasn't about to be anyone's unwitting pawn-- not to mention some Hungarian Billionaire understood for sowing discord and strife throughout the world. Oh, but we'll be addressing George Soros later in this book. In the meantime, it's enough to understand that the man uses the Hegelian Dialectic to his benefit: synthesis, thesis, and reverse. In essence, Soros establishes opposed groups to eliminate with each other, which results in the weakening of the primary population, developing disunity, and promoting hatred amongst individuals, all to press everyone along to some established end.

So while the "directly, white males" at the Unite the Right rally were absolutely all reacting to the same, extremely genuine phenomenon of anti-white hatred (cultivated and moneyed by the likes of Soros), the reality is, they were all being used in the very same way as the Antifa foot-soldiers they claimed to be fighting. Everybody present at the rally that day was a helpful moron, driving the wedge of division more profound into the American soul.

Trump understood this, and would later on state of the catastrophe: What about the 'alt-left' that came charging at, as you say, the 'alt-right,' do they have any regret?

What about the reality they came charging with clubs in hands, swinging clubs? Do they have any issues? I think they do.

And:

You had a group on one side that was bad, and you had a group on the other side that was also too violent. No one desires to say it, but I will state it right now. See, Trump understood the reality of the situation on the ground that day, so many did not. And while his challengers in the Mockingbird Media were eager to make some type of racist association between Trump and the "Alt-Right," Trump's main concern was keeping the nation together and not permitting the media to exploit the occasion to develop more division-- division which had been intentionally and purposefully planted and fostered throughout Obama's tenure in office, both by governmental firms and NGOs, through the similarity lots of, numerous Soros-backed groups.

The strategy was to design their tactics on what had currently taken place overseas, in locations like Europe and different Baltic states, with numerous "color revolutions." Even a brief search online these days will reveal the manifold connections to Soros-backed groups to even the most dubious skeptics. Soros poured billions over several years into whatever from Black

Lives Matter marches, to the so-called Women'sMarch, and well beyond.

Top-level Insider Anon would say, of Soros, when asked by an Anon:

Why is Soros pushing all these opportunities of degeneracy such as Feminism?

- Strategies of stress.

He isn't an anti-white man for some inexplicable reason. He is pro-division and pro-tension, to get the masses concentrated on each other rather than the regime that is fucking them.

Crafty challengers need careful strategies to get rid of. It's very appealing for some to think, "Why not just crush our enemies?" The Right had essentially forced Trump into the workplace, and was now appearing in force worldwide. And let's face it; they might probably just run over the Left underfoot, if they were only enabled. That would inevitably lead to something like a civil war. If the objective of the likes of Soros and the Cabal is to plant division to trigger damage, and an overall weakening of the nation, doing so would only even more advance the program of evil. The effective action to counter solve is to announce and show unity instead. Understanding that those on the Left and the Right had been successfully brainwashed and demoralized through years of conditioning, Trump picked the most efficient path, announcing that there were terrible stars on both sides, refusing to blame just one side, which would serve to give aside from the "moral high ground," in effect, perpetuating the department and endorsing.

Again, this becomes part of why I wrote this book to help bridge the gap, bring people into the light, and help them see our common enemies who are so great at setting us at each other's throats.

However, the Cabal was refrained from doing combating, not by a long-shot. On August 30, bystanders would capture footage of a driver losing control of their lorry at the very minute President Trump's motorcade pass by on its way to a rally in Springfield, Missouri. The car emerged from the woods and careened down a hill, directed right at the motorcade. The vehicle stopped when it bottomed out on a drainage ditch before stalling out at the side of the roadway.

Q would, some months later, verify that the CIA has classified innovation that enables it to take control of specific kinds of automobiles remotely, and yes, this was an effort on the president's life (among many).

Yes, we are now in the remote-controlled assassination zone. And if that sounds like sci-fi conspiracy theory territory, just keep in mind that in 1975, the presence of the CIA's "Heart

Attack Gun," which fired frozen darts of undetectable poison (and which mimicked a heart attack in its target) was disclosed openly before the Senate. And you much better think that the approaches and technologies at the disposal of the Deep State have considerably advanced in the intervening forty-plus years since that initially, unintentional disclosure.

But as soon as again, we need to continue with our timeline. On September 18, Donald Trump Jr. would drop his Secret Service detail.

Q would later describe why: On September 25, Trump Jr. would restore his Secret Service security. The issue, whatever it specifically had been, was now resolved, and it was safe for him to regain his security information. But then came the first big public crisis of the Trump administration.

The official story is that of a person called Stephen Paddock, raised fourteen AR-15s, eight AR-10s, a bolt action rifle, a revolver, and cases upon cases of ammunition to his space for six days before finally snapping, breaking out two windows made from hurricane-resistant glass with a hammer, and dumping over 1,100 rounds down into the performance crowd, around four-hundred. Fifty meters listed below, ultimately eliminating fifty-eight people and hurting over four hundred, while likewise trying to spark a jet fuel tank some 2,000 feet away. Images of Paddock, dead on the ground, would quickly leak on the internet.

And this is where the questions began for Anons!

Named the "most dangerous mass shooting in America," the occasion only didn't entirely build-up to this day; there's been no official motive listed regarding why Paddock would do what he had done. Add that to the truth that the footage of the shooting plainly showed muzzle flare in both broken windows (regardless of the police report saying there was no second shooter), the bizarre interview provided by his brother the following day, the existence of black vans on the ground, and the odd interview offered by one Jesus Campos, security personnel at the Mandalay Bay who had been shot as soon as, when probably Paddock had fired thirty-five bullets through the door when he check on the commotion.

Campos would go on Ellen later on, together with someone who can just be explained as a handler, and give among the strangest interviews I've ever seen on TV. So weird was the interview, and so different-looking was "Campos" on TV from pictures we had been seen with earlier, there was speculation as to whether this was even the same Jesus Campos being presented to us, or some kind of Deep State body-double being used to shill a central narrative.

And there was, of course, the caution Anons had gotten about Las Vegas just a couple of weeks prior that had motivated them to keep digging. Then, on October 25, Stephen Paddock's sibling would be detained for belongings of kid porn and the sexual exploitation of a minor, leading some Anons to dig even more challenging and show up familial connections Bohemian Grove. The Paddocks owned an estate just outside the Grove, a fact revealed by independent private investigator Jake Morphonios at Blackstone Intelligence, leading some to question if the relations were Cabal possessions, leveraged to get, ship, and transport "resources" for all sorts of illicit deeds. Morphonios would, in the week of his investigations, have his channel eliminated from YouTube, censored after I started enhancing his videos beyond the YouTube community. This kind of censorship has now become nearly associated with the extreme Left in Silicon Valley; the primary method they perform their affairs to silence dissent, functioning as publishers instead of open platforms (regardless of all congressional testament to the contrary).

Not only that, but MGM officers had discarded two-hundred and fifty million dollars worth of stock thirty days before the shooting, as had Soros, who had purchased up 1.35 million dollars worth of puts against MGM stock some sixty days before the strike.

But the story didn't end there. Survivors began passing away, with one death coming over a year later, when a Las Vegas survivor was captured in yet another mass shooting, this time in Thousand Oaks, California, one of thirteen who would end up perishing that evening. And then Anons discovered video footage of a VIP being escorted out of the Tropicana by SWAT operators.

I can just start to sum up the weirdness, and the depth of examination Anons did during that time, but the except it is this: Paddock was no the only shooter. Numerous Anons quickly concluded that he was an arms dealer working for the FBI. He was brokering a handle, well, the majority of Anons who checked out the subject figured it was some type of Saudi counter-coup terror/assassination operation.

Remember how Trump had traveled to Saudi Arabia and brokered an offer with the new king there? This was the action of the faction opposed to that new king, and yes, there were factions within our government supporting this operation, particularly by supplying weapons and ammo to terrorists.

And see how the VIP remains in the Tropicana?

Yeah, that was the massive problem with these prospective assassins. That guy, obviously a member of the Saudi Royal family, was the target. He was supposed to be in the Mandalay Bay gambling establishment; however, he had gone, on an impulse, to the Tropicana. However, by that point, the assassins' cover had been blown by ... many think it was Mandalay Bay security personnel, Jesus Campos.

The terrorists would fire upon Campos, mistaking him for a police officer, discharging some 200 rounds through the thirty-second flooring hotel room door, lodging one bullet in Campos' leg.

Campos would pull away and radio for help, suggesting word was out now, and the clock was ticking. The terrorists are required to produce an interruption to leave. They broke the windows, and numerous shooters opened fire at the crowd listed below. One spotted a jet fuel tank in the range and began firing at it, hoping to develop a gigantic fireball to sidetrack from their place. They also eliminated Paddock, making it appear like a suicide so that he might take the fall.

A similar story is distributed throughout/ pol/ by somebody claiming to be Q in an engaging post (but who most likely isn't Q). Still, the information set out in the drops is very thought-provoking and worth noting, even if the source is dubious.

One can only hope the real story about Las Vegas will eventually pertain to the surface area; however, all the proof I have seen indicate the official narrative being a carefully crafted fiction.

On October 5, 2017, George Papadopoulos would plead "guilty" to lying to the Feds about his communications with other foreign nationals, to enter into a plea deal, and serve all of fourteen days in prison. However, since this writing, he is presently thinking about recanting his plea offer, considering that it's now coming out that certain exculpatory proof might have been deliberately kept from him by the FBI.

On October 6, Trump would ask his "famous" (at least in Q-circles) "Calm Before the Storm." Surrounded by military leaders and their better halves, who were all present for dinner later on that evening, Trump asked the professional press photographers that existed:

" You guys understand what this represents? Maybe it's the calm before the storm.".

" What's the storm?" asked one bewildered reporter. " Could it be the calm before the storm," he responded, with a characteristic sly smirk on his face.

Really few people in the space, if any other than Trump, knew what he implied at the time. However, there in that room, surrounded by the top military minds in the nation, Trump gave the order for the 'Q' operation to go active. And this was far from the only Q-reference Trump would drop during the next year and a half, for those paying attention. Trump would even take to trolling the media using Twitter, tweeting out the phrase "Scott Free," which likewise occurs to be the name of Ridley Scott's production company, which had produced White Squall. In this movie, Q had ripped his preferred catch-phrase from, "Where we go one, we go all." It was one in a long line of winks-and-nods to Anons, over a year after their cumulative undertakings had started.

Naturally, the media's only response was to play dumb and wax pedantic, after months and months of declining to ask anybody in the Trump administration about the integrity of Q.

Had the media done its job and even tried to approach the issue truthfully, they would have made the connection themselves. Heck, they make the connection; however, they just refused to tell you about it, choosing to keep you in the dark, rather. And this wasn't the very first time something like this occurred, not by a long shot. There are dozens, if not numerous circumstances like this, I could reveal you. No, the media wished to keep you in the dark, not just because they were Mockingbirds charged by the CIA with opposing Trump at every turn, but likewise since numerous of them already had the unredacted FISA warrants from so long ago, demonstrating that they were complicit in the treasonous cover-up. You're discussing journalist after journalist guilty of devoting sedition, if not outright treason. And so, they lied to you. They actively kept you in the dark so you wouldn't revolt. They lied to you to conserve their sorry hides and spun a web of lies, wishing to avert the inevitable, hoping that the truth would never see the light of day.

And yet, here we are.

The product of years of collective effort and planning, the Q operation would go live twenty-three days later, when Q would make his first post on/ pol/. On October 28, 2017, Q's very first main post read:

Now, this has been mostly misconstrued by many critics, that I've frequently questioned if it was intentionally "misconstrued" to lead individuals astray and away from Q. On the other area, to the uninitiated, it appears like Q is predicting that Hillary Clinton would be apprehended on October 30, 2017. That never took place, so how could anybody trouble with QAnon all these years later on?

See, this is how silly many so-called "reporters" are. They don't comprehend how a Chan-based forum works, and the answer is straightforward: Q didn't compose that part. A random Anon wrote that entire upper section on/ pol/, just barfing out whatever rubbish he desired to publish that day. The text listed below that false prediction? The part about the passport being flagged, and the extradition order in effect in case of HRC making a run for it? That's Q's real post. Q was reacting to the initial Anon, fixing him.

Q started by authoritatively informing the board that Hillary was under constant surveillance and wasn't going to have the ability to run anywhere. She was being tracked, and there was no escape for her. (In fact, comprehending that none of these individuals will getaway is among the most important pillars to include your understanding of Q.

Depending on where we are in the timeline when you read this, and how far along Q's plan has advanced, there might still be exceptional or even continuous arrests. Nobody included is escaping, and by a specific point in history, all traitors will remain in jail.)

For the record, Q also forecasted riots if a cross-border run was attempted, and that, when the arrest lastly takes place, it will be the military managing the details of that operation.

Q would also go on to add, in that very same thread:

And this was the start of Q.

Over the coming months and weeks, Q would regularly publish intel drops similar to the ones above, beckoning Anons to follow him more profound and deeper into the rabbit hole, crafting eighty-three posts in the first week alone. And you may likewise be picking up on Q's unique design of writing, which can practically be described as Socratic and sporadic. The truth is, even this stylistic option was deliberate. Think back to the Trump Jr./ Secret Service drop. What did Q state?

" These questions and keywords are framed to reduce sniffer programs that constantly absorb and examine data, then pushed to z terminals for eval. Think keys on steroids.".

Not to get too technical here, but the Deep State had supercomputers at their disposal that were continually trawling the internet, publishing in online forums, and disrupting communications to mold and form the story of the nation. Several strategies were utilized to achieve this, but yes, these supercomputers could imitate natural speech and engage with people on several topics, basically passing the Turing test, fooling users into thinking they were talking to real individuals. Not only would these computer systems do this, but they would do it with multiple accounts to participate in something called "consensus cracking." It's one thing to have a web argument with someone. It's another to have five or 10 "individuals" screaming you down, saying you and your only viewpoint are wrong/radical/stupid/. When the "right" consensus was established, the bots would proceed to the next target (after all, CPU cycles are still a minimal resource-- even for leading secret supercomputers).

And "keys" here refers to XKeyScore, which was an NSA application that generally allowed the NSA to draw down all the information crossing the internet, anywhere in the world, and shop it in their massive archive in Utah.

All classified and indexed. The program was disclosed by Edward Snowden in 2013, which resulted in, according to Q, the NSA being seriously paralyzed in its ability to perform SIGINT operations. Before you go thinking Snowden is a hero, let me tell you, that guy is a traitor, and his factors for disclosing the program before running away to "Russia" (he left to Hong Kong) were to give the CIA and the Cabal an edge when it came to OpSec. Keep in mind Hillary's private, unlawful e-mail server? The one filled with blackmail? The one she was offering Special Access Programs to other countries with? Oh, did I mention that little factoid yet? One of the significant factors Hillary set up an insecure server was to enable foreign nationals access to our SAPs and other classified intelligence.

So, somebody may contribute to the Clinton Foundation, and in return, they would be informed how to access files on the server. It was a fiendishly devilish pay-to-play arrangement (and believe me when I state this is just the idea of the iceberg when it concerns Hillary's treasonous activities).

Hillary wasn't the only game in town. Obama had his e-mail servers too. Eric Schmidt, co-founder of Google, went to North Korea to assist establish one of these private e-mail servers (because North Korea is nothing like what you've most likely been told it is. Don't worry, we'll go over that in detail later, too). And at first, the NSA was using their critical score program to spy on the illegal activities of these Cabal-affiliated politicians and strategy ahead.

It would be pretty funny if it weren't so ill; to avoid surveillance, Q would inform us, these different Cabal actors would resort to utilizing Gmail drafts (because, once again, Eric Schmidt had set up a personal Gmail server for them all) to interact with each other. They'd compose up a draft, conserve it, never send it, and after that, give the signal for the next individual to log in and check out the draft. That was one method they attempted to navigate the NSA's monitoring programs. They even tried to use "game comms," as Q has informed us. They utilized the likes of XBOX Live, Playstation Network, and different mobile game chat spaces to attempt and go incognito with their communications. (Thankfully, it didn't work.).

So when Q states "believe keys on steroids," it implies there was a program on Cabal supercomputers that was even more powerful than what the NSA had formerly had access to, before Snowden occurred and paralyzed them with a little bit of publicity. Q had to skirt around that through bland, Socratic phraseology, lest the Cabal computer systems detect what was going on and overwhelm the boards with a flood of spam and sound.

Oh, and if you were paying attention at the time, you'd recognize Eric Schmidt stepped down from Alphabet (the parent corporation of Google) the very same day (December 21, 2017) President Trump would sign the executive order entitled "Blocking the Property of Persons Involved in Serious Human Rights Abuse or Corruption," mandating overall property seizure for anyone associated with such criminal activities.

Schmidt resigned that really day to safeguard the company he had helped develop (with the assistance of the CIA, through its devoted tech incubator, In-Q-Tel). Schmidt would, later on, make an appearance in June 2018 during Inspector General Horowitz's testament before your home and Senate Judiciary committees. He would be sitting on the edge of his seat, the entire time

More tips on the "pre-Q" timeline:

Comparable to what occurred with Schmidt above, on October 30, it was announced that Paul Manafort would be prosecuted as part of Mueller's special counsel investigation. This is the day Tony Podesta would resign from The Podesta Group. November 9, 2017, all of the Podesta Group's employees would be informed that they needed to discover brand-new jobs because the Podesta Group would disappear come the new year. Kimberley Fritts, the Podesta Group's chief executive and second-in-command, would soon but reanimate the company as Cogent Strategies, taking many of the Podesta Group's former hires and clients with her, basically reincarnating the Podesta group under her management, but leaving behind all the legal baggage in the process.

Now, this isn't a complete timeline of every single event that occurred throughout the time leading up to and following

Trump's governmental project, and it's not suggested to be. Entire books have been composed, dissecting the layers of intrigue surrounding these events (I mean Dan Bongino's Spygate, in specific), and new information continues to emerge with each passing week. However, what this timeline is supposed to offer you is a general view of what Anons were seeing during this time, what connections we were making, and what discoveries we were digging up, because honestly, much of this was either intentionally mocked or purposefully buried by the Legacy Media. And I know I keep saying it, but believe me, the media is not your friend.

Trump labeled them "Fake News" and "the enemy of the people" for a reason. They do not have your benefit at heart. If you're reeling from whatever I simply told you, I wouldn't be shocked. Imagine how Anons felt this entire time, all at once, furious and reviled by the Mockingbird Media. And yet, they fight on, dogged in their pursuit of the truth, they are working not for acknowledgment but out of love for their country, for their individuals, and their desire to restore the Republic to the former splendor enshrined in its ideals. They desired the very same thing Trump chose: to Make America Great Again (which is why they assisted meme into the workplace in the very first place)!

Trump's unspoken genius in all this remained in leveraging the power of Anons, a decentralized, digital volunteer army, to achieve this objective.

What do we call this movement the QAnon operation? What, specifically, was this movement of daily Anons and patriots attempting to accomplish, and how did it plan to accomplish its objectives?

QAnon is a top-level intelligence operation run in combination with the NSA and Military Intelligence, put in place by President Trump as a way to bypass the media and develop a direct interaction backchannel with individuals (by beginning specifically with his most emotional, devoted, and smart fans-- the Anons), to topple an ancient cult/Cabal that had, as its goal, the complete damage of America. Making use of a Socratic design of writing, Q would begin slow-rolling disclosures about these Cabal stars and their wicked strategies, along with reframing certain inaccurate. Yet, typically held presumptions (and correcting lies, when fit), to "awaken" individuals to the truth that had been concealed from them for decades.

The supreme objective of all of this was to reach a tipping point, where a specific emergency of individuals would get a level of prerequisite knowledge previously overlooked worldwide, developing, in essence, a decentralized intelligence firm comprised of numerous thousands of Anons (if not millions), running 24/7, all dealing with each other to research, write, distribute, and meme non-stop, not only to counter the nationwide stories, however, to develop a "safety-net" of psychological and emotional support for when the rest of the population would be unwillingly (a minimum of in the beginning) pushed into the light by events that would begin to appear around them such as mass arrests, military tribunals, and even executions of previous politicians. (And if you wanted to get more esoteric, there's even some out there who think Q was building a morphogenetic field, essentially, a quantum description for what some might call a "collective consciousness" that is, honestly, beyond my present level of understanding.

Though I will confess, I think it well within the realm of possibility, evaluating what I have actually seen and checked out, therefore far.).

My role in all this was to follow Q with every drop, remain active on the research study boards, posting whenever necessary, attempting to determine what precisely Q was talking about (however, due to the nature of Q, this often proved to be an overwhelming job), and disseminate my findings online, both on my site, and my social networks profiles-- in a method that lots of people discovered both engaging. Picturing from my knowledge and the expertise of seasoned Anons, I would dissect Q's drops and curate them in such a way as to tailor them for mass intake. These efforts ultimately resulted in me turning into one of the most followed and most prominent Q-supporters in the world, with Q even pulling images from my website on event, highlighting images of followers wearing the shirts and hats I had started to produce Q-related mottos and symbiotic relationship. And I don't state any of that to toot my own horn. I was typically inaccurate in my analyses, attempting as I might keep pace with Q. But one thing my readers valued was that I would always try to explain when I was hypothesizing, that I would admit when I was wrong, and do my best to correct in practice. It was not a little task, and it was a few of the most challenging and crucial work I might have ever carried out. In essence, I became an extensive and recognizable "node" in this QAnon network, of which I am delighted to be a part.

And Q was no mere PR project. Lives were at stake. Our enemies were genuine, significantly embedded, and exposing them would require a "Great Awakening," worldwide, resulting in changing history. Evildoers would be exposed and eventually assembled for sentencing at military tribunals, considering that the regular justice system was far too corrupt and subverted by bad stars at this time. If we succeeded in our efforts, this would lead to the restoration of the Republic and the dawn of a new Golden Age for America and even the world.

Q would even speak about suppressed and concealed innovations, stirring the creativities of Anons worldwide as he verified the presence of things like the Secret Space Program and promised disclosures that would blow individuals' minds. As soon as again, we'll have to save that conversation for the very end.

Things had gone so awry throughout the Obama years, the original plan being fielded by the top brass, the initial Plan A, was for a military coup, where Obama would have been toppled by force. See, military intelligence had long been keeping track of the scene, and whatever I've informed you therefore far was known to them years earlier. They believed it might be needed, as early as 2013, to depose Obama from the workplace in a military coup merely and summarily execute him.

There would have been rioting, yes. The expense to America would have been terrible, yes. The Republic would have been protected, and millions of lives would have been saved as a result.

However, vigilance won out, and persistence took the day. They chose to hold back. An election was a few years away and if they could discover the ideal prospect to back, and if they could persuade him to run, and if they might reduce the widespread citizen scams, and if they might discover a method to have him attract sufficient individuals, and if they might win the nomination, and if they might prevent the media, and if they could keep him safe from the constant hazard of assassination, well then they might simply have the ability to manage a completely legal, bloodless coup, and wind up driving this cult from the halls of power as soon for all.

After all, if, in the end, the bloodless way stopped working, they could attempt the bloody path again. This course was more sensible. However, it was likewise more distressing for everyone included. They'd figure out how to deal with the Cabal later if that all worked.

If you're reeling from that summation, as I'm sure lots of in America are by now, it's best to get used to the sensation, because it's not going to go anywhere as long as you've got this book in your hands. Essentially, when you enter the world of QAnon, you rapidly discover that nearly every presumption you had about the way the world works, whatever you thought you knew, was wrong in some method, which this was by design. The sensation is dizzying, at least when you're mentally connected to a particular result (or a specific event, or politician, instead of perfects flexibility and liberty). Conquer those attachments, however, and the ride soon becomes exciting!

So, having effectively leveraged this latent power, this mass of Americans sitting at their computer systems, yearning to assist in some way, any way they could, the Q motion handled its final kind: a decentralized, anonymized, online research study effort surrounding the questions and concerns raised by interactions with a representative (or group of representatives) embedded deep in the Trump administration, running at the most significant tiers of federal government intelligence, to bypass the media and remove the Cabal.

But that hardly does the size and scope of what's taking place here any justice. And beyond that, Anons, naturally, had concerns. Could Q be trusted? What's the nature of the hazard facing the country? Can we rely on the Plan? There had been other expert leakages before. Why Q, and why now? Why follow him?

Why did I follow him?

Trump represented an existential hazard to the establishment from the very minute he started his candidateship. I said earlier that I understood almost immediately that this election was like no other election in our whole history. The discontent and the discord made it clear that this was unlike anything we, the individuals, had ever seen before. The election wasn't quite the success we, on Trump's side, initially believed it was. It was clear from that day on that Trump's victory had been a declaration of war, which war was about to enter its next stage

.

CHAPTER TWELVE

It's Time to Wake Up

If you are ready to provide up the ridiculous rage you are surrounded by, get up and join the forces of Light. We invite you.

We are not a political party. There is corruption on both sides of the aisle. The majority of us are Independents in some sense as we think of ourselves. Rather, we are a team of awakened individuals working together to find and expose the fact that has been hidden from us and to get rid of evil and corruption. Our goal is to secure others, to share the truth, and to restore peace of mind. We have good friends and advocates all over the world.

Here are ten things you can do to help and awaken others in the war we are battling versus the Deep State.

1. Love and support our Nation, our Constitution, and yes, our President. Donald Trump has quit the life he could have had to play a vital role in freeing us from the darkness. He can't do it alone. Supporting him is the least we can do.

2. Get an education. You can capture up with past stories that the media has fixated on. Follow independent journalists. Subscribe to their channels.

3. Share what you're learning. Tell your loved ones. Send out posts, e-mail, Tweets, and so on, sharing news, videos, memes. Have discussions. Give this book to somebody you appreciate. Ask When they are done reading, them to share it. Purchase more copies and give away.

4. Pray for our leaders, our families, our communities, our kids, and our motion. Please pray for protection from those who would hurt us and for the power to get rid of evil. Among the things we've found out is that evil is real. Many of us are Christian, and we seek God's help daily.

5. Be there for loved ones as they awaken. They will be in different phases of disbelieve, denial, worry, anxiety, anger, and misconstruing as they process the new realities. Be tolerant.

6. The Deep State will state and do ANYTHING to retain power. False flag occasions, possible biological risks, violent mob actions, and so on are genuine possibilities. If you see anything suspicious, please report it. Avoid violent confrontations. Stay informed.

7. Be prepared. Communications might break down. The banking system might be offline. This isn't intended to frighten you. It is just to say it is smart to get ready for breakdowns and delays in times like these.

8. Give peace a possibility. The Deep State has been the concealed hand in disputes and wars all over the world. They

215

gain from conflict and turmoil in many ways. While countries must be all set to safeguard themselves, as we eliminate the bad players, we lead peace and success.

9. Join us in developing a promising future. Whether we realized it or not, we have been working indirectly for the Deep State as they

have stolen from us in numerous methods. As their grip damages, some of the stolen resources will be gone back to us, and we will have access to innovative technologies they've concealed from us and kept for themselves. Much better days are ahead.

10. Get included. This is an entirely voluntary motion. We contribute what we are good at, what we are relocated to do. We do something about it where we see we can make a difference. There is a place for you too. Welcome aboard, Patriot.

QAnon's messages are typically conveyed using code, abbreviations, and with both military and political terminology also. In turn, the subcultures of Reddit, 8Chan, and even YouTube have their language.

CHAPTER THIRTEEN

The Resistance Is On

Many individuals wouldn't provide "shills" (paid antagonists) the time of day. I decided to tackle this issue daily on the boards in a different way. In my mind, I believe deep down there is something inside everybody that should need to understand the truth and who should have a good life and desires unto others.

They have been attempting to bring the world to its knees to bring about the "New World Order." They have made it well known for their strategies. There is an evil that our world is facing, beginning with the initial 13 wealthiest households, whose families date back 6000 years to Babylonian times. These families are some of the most twisted.

Satanic individuals out there.

They essentially have every opportunity of "kill order" working in their favor. That consists of all platforms of Media/ TV/ Movies for Mind Control (with their Luciferian meaning planted everywhere, like the pyramids with an all-seeing eye in the middle), Food Giants for GMO/slow kill, Vaccine Industry for Agenda 21/ depopulation, water fluoridation for/ calcification of the pineal gland, H.A.A.R.P.

Weather changes for producing natural disasters, etc. They profit on their own in many ways. It's disgusting to think of.

This is not even getting into the MK-Ultra programs that they use with False Flags around our country and the world to push their agenda on and through the media, political leaders, soldiers, stars, artists, and more.

This does not include the operations they have used for many years with the CDC/unexpected illness breakouts and the creation of diseases (Aids, Polio, STDS, Lyme Disease), using countries/entire villages as their lab rats. A number of the outcomes never see the light day.

This doesn't include owned or contracted organizations had that "legally' take, steal or entice children for the sake of using them as sex servants, or slaves camps/mines, using them like toys in their pedophilia fantasies, and then to compromise them in their cult occasions. And then they have the nerve to blast it in your face as they perform in films like "The Dark Crystal," "Indiana Jones and the Temple of Doom," "Monsters, Inc." (The Fear Meter), etc. revealing how to collect adrenochrome that gives them some form of high and younger looks. We can't forget organ harvesting operations, which are big cash (Planned Parenthood).

When you start seeing the press release from the grip of the enemy, and their narratives start changing as we shine the light on these Elites, join us somewhat of keeping them up like a pack of canines.

You will understand that the world is about to get a whole lot more " intriguing" as those who have done us all wrong for years will finally be addressing for the crimes against humanity they have been involved in.

Here are the truths. For many years, from points of power, all the way to big-screen movies and every perch between, our history to the present day has attempted to alert us about the "bad gamers" working to destroy our nation and eventually the world. We simply had to listen!

A Fierce Patriotic Passion.

When this "Q" movement began, and everyone was up in arms questioning the direction Qanon was trying to take them or waiting around questioning when the next crumb would fall. I understood somebody needed to speak up with a little guidance.

I believe more people need to be focusing on the underlying cause/reason for "Q" to be doing what he or they is doing, the factor our country and the world is in a complete uproar. You don't learn that by simply connecting puppets to puppets. You do that by beginning at the base of all of it, "the structure," and work up. I can tell you doing it the way everyone is assuming must be done resembles a train wreck and when you stand back after a couple of months, look at who you are connected to.

This web resembles the size of the world, and each lousy gamer has thousands of connections to somebody else. Think of a "program" that was written 200 years earlier. Now imagine how numerous people are associated with that one primary goal. You need to understand that the primary objective initially and understand what's going on.

This is way bigger than the U.S. This is way bigger than Q, Trump, or a memo. We require to do good by them by examining the shit out of the original players, the ones who made all this possible. They formed the genuine "Secret Societies," and through those societies, they developed the most twisted framework to kill off 80 percent or more of the world's population. All these puppets are either descendants of the members of these societies, or well linked that relied on advocates.

Some households into a cult confronted. These households can be found worldwide, and the neighborhood should be investigated to the max for bribery, laundering, trafficking of drugs and humans of all kinds.

This is how we stay focused and ahead of the Q phenomenon, instead of scattering our brain all over the place. Q is mainly dropping these crumbs to connect to current events that link in the red stars they are trying to take down in due time. Our task is "red pill" the public within and around our country and the world.

I've got a strategy to get this rolling into something enormous. That is by dividing people into work classifications that can interact effectively and work all the time on things such as Meme Productions, Social Media Teams, Investigative Researchers & Bloggers, and Semi Community Organizers for a Mobile Movement so we can help press the vetted information that we discover, and we end up being a Go-To Source For Investigative Info when other news or when trusted sources become reluctant or unable to do individuals' work

The Battle For Our Souls and The Earth, Discover How The New World Order and Illuminati Hijacked The World And Control Your Mind

Simon Smith

All trademarks inside this book are for clarifying purposes only and are possessed by the owners themselves, not allied with this document.

Disclaimer

All erudition supplied in this book is specified for educational and academic purposes only. The author is not in any way responsible for any outcomes that emerge from utilizing this book. Constructive efforts have been made to render information that is both precise and effective. Still, the author is not to be held answerable for the accuracy or use/misuse of this information.

Foreword

I will like to thank you for taking the very first step of trusting me and deciding to purchase/read this life-transforming book. Thanks for investing your time and resources on this product.

I can assure you of precise outcomes if you will diligently follow the specific blueprint I lay bare in the information handbook you are currently checking out. It has transformed lives, and I firmly believe it will equally change your own life too.

All the information I provided in this Do It Yourself piece is easy to absorb and practice.

CHAPTER ONE

What Is Qanon

President Trump has spoken of how advocates of the QAnon conspiracy theory, which has grown online in the US, appear to like him so much.

Mr Trump told reporters that he didn't understand much about the movement, but added that he had heard that "these were individuals who love our country."

The movement faces a crackdown from Facebook and Twitter, who have taken steps against many accounts and web addresses linking to videos and websites spreading out QAnon's bizarre ideas.

At its heart, QAnon is an extensive, unproven conspiracy theory that says that President Trump is waging a secret war against elite Satan-worshipping pedophiles in government, the media, and business.

QAnon believers have speculated that this battle will cause a day of reckoning where prominent people such as former presidential candidate Hillary Clinton will be detained and executed.

That's the basic story, but there are numerous offshoots, detours, and internal arguments that the comprehensive list of QAnon claims is massive - and often inconsistent. Adherents draw in news events, historical facts, and numerology to establish their improbable conclusions.

Where did it all start?

In October 2017, an anonymous user put out a couple of posts on the message board 4chan. The said user signed off as "Q" and claimed to have some form of US security approval referred to as "Q clearance."

These messages or posts became referred to as "breadcrumbs" or "Q drops," often written in cryptic language supported with pledges, slogans, and pro-Trump themes.

"Where we go one we go all," typically abbreviated as "WWG1WGA!" is one of the most popular QAnon slogans

Do you think nobody genuinely believes it? Thousands do. The quantity of traffic to mainstream social networking websites like Twitter, Facebook, Reddit, and YouTube has exploded since 2017, and indications are to the effect that the numbers have increased even more throughout the coronavirus pandemic.

Judging by social networks, many individuals believe in a minimum of some of the bizarre theories provided by QAnon. Its appeal hasn't been decreased by events that would appear to debunk the entire thing. For example, early Q drops concentrated on the investigation by special prosecutor Robert Mueller.

QAnon fans claimed Mr Mueller's inquiry into Russian interference in the 2016 United States election was truly a fancy cover story for examining pedophiles. The attention of the conspiracy theorists wandered somewhere else when it concluded with no such bombshell discovery.

Real believers assert that deliberate misinformation is sown into Q's messages - in their minds making the conspiracy theory impossible to disprove.

QAnon followers bring flags and banners to rallies in support of President Trump

What result has it had?

QAnon fans drive hashtags and co-ordinate abuse of seen enemies - the political leaders, press reporters, and celebs that they assume are concealing for pedophiles.

It's not just about threatening messages posted online. Twitter stated that it acted against QAnon due to its potential for "offline damage."

Many QAnon followers have been nabbed after making threats or engaging in offline activities.

In one substantial case in 2018, a significantly armed man blocked a bridge over the Hoover Dam. Matthew Wright eventually pleaded guilty to a terrorism charge at a later date.

Researches reveal that most Americans haven't come to be mindful of QAnon. For a lot of supporters, it forms the structure of their support for President Trump.

In the past, Mr Trump had retweeted QAnon followers, and last month his child Eric Trump published a QAnon meme on Instagram.

How famous is a pro-Trump conspiracy theory?

It's quite most likely that a QAnon fan - or someone considerate to the conspiracy theory - will be in the future United States Congress.

If you're spending a great deal of time on the internet nowadays-- and thanks to the pandemic, a great deal of us are-- you've probably become aware of QAnon. This extending net conspiracy theory has remained dominant amongst a few of President Trump's followers.

Unless you're online, you likely still have inquiries regarding what exactly is taking place.

QAnon was once an edge phenomenon-- the kind most individuals might safely neglect. However, in present times, it's gone mainstream. Twitter, Facebook, and different other social media networks have been significantly flooded with QAnon-related false information. QAnon followers have also been attempting to attach themselves to different other lobbyist causes, such as the anti-vaccine and anti-child-trafficking motions, to increase their rankings.

QAnon has additionally permeated into the offline world, with some followers charged with terrible criminal offenses, including one QAnon follower implicated of killing a mafia manager some time ago and one more that was accused of threatening to eliminate Joseph R. Biden Jr., the presumptive Democratic presidential candidate. The Federal Bureau of Investigation has warned that QAnon positions a possible residential risk.

Not too long ago, QAnon got to a new turning point when Marjorie Taylor Greene, a well known QAnon supporter from Georgia, won a Republican ticket in a heavily conventional district, setting her up for a near-certain election to Congress in November. After Ms Greene's win, Mr Trump called her a "future Republican celebrity."

QAnon is an incredibly intricate theory, and you can fill a whole book discussing its various tributaries and sub-theories. Below are some common points you should understand.

What is QAnon?

QAnon is the umbrella term for an expansive collection of internet conspiracy theory concepts that affirm, incorrectly, that the world is run by a cabal of Satan-worshiping pedophiles that are outlining against Mr Trump while running an international child sex-trafficking ring.

QAnon fans think this internal circle consists of leading Democrats, including Hillary Clinton, Barack Obama, and George Soros. Some entertainers and Hollywood celebrities like Oprah Winfrey, Tom Hanks, Ellen DeGeneres, and religious figures including Pope Francis and the Dalai Lama.

Many believe that, along with molesting children, members of this team kill and eat their victims to remove a life-extending chemical from their blood.

According to QAnon tradition, Mr Trump was recruited by leading army generals to compete as president in 2016 to break up this criminal conspiracy, finish its control of politics and the media, and bring its members to justice.

Since it began, QAnon has integrated aspects of several other conspiracy theory communities, including the claims about the assassination of John F. Kennedy, the 9/11 "truther" movement, and the presence of U.F.O.

QAnon Anonymous, a podcast regarding the QAnon movement, calls QAnon a "big tent conspiracy theory" because it is developing and includes new functions and claims. The presence of a worldwide pedophile cabal is the core tenet of QAnon, and the one that most, if not all, of its fans, believe.

How did this all start?

In October 2017, a post appeared on 4chan, the notoriously dangerous message board, from a private account calling itself "Q Clearance Patriot." This poster that came to be known just as "Q," claimed to be a high-level knowledge officer with accessibility to classified details regarding Mr Trump's battle against the global cabal.

Q forecasted that this battle would soon culminate in "The Storm"-- a designated time when Mr Trump would lastly uncover the cabal, punish its members for their criminal activities and also bring back America to success.

Why is it called 'The Storm'?

Mr Trump commented with senior military leaders in 2017 that QAnon fans have suggested as evidence of the president's technique to separate a cabal.

Mr Trump remarked with elderly army leaders in 2017 that QAnon believers have aimed to as evidence of the head of the state's strategy to break up a cabal.

It's a reference to a puzzling statement Mr Trump made during an October 2017 image op. Posturing together with army generals, Mr Trump claimed, "You people know what this stands for? Possibly it's the tranquillity before the storm."

QAnon believers referred to that moment as evidence that Mr Trump was sending out coded messages concerning his strategies to divide the cabal, with the help of the armed forces.

Who is Q, and what are 'Q Drops'?

Q's identity is still unidentified, although there have been hints and supposition concerning it for many years. Some guess that a solitary web troll has been posting as Q the whole time; others state that several people are included in posting as Q, or that Q's identity has changed with time.

Making things a lot more complicated is that Q's online home base has changed many times. Q's posts originally appeared on 4chan. They moved to 8chan, where they remained until that site was taken offline last year after the El Paso mass shooting. They currently survive on 8kun, a site run by the former proprietor of 8chan. Each of these sites uses a system of identification verification known as a "tripcode"-- basically, a distinctive digital signature that proves that a collection of confidential posts were written by the very same person or people.

" Drops" are what QAnon followers call Q's posts. There have been almost 5,000 of them up until now, and a whole lot of them take the form of a message that is cryptic code.

Many of QAnon fans make use of "Q Drop" apps that collect every one of Q's messages in one place and share them each time a new message gets here. (One of these apps struck the top 10 paid applications in Apple's App Store before it was taken down for breaching guidelines of companies.) They then post these drops in Facebook groups, chatrooms as well as Twitter strings, and start speaking about or debating what everything means.

Is QAnon the same thing as Pizzagate?

QAnon has been explained as a "big-budget follow up" to Pizzagate because it takes the preliminary Pizzagate conspiracy theory-- which proclaimed, incorrectly, that Mrs Clinton and her cronies were running a child sex-trafficking ring out of the basement of a Washington, D.C., pizza restaurant-- and also includes a lot more layers of story on top of it.

Many people rely on both theories, and for many QAnon followers, Pizzagate represented a sort of conspiracy theory on-ramp.

One new element in QAnon is a rage of particular and clear predictions about when and how "The Storm" would play out. For years, Q has expected that mass arrests of cabal participants would take place on certain days, that specific government records would reveal the cabal's misbehaviors, which Republicans would win several seats in the elections.

None of those predictions came true. Most QAnon fans didn't care. They simply discovered ways to reframe the story and forget the disparities and carried on.

How many individuals believe in QAnon?

It's difficult to say, since there's no official membership directory website; however, the number is not small. Also, if you count simply the die-hard QAnon followers-- excluding "QAnon-lite" followers that may strongly believe in a deep state story against Mr. Trump, but not a cabal of child-eating Satanists—the actual number might be at least in the thousands.

Some of the most prominent QAnon groups on Facebook have greater than 100,000 members each, and Twitter lately revealed it was doing something about it to restrict the reach of more than 150,000 QAnon-associated accounts. A current record by NBC News found that Facebook had implemented an inner research study of QAnon's existence on its platform. It reached the conclusion that there were many QAnon groups, with many members between them.

That number has more than likely grown throughout the pandemic, as people stuck indoors count on the internet for home entertainment as well as socializing and get pulled into the QAnon neighborhood. A recent short article in The Wall Street Journal found that subscription in 10 big Facebook groups devoted to QAnon had expanded by even more than 600 percent since the commencement of lockdowns.

Why are some individuals attracted to the QAnon movement?

A common misunderstanding is that QAnon is just a political movement. It works, for individuals that count on it, as both a social community and a source of entertainment.

Some individuals have compared QAnon to a substantial multiplayer online game, given the way it welcomes individuals to co-create a sort of everyday reality filled up with recurring characters, changing storylines, and also sophisticated puzzle-solving missions. QAnon has also been linked or compared to a church, in that it provides its supporters with a social support framework and an organizing narrative for their day-to-day lives.

Adrian Hon, a game designer that has written about QAnon's similarity to alternate-reality games, claims that followers "open an impressive fantasy world of secret wars as well as cabals and Hillary Clinton controlling things, and it offers hassle-free explanations for things that feel strange or wrong regarding the world."

What function have social media networks played in QAnon's appeal?

Despite the truth that Q's blog posts show up on fringe message boards, the QAnon phenomenon attributes much of its appeal to Twitter, Facebook, and YouTube, which have enhanced QAnon messages and recommended QAnon pages and groups to new individuals via their algorithms.

Additionally, QAnon believers have used social networks to harass, terrify, and threaten their perceived adversaries, and to seed other types of misinformation that influences public debate.

Many of the most popular conspiracy theories on the internet in recent times, such as "Pandemic," a documentary containing dangerous and false claims regarding Covid-19, and a viral conspiracy theory that wrongly declared that Wayfair, the online furniture company, was involved in the trafficking of children-- have been popularized and amplified by QAnon followers.

A few of these networks have started trying to eliminate QAnon content from their platforms. Twitter recently banned several QAnon accounts, stating that they had been involved in coordinated harassment. Facebook has taken down almost 800 QAnon groups and restricted many QAnon-related pages, groups, and Instagram accounts.

Haven't there always been unlikely conspiracy theory concepts concerning powerful elites?

It's a fact that much of QAnon's subject matter is recycled from earlier conspiracy theories. However, QAnon is fundamentally an internet-based movement that functions differently and at a different scale than anything we have seen or experienced before.

For beginners, QAnon is deeply participatory in such a way than some other well-known conspiracy theories have been. Supporters meet in Facebook groups and chat rooms to decode or interpret the latest Q posts, discuss their ideas regarding the news of the day, and bond with their fellow supporters. The Atlantic has called it "the birth of a new religion."

There's similarly the crucial danger of what QAnon supporters or followers believe. It's one thing to be involved in a polarized political discussion with heated disagreements; it's another to have a fraction of Americans who believe, with overall sincerity, that the leaders of the opposition party are cannibalizing and kidnapping innocent children.

Add those terrible, paranoid fantasies with the fact that QAnon supporters have been charged with committing grievous crimes in Q's name, and it's not a surprise people are worried.

How has President Trump responded to QAnon?

Mr. Trump is the leading and heroic figure in QAnon's major narrative-- the courageous patriot who was selected to save America from the international cabal. As a result, QAnon believers parse Mr. Trump's actions and words carefully, searching for hidden meanings. When Trump mentions the number 17, they indicate that he is sending secret messages to them. (Q is the 17th letter of the alphabet.) When he puts on a pink tie, they see it as an indication that he is releasing trafficked children.

It's uncertain whether Mr. Trump understands the mystical details of the QAnon theory or not. But he has embraced the movement's followers, saying in a White House press briefing that "I've heard these are people that love our country." He also refused to disavow or denounce the movement when questioned about his support for Ms. Greene, the QAnon-affiliated congressional prospect. And he has shared posts from QAnon followers lots of times on his social media accounts.

For months, QAnon followers hijacked the #SaveTheChildren campaign, which began as a fund-raising campaign supporting a legitimate anti-child-trafficking organization-- as a recruiting strategy.

What they're doing, essentially, is using overemphasized and false insurance claims about child trafficking to bring in the interest of a new audience- most likely worried mothers and fathers. They attempt to guide the discussion to QAnon chatting factors-- mentioning that the featured children are trafficked. For instance, results from the fact that the global cabal intends to accumulate a life-extending chemical from their blood.

This particular technique has explicitly been problematic for legitimate anti-trafficking groups, who need to take care of blocked hotlines and extensive misinformation as QAnon has latched on to their concern.

Just posting #SaveTheChildren does not mean your pals are QAnon believers. They might have just found an article regarding child trafficking that reverberated with them and chose to share it. They, and you, must recognize that those blog posts are part of a collective QAnon strategy.

Background on Qanon

QAnon is a remote conspiracy theory preferred amongst various extremists and some public advocates of President Trump.

QAnon, which showed up in 2017 on 4chan, is primarily and initially an online trolling and disinformation movement. While it is difficult to figure out the size of the movement, it is likely that QAnon followers number in the tens of thousands.

Supporters follow the Q and believe a shadowy cabal of paedophiles is controlling world governments.

The QAnon theory is huge and anti-government; its supporters proactively plant fear regarding autonomous organizations.

While the ADL does not think that all QAnon followers are usually extremists, this is a dangerous concept that has inspired terrible acts.

QAnon is a globally, incredibly innovative and wide-reaching conspiracy theory that has taken place within some components of the pro-Trump activity. It is a mix of both reputable and unique concepts, with significant touches of antisemitism and xenophobia.

The said theory declares that nearly every head of state in existing American background until Donald Trump has been a creature implemented by an international elite of power brokers heck bent on developing themselves and maintaining their

Satanic child-murdering sex cult. Q refers to "Q clearance" or "Q gain access to consent," terms used to explain a top-secret clearance level within the Department of Energy.

According to QAnon custom, this international elite, described as "The Deep State" or "The Cabal," control not just world governments, but the Catholic church, the banking system, the farming and pharmaceutical markets, the media and movie industry; all working to keep people of the world negative, enslaved and ignorant.

Connection to Mainstream Politics

Even with a considerable lack of any kind of sustaining proof, QAnon has efficiently made the jump from the paranoid catacombs of online subculture right into America's mainstream conventional movement. As the QAnon ideology has obtained a larger audience, a cottage market of food supplements, merchandise, and way of life assistance has emerged in addition to it, all rooted in the well profound distrust in government, established sciences, and traditional media. It has reeled in a following of private citizens, ravenous grifters, and politicians, as well as substantial support within various other extremist movements, mainly the militia and anti-government movements.

QAnon adherents have been linked to acts of murder, physical violence, kidnapping, and public disturbance. In 2020, the novel coronavirus gave extra straw for QAnon supporters who eagerly folded the pandemic into their paranoid worldview.

In January 2020, twenty candidates competing U.S. Congress publicly supported the QAnon conspiracy theory. While some have been defeated or left, and it is unlikely that much of those staying will win, the ubiquity of the theory stands out. It is fretting that support for QAnon has become merged with allegiance to President Trump, perpetuating a belief that his political rivals are bogus adversaries of humanity.

The QAnon movement has attached itself to the sense of unfair treatment and persecution felt not just by advocates of President Trump but regularly voiced by the head of state himself. While the President has not directly accepted QAnon, he has actively advanced the narrative that there are treacherous forces within the democratic party and the government.

What followers believe

QAnon consists of various comprehensive and complex conspiracy theories; it is a host of reasonably diverse theories touching on everything from the fabricated death of JFK, Jr. to

Satanic blood rituals and nuclear deterrence, tenuously focused around the idea that a global cabal of high-powered culprits manages culture.

This kitchen sink method is a significant reason why QAnon has gotten such a considerable adhering to in its fairly short life; it imagines a significant tent conspiracy theory with the ability of accomodating all sort of theories and around the globe events.

It's not all doom and gloom: QAnoners also think there are tremendous forces at play, women and men working within the government to prevent the Deep State. QAnon supporters refer to such people as the "white hats."

The internet has offered these likely saviors a new opportunity to share the reality outside the strictures of the Deep State-controlled "mainstream media." Mobile phone, email, and social networks have made it simpler to share what followers think to be the facts regarding Deep State criminal offenses and have made the criminals trackable and their illegal activities deducible.

In the considerably hash-taggable world of QAnon, this development created #ThePlan. This improbable pipe dream discusses not just the presidency of Donald Trump but also the resistance to his government by the forces QAnon wants to defeat.

According to Q, the mystical expert who is "trickling" this information to the public, the white hats stopped Hillary Clinton and Barack Obama from winning the 2016 election. As the theory goes, the Democratic elites needed to win the presidency to pay back funds the Clinton Foundation extracted from various other countries under the guise of 2010 emergency quake aid to Haiti. Instead of helping desperate Haitians, the Clintons used the money to fund a substantial child sex trafficking process from the disaster-stricken country.

Luckily, the white hats recognized the only individual they consider ethical and honest enough to withstand the wickedness of the Deep State: then-candidate Donald Trump

Since the Trump's election, Q and the white hats have been involved in what they considered an impressive fight with the Deep State. The reliable conclusion of the Plan rests on many expected secret charges, apparently to be put together by the Department of Justice against prominent Democrats, elites, and Hollywood celebs.

When these indictments are revealed, they believed the criminal activities of the elites would be exposed, and they will without delay, be restrained, and sent out to Guantanamo Bay.

Many aspects of QAnon lore mirror longstanding antisemitic tropes. The belief that a global "cabal" is truly involved in rituals of child sacrifice has its origins in the antisemitic trope of blood libel, which is the theory that Jews murder Christian children for ceremonial purposes. Furthermore, QAnon has an embedded hatred for George Soros, a name that has so much become associated with perceived Jewish meddling in global affairs.

Furthermore, QAnon's ongoing addiction with an international elite of loan providers additionally has deeply antisemitic touches.

CHAPTER TWO

The Origin of Qanon

On Saturday afternoon, on October 28, 2017, a message appeared on 4chan's exceptionally racist, xenophobic, and sexist forum. Sandwiched between racist discourse and a post making speculations about a non-existent Hilary Clinton sex tape, the post supplied a news flash: "HRC extradition currently in motion effective the previous day with various countries in case of cross border run." Over the following couple of days, the user collected cryptic forecasts referencing the Mueller probe, the Clintons, Soros, and Obama, and hinted at a large conspiracy theory within the U.S. government.

Lost in the din of 4chan, the posts were brought to the attention of #pizzagate adherent Tracy Diaz who eventually shared them with her audience.

After that, discussion boards devoted to Q turned up on Reddit, broadening the audience for the new conspiracy theory. Not only was Reddit considerably even more pleasant than the overwhelming boards on 4chan, it presently had a growing community of conspiracy theorists that were happy to take the QAnon sphere and keep it up. From there, the theory spread to a lot more mainstream platforms like Facebook, Twitter, and YouTube, where individuals, both fake and real, shared and intensified the theory.

As the theory became increasingly widespread, the Q logo became common view at Trump rallies where followers parsed every word and motion from the President, seeking pointers regarding the Plan or Q. Even Trump joined the move retweeting of notable QAnon slogans or followers.

Followers and Leadership

Nobody understands who is actually behind the QAnon conspiracy theory, although rumors are abundant. From the initial posts in late 2017, Q's identity has thwarted the groups of self-proclaimed Q researchers who fanatically read every detail of every post. Because of the anonymous nature of the message boards where Q posts, the real identity of the poster is almost impossible to determine.

QAnon followers proclaim Q is a person, or persons, within the leading tiers of government with accessibility to highly delicate information, that have chosen this time to expose the suspicious conspiracy outlined in The Plan. There is no evidence to suggest that the entity behind the posts is a government employee or has accessibility to secret information. Q's "details" are so confusing and obscure that the author can be anyone.

In various posts, Q urges their audience to put the pieces together themselves, or "paint the picture," making it possible for QAnon supporters to fill the many blanks with their very own musings and concerns. This establishes the effect that Q is presenting vital details while offering practically nothing.

Some Q researchers believe that Q is a young man in his twenties called Austin Steinbart, who is uploading from the future, using quantum computing. In the QAnon world, this appears as likely as anything else.

When it was exposed in early April that Steinbart had been imprisoned for extortion and probably suffered mental problems, the Q community considered it both definitive evidence that he was Q and straight-out proof that he wasn't.

CHAPTER THREE

History Of Illuminati

The Order of the Illuminati was an Enlightenment-age secret society established by Adam Weishaupt on 1 May 1776, a university professor, in Upper Bavaria, Germany. The movement include advocates of freethought, secularism, sex, liberalism, and also republicanism equal rights, hired from the German Masonic Lodges, that looked for to educate rationalism through enigma schools. In 1785, the order was penetrated, separated, and reduced by the government reps of Charles Theodore, Elector of Bavaria, in his preemptive campaign to neutralize the risk of secret societies before winding up being dens of conspiracies to topple the Bavarian monarchy and its state religious beliefs, Roman Catholicism. There is no evidence that the Bavarian Illuminati survived its reductions in 1785. In the late 18th century, reactionary conspiracy philosophers, such as Scottish physicist John Robison and also French Jesuit clergyman Augustin Barruel, started hypothesizing that the Illuminati had withstood their reductions and has come to be the masterminds behind the French Revolution and the Reign of Terror. Throughout the 19th century, fear of an Illuminati conspiracy was a real concern of the European gentility. Their oppressive reactions to this unproven fear provoked in 1848 the changes they sought to prevent.

1. Early evidence.

When we talk about the Bavarian Illuminati, we're speaking about the group that a man called Adam Weishaupt established in Bavaria, a southern state in Germany, back in 1776. Particularly he founded it on May 1st, 1776, called May Day or Walpurgis Night, a date celebrating an old conference of sorcerers and witches. May Day is likewise a major Communist vacation that celebrates the "workers of the world." Almost 200 years after Adam Weishaupt ceremoniously founded the Illuminati on this day, Anton LaVey ritualistically shaved his head. He founded the Church of Satan on May 1st, 1966, to commemorate this occult vacation.

The Bavarian Illuminati was essentially a reorganization and modernization of the corrupted ancient Mystery Schools. Weishaupt was a lawyer like so many corrupt politicians today, and in 1772 when he was twenty-four-years-old, he ended up being a law teacher at Ingolstadt University in Bavaria, Germany. A few years later, he ended up being the dean of the law department and began developing his strategy to release the Illuminati.

He got his inspiration for forming his secret society from both the Rosicrucian manifestos and from the Jesuits (the zealous elite Catholic Society of Jesus founded in 1540). The Rosicrucian manifestos were books that first appeared in 1614 in Germany, and explained an "unnoticeable brotherhood" committed to the pursuit of knowledge and Hermetic and alchemical magic. No such secret society existed. However, the Rosicrucian manifestos planted the seeds for such a thing in men's minds, which was the author's purpose (although not the despotic sort of organization that Adam Weishaupt developed).

Weishaupt used his position at the university to start hiring others and students to join him in his Test to topple the ruling monarchs of his day and install a global communist system with him and his inner circle of partners as the brand-new rulers. Originally he called his group the Perfectibilists, implying they intended to "perfect" man by facilitating his "development." Still, the name Perfectibilists was Quickly altered to the Illuminati to harmonize the "enlightenment" style of the era, given that Illuminati is Latin for "the enlightened ones." While he was growing increasingly effective at broadening his network and influence, it was only a matter of time before his secrets started to slowly leakage out.

It's indisputable that original copies of Adam Weishaupt's works were found and released for all to check out. This is completely confessed in traditional history books and encyclopedias, although few individuals care to put in the time and look. Today, well over one hundred original documents are kept at the State

Museum in Ingolstadt, Germany, where they are on a public display screen.

Originator, Adam Weishaupt, composed under the pseudonym "Spartacus," and all other members used pseudonyms too, although numerous were identified after their letters were found and some defectors came forward. In1784, eight years after the Illuminati were formed, a defector called Joseph Utzchneider provided many documents to Duchess Dowager Maria Anna, cautioning her of the organization and their goals of overthrowing the government and destroying religious beliefs. The Duchess, who was the sister-in-law of the Duke, handed them over to her brother-in-law Duke Karl Theodore, the leader of Bavaria.

A seemingly bizarre tale concerning the discovery of more initial writings includes a story about how an Illuminati member was struck by lightning and killed; when his body was taken a look at the coroner, some files were found to be packed in a concealed pocket sewn into his clothing. When he saw the composing on the wall that authorities were closing in on him, Adam Weishaupt ran away Bavaria in 1785 and headed to a neighboring province. He and his friend Jakob Lanz. When Lanz was riding on horseback on their way to Regensburg was struck by lightning and killed.

While this story is so bizarre, it's reasonable for people to dismiss it as a misconception; however, several historical sources report precisely what occurred. But regardless, a treasure chest of files was also found by other means as well.

On October 11th, 1786, authorities searched the home of Xavier von Zwack, situated in the city of Landshut (45 miles from Ingolstadt), where they found over two hundred letters including membership lists, signs, carvings used to fake various wax seals used by princes, nobles, clergymen, and merchants; instructions on counterfeiting, dedicating suicide, recipes for poison, an abortion tea, invisible ink, and directions for developing an explosive strongbox that would explode and damage anyone that opened it without consent. One paper listed a method for filling a room filled with a fatal gas if they desired to kill somebody without getting their hands filthy. The government published these documents in a report titled Some Original Works of the Order of the Illuminati (Einige Originalschriften Des Illuminaten Ordens in German)

In the year 1787, cops searched the castle of Baron de Bassus and found more documents which were then released as a Supplement of Further Original Works. The next year in 1788, Johann Faber published The Genuine Illuminati [Der ächte Illuminati], which exposed the routines for the Preparation, Novitiate Degree, Minerval Degree, the Minor and Major Illuminati Degrees.

In 1789 a French journalist named Jean-Pierre-Louis de Luchet published a book titled Essay on the Illuminists (Essai sur la

Secte des Illuminés), which denounced the Illuminati and said they managed Masonic lodges throughout Europe.

In 1794 Illuminati whistleblower Ludwig Adolf Christian von Grolmann published The Latest Work Of Spartacus and Philo (Weishaupt's and Baron von Knigge's code word) Die Neuesten Arbeiten Des Spartacus Und Philo, exposing the tricks of the Illuminati Dirigens degree (Scottish Knight degree) which selected men to run Masonic lodges so they could recruit new members from within Freemasonry.

In 1797 a French Jesuit priest called Abbe Barruel published a series of books on the French Revolution because he thought it was the outcome of the Illuminati, stating, "The third conspiracy.

Barruel considered, as others still do today, as to whether Weishaupt was the mastermind behind the conspiracy, or whether he was dealing with or for someone else. "It is not understood, and it would be challenging to find, whether Weishaupt ever had a master, or whether he is himself the excellent owner of those monstrous teachings on which he founded his school," he composed.

A man called John Robison, a science professor (called natural philosophy back then), living in Scotland, published a prolonged book about the Illuminati in 1798 titled Proofs of a Conspiracy, one of the first books composed English about the organization.

Before writing his book, he was asked to join them; however, after looking into the group, he realized he didn't want to have anything to do with them and, after that, chose to compose his book wishing to expose them. In Proofs of a Conspiracy, he also consisted of English translations of much of the confiscated Illuminati documents.

Robison composed that, "A collection of initial documents and correspondence was discovered by browsing your home of one Zwack (a member) in 1786. The list below year, a much larger collection, was discovered at your home of Baron Bassus. Since that time, Baron Knigge, the most active member next to Weishaupt, published an account of a few of the higher degrees, which had been formed by himself."

He alerted, "An association has been formed for the express function of rooting out all the religious facilities and reversing all the existing governments of Europe.

Zealously and systematically, until it has become almost alluring." He continued, "I have seen that this association still exists, still operates in a trick, which not just some appearances amongst ourselves show that its emissaries are venturing to propagate their detestable doctrines among us, but that the association has Lodges in Britain corresponding with the mom Lodge at Munich since 1784.

Original Five Members

- Adam Weishaupt (codename: Spartacus) Andreas Sutor (Erasmus Rotero-damus)
- Bauhof or Baubof (Agathon).
- Franz Anton von Massenhause (Ajax)
- Max Elder von Mer] (Tiberius).

Primary Goals.

The original leading five objectives of the Illuminati were:

1) Abolish the Monarchy and change all federal governments.

2) Abolish personal property and inheritance.

3) Abolish patriotism, along with individuals' national identity and national pride.

4) Abolish the family, marriage, morality, and then have the government raise and indoctrinate the children.

5) Abolish all religions.

These are the very same goals that would be detailed around seventy years later in the Communist Manifesto (1848) and make up the foundation of communism since Weishaupt no doubt inspired Karl Marx.

More contemporary objectives consist of a universal one-world digital currency; a Big Brother Orwellian monitoring state; the elimination of the 2nd Amendment and ending citizens' gun ownership (leaving just police and military to be equipped); executing an all-powerful nanny state socialist federal government; all leading up to the unveiling of a "messiah" who will claim to be God and offer individuals immortality here in the world, stating he has "brought back humanity" to our "pre-fallen" state so we can live forever through using cybernetic Transhuman innovation on the new "Heaven on earth" he has created.

Deposition for the Court.

In 1785, three previous members, Joseph Utzschneider, George Grunberger, and Johann Cosandey, composed a joint deposition for the court. They supplied info about a few of the Illuminati's goals and viewpoints that males in the first couple of degrees were taught. Of all, "The Illuminee who wants to rise to the highest degree needs to be complimentary from all religions; for a religionist (as they call every guy who has any faith) will never be confessed to the greatest degrees."

The 2nd concept exposed to the starts was that the ends validate the ways. "The welfare of the Order will be a validation for calumnies (defamatory, declarations), poisonings, assassinations, perjuries, treasons, disobediences put merely, for all that the bias of men lead them to call crimes.

One should be more submissive to the Superiors of the Illuminati than to the sovereigns or magistrates who govern individuals. When they do not direct them, the governors of countries are despots. They can have no authority over us, who are free men.

They called the Patent Exitus, or the "doctrine of suicide," was also taught as an honorable way anyone captured could leave prosecution and prevent themselves from exposing the Order's secrets.

The deposition exposed, "The Superiors of the Illuminati are to be looked upon as the most ideal and the most enlightened of men; to be amused even of their infallibility."

It remains in these political and moral principles that the Illuminati are educated in the lower degrees. It is according to how they imbibe them and show their commitment to the Order.

Their testament continues, the Illuminatispread out through practically every province under the cape of Freemasonry; because it sows division and discord between moms and dads and their children, in between Princes and their subjects, and amongst the most sincere buddies; because occasionally it would install partiality on the seats of justice, as it continually prefers the welfare of the Order to that of the state, and the interests of its adepts to those of the profane."

" Experience had persuaded us that they would quickly be successful in perverting all the Bavarian youth. The leading feature in the generality of its activities was irreligion, wickedness of morals, disobedience to their Prince and their moms and dads, and overlooking all useful research studies. After retiring from the Order, the Illuminati calumniated us on all sides in the most notorious manner. Their cabal made us fail in every request we provided, prospering in rendering us despiteful and repellent to our superiors, they even carried their calumnies [defamatory statements] Far as to pretend that one of us had committed murder.

Four Pillars of the Illuminist Agenda.

The "Four Pillars of the Illuminist Agenda are:.

1. Prompt and oversee a devastating "clash of civilizations," pitting religious beliefs, ethnic groups, country, and states against one another;

2. End American sovereignty and combine the U.S.A. into local and global systems of governance;

3. Change the United States into a Third World culture, crushing America's middle class, collapsing its economy, and making its

desperate citizens voluntarily subservient to illuminist management and solutions;

4. Develop a dictatorial, Masonic inspired Zionist Global Empire.

CHAPTER FOUR

'The Cult that Hijacked the World

The greatest risk to this nation hinges on their big ownership and impact in our pictures, our press, our radio, and our government.

Preciselysixty years later, the Illuminati Zionist Mossad is a prime suspect in the "false flag" assault on the World Trade Centre created to promote more war.

Zionists were also behind America's entrance into 'World War One. They made a trade-off. America will go into the war as Britain takes Palestine from Turkey. History repeats itself since it follows a ready script. Rothschild banking organization did not reveal its purpose to topple Western civilization; it went ahead and did it. The Rothschilds assert to stand for the Jewish individuals, but there has never been a vote.

For over 200 years, they have used Jewish teams and Freemasons to provoke battle to progress their world government tyranny.

The war must be conducted in such a way that Islam (the Moslem Arabic World) and political Zionism (the State of Israel) mutually damage each other" by combating to the point of full physical, ethical, affordable, and also spiritual.

The stage is being embedded in the Persian Gulf, Eastern Europe, and the Caucuses for anuclear conflagration pitting Russia, China, and Iran against the U.S., the EU, and Israel. The Rothschilds regulate both sides. On a cosmic degree, the story is to pirate humankind and divert it to the service of Satan and his adherents.

Today, even after the debacle in Iraq, Zionists lobby for a strike on Iran. Zionism is controlled by "the Order of the Illuminati," representing a team of dynastic family members, generational Satanists, related to the Rothschilds and European aristocracy, united by Freemasonry, marriage, and money. This cult sterns from the Satanic Jewish Sabbatean-Frankist movement described later on in this quantity. While it frequently displays derision for non-Jews, this cult intermarries strategically with other generational Satanists. It takes over riches, power, culture, and functions to prevent moral and scientific growth. It is re-engineering humanity to be serfs ina Neo-Feudal World Order.

Our human experience is mostly the product of a spell they cast by "education and learning" and mass media. Our social and political mindsets are given to us.

" Mary Anne," a previous prominent member of the Illuminati, stated she was told the cult goes back to ancient Babylon and the Tower of Babel (which appears like today EU parliament.) When God foiled the Cabalists' plans for a tower reaching to paradise, they prompted their centuries-long vendetta against and promised to hijack His Creation.

The Cabalists were relatively few, so they decided to dominate using Gold, i.e., economic domination.

In1773, Amschel Mayer Rothschild, an orthodox Jew that never transformed his clothes, assembled a meeting of 12 famous Jewish lenders. They improved their program by baiting the hook with the spurious pledge of liberty, fraternity, and equal rights: The 1848 Communist Manifesto, which demands the theft of personal residential or commercial property and the destruction of freedom and household for" equal rights," shows their Satanic schedule.

In1776, they assigned Adam Weishaupt to rearrange the Illuminaticombined with Freemasonry in 1782. According to Andre Krylienko, Freemasonrywas used "to employ non-Jews knowingly or unknowingly in the service of Jewry."

The Cabalistic bankers were behind the innovative activities of the 17th- 20thCenturies in addition to each respective reign of horror. Throughout history, they have pursued bad grudge against humankind. They finagled a monopoly on credit history(laying hold of the federal government's right to produce money) and have used it to overcome the world. Considering that they produce cash out of nothing, they think they are God. This harmonizes with Messianic Jewish, and Cabalistic prophesies. Basically, for cooperation in their wicked strategy, they let fellow Jews and non-Jewish Freemasons on their rewarding racket.

Ina well-known statement, Georgetown University professor Carol Quigley, an insider who was Bill Clinton's coach, claimed the central bank plan is "absolutely nothing much less than to develop a world system, to be able to dominate the political system of each nation."

Hope and Tragedy

The Illuminati manage the Establishment in Europe, America, and also a lot of the globe. Its secret war against humankind is created to make us acquiesce in their tyranny; by possessing the leaders on both sides and the media, they begin all major battles and determine their outcome. They are accountable for revolutions anxieties and the battle on terror. Jewish groups are one of their tools.

1920, Oscar Levy, a Jewish philosopher, stated, "there is rarely a modern-day event in Europe that can not be mapped back to the Jews. Jewish elements provide the driving pressures for communism and industrialism, for the product and the spiritual wreck of this globe' in Levy condemns the "intense optimism of the Jew" for the revolutionary mayhem. These innovative Jews do not understand what they are doing, but they are more unconscious sinners than voluntary wicked doers.

"Anti-Semitism"

I think everyone has a straight connection with the Creator, no matter their religion or lack thereof. We all have a spur of the Divine within. I judge each individual by his feedback to his Divine calling, not by his religious beliefs, ethnic background, or race.

The majority of Jews are uninformed of the Illuminati agenda. They are manipulated and endangered, like everyone else. All Americans are linked to battle crimes in Iraq by their taxes. The average American had no say in the inception or implementation of this battle. Organized Jewry doesn't represent me anymore than the U.Sgoverrunent stands for Americans. Both have been pirated by the Illuminati banksters. The Illuminati hides behind the skirts of average Jews. The cult that hijacked the globe is the tiny nucleus of Cabalistic bankers and Masons based in London and directed by the House of Rothschild.

They control with their refined control of large firms (cartels – precisely money, oil, security, pharmaceuticals, media), government, mass media, secret societies, knowledge companies, the military, legislation, churches, foundations, NGO's and education.

Chatham House in London (The Royal Institute of InternalMatters) and Pratt House in New York (Council on Foreign Relations) are two main control mechanisms. Illuminati power is omnipresent, yet the masses do not also know it exists.

Lately, Doreen Dotan, a Jewish female from an Illuminati history, uploaded a talk on YouTube claiming she is tired of blaming the Rothschilds and Warburg. Unlike this brave female, ordinary Jews have been obsequious.

Professor Albert Lindemann composed that Jews do not intend to comprehend their past.

Absolutely nothing happens without the true blessing of money; most people "go along to get along" unaware of the big image. They instinctively accept ideological backgrounds and teams that advance their product interests.

The Communist term, "useful idiots:'

The knee jerk charge of "anti-Semitism" is generally a ploy to keep individuals oblivious of the Illuminati conspiracy theory. Nobody is supporting or pardoning genocide. The charge is used to suppress opposition. The concern is actually regarding a monopoly of debt, power, riches, as well as society. The bankers are worried only about their preeminence and that of their SabbateanFrankist-Illuminati cult. This isn't regarding the ordinary Jewif the Jewish leaders can not acknowledge any type of authenticity to anti-Semitism because they have no intention of changing course. Hence they act it is encouraged by "bias:'.

Organized Jewry (Neocons, Zionists, B'nai Brith) has the self-consciousness of a snake devouring a mouse. It pertains to the death spasms of the mouse as "disgust:' Increasingly, we are instructed to accept the snake's perspective, even we are the mouse.

We have already contrived to possess ourselves of the minds of the goy communities, they all come near looking through the spectacles we are establishing astride their noses.

Talmud And Cabala.

Judaism has been hijacked. Initially, Judaism was based on Moses' vision of God as a universal ethical force. This is the only Judaism I understand. I have constantly intuited that life is neither meaningless nor arbitrary but regulated by intrinsic ethics and spiritual regulations. This led to creating "Scruples," the game of day-to-day moral dilemma, in 1984.

Judaism today is based upon the Talmud, which is composed of the analyses of "sages"(Pharisees) throughout the Babylonian exile 586 BC to 1040. Generally talking, the Talmud negates the spirit of Moses and also takes precedence over the Old Testament.

Jesusreviled the Pharisees as hypocrites, phonies, and also a "generation of vipers." He said they nullified God's Commandments "training for teachings the rules of men:' (Mark 7:6 -8). He implicated them of worshipping the devil: "Ye are of your father the evil one, and the desires of your father ye will certainly do." (John 8:44).

Elizabeth Dilling (1894-1966), a bold Christian whose see to Soviet Russian 1931 inspired a 20-year study, revealed Judaism's a lot of very closely secured secret, its supremacism, and also disgust for non-Jews, especially Christians.

The adversary runs by deceiving and damaging good individuals. According to Dilling, the Talmud is started on the presumption of Jewish supremacy.

The non-Jew ranks as an animal, has no legal property rights, and also no lawful civil liberties under any code whatever. 'Milk the gentile' is the Talmudic rule, yet don't get captured in such a way regarding jeopardize Jewish passions.

Summarized, Talmudism is the quintessence of distilled hatred and discrimination, without reason, against non-Jews. The

Talmud is defined by "obscenity and also more obscenity, an establishing up of laws seemingly to design circumvention, and evasions; indulge in sadistic ruthlessness; turnaround of all Biblical ethical teachings on theft, murder, sodomy, perjury, treatment of parents and kids.

The Talmud most certainly adds to anti-Semitism. Dilling writes: "The mindset resulting from such teachings has been frowned at by non-Jews in nations and also centuries. Such hatred, nonetheless, is continuously depicted by Jews as 'persecution of the jews:"

What fault could the Pharisees place with a gospel that preaches human brotherhood and putting others before yourself? Response: It rejects their unique insurance claim. They'recontending with Christ to be God themselves. Hence the Talmudic disgust Christ.

Dilling writes: "The Jewish Cabala with its non-existence of wickedness, its deification of man, is a resource book of modern-day 'isms:"

The Cabala depicts the accomplishment of global consistency in terms of facilitating sex-related union of male and female deities. It teaches that "arousal below provokes arousal above." It provides the basis for the Illuminati sex cult mirrored in the Illuminati symbol, the dot in a circle, signifying the penis and vaginal canal. It is seen in the propensity for homosexuality and pedophilia among beginners.

Whether a sorcerer is White Magic or Black Magick, their keystone of belief and thought is the Cabala. He will be basing his technique when Antichrist develops the occult on the Jewish Cabala. Hence, the paradox is that when Antichrist strides out of the newly-built Jewish Temple after devoting the "Abomination of desolation" and begins his initiative to massacre every Jew in the world. The Jewish Cabalawill has offered the primary inspiration for his efforts! The Cabala developed the foundation of Adolf Hitler's occult beliefs, so this dreadful paradox will undoubtedly strike the Jewish people two times in global history."

CHAPTER FIVE

Why are the Jews Always Blamed?

One can't talk about the Illuminati at any length without coming across anti-Semitism. For a minority of those who are obviously against the New World Order or Illuminati, the Jews are at the heart of every problem and the peaks of power. The "Jewish bankers" and the "Jews in Hollywood" control all of it, they say. Some still believe that The Elders of Zion are genuine Jewish documents that show the Zionists' sinister strategies, and the fact that the Illuminati is managed by Jews at the top.

The Protocols are a class of important documents written from a Jewish point of view that layout the required steps for world supremacy. They explain the need to manage or control the banking system, the media, and political institutions to achieve these goals. They are the Illuminati plan or strategy for control written from the Jews' perspectives.

When the documents were "discovered," in 1905, word went out that they were created by a governing body of the Jews, and the Protocols have been used since then to promote hate against the Jewish people. Hitler had the belief that the Protocols were authentic or genuine, and today, some still believe that is the case.

One source of anti-Semitism is derived from the idea that some Jews think they are God's picked people and God's favorite race of humanity. Many people see the Jews who hold these views as racist and Jewish supremacists. Many Jews believe that God offered them the land of Israel right in the Middle East, and that the Palestinians than have no rightful claim to it continues to cause conflict today as the two cultures kill and argue over whose land it truly is.

Some see the main theme of Judaism as being secretive, and an inner circle of Jews privately controlling the religion and international banking. Certainly, the Jewish Pharisees (the spiritual teachers in the past) kept the spiritual teachings about Judaism to themselves. They actively kept the masses ignorant and uninformed about God's nature and the Torah (the Old Testament). Jesus denounced this control, and the primary focus of his entire teaching was that individuals didn't require the Pharisees to have a connection with God and that they could have direct or straight access to God themselves. It didn't require a "middle man."

Some point to the Talmud and Cabala as a continuation of the monopolization of spiritual information on the part of the Jews and see parts of the Talmud as Jewish supremacist in their teachings and provide justification for some Jews to think that their race is the one divinely ordained by God to rule the world.

An unorthodox analysis of the Book of Genesis and the Fall of Man also fuels anti-Semitism. Followers of the serpent seed theory believe that Satan or the devil had sex with Eve right in the garden of Eden and caused Eve to conceive with Cain, making him half-human, half Devil. Later, as the said theory claims, Adam and Eve eventually conceived a child of their own, being Abel. The theory continues that Cain is the head of the Jewish people, and hence they are all descendants of Satan.

Some white supremacists believe that white individuals, or Aryans, are God's selected race, and that the Jews are wrongly declaring they are the selected ones. This holds with the Christian Identity movement, who are racist Christians who see themselves as the real heirs to God's true blessings and see the Jews as fakes and the enemies.

In the Book of Revelation chapter 2, verse 9, the Bible states, "I know your afflictions as well as your poverty-- though you are rich! I know all the slander of those who claim they are Jews and are not, but are instead, a synagogue of Satan."

Later on, in chapter 3, verse 9, Jesus states, "I will surely make those who are from the synagogue of Satan, who claim to be Jews while they are not, but are just phonies-- I will cause them to come and fall at your feet and acknowledge the fact that I have loved you."

These are two compelling passages that those who frequently target the Jews as being the root of the world's problems will use as evidence that even Jesus saw that fake Jews were attempting to deceive the people regarding their real beliefs and motives.

Christian Identity's beliefs are similar to British Israelism, which teaches that Europeans (whites) are the literal descendants of the Israelites through the ten groups or tribespeople that were taken into slavery by Assyria armies.

These beliefs emphasize that Jesus was an Israelite from the people of Judah, and that white European Israelites are still the chosen people of God. They believe that those which many people call modern-day Jews are not descendants from the Israelites nor Hebrews but are instead, Khazars who descended from people with Turco-Mongolian blood.

Adolf Hitler most likely subscribed to these theories, and they were eventually used to validate the actions of the Holocaust. A few of Aryan Nation organizations and other white supremacist groups incorporate similar beliefs and are used to support their actions and ideologies.

Some Christians seemingly subscribe for what is referred to as replacement theology, which teaches that people who diligently follow all the teachings of Jesus and end up being Christians are God's chosen. The church or body of Christ replaced the Jews as the chosen people. This is certainly not mainstream Christianity, which teaches that the Israelites are God's chosen ones. Followers of replacement theology aren't necessarily racists or white supremacists and should not be confused with Christian Identity followers.

While the Jews continue to be at the center of controversy and blame regarding their alleged control of the Illuminati, it ought to be stressed that members of all races are discovered within the hierarchy of power. While it is easy to explain wealthy Jews, or influential Jews in Hollywood and the media, it is more efficient to point out the corrupt nature of somebody's soul, instead of their racial heritage. While there are Jews who arrogantly place themselves and their value above all others just because of their racial identity, there are many more who see themselves as many individuals do, that of members of the humanity and equivalent to all others despite race or faith.

Is the New World Order "Jewish"?

Let us start by explaining what the "New World Order" means;

The central point of the New World Order is the interest of the world's prominent central bankers to convert their huge financial power right into long-term worldwide organizations of social and political control.

Their power is based upon their apparent monopoly over credit. They make use of the government's credit score to print money and also call for the taxpayer to shell out billions in interest to them.

Central banks such as the Federal Reserve pretend to be institutions of government. They are not. They are independently owned by probably 300 families. The bulk of these households must be Jewish or part Jewish.

Central banks also regulate or manage the supply of credit to individuals and businesses.

Are "the jews" responsible?

The New World Order can be seen as a hydra-headed monster. The bankers effectively work through several fronts such as Socialism, Liberalism, Communism, Feminism, Neoconservatism, Freemasonry, and Zionism. Unknown to many participants, these "modern" movements are all privately devoted to "globe change," a euphemism for banker hegemony and Satanism.

The bankers manage or control the major corporations of the world, intelligence agencies, media, foundations, think tanks, and universities. They are in charge of suppressing the truth. Jews figure conspicuously in all of this, a cause of anti-Semitism. Indeed, many other people are seeking "success" as well.

The bankers also operate through countries. They are largely liable for American and British expansionism, whose purpose is to take over the world's wealth.

The British social critic, Hilaire Bellocwsz, in his book "The Jews" (1922), writes that the British Empire stood for a partnership or union between the British aristocracy and Jewish financing.

"After Waterloo [1815], London then became the money market as well as the world's clearinghouse. The rate of the Jew's interests as a monetary dealership and the interests of this wonderful commercial polity estimated increasingly more. One may claim that by the last third of the 19th century, they had become virtually identical:'.

The confluence of British and Jewish interests also extended to a marital relationship.

After two generations of this, with the opening of the twentieth century, those of the great territorial English households or families in which there was no Jewish blood was the exception.

" In many of them was the pressure essentially significant, in a few of them so strong that though the name was still an English name and the customs those of a complete English lineage of the long past, the character and the physique had become entirely Jewish ... ".

The British and Jewish objective of world domination was similar and made use of Freemasonry as a tool. Specifically, Jewish institutions, such as Freemasonry, were particularly strong in Britain, and there emerged an active political culture, and inevitably to verify of incredible significance, wherein the British nation was accepted by foreign governments as the main guard of the Jews in other nations.

It was Britain which was anticipated to step in anywhere Jewish persecution took place and to support the Jewish economic powers throughout the world, and to get in return the benefit of that connection:'

The New World Order is an extension of the British Empire, in which exclusive British, American as well as Jewish imperial interests are tantamount.

CHAPTER SIX

InductingNewMembers

Various places were used for hiring brand-new members. Once somebody revealed interest to an existing member about his desire to topple the king, that person was "thoroughly observed in silence." If, after factor to consider by the council, "the Novice" as they were called, were believed to be a possible possession, he would be given a coach and welcomed to a conference.

One correspondence between members reads, "I will therefore push the cultivation of science, especially such sciences that might have an impact on our reception in the world, and might serve to remove barriers out of the way. Only those who are surely valid will be selected from amongst the inferior classes for the higher mysteries. And in particular, every individual shall be made a spy on another and all around him."

After given preliminary approval by the council, the Novice would be revealed "specific portions" of the goals and rules of the Order and was advised to provide a weekly account in writing of his development as he brings out his regulations. At this moment, he was not enabled to take physical ownership of any material and needed to read it in the Mentor's house just to make sure they would not turn it over to authorities, providing concrete evidence of the conspiracy.

High-level member like Baron Von Knigge confesses, "As a rule, under the veil of secrecy, harmful teachings and dangerous strategies can be accepted as well as noble objectives and profound knowledge; since not all members themselves are notified of such depraved intents, which in some cases tend to lie hidden below the beautiful facade, and it is unworthy of an intelligent man to work according to a plan, which he does not see.

Another original correspondence boasts, "Nothing can leave our sight; by these ways, we will readily find who are pleased, and get with relish the strange state-doctrines and spiritual viewpoints that are laid before them; and, at last, the trustworthy alone will be confessed to a participation of the fundamental maxims and political constitution of the Order. In a council made up of such members, we will labor at the development of means to drive by degrees the opponents of reason and humankind out of the world, and to establish a peculiar morality and religious beliefs fitted for the great society of humanity.

In perhaps the most ominous initiation to the greater levels, a prospect was informed they needed to show their commitment to the Illuminati by killing someone who betrayed the Order. The prospect was taken before a man bound and gagged who was stated to have betrayed their oaths and then handed a knife and blindfolded before being positioned in front of the supposed traitor who they were then ordered to stab. Once the prospect stabbed the "person" in front of them, the blindfold was removed to expose that the "traitor" had been switched with a sheep, and the entire charade was a test of their commitment.

If the candidate refused to perform the "murder" of the supposed "traitor," then they were told they passed the test anyway; however, he will never be permitted to continue to a higher level and never relied on with any much deeper secrets because they had revealed they would not kill for the Order.

Contingency Plans if Discovered.

A great deal of individuals declare that because some Illuminati members were discovered and a lot of their works released, that they just offered up and disappeared from that point on; however, the Duke of Bavaria's 4th Edict and the Illuminati's writings recommend otherwise. Weishaupt wrote, "By this strategy, we shall direct all humanity. In this way, and the most basic ways, we will set all in motion and flames. The professions must be so allotted and contrived that we may, in secret, affect all political transactions.

There must not be a single function that ever comes in unclear sight, which may betray our objectives against faith and the

State. One should speak sometimes one way and in some cases another, but so as never to contradict ourselves, and so that, concerning our real way of thinking, we may be impenetrable.

This can be done in no other way, however, by secret associations, which will by degrees, and in silence, possess themselves of the government of the States, and use those ways for this purpose.

Quickly after the Illuminati were found, and thought by lots of to have been damaged, Joseph Willard, President of Harvard University, alerted, "There suffices proof that several societies of the Illuminati have been established in this land of Gospel light and civil liberty, which were very first organized from the grand society, in France. They are doubtless secretly making every effort to undermine all our ancient institutions, spiritual and civil. These societies are carefully leagued with those of the same Order in Europe; they have the same object in view. The enemies of all order are seeking our mess up. Needs to extramarital relations generally dominate, our self-reliance would fall naturally. Our republican government would be obliterated."

Willard was just among many Americans, consisting of George Washington, who thought the Illuminati survived the desired purge and continued to work under cover of Freemasonry and other organizations.

CHAPTER SEVEN

How The New World Is Controlled

Using Feminism to Breakdown Families

Because among the Illuminati's original goals was to separate the standard family so children would be raised and indoctrinated by the government, they prepared on manipulating women through what would later be referred to as feminism, encouraging them to rebel against their duties of domestic management and motherhood.

There is no other way of influencing men so powerfully as by methods of the women, it will be an immense relief to their enslaved minds to be devoid of anyone bond of restraint, and it will fire them the more and cause them to work for us with zeal, without understanding that they do so; for they will just be indulging their desire of personal adoration.

What this implies is they prepared on changing women into self-centered, narcissistic, pleasure looking for sluts, and promote this habits under the banner of "freedom," so instead of raising their children and keeping their families in balance, they would have the government raise their kids while turning against their husbands and interrupt the family unit in hopes of redirecting people's commitment and love to the State instead of each other.

In most modern-day times, this same method has been applied to promote the feminist motion in the 1970s through the production of Ms. Magazine and the push to demonize stay-at-home moms. Kim and other skilless skanks are promoted as a good example. However, they have no genuine value and are talentless and useless idols promoted by the mainstream media as modern-day royalty. The hypocrisy of feminism is remarkable. For instance, feminists who sob about sexism and the "culturally programmed gender roles" only wish to quit the functions society expects of them, while still requiring guys to continue following theirs.

Women who whimper about "mutual rights" still expect men always to buy them pricey gifts. Females who do not feel they must know how to cook still feel guys ought to fix things around the home and detect their problems. And obviously, feminists who announce they want to end the gender functions still anticipate their male to cough up thousands of dollars on a diamond engagement ring when the courtship is on the road to marriage. Feminism is a one-way hypocritical double standard street that not just targets males, but likewise, other ladies who resist succumbing to this cultural Marxism.

Mothers who choose to be stay-at-home mamas and raise their children or who delight in cooking for their household are labeled "victims" of a "male-dominated ideology." Feminism pressures females to put their kids over to daycare centers and trade-in working around the home for being stuck in a cubicle being in front of a computer system all day. Feminism has caused an entire generation to be raised in single-parent houses with lots of mothers turning to government assistance, costing the taxpayers countless dollars and not to discuss tens of millions of children maturing without the assistance and supervision of both parents.

Adam Weishaupt himself was an unfaithful partner who impregnated his partner's sis, which he exposed in among his correspondences. In hopes of killing the child to conceal the adulterous habits, he gave his sister-in-law an "abortion tea," It appears from his letter about the issue that he likewise consistently punched his mistress in the stomach hoping to abort the kid.

" I am now in the most awkward scenario; it robs me of all rest, and makes me unfit for everything. I am at risk of losing at the same time my honor and my credibility, by which I have long built." he composed.

Using Schools to Indoctrinate the Youth.

Autocrats throughout history have understood that if they efficiently preserve their power, they must indoctrinate the youth with their brand of propaganda to guarantee as the children come of age, they will blindly support the leader and his ideologies. Adolf Hitler used the Nazi Youth program to brainwash kids starting at a young age; the Taliban in Afghanistan prohibited ladies from going to school at all to keep them oblivious; and North Korea's strict control of their education system are just a few examples of this in our contemporary age.

" We must win the typical individuals in every corner," the original Illuminati writings readout. "This will be acquired chiefly utilizing the schools, and by open, hearty behavior, program, condescension, popularity, and toleration of their prejudice, which we will root out and eliminate during the leisure time.".

The brainwashing of students by the public school system is clear today with programs like Common Core and the promotion of the Big Government baby-sitter state and the gay lifestyle while demonizing the Second Amendment right to bear arms and belief in God. Being a Christian in public schools is not only frowned upon, but outright mocked, and positively discussing the word "God" or "Jesus" has essentially been prohibited.

Charlotte Iserbyt, who was the head of policy at the Department of Education during the Reagan administration, found how tax-exempt structures were shaping the American education system to remove critical thinking and innovation by turning trainees into zombies who only regurgitate what they're told. She published her findings in her book "The Deliberate Dumbing Down of America." Iserbyt and others assert that Skull& Bones runs the Department of Education, which determines what is taught to the kids. Skull & Bones also manages the American Historical Association, which determines the "main" variation of American history by thoroughly crafting a typically one-sided and prejudiced view of what occurred.

While the vast majority of students who participate in public schools are mainly worried about the newest teen idol, their favorite professional sports groups, or merely getting high and drunk, children of the elite are taught team building, networking skills, and other tools to prepare them to quickly advance up the social hierarchy once they enter the "real life.".

The Illuminati has mostly funded this school and utilized it to educate their kids and prepare them for their duties later on in life. In.

1930 Edward Harkness (a member of Skull & Bones' sister organization Wolf's Head) donated 5.8 million dollars to the school under the condition that their approach of teaching students would change to what he called the Aristotelian technique of antiquity. Harkness was the 2nd biggest investor in Rockefeller's Standard Oil in the early 1900s and remained in John D. Rockefeller's inner circle.

The Rockefeller family has been one of the most effective Illuminati families for generations, and the "Aristotelean technique of antiquity" that Edward Harkness paid to carry out at Philips Exeter Academy was based on the ideology of the Greek thinker Aristotle (a trainee of Plato) who believed that the majority of people were too dumb to govern themselves and that society needs to be structured in such a way that "theorist kings" should rule and decide what was best for individuals.

Controlling the Media

Weishaupt knew the power of info, and back in his time, there was no tv, radios, or Internet. Still, there were books, libraries, and reading clubs, and he understood how essential it was to control them if he wanted to manage what information reached the minds of the public. In one correspondence, he composed, "By developing reading societies, and subscription libraries, and taking these under our instructions, and supplying them through our labors, we might turn the public mind to the way we want." He goes on to write, "In like manner we need to attempt to obtain an influence in the military colleges, the printing-houses, booksellers stores, chapters, and simply put in all offices which have any impact, either in forming, or in handling, or in directing the mind of man."

Another letter written by a different member recognized as Cato [real name Xaver von Zwack] explains, "We get all the literary journals. We take care, by well-timed pieces to make the citizens and the Princes a bit more discovered for certain little slips."What this suggests is they planned to use the newspapers to assault their enemies. "A little bit more discovered for particular little slips" indicates to highlight and enhance anything officials have said or done that can be used against them.

Those who directed these societies had control of the material being read out and talked about. It ended up being an ideal vehicle to instill extreme or subversive views.

Today, much of the American mainstream media and other outlets in countries worldwide are under the control of the government. In some nations, the State-controlled tv is apparent; however, in places like America, such control is done more discreetly, leading several people to believe that it is an "independent and complimentary" press.

In 1975 a congressional investigation discovered the CIA had every editor from the major news outlets in their pocket. The Church Hearings, as they were called, revealed the government was investing a billion dollars a year (in 2014 dollars) to covertly pay editors and press reporters to work as gatekeepers and propagandists for the establishment. The program was dubbed Operation Mockingbird.

President Obama designated a Harvard Law professor called Cass Sunstein to a cabinet-level position to establish numerous fake social networks accounts and "troll" the comments section of news, YouTube videos, and Facebook pages in attempts to reject newspaper article the White House thought were damaging to the establishment. One of Edward Snowden's leakages revealed that the NSA took things even further by having paid trolls bother and defame individuals online, who the facility idea was causing too much difficulty for the government's.

The NSA likewise established innovation to spoof e-mails, SMS messages, inflate or deflate the view depend on YouTube videos, adjust the ranking of sites, manipulate the outcome of online polls, or merely shut down somebody's social networks presence entirely for counterfeit "regards to service" offenses.

For decades both the Pentagon and the CIA have had whole departments devoted to working with Hollywood to assist produce major tv shows and movies literally.

Infiltration of Freemasonry

Illuminati frontman Adam Weishaupt loved the idea of using existing secret societies to assist growing organization, saying, "Nothing can bring this about but hidden societies. Hidden schools of wisdom are how free men from their bonds. Among the main vehicles used to conceal and further their program wasFreemasonry. Already an established occult organization in his time, Weishaupt had goals of using the fraternity for his means. In July 1782, he infiltrated Freemasonry and presented what he called Illuminated Freemasonry. Using the existing structure of Freemasonry, he created factions that were dedicated to his cause, and with their brutality and fascination, his fans Quickly took control of the highest levels within lodges across Europe.

I declare, and I challenge all humanity to oppose my statement, that no guy can give any account of the order of Freemasonry, of its origin, of its history, of its things, nor any description of its signs and mysteries, which does not leave the mind in overall unpredictability on all these points.

Understanding the power of declaring to have possession of a great secret, he knew how men might be manipulated into doing his bidding, intending to have the terrific secret sooner or later revealed to them. "Of all the means I know to lead guys, the most effective is a concealed mystery. The craving of the mind is alluring, and if once a man has taken it into his head that there is a secret in a thing, it is difficult to get it out, either by argument or experience. And after that, we can so change concepts by simply altering a word." 81.

Among the most popular books on the definitions of Freemasonry's symbols also confirms that Weishaupt successfully penetrated the fraternity and presented his plot to the inner circle. The Lexicon of Freemasonry was first published in 1845 by Albert G. Mackey, a 33rd degree Freemason, who was one of the most popular scholars on the topic of Freemasonry in his day. The book includes an alphabetized list of the majority of Masonic symbols accompanied by a comprehensive description of their esoteric significance.

In the entry on the Illuminati, Mackey admits, "Weishaupt was a radical in politics, and an infidel in faith; and he organized this association, not more for functions of aggrandizing himself than overturning Christianity and the institutions of society. Many Freemasons, misled by the building and construction of his first degrees, were lured into the order.

Barcoding The Population

Devoted Mikkelson, writing at Snopes, states: "THE EAN-13 barcode system is used in 85 countries, making it the most popular item scanning system of its kind worldwide. It works by representing numbers as a series of seven vertical lines. Each of the seven lines is either black or white, and the sequence of lines forms a pattern that is acknowledged as a specific digit when scanned by a computer.

The American Civil Liberties Union says of this inflammatory affair: "To have a record of everywhere you go and whatever you do would be a frightening thing. As soon as we let the government and companies go down the road of nosing around in our lives, we're going to lose all our privacy rapidly." Do we all have to get barcodes tattooed on our flesh one day like products in a supermarket?

The Inquirer echoes these issues: "The idea of implanting a microchip into a person, whose individuality information and delicate personal information are on the chip (which could also pinpoint the specific realtime area of the wearer) is developing a lot of debate.

There is concern amongst different sectors of society that this 'human barcoding' would curtail individual civil liberties and break the person's constitutional flexibility and right to personal privacy, confidentiality, safety, and security. There is also the fear that this innovation could be used by unethical individuals or bad guys, by contending corporations, or even by some agencies in the government, for unlawful details event or surveillance, or some immoral goals.

CHAPTER EIGHT

New world order

With the cold war at an end, there was a need for a new world order. These came in several varieties. The earliest was published by the non-governmental South Commission, chaired by Julius Nyerere, including leading Third World economic experts, government coordinators, and other people. In a 1990 study, the Commission reviewed the current record of North-South relations culminating in the catastrophe of capitalism that swept through traditional colonial domains in the 1980s. Apart from the Japanese sphere in East Asia, where states are effective adequate to manage not just labor, as is the norm, but also a capital.

The South Commission observes some gestures toward Third World issues in the 1970s, "unquestionably spurred" by concern over "the freshly discovered assertiveness of the South after the increase in oil costs in 1973." As this problem abated and terms of trade.

The core industrial powers lost interest and turned to "a brand-new type of neo-colonialism," monopolizing control over the world economy, undermining more democratic elements of the United Nations, and in necessary proceeding to institutionalize "the South's second-class status" the natural course of occasions, given the relations of power and the cynicism with which it is exercised.

Examining the unpleasant state of the conventional Western domains, the Commission required a "new world order" that will react to "the South's plea for justice, equity, and democracy in the international society," though its analysis provides little basis for hope.

The prospects for this call are revealed by the attention accorded to it, or to the report usually, which likewise passed silently into oblivion. The West is assisted by a different vision outlined forthrightly by Winston Churchill as an earlier New World Order was being constructed after World War II.

The government of the world should be delegated to satisfied nations, who wanted absolutely nothing more on their own than what they had. There would always be a risk if the world-government were in the hands of hungry nations. None of us had any factor in seeking for anything more. The peace would be kept by peoples who lived in their way and were not enthusiastic. Our power positioned us above the rest. We were like rich men dwelling at peace within their habitations.

To rule is the right and duty of the rich men dwelling in deserved peace. It is just essential to add two footnotes. Initially, the rich men are far from lacking ambition; there are constantly brand-new ways to improve oneself and control others. The financial system practically requires that they are pursued, or the laggard falls out of the game. Second, the fantasy that nations are the stars in the global arena is the basic doctrinal camouflage because within the rich countries, as within the hungry ones, there are radical differences in privilege and power. Removing the remaining veil of misconception from Churchill's prescription, we derive the guidelines of world order: the rich men of the abundant societies are to rule the world, competing among themselves for a greater share of wealth and power and mercilessly reducing those who stand in their way.

These are truisms.

As explained over two hundred years earlier by Adam Smith, the often-misrepresented hero of Western self-congratulation, the rich men follow "the vile maxim of the masters of humanity" "All for ourselves, and absolutely nothing for other people." They naturally use state power to achieve their ends; in his day, the "makers and merchants" were "the primary designers" of policy, which they created to guarantee their interests would be "most peculiarly took care of," nevertheless "severe" impact on others, including the general population of their societies. If we do not embrace Smith's method of "class analysis," our vision will be blurred and distorted. Any conversation of world affairs that treats nations as actors are at best misleading, at worst pure mystification, unless it acknowledges the important Smithian footnotes.

As in any intricate system, there are even more nuances and secondary effects; however, in reality, these are the basic styles of world order. There is no little merit in the description of world order, brand-new and old, as "codified international piracy."

America's loyal subsidiary in keeping the starving countries under control is less burdened by the need for prettifying the message than Washington and its domestic chorus. Britain can appeal to a royal tradition of refreshing honesty, unlike the United States, which has chosen to do the attire of saintliness as it proceeds to squash anyone in its course. This position is called "Wilsonian idealism" in honor of among the fantastic exponents of violent military intervention and imperial repression, whose ambassador to London complained that the British had little use for his mission to remedy "the moral imperfections of foreign nations."

Britain has constantly "demanded booking the right to bomb niggers," as the distinguished statesman Lloyd George put the matter after Britain had ensured that the 1932 disarmament treaty would put no barrier on the aerial bombardment of civilians, unwilling to relinquish its major gadget for controlling the Middle East. Winston Churchill had articulated the fundamental thinking. As Secretary of State at the War Office in

1919, he was approached by the RAF Middle East Command in Cairo for authorization to utilize chemical weapons "against recalcitrant Arabs as an experiment." Churchill authorized the experiment, dismissing qualms as "unreasonable": "I do not understand this squeamishness about the use of gas," he reacted with annoyance. Chemical weapons were merely "the application of Western science to modern-day warfare," Churchill discussed. "We can not in any situations acquiesce in the non-utilization of any weapons which are readily available to obtain a fast termination of the condition which dominates on the frontier." Toxin gas had currently been used by British forces in the North.

The British style grew again as racist frenzy swept the West during the Gulf conflict of 1990-91. John Keegan, a popular British military historian and reporter, detailed the typical view succinctly: "The British are used over 200 years of expeditionary forces going overseas, fighting the Africans, the Chinese, the Indians, the Arabs. It's simply something the British take for granted," and the war in the Gulf "rings extremely, extremely familiar royal bells with the British." Britain is therefore well-placed to carry out the Churchillian objective, which the editor of the Sunday Telegraph, Peregrine Worsthorne, termed the "new job" for "the post-Cold War world to help sustain a world and develop order stable sufficient to enable the innovative economies of the world to function without continuous interruption and hazard from the Third World. a job

Soon after the South Commission required a "new world order" based on democracy, justice, and equity, George Bush appropriated the phrase as a rhetorical cover for his war in the Gulf. As bombs were moistening Baghdad, Basra, and miserable conscripts hiding in holes in the sands of southern Iraq, the president announced that the United States would lead "a brand-new world order, where varied countries are accumulated in common cause, to attain the universal aspirations of humanity: peace and security, flexibility and the guideline of law."

We are entering an "era loaded with the pledge," Secretary of State James Baker proudly revealed, "one of those uncommon changing minutes in world history."

The message was elaborated by Thomas Friedman, chief diplomatic correspondent of the New York Times. The principle directing President Bush in the Gulf war, Friedman discussed, was that unless global limits between sovereign country states are respected, the alternative is chaos thinking, possibly, of Panama, Lebanon.

Finally, the world is about understand that "the free enterprise is the wave of the future, a future for which America is both the design and the gatekeeper.

It is George Bush's "new world order" that resounded, not the plaintive plea of the South, unheard and unreported. The response to the two near-simultaneous requires a New World Order reflects, obviously, the power relations.

We can value the nature of these "dreadful misfortunes" by looking at the earliest victims, Haiti and Bengal, explained by the European conquerors as flourishing, richly endowed, and largely populated, later a source of massive wealth for their French and British despoilers, now the real signs of misery and despair.

We learn more by looking at "the first nest of the contemporary world," Ireland, deindustrialized and significantly depopulated, in part through the rigid application of spiritual "laws of political economy," which forbade significant support.

The European conquest is typically described in more neutral terms by those who set the guidelines: hence we refer euphemistically to developed and developing societies or the North-South divide.

CHAPTER NIGHT

The "Q" Claims

Claims need proof to back them up, that needed cogency of evidence which can prove beyond a shadow of a doubt, mathematically or philosophically, the establishment of those statements as reality.

On this topic in specific, the weight of these posts and the power they hold relating to our extreme liberty. The claims we make and the implications therein need bodies of proof that support those claims as genuine.

In the world of Q, proofs are as good as gold. We are going to run you through some of the best Q proofs, that in our viewpoint, lend reliability to the reality that Q is an individual or group of people who are close to President Donald Trump.

When we first learned more about this Anon publishing on the boards, different of us were ecstatic because we had been investigating this kind of content for several years. This line of research brings with it the ire of the establishment, and Q was no exception.

Early on, there was very little pushback, as the media desired to guide as straightforward as possible, and Q's messages were not as popular, nor as prevalent as today. Now, with Q gaining a more significant foothold in the conscious awareness of more individuals, proofs are more needed than

ever.

As long as Q has been publishing, Anons on the boards have been taking those posts, integrating them with tweets by POTUS along with news and real-life events, to develop evidence. Evidence is our evidence, our argument of truth that establishes the validity of these posts. The number of evidence you can create from various posts, tweets, future news, and world occasions is staggering. Q's post has yet to be proven real; lots of more crumbs have been dropped in its wake that have been. These crumbs, taken by other Anons and organized into pictographic memes, have given us the body of proof needed to establish, with statistical certainty, the legitimacy of the anonymous Q.

•   Not Lord Voldemort, But Close

As far back as November of 2017, Q had published regarding Arizona Senator John McCain, who eventually known mostly as NO NAME because "we do not like to say his name," as exposed in Q post 357. Senator NO NAME first appeared in post 436 on December 22, 2017, in a post that laid out the strategy to remove the President through the "insurance plan" found in the Strzok-Page text messages.

The "insurance coverage" was hinted as having begun with Hillary Clinton and the DNC's funding of the Steele Dossier as pointing to NO NAME in disseminating it to Buzzfeed and other media outlets.

The post is an example of "future proves past," an expression used frequently by Q, since we pertained to find out that HRC and the DNC performed for the dossier, and it remained, in fact, a long-time associate of NO NAME who first gave the dossier to the press. This was also the first time an " insurance coverage" was mentioned in the posts and months before being exposed to the media. From that point forward, the name McCain was hardly ever spoken, either by Q or the President.

McCain vanished from the general public eye in Dec. 2017, nearly immediately after Q started publishing. In a February 11, 2018 post, 732, Q published an image of NO NAME with ISIS rebels in Syria, in addition to, "We do not state his name returning to Primetime wonder if his so-called illness or condition will flare up," in referral to McCain taking a leave of absence and eventually passing away, as the mainstream story would go.

Again, Q knew before the media or anyone else did. Throughout the year, Q released regarding the anonymous Senator, consisting of post-1706 that stated, "no-name returning to headlines," and days later, the media was awash in the news covering his stopping working condition. Q was right each time.

On August 13, 2018, the New York Times had published concerning a speech President Trump made, introducing the John S. McCain National Defense permission act for the financial year 2019. In an article in the New York Times on August 13, 2018, it was reported that President Trump made a speech in front of soldiers and Senior Military leaders at Fort Drum in New York City.

The President spoke for 28 minutes without discussing McCain's name, calling it the most significant investment in our military and our warfighters in modern-day history. President Trump never references John McCain's military service, nor his decades-long career in the Senate.

Some may state it has a coincidence; however, going out of your way not to mention an individual's name, the name that adorns the costs you're hailing, is a little unusual.

How Much Evidence Do We Need?

A question Q presents frequently is, "How frequent is the coincidences before it is mathematically impossible?" Over the past year or more of posts, there have been a lot of coincidences that it is beyond mathematical possibility that Q is not with President Trump, or in his administration at the least.

Another difficult coincidence was from post 521 on January 13th, 2018, in which Q published, "Do you TRUST the chain of command?" 2 days later, on January 15, the United States Department of Defense (@DeptofDefense) tweeted a post regarding a program airing that night on The National Geographic Channel, using the hashtag #chainofcommand. When the program aired, a scene with a coffee mug with a big letter Q emblazoned on it! Some may suggest that this is merely a coincidence; however, we reiterate the prospects? Some evidence was posted on May 10th, 2018. On that day, Q published on his private board posts numbered 72 through 76.

Some might remember President Trump had negotiated with North Korea at that time to secure the release of three American detainees being held there.

On the day of the release, President Trump posted on his Twitter a video of the three hostages returning home. In that video, there were two fire engines with their booms extended, holding a big American flag in between them. That same day, Q posted a photo of an American flag, post 7 4 on Patriots Battle, with the words, "Castle Lock," listed below.

In another remarkable coincidence, the fire engine holding up the flag on the right when the hostages came home had a big Q7 4 on the side of it. That, my pals, is too coincidental for our taste!

There have been many times over the past year where people in the growing audience have snapped against Q, tossing doubt on his legitimacy. What are the odds on a day Q is releasing posts 72 through 76, that there would be a video launched by President Trump that has Q 7 4 in it?

Due to all of the push back we have gotten since this movement began, we did due diligence every time Q's validity was concerned, with the Q7 4 being no exception. To validate the likelihood that a fire engine would be identified as Q7 4, times were invested reading images of fire engines. Yet, we could not find any fire engine at all that had one letter and two digits. Most fire engines discovered had 3 or 4 letters in their identifier, so the reality that fire truck had Q7 4 on it is odd enough, add to the fact that Q7 4 was the middle post that day, and the chances are almost impossible.

On April 24th, 2018, post-1254, Q posted:.

Is Iran next " Mark it down" Bigger problems than ever in the past Sig to Iran?

Q coincidentally, roughly two-weeks in the future, May 8, 2018, President Trump offered remarks on the joint comprehensive plan of action relating to Iran. Because speech, he states quote, "It will have larger problems than it has ever had before." When again, we have a post where Q gave us foreknowledge of a declaration that President Trump would make ahead of time.

Another one of our favorites began at Easter. We admit this one is a little bit ludicrous, but if anything, it increases the possibility of its credibility. An anon on Schan asked, "possibly Q can work the phrase, 'Idea Top' into the SOTU (State of The Union speech)," as the State of the Union Address was arranged for January 30th, 2018 at 9 p.m. EST. Nevertheless, this demand came only the night before on January 29th at 6:56 p.m releasing an expression called "Tip Top."

In our opinion, the State of the Union Address was probably already well completed at that point.

Quick forward to April 2nd, 2018, when Q was reacting to an anon on the board who stated, "Tiptop tippy-top shape," and Q responded to, "It was requested, did you listen today? Q."

Q was referring to President Trump's resolving the nation on Easter Sunday, in the White House balcony with First Lady Melania Trump and an Easter Bunny. Perhaps more specifically, the Easter Bunny was an assistant in a rabbit fit with freaky looking glasses.

"We keep it in tip-top shape; we sometimes call it tippy-top shape.".

Using this expression was so odd, and the repeating was seen by anons as being done to match the requested phrase. What are the odds that a President of the United States would ever use the words, great tippy-top, in a sentence?

The number of times in your life have you heard anyone use that phrase? Even for those who were on the fence about Q saw that one as a clear indication that President Trump was talking straight to us.

On November 14th, 2017, Q published the full text of the Lord's Prayer, which stood out when there was no context or significance provided for the post. On December 8th, 2017, news broke that Pope Francis had proposed a small change to the words of The Lord's Prayer.

The next day, December 9th, 2017, in post 306, Q published, Which version? Why is this relevant? What simply came out re: The Lord's Prayer? As you can see, Q meant something regarding The Lord's Prayer less than a month before anybody understood. It's yet another evidence of foreknowledge that Q has on world occasions.

In yet another proof relating to world events, specifically concerning the Pope, was a post.

On April 3rd, 2018. In post 997, Q stated, Pope, will be having a terrible May.

Within a month later, May 18th, stories started to distribute around the Internet under the heading, Every Bishop in Chile Sends Resignation to Pope Francis, due to the issue of sexual assault claims facing priests in Chile. These accusations supposedly took place and were subsequently concealed by the top leadership in the Vatican, presumably as much as and including the Pope.

Every bishop in Chile simply resigned over the child sex abuse scandal.

Considering Q's propensity for telling us about happenings ahead of time, such as the Pope's dreadful May that was followed by the resignations of Chile's Bishops, what else has Q informed us about ahead of time? On January 19, 2018, in post 559, Q published, HUSSEIN CABINET I STAFF Who used personal email addresses? Q went on to list many sets of initials that stood for: Loretta Lynch, Hillary Clinton, James Corney, James Clapper, Chuck Schumer, Andrew McCabe, John McCain, Rod Rosenstein, Susan Rice, John Brennan, Huma Abedin, and Valerie Jarrett, after which asking, Did Hussein use a private e-mail address? These Obama administration officials, listed by Q, were all part of Crossfire Hurricane, the operation to keep President Trump from getting post-election access to the White House.

From the Inspector General's report dated June 14, 2018, it was revealed that FBI analysts and district attorneys informed us that previous president Barack Obama was one of the 13 individuals with whom Clinton had direct contact using her Clintonemail.com account. Obama, like the other high-level federal government authorities, used a pseudonym for his username on his Clintonemail.com account.

Coincidentally, all of the individuals noted in this post are either removed from the workplace, under examination, or about to be under. Suppose they are not already under a sealed grand jury investigation. As early as November of 2017, we saw quotes like this by Q, far before any removal or criminal disclosures. Those who have been listening to Q have been an action ahead of the general public discoveries.

As you can see, the number of coincidences continued to install. As the evident "coincidences" grew in number, so did the pushback against Q and his validity. On July 24th, 2018, in post-1682, the line of Q's post read, "Sea to shining sea." That night, President Trump was going into the phase as he normally does, while the song, "God Bless the U.S.A." by Lee Greenwood, played. As many people know, there is a line in the lyric that states, "From sea to shining sea." As soon as again, coincidentally, right before the song yell the words "sea to shining sea," President Trump put his finger to his ear as if to say, listen up! He pointed up with both hands as the words rang through the arena.

At another rally on June 20, 2018, President Trump strolled down to the stage and right as much as an individual in the crowd who had a huge Q on their t-shirt and pointed directly at him. Later, Q posted the image that the Anon took President Trump, pointing directly at him. On multiple celebrations,

President Trump has gone on phase and made the hand gesture of drawing up a Q, rather certainly for us anons.

There have been countless mainstream short posts, well over hundreds, that have gone out of their method to try to discredit Q.

Not one pundit will ask President Trump the one question all of us want them to ask, "President Trump, do you understand anything about this person or entity that is Q Anon?" There has been so much media buzz (most of it negative) about Q; one would believe at least one press reporter would try to discredit Trump and Q by asking the question.

As stated previously, every single time there was a question of Q's credibility, we went out of the way to make sure absolutely nothing was reported to audiences that were phony or fraudulent. Early on as a means of recognition, Q began to use an identifier understood on Schan as a "tripcode," as a suggests to make sure that we know we are checking outposts from the same poster each time. As Schan is normally a confidential board, the journey code was vital in learning who to trust, as only Q (or the group of individuals publishing as Q) might use it. This tripcode system is not a basic cipher; for instance, if you enter an A 3 times, the very first one may be an equals X, however the second time may be an equates to an enigma, and so on. So the trip code is not extremely easy, but not substantial.

The Deep State that President Trump and Q are fighting have very great resources and access to excellent computing power with powerful decryption and hacking tools, so given time, it is possible to crack.

Operatives made it their mission to attempt to make use of Q and his/her trip code, as getting to the account would indicate potential control of the movement. On one occasion, Q's tripcode was exposed, and over time it became needed to change it on numerous extra events.

Along with the method, nevertheless, Q kept providing proofs, even presuming as to hold some proofs back for months at a time. After the trip code was exposed, there was much discussion relating to the continued integrity of the details Q was supplying.

Was this still really Q? Many individuals headed out of their method to reveal the tripcodes were not protecting, inferring anybody could publish under it if they figured out the code.

CHAPTER TEN

The Political-EconomicOrder

Through this long era, there have been several significant changes. The Second World War brought one crucial difference: for the first time, a single state had such frustrating wealth and power that its leaders could realistically develop and implement a global vision. As the war ended, the United States held about half of the world's wealth and was its most tremendous military power, taking pleasure in extraordinary security; it had no enemies close by, controlled both oceans in addition to the wealthiest and most developed regions throughout the seas, and controlled the world's significant reserves of energy and other vital resources.

The United States had long been the world's leading industrial power. The war badly harmed all others, while in the United States, uniquely immune from the war's devastation, production grew, nearly quadrupling in scale.

From the beginning of World War II, U.S. strategists and planners knew that they would be in a position to get much of the world organized. Naturally, they planned to make use of these opportunities. From 1939 through 1945, comprehensive research studies on the postwar world were conducted by the Council on Foreign Relations, which combines worldwide oriented business and financial circles and top-level State

Department planners. They created what they called a "Grand Area," an integrated world economy that would meet the needs of the American economy and provide it with "the elbow room' ... needed for surviving without significant readjustments". That is, without changing the domestic circulation of power, control, ownership, and wealth. The organizers sought "national security," but in the broad sense discussed earlier, which has little to do with the security of the country.

It was first assumed that Germany would survive as a significant center of power. The Grand Area, then, was to be a non-German bloc, which was to incorporate at a minimum the Western hemisphere, the Far East, and the former British empire, to be taken apart along with other local systems and incorporated under U.S. leadership. On the other hand, the United States extended its regional systems in Latin America and the Pacific, leaving out standard colonial rulers. As it became clear that Germany would be defeated, Grand Area planning was modified to include the German bloc. A fly in the ointment was the Soviet Union, and China afterward, to be handled by "containment" or "rollback," in the framework earlier discussed.

The structure of the Grand Area was analyzed with some care, later developed in government preparation studies as events took their course. Top of the list for international planners were the prosperous industrial societies. In the context of their needs, the standard colonial domains were assigned their precise roles.

317

A prominent issue was the problem of the Communist states, which had left their third World status; this was the core problem of the Cold War, gotten rid of with the reintegration of China and the Soviet Union into the global economy as mostly subordinate sectors. Always in the background was the future of the United States itself. Its society was to be reshaped in a particular way, one that would, it was hoped, become a model for the industrial world. This last topic deserves a close consideration for what it exposes about the dominant social forces and their thinking.

1. Securing the Home Front

The Enemy Within

The problems occurring at home were partly ideological and social, partly economic. The Great Depression of the 1930s had brought about a major obstacle to business dominance, a huge shock; the prevailing presumption had been that the danger of labor organizing and popular democracy had been buried permanently.

After some preliminary cautions, the Wagner Act of 1935 gave rights to workers who won about half a century earlier in England and some other places. That victory for the working individuals and democracy sent out a chill through the business community. The National Association of Manufacturers (NAM) warned of the "danger dealing with industrialists" in "the newly found political power of the masses." That must be reversed, and "their thinking ... directed" to more valid channels, or "we are heading for adversity," the NAM cautioned.

A corporate counteroffensive was quickly released, often using the usual recourse to state violence, but rely more on thought control: "scientific methods of strike-breaking" and "human relations"; campaigns to mobilize the public against "outsiders" preaching "anarchy and communism" and seeking to disrupt the various communities of sober working-men and farmers, housewives tending to their families, hard-working executives toiling day and night to serve the people-- "Americanism," in which all share alike in happiness and harmony. The project relied and built on earlier propaganda successes of the Public Relations (PR) industry, an American development, which had beaten back a wave of anti-business belief or sentiment in the early face of the century and assisted in establishing business dominance after World War I, conclusively it had been thought.

The latter accomplishment was helped by the experiences of the very first government propaganda agency, Woodrow Wilson's Creel Commission, which had assisted in transforming a pacifist nation into a jingoist warmonger when Wilson chose to go to war. The propaganda accomplishments considerably impressed the American business world and others, including Adolf Hitler. He associated Germany's defeat to its ineptitude on the propaganda front in contrast with the Anglo-Americans. Wilson himself was described as "the terrific generalissimo on the propaganda front" by Harold Lasswell, among the leading figures of modern political science, who began his profession with queries into propaganda and its uses in the West. Like other great investigators, he acknowledged that propaganda was of greater value in more democratic and complimentary societies, where the general public can not be restrained by the whip. Keeping to prevailing norms, he promoted the more advanced usage of this "new technique of control" of the public, who are a hazard to order because of the "lack of knowledge and superstition [of] ... the masses."

As he discussed in the Encyclopaedia of the Social Sciences, we must not give in to "democratic dogmatisms about men being the best judges of their interests." They are not; the very best judges are the elites-- the rich men of Churchill's wealthy nations-- who should be ensured the means to impose their will, for the common good.

Like other leading intellectuals, and the business world, Lasswell shared Secretary of State Lansing's worry of the "oblivious and incapable mass of humanity," and the obvious risk of letting them become "dominant in the earth," or perhaps influential, as Lansing (erroneously) believed the Bolsheviks intended. Articulating these concerns, the leading progressive intellectual Walter Lippmann, the dean of American journalism and a noted democratic theorist and commentator on public affairs, encouraged that "the public should be put in its place" so that the "responsible men" may "live free of the trampling and the roar of a confused herd."

In a democracy, Lippmann held, these "meddlesome and oblivious outsiders" do have a "function": to be "interested spectators of action," but not individuals lending their weight occasionally to some member of the leadership class (elections), then returning to their individual or private concerns.

Lippmann represents the more progressive fringe of opinion. At the reactionary end, we discover those mislabeled "conservatives" in contemporary ideology, who reject even the spectator role. So, the attractiveness to Reaganite statist reactionaries of private terror operations created to leave the domestic population ignorant, along with censorship, agitprop on a unique scale, and other steps to ensure that an interventionist and powerful state will not be bothered by the rabble.

As Bakunin presciently observed over a century ago, this conception was common to the two major propensities amongst the rising "new class" of intellectuals: those who would end up being the "Red bureaucracy," instituting "the worst of all despotic governments"; and those who see the path to opportunity and authority in service to state-corporate power. In the West, the "responsible guys" are guided by a user-friendly understanding of a maxim developed by David Hume as one of the First Principles of Government: to make sure that "the few govern the many" and to guarantee "the implicit submission with which men resign their own beliefs and passion to those of their rulers," the government should control thought; "'It is, therefore, on opinion only that government is founded; and this maxim reaches the most despotic and most military governments, in addition to the most free and most popular"-- in reality, much more to "the most free and most popular," for obvious reasons.

Bakunin's analysis brings to mind much earlier reflections by Thomas Jefferson; rather, intriguing connections can be drawn from classical liberal thought to the libertarian socialists of later years, who typically saw themselves as its natural inheritors, the leading anarchosyndicalist Rudolf Rocker for one.

In his last years, Jefferson had major concerns about the fate of the democratic experiment. He compared "aristocrats and democrats." The aristocrats are "those who fear and wonder about the individuals, and desire to draw all powers from them into the hands of the higher classes." The democrats, on the other hand, "relate to individuals, have confidence in them, value and consider them as the safe & truthful, altho' not the most wise depository of the general public interest." The aristocrats were the supporters of the increasing capitalist state, which Jefferson concerned with much ridicule because of the apparent contradiction between democracy and capitalism (whether in the state-guided Western design or some other), particularly as new business structures-- the "banking institutions and money incorporations" of whom he had cautioned-- were given increasing powers, primarily by judicial decision. The contemporary progressive intellectuals who seek to "put the public in its right place" and are free of "democratic dogmatisms" about the capability of the "meddlesome and oblivious outsiders" to get in the political arena are Jefferson's "aristocrats," democratic only by comparison with the rest of the operative spectrum. Jefferson's worst fears were more recognized as the spectrum of viewpoint settled into its contemporary variation, accommodating to power and its.

It is not that the democratic ideal collapsed totally; rather, it was marginalized, though it remained alive in popular motions and was articulated by some intellectuals, most prominent amongst them, perhaps, America's leading twentieth-century theorist, John Dewey. Dewey acknowledged in his later years that "politics is the shadow cast on society by big business," and as long as this is so, "the attenuation of the shadow will not change the substance." Reforms are of limited energy; democracy requires that the source of the shadow is eliminated, not only because it dominated the political arena but also because the very institutions of private power weaken democracy and liberty. Dewey was specific about the anti-democratic power he had in mind: "Power today resides in control of the ways of production, exchange, transport, promotion and communication. Whoever owns them rules the life of the nation," even if democratic types remain: "business for private revenue through private control of banking, land, industry, enhanced by command of journalism, press agents and other ways of publicity and propaganda"-- that is the system of real power, the source of browbeating and control, and till it is relaxed, we can not talk seriously about democracy and freedom. In a free and democratic society, workers must be "the masters of their commercial fate," not tools rented by businesses, a position that traces back to leading thoughts of classical liberalism articulated by Wilhelm von Humboldt and Adam Smith, amongst others. It is "illiberal and immoral" to train children to work, "not easily and wisely, but for the sake of the work earned," in which case their activity is "not free because it is not freely participated in." Industry should be altered "from a feudalistic to a democratic social order," based on workers' control and federal organization in the style of G.D.H.

Cole's guild socialism and much anarchist and left-Marxist thought. As for production, its "supreme objective" is not the production of items but "the production of totally free people associated with one another on regards to equality," a conception inconsistent with contemporary industrialism in its state capitalist or state socialist varieties, and once again with roots in classical liberal ideals

Dewey likewise had no impressions about the covert premise that lies behind the self-serving rhetoric about "responsible guys," "Great minds," "sensible men," "aristocracy of intellect and character," and so on. Lippmann, for example, did not ask why he was among the "responsible men" but not Eugene Debs, who, far from signing up with that august business, was serving a ten-year jail sentence. The answers are not tough to find, even if unmentioned.

With the constricting of the doctrinal system throughout the years, essential libertarian concepts now sound exotic and extreme, perhaps even "anti-American." It is well to bear in mind, then, that they are "as American as apple pie," with origins in traditional thinking that is ritually lauded though distorted and forgotten. This is a crucial function of the degeneration of democracy in the current period, at the intellectual as at the institutional level.

Business propaganda makes its distinctive contributions to these processes. Consider an essay by Michael Joyce, president of the Bradley Foundation, one of the foundations dedicated to narrowing the ideological spectrum, especially in schools and colleges.

Joyce begins with rhetoric drawn from the libertarian left, condemning the narrow sense of citizenship that restricts it to the "episodic, irregular, albeit boring, duty" of voting, after which the person "is expected to get out of the way, and let the professionals or experts take charge." He advocates a richer concept of citizenship, participation in civil society, outside "the political sphere." Here "citizenly activity ... takes place not episodically or rarely, just like voting, but frequently and constantly": in the market, working, making money, domesticity, churches, fraternal and sororal lodges, PTA meetings, and other such "tasks" of "good people.".

As the uplifting tale unfolds, the "political sphere" vanishes from view, delegated forces unidentified and hidden-- or almost. Joyce does caution against "conceited, paternalistic social scientists, bureaucrats, professionals, and therapists, who claim special right to minister to the harms inflicted by hostile social forces," forming the "puffed up, corrupt, central bureaucracies" of the "nanny state"; "corrupt intellectual and cultural elites in the universities, the media, and in other places," who denigrate "standard moderating structures" as "benighted" and "reactionary"; "expert elites" who "require more government programs-- and more bureaucratic experts and experts to minister to the hurts allegedly inflicted on hapless victims by industrialism, bigotry, sexism, and so on-- in the course removing more authority from citizens and civil institutions yet.".

The person, then, need to go back to the wholesome job of searching for a task and going to church, while the "nanny state" is rid of the therapists and social scientists who now run the world and left in the hands of some missing force. Entirely missing from the picture are the real centers of concentrated wealth and power, the people and institutions that identify what takes place in the social and economic order and mostly control the state, either by direct involvement or imposition of narrow restraints on political option, converting governmental authority into an effective and interventionist "nanny state" that takes care of their requirements with much solicitude. In short, the PR operation is more or less the analog of an account of Soviet Russia that ignores the Kremlin, the military, and the Communist Party. It would be difficult to carry off the farce; here it is rather easy, an interesting truth, which reveals the performance of service-- run believed control, to which vast resources and thought have been committed for lots of years. Liberal Democrats play rather similar video games, a matter to which we return.6.

In the more liberal societies, state controls are hardly ever exercised straightly. George Orwell once wrote, "The sinister fact about literary censorship in England," "is that it is mainly voluntary. Undesirable ideas can be silenced, and inconvenient facts kept in the dark, without any requirement for any official ban." The desired outcome is obtained in part by the "basic indirect arrangement that 'it wouldn't do' to point out that specific fact," in part as a basic effect of centralization of the press in the hands of "rich guys who have every intention to be dishonest on specific important topics." As a result, "Anyone who challenges the dominating orthodoxy finds himself silenced with unexpected effectiveness." About ten years earlier, John Dewey had observed that critique of "particular abuses" of "our un-free press" is of minimal value: "The only truly basic approach to the problem is to inquire about the essential impact of the present financial system upon the whole system of publicity; upon the judgment of what news is, upon the selection and removal of any matter that is published, upon the treatment of news in both editorial and news columns." We should ask "how far authentic intellectual freedom and social responsibility are possible on any large scale under the existing economic regime." Not far, he judged.

The leading student of business propaganda, Australian social scientist Alex Carey, argues convincingly that "the 20th century has been identified by three advancements of high political importance: the growth of democracy, the development of business power, and the growth of corporate propaganda as a method of safeguarding corporate power against democracy." The corporate counteroffensive of the late 1930s is among many striking illustrations that he provides for this thesis.

The ways for controlling the "public mind" were much extended by the recently readily available technology of radio, rapidly taken control of by the corporate sector in the United States, unlike the other advanced countries, which were less under business domination for a range of historical reasons. The war put the job of reversing the democratic 2 nd thrust of the 1930s on hold, but it was used powerfully as the war ended.

Huge PR campaigns employed the media, cinema, and other gadgets to recognize "capitalism"-- indicating state-subsidized private power with no infringement on managerial prerogatives-

- as "the American way," threatened by dangerous subversives. The method of whipping up worry and hatred of "foreigners," "communists," "anarchists," and other miserable creatures was, obviously, long familiar, virtually second nature to propagandists in a political culture with unusual Manichaean strains from its earliest days, one that can make the ranting of NSC 68, or the principle "un-American." Apart from the previous Soviet Union, where "anti-Sovietism" was the most significant criminal offense, there are a couple of intellectual communities that could treat with respect deceiving and ridiculous works on "Anti-Americanism," raging about departures from sufficient servility to the Holy State. A book on "anti-Italianism" would just generate ridicule in Milan or Rome, as in any society with an operating democratic culture.

Acknowledging these peculiarities of American political culture, the U.S. Chamber of Commerce distributed more than a million copies of its handout "Communist Infiltration in the United States" immediately after the war, together with another entitled "Communists Within the Government."

In April 1947, the Advertising Council announced a $100 million campaign to use all media to "sell" the American economic system-- as they conceived it-- to the American people; the program was formally described as a "major job of educating the American people about the economic facts of life." Corporations "started comprehensive programs to indoctrinate staff members," the leading business journal 'Fortune' reported, subjecting their captive audiences to "Courses in Economic Education" and checking them for commitment to the "capitalism" system- that is, "Americanism."

A survey carried out by the American Management Association (AMA) discovered that many business leaders regarded "propaganda" and "financial education" as associated, holding that "we desire our people to think right." The AMA reported that Communism, socialism, and particular political celebrations and unions "are typically typical targets of such campaigns," which "some employers see ... as a sort of 'fight of commitments' with the unions"-- an unequal battle, given the resources available, consisting of the corporate media, which continue to offer the services free of charge in methods to which we return.

Others jumped into the fray. As is well understood, the United States is distinct amongst commercial societies in doing not have detailed health insurance. Truman's efforts to bring the nation into the modern-day world were bitterly assaulted by the American Medical Association as "the primary step" towards "the sort of regimentation that led to totalitarianism in Germany and the downfall of that nation."

Association's journal knocked "medical soviets" and the "gauleiters" who would run them and warned that advocates of national healthcare and insurance coverage were inciting a socialist revolution. Its marketing firm introduced the biggest campaign in American history to beat proposed legislation, comprising phony quotes from Lenin, interesting Protestant clergymen on-premises that Christianity is threatened by political leaders weakening "the sanctity of life," and dispersing 54 million pieces of propaganda targeting different groups. The slogan of the nationwide PR campaign was "The Voluntary Way is the American Way." Its standard theme was: "American medication has ended up being the blazing centerpiece in an essential battle which may determine whether America stays complementary or whether we are to end up being a socialist state." The heresy was peacefully whipped.

With the expenses of the highly inefficient and bureaucratized capitalist health care program becoming a severe concern for business, the problem of healthcare entered the government-media plan in the 1990s-- which is why we now find posts in the traditional press mocking the propaganda campaigns of earlier years. The Clinton administration sought health reforms but keeping strictly to two vital conditions.

1) the result must be significantly regressive, unlike tax- or even wage-based programs; and 2) big insurance provider need to remain in control, adding significantly to the expenses of health care with their big marketing expenses, high executive salaries, and profits, along with the expenses of their elaborate bureaucratic systems to micromanage to make sure every little healthcare and the intricate governmental regulatory device required to keep the intricate system based upon private revenue functioning with a minimum of some regard for public requirements--" handled competition." The code expression used to camouflage these obstacles to a much more fair and efficient government-run strategy is that the latter is " politically impossible." The significant popular assistance for some variety of nationwide healthcare is, therefore, unimportant.

Media coverage keeps well within the bounds set by state-corporate power. Hence a front-page New York Times short article on the public issue for healthcare reform mentions in passing, near the end, that 59 percent of respondents prefer a model "that Mr Clinton has declined; a Canadian-style system of national medical insurance spent for with tax money." The figure is remarkably high, given near-unanimous government-media termination of this alternative, which is off the list. The Boston Globe presented a "user's guide" to the baffled public, attempting and identifying to clarify the concerns that are under discussion. These are the six "assisting stars" presented by President Clinton-- omitting, of course, the two unmentionables. The press reporters quote professionals who challenge the "bewildering" intricacy of the propositions in comparison to "the simpler government-run system" utilized elsewhere, but mention that this is not appropriate: "It is tough to prevent intricacy if one begins with the premise, as both Clinton advocates and his critics do, that a simpler government-funded health system is not an alternative." Considering that critics and advocates agree that we should have "handled care," no classification remains to consist of those who disagree (including, it appears, most of the population, not to mention grass-roots organizations, members of Congress, medical experts, etc.)-- other than, maybe, "anti-American.".

The past week, the same journal gave extensive front-page coverage to a nationwide survey it carried out with the Harvard School of Public Health that determined public reactions to 3 options: handled care, individual private care, and Medicare, the nationalized system for the senior. The post compares reactions to the first two options, finding little significant distinction ("excellent news for the White House"). Data are cited showing that Medicare wins conveniently on quality of care, ease of use, and the majority of other steps, as it does on administrative expenses and other elements ruled out. And undoubtedly, the reader will discover that "one striking finding is that elderly Medicare customers were the most pleased of all guaranteed Americans on practically every step of medical care and insurance coverage system quality," a result that "some interpret" as an argument in favor of national health insurance coverage. But it is the ineffective and extremely regressive alternatives that deal with the corporate-financial world that stay on the program.

Since the 1940s, when major opinion surveys began asking people's attitudes toward a universal health program, "the bulk or big pluralities have consistently supported it," Vicente Navarro observes, "even at the expense of paying higher taxes." In 1989-90, support for a tax-based national health plan was in the 60-70 percent range (69 percent in February 1992). The high administrative costs and limited coverage of U.S. health care do not result from some curious function of American culture or popular desires, as always declared by scholars and journalists, however from the structures of power and propaganda, notably the weak point of the labor movement and organization control of the doctrinal institutions.11.

Postwar propaganda projects joined numerous other impressive successes recorded with pleasure by organizations. The Chamber of Commerce reported that its attack on supposed

Communists in the federal government "led to Truman's loyalty program"--" insufficient however still a commitment program," hence addressing least part of the method towards removing individuals who might be lured to assist the bad "ransack the rich," even if not yet far enough. Another example was the fate of the Office of Price Administration (OPA), which had kept products within reach of the general public during the war.

A huge campaign by the NAM and the Chamber of Commerce decreased public support for OPA from 80 percent in February 1946 to 26 percent about eight months later on. President Truman was required to end its operations in the face of what he explained as a huge business campaign "to destroy the laws that were securing the consumer against exploitation." By 1947, a State Department public relations officer could celebrate that "smart public relations [has] paid off as it has before and will once again." Popular opinion "is not moving to the right, it has been moved-- skillfully-- to the right." "While the remainder of the world has transferred to the left, has confessed labor into government, has passed liberalized laws, the United States has become anti-economic change, anti-social change, anti-labor.".

A few years later, sociologist Daniel Bell, then an editor of Fortune magazine, observed that "it has been market's prime concern, in the post-war years, to change the environment of viewpoint introduced by ... the anxiety. This 'free enterprise' campaign has two important goals: to rewin the commitment of the worker which now goes to the union and to halt sneaking socialism," indicating the mildly reformist commercialism of the New Deal. The scale of business PR projects was "staggering," Bell noted. One significant impact was legislation that dramatically limited union activity, resulting in the decline of unions today. Extensive is the campaign that Labor Secretary Robert Reich, at the liberal fringe of the Clinton administration, informs us that "the jury is still out on whether the standard union is necessary for the new work environment," what the press calls "the high-performance workplace of the future" that state-corporate authority is creating. "Unions are O.K. where they are. And where they are not"-- which is practically all over by now-- "it is not clear yet what sort of company need to represent workers," Commerce Secretary Ronald Brown, another "New Democrat," elaborates.

A parallel attack on the independent idea, part of the "just suppression" that Truman's leading advisors required in the Cold War context, was successful as soon as again in mainly eliminating any open obstacle to company domination. Much of

337

the intelligence community and labor bureaucracy worked together with enthusiasm. The campaign is frequently mislabeled "McCarthyism"; in reality, Senator McCarthy was a latecomer who made use of an environment of repression currently developed, triggering severe damage before he was gotten rid of from the scene.

These efforts restored the environment of the 1920s in large steps. The disintegration of discipline under the impact of the popular ferment of the 1960s elicited restored hysteria and much more dedicated efforts to develop doctrinal controls.

A congressional inquiry was notified that by 1978, American organization was spending $1 billion a year on grassroots propaganda. These efforts were supplemented by what Carey calls "tree-tops propaganda," targeting informed sectors and looking to eliminate any articulate risk to business supremacy. Techniques ranged from endowed Professorships of Free Enterprise in universities to massive propaganda campaigns against the typical run of targets: taxes, business regulation, welfare (for the poor), pointy-headed "bureaucrats" interfering with the imaginative entrepreneur, union corruption and violence, evil apologists for our opponents, and so on.

The impacts have been dramatic, as the "l-word" ("liberal") followed the "s-word" (" socialist") into oblivion. The conservative conquest of ideological institutions is, of course not total, a catastrophe to the totalitarian mentality, reflected in the fantastic and often rather funny campaign raging in the United States and Britain to safeguard the ramparts from a takeover by "left fascists," omnipotent because they have still not been thoroughly rooted out. Signs that the labor movement has not been fully tamed arouse similar hysteria, highlighted in late 1993 in fascinating ways, to which we return. That advanced electoral democracies ought to display such propensities is entirely natural, for reasons currently kept in mind.

Functioning democracy is feared a lot more at home than abroad. Efforts of previously marginalized sections of the population to go into the political arena in the 1960s were condemned by frightened liberal elites as a "crisis of democracy." The resulting "ungovernability" can just be overcome by restoring popular sectors to passivity and obedience; the Trilateral Commission advised in its very first major study, The Crisis of Democracy. The Commission, established by David Rockefeller, brings together liberal internationalist elites from the United States, Europe, and Japan; Jimmy Carter was a member. His administration was drawn nearly totally from the Commission. The American rapporteur, Professor Samuel Huntington of Harvard, looked back with some nostalgia to the golden age when "Truman had been able to govern the country with the cooperation of a reasonably little number of Wall Street bankers and lawyers," so that democracy functioned smoothly, with no "crisis." Worry of the "oblivious and meddlesome outsiders" articulated by business leaders, federal government officials, and lots of leading intellectuals can be traced to the earliest modern democratic revolution in seventeenth-century England. It has not stopped since.

Nor commits to "historical engineering," to borrow the term invented by American historians as they enlisted in "Generalissimo Wilson's" ideological crusade. This phenomenon provides much insight into the Western political culture and what we can prepare for as it creates a new order with fewer obstacles on decision-makers. We might stop briefly to take a look at a couple of normal cases of the business of reshaping recent history to a form better for domestic power.

.

CHAPTER ELEVEN

The Contours of the New World Order

Structures of governance tend to coalesce around domestic power; in the last couple of centuries, financial power procedure continues. In the Financial Times, BBC economics correspondent James Morgan describes the "de facto world government" that is taking shape: the IMF, World Bank, G-7, GATT, and other structures designed to serve the interests of TNCs, banks, and financial investment companies in a "new royal age." At the other end of the bludgeon, the South Commission observes that "the most powerful nations in the North have ended up being a de facto board of management for the world economy, protecting their interests and enforcing their will on the South," where federal governments are then left to deal with the wrath, even the violence, of their people, whose standard of lives are being depressed for the sake of preserving the present patterns of operation of the world economy" that is, today structure of wealth and power. An important function of the rising de facto governing organizations is their resistance from popular impact, even awareness. They operate in trick, developing a world subordinated to the requirements of investors, with the general public **"put in its place,"** the threat of democracy lowered. This reversal of the growth of democracy over the previous centuries is a matter of no small significance, together with the new forms of perversion of classical doctrine in the world.

These advancements are naturally regarded with many issues throughout the South, and the growing Third World at home must be no less bothered. In the last address to the Group of 77, Chairman Luis Fernando Jaramillo considered the "hostile global environment" and the "loss of financial and political standing" of the developing nations "in the so-called New World Order at the dawn of the 21st century," as factors that trigger genuine hardship that contrasts dramatically with the "ecstasy" engendered by the end of the Cold War, financial liberalization programs, and the GATT arrangement.

The strategy of the rich, he observed, is "plainly directed at strengthening more and more the economic institutions and firms that run outside the United Nations system," which, with all its severe defects, stays "the only multilateral mechanism in which the developing nations can have." On the other hand, the Bretton Woods institutions (World Bank, IMF, etc.) are being made "the center of gravity for the primary financial decisions that impact the developing countries" are marked by "their undemocratic character, their lack of openness, their dogmatic principles, their lack of pluralism in the argument of ideas and their impotence to influence the policies of the industrialized nations" whose dominant sectors they serve, in reality.

The new World Trade Organization established by the most current GATT agreements will align itself with the World Bank and IMF in "a New Institutional Trinity which would have as its specific function to control and dominate the financial relations that devote the establishing world." At the same time, the developed nations will make "their deals outside normal channels," in G-7 meetings and somewhere else.

A comparable perception was revealed by the conference organized by Jesuits in San Salvador in January 1994. Its report concludes that "Central America today is experiencing globalization as more terrible pillage than what its individuals underwent 500 years ago with the conquest and colonization," a comment that generalizes too much of the "developing world." The new dominant force is not the market but rather "a strong global state that determines economic policy and prepares resource allowance. The IMF, World Bank, Interamerican Development Bank, U.S. Agency for International Development, European Community, UN Development Program, and their ilk are all state or interstate institutions of a transnational character that has much advanced economic influence over our nations than the marketplace."

A consequence of the globalization of the world is the rise of new governing institutions to serve the interests of global financial power. Another is the spread of the two-tiered Third World social design to the industrial world. The United States is taking the lead, another repercussion of the uncommon power and class awareness of the company sector, which could resist the social contract that popular battle has accomplished somewhere else. Production can be moved to low-wage areas in the global economy.

A UN report on transnationals (UNCTAD World Investment Report 1993, WIR) estimates that TNCs control one-third of the world's private sector efficient possessions. Their overseas financial investment is "a bigger force in the world economy than world trade." Tony Jackson reports in the Financial Times, with $5.5 trillion in sales outside the country of origin compared with $4 trillion of overall world exports (consisting of the huge circulation of in transform "exports"). These figures, trade analyst Chakravarthi Raghavan states, "do not show the number of companies that transnational activities and, with little or no [foreign direct financial investment, FDI], apply control over foreign efficient properties through a variety of non-equity arrangements-subcontracting, franchising, licensing, and so on, as well as through strategic alliances." The WIR reports that FDI is extremely focused, with about one percent of TNCs owning over half of the FDI stock or overall affiliate possessions. It keeps in mind even more than the 1993 GATT contracts increase the rights of TNCs to pursue their activities, which are "advancing the economic combination of the worldwide economy on a scale and at a pace that is extraordinary," Raghavan observes.

On the other hand, they impose no corresponding obligations on TNCs. Likewise, the World Bank releases standards for the treatment of personal FDI by host governments, but "they do not handle the obligations of foreign financiers, except in very basic ways," the WIR explains. Efforts to develop a Code of Conduct for TNCs broke down in July 1992; "This brings to an official end the most detailed effort to produce a well balanced and worldwide framework for FDI," the WIR keeps in mind.

From 1982 to 1992, the two hundred top corporations boosted their share of global Gross Domestic Product from 24.2 percent to 26.8 percent, doubling combined revenues to nearly $6 trillion, with the leading 10 taking nearly half the profits of the leading two hundred, an underestimate of concentration, since it does not appraise privately owned giants such as Cargill, UPS, and others. Meanwhile, the world's leading five hundred companies "have shed over 400,000 workers yearly over the past years notwithstanding the rise of their combined incomes," Frederic Clairmont and John Cavanagh observe. The phenomenon is reflected in the United States; in 1992, the first year of a mild recovery, the service pages reported that "America is refraining from doing well; however, its corporations are doing just great," with corporate revenues "striking brand-new highs as revenue margins expand."

The strength of personal power and the shady character of "trade" is highlighted even more in an idea of the National Academy of Sciences that "exports" from the United States be determined in regards to total sales of U.S.-based firms, anywhere the factories are located.

In an essential vital analysis of the GATT, World Bank financial experts Herman Daly and Robert Goodland mention that in prevailing economic theory, "companies are islands of main planning in a sea of market relationships." "As the islands grow," they keep in mind, "there is no factor to claim triumph for the marketplace concept," particularly as the islands approach the scale of the sea, which departs drastically from free enterprise principles, and continuously because the powerful will not submit to these damaging guidelines.

U.S. attitudes towards "open market" are shown even more by its dependence on embargo and sanctions as weapons against its Third World enemies from democratic capitalist Guatemala and Chile to Cuba, Vietnam, Nicaragua, and other criminals. Of 116 cases of sanctions used since World War II, 80 percent were initiated by the United States alone. These procedures, which radically break free trade doctrine, have frequently received worldwide condemnation, including decisions of the World Court and GATT council. Hence the United States might retaliate if it feels that Nicaragua discriminates against it.

Nicaragua can impose sanctions on the United States and even demand the reparations required by the World Court, abandoned by Nicaragua under U.S. danger. As acknowledged by the founders of the Chicago school before it was taken control of by ideological extremists, "liberty without power, like power without liberty, has no compound or meaning," another truism muffled in the enthusiastic "free enterprise" chorus.

Evaluating Chile's "economic miracle," Latin Americanist Cathy Schneider remarks that, quite apart from the standard economic functions of market reforms, significantly increasing poverty rates, inequality, and the transformation of the financial and political system has an extensive effect on the world view of the common Chilean.

 Many Chileans today, whether they own a little, precarious business or subcontract their labor on a short-lived basis, work alone. They are dependent on their effort and the growth of the economy. They have little contact with other employees or with neighbors, and only limited time with their household. Their exposure to political or labor companies is minimal. Except for some crucial public-service sectors such as healthcare [which the fascist rulers were not able to demolish in the face of widespread resistance], they lack either the resources or the disposition to face the state. The fragmentation of opposition neighborhoods has achieved what brute military repression could not. It has transformed Chile, both culturally and politically, from a country of active participatory grassroots neighborhoods, to a land of disconnected, apolitical individuals. The cumulative effect of this change is such that we are not likely to see any collective difficulty in the nearest future.

Today era stimulates memories of essential periods of the past. The passionate resort to classical (now "neoliberal") financial doctrine as a weapon of class war is a striking example. Another is the resort to brand-new innovation to develop a kind of "development without individuals," not as an effect of the nature of innovation or the pursuit of effectiveness and cost-effectiveness, as David Noble has shown in crucial work-noting, for example, that the extreme inefficiencies of automation needed to be masked through the typical resort to the Pentagon system of public aid and market distortion. As in the early industrial transformation, the innovation is created to increase revenue and power, ownership, and supervisory control at the cost of significant work, freedom, human life, and welfare; other social arrangements might develop its liberatory capacity.

The nature of the experiment is illustrated by a report of the International Labor Organization, which approximates that about 30 percent of the world's workforce was unemployed in January 1994, unable to earn enough to sustain a minimum standard of life. This "long-lasting relentless joblessness" is a crisis of the scale of the Great Depression, the ILO concludes.

Vast unemployment persists together with big needs for labor. Wherever one looks, there is work to be done of excellent social and human worth, and there are a lot of people excited to do that work. The financial system can not bring together essential work and the idle hands of suffering people. Its concept of "financial health" is geared to the needs of earnings, not the requirements of individuals.

In short, the economic system is a devastating failure. It is hailed as a grand success, as it is for a narrow sector of privileged individuals, including those who state its virtues and accomplishments.

How far can this go?

Will it indeed be possible to construct an international society on something like the Third World design, with islands of fantastic opportunity in a sea of misery, fairly large islands, in the richer nations, and with controls of a totalitarian nature within democratic forms that significantly become a facade?

Or will popular resistance, which must itself end up being internationalized to be successful, be able to take apart these developing structures of violence and domination, and bring forth the centuries-old procedure of growth of flexibility, justice, and democracy that is now being terminated, even reversed?

These are the significant concerns for the future!!!

CHAPTER TWELVE

Fixing the Fight

Many people who are a member of a particular political party believe that whatever that their party does or stands for is right, which whatever that the opposing party stands for is wrong. This same "us vs. them" attitude, is also directed towards popular members in each political party and party leaders. Republican fans think that the Democratic celebration and management are foolish, inexperienced, and often criminal while thinking that members of the Republican party are saints and have the individuals' best interests in mind. The same is real of Democratic advocates because they blindly view their party as above reproach and see the opposing party as incompetent, ideologically incorrect, and sometimes criminal.

This false, left/right paradigm averts many people from seeing that the same private interests control the management at the top of both political parties. The Illuminati own both horses in the race, so to speak, as was highlighted in the 2004 governmental election when both John Kerry and George W. Bush were taking on against each other for the presidency. Both are members of the ultra-elite Illuminati branch, the Skull and Bones society.

The man credited with founding the Illuminati in 1776, Adam Weishaupt, wrote, "By this strategy we will direct all humanity.

In this manner, and by the most basic methods, we shall set all in motion and flames. The occupations should be contrived and so allotted, that we may, in trick, influence all political transactions."

" This can be performed in no other way, however by secret associations, which will by degrees, and in silence, possess themselves of the government of the States, and use those methods for this function."

"The Order will, for its own sake, and for that reason definitely, place every man because circumstance in which he can be most reliable. The pupils are encouraged that the Order will rule the world. Every member therefore becomes a ruler.".

Sciences may have an impact on our reception in the world, and might serve to get rid of challenges out of the way. Only those who are assuredly appropriate subjects will be selected among the inferior classes for the greater mysteries. Specifically, every individual will be made a spy on another and all around him.

Nothing can leave our sight; by these means, we will readily find those who are satisfied and relish the strange state-doctrines and spiritual opinions that are laid before them; and, at last, the trustworthy alone will be admitted to the involvement of the fundamental maxims and political constitution of the Order.

" In a council composed of such members we shall labor at the contrivance of ways to drive by degrees the enemies of factor and mankind out of the world, and to establish a strange morality and religious beliefs suitable for the great Society of humanity.".

High-level Republicans and Republican presidents are the right foot of the Illuminati, and Democrats are the left foot. One foot takes an advance, then the other, and the procedure is repeated as the two feet interact to move the Illuminati forward to accomplish their objectives. Both liberal and conservative political leaders are privately aiding. This is why we find politicians and presidents whose actions are inconsistent with their party or the pledges they made on the project path. George W. Bush, a supposed conservative, increased government investing more than all previous administrations combined. While always talking about keeping America safe from terrorists, he declined to increase border security. He knocked the Minute Men, who voluntarily patrol the U.S. Mexican border, as "vigilantes."

The owners of the NFL (National Football League) couldn't care less which group wins the Super Bowl each year, because no matter which team it is, the NFL earns money. The Illuminati is the same way when it comes to politics. The president of the United States resembles a manager at a junk food dining establishment. He seems to be the one in charge and takes the impact of client problems, but he is simply working for someone who the people will never see or never hear about. The junk food manager is working for the franchise owner, just as the president of the United States is merely a spokesperson who is carrying out the orders and plans of his employer, which stays unseen by the public. This boss is obviously, the Illuminati.

CHAPTER THIRTEEN

Spiritual Beliefs

It is typically said that the Illuminati is "satanic" or Luciferian, which seems astounding to somebody new to this material as the majority of people understand that such claims are frequently met suspicion, disbelief, or outright ridicule. When one takes a more detailed look and understands simply what Satanism and Luciferianism are, such claims might not just seem reasonable; however, they are undeniable. First, we should take a look at the story of Adam and Eve to start to comprehend this.

While Christians, Jews, and lots of others think that the first humans disobeyed God in the Garden of Eden by following the advice of Satan, the Illuminati (and every occult association, fraternity, or secret society) thinks that Satan saved Adam and Eve from enslavement to God, who they state was keeping back Mankind's right capacity and keeping Adam and Eve sent to prison in ignorance.

Many religious beliefs have an esoteric and an exoteric doctrine, one analysis for the masses, and another teaching with more in-depth or various interpretations for the scholars or religious insiders, often called "adepts" or "the elect." In Judaism, this "second" teaching is called the Midrash, which goes "beyond" the "basic" and "legal" analyses of the Torah (the Old Testament) and gives an "expanded view" of the Bible's stories.

In a book, The Wisdom of the Knowing Ones, Manly P. Hall explains, "all of these faiths had been divided into two areas, one of which was for the general public and the other a mystical or esoteric custom for a few who were ready to consecrate their lives through a procedure of internal enlightenment. For the many, there was obedience to the kinds and letters of religious law. For the few, there was an insight into the much deeper significances of these things byways of which orthodoxies were transformed into great spiritual systems."

Lucifer and Satan.

The biggest trick of the Illuminati is that they believe Satan is great because, in their view, he is the "exceptional God." This secret has enhanced them with remarkable power. Helena Blavatsky, in her 1888 book The Secret Doctrine, discusses, "Thus Lucifer-- the spirit of Intellectual Enlightenment and Freedom of Thoughts metaphorically the assisting beacon, which assists male to find his way through the rocks and sandbanks of Life, for Lucifer is the Logos in his greatest."

She continues, "Lucifer is terrestrial and magnificent light, the 'Holy Ghost' and 'Satan,' at the same time, visible area being filled with differentiated breath undetectably; and the Astral Light, the manifested efforts of two who are one, directed and attracted by ourselves, is the karma of humanity, both a personal and impersonal entity. The Fall was the result of man's knowledge, for his 'eyes were opened.' Indeed, he was taught wisdom and the surprise knowledge by the 'Fallen Angel.'

And now it stands proven that Satan, or the Red Fiery Dragon, the "Lord of Phosphorus" (brimstone was a doctrinal enhancement), and Lucifer, or 'Light-Bearer,' remains in us: it is our Mind, our tempter and Redeemer, our smart liberator and Savior from pure animalism. Without this Quickening spirit, or human Mind or soul, there would be no distinction between guy and monster."

The Secret Doctrine states, "For no one, not even the greatest living proficient, would be allowed to, or could even if he would provide promiscuously, to a mocking, unbelieving world, that which has been so effectively concealed from it for long eons and ages."

Such views can likewise be thought about Gnosticism, a philosophical belief that a lower level wicked god called the Demiurge developed human beings as slaves. To complement the enslavement, they should be given the secret knowledge (gnosis) from a higher God (Satan). Manly.P. Hall explains, "Gnostics never wanted salvation from sin (initial or other), but rather they desired release from unconsciousness and incomprehension, whereby they indicated mostly lack of knowledge of spiritual truths. Redemption (or freedom) is a prospective present in every man and woman, and it is not vicarious, however, individual. The great Messengers of the

Light concerned stimulate this perspective, and they do not live by their death, however, by their lives."

Those who believe they have found this "secret to life" frequently keep it contained within occult fraternities, wanting to keep the large majority of people oblivious of their supposed "reality" so they can keep others from ending up being "enlightened" so they can more quickly benefit from them. This sort of spiritual supremacism frequently results in Social Darwinism, which is the viewpoint of the survival of the fittest. These people have no concern for their fellow guy; however, they are conceited, megalomaniacs who see themselves as Gods due to Satan's trick. This supremacy complex is communicated by the "do what thou wilt" approach that Aleister Crowley and Church of Satan founder Anton LaVey preached, which suggests "do whatever you want" because you are your own God.

In his authorized bio "The Secret Life of a Satanist," it was exposed that Anton LaVey wasn't concerned if Satanism motivated individuals to devote mass murder. It checks out, "Anton LaVey preserves that he isn't truly worried about allegations of people killing other individuals in the name of Satan. He swears that each time he reads a new killing spree, his only response is, 'What, 22 people? Is that all? There will unquestionably be more Satanically-motivated murders and criminal activities in the sense that The Satanic Bible informs you 'You do not need to take any more shit.'"

LaVey likewise admired a homosexual serial killer from the early 1900s named Carl Panzram, who killed at least twenty-two people, and who claimed to have raped one thousand men. "The only way I would like to.' help' the great majority of individuals is the same method Carl Panzram' reformed' individuals who attempted to reform him. It would be most merciful to assist them by easing them of the life they seem to dislike so much. People ought to be delighted I'm not a humanitarian I'd probably be the most wicked mass murderer the world has ever known," LaVey stated.

Richard Ramirez, the "Night Stalker" serial killer from Los Angeles, and Charles Manson were interested in Satanism. Ramirez notoriously drew a hellish pentagram on the palm of his hand throughout his trial and would scream "Hail Satan!" to electronic tv cameras and press reporters.

Because Satanists do not think in an afterlife or an all-knowing, all- effective God, they are not interested in any type of magnificent retribution for their actions. They are thus inspired even more to ruthlessly make the most of others, considering that they think is the "survival of the fittest," which "might be ideal" as they see themselves as Gods.

This "royal trick" of Satanism will likely one day soon be exposed to the world after being practiced in secret for countless years. The Illuminati and the counterfeit (anti) Christ will likely openly expose Satanism as the new World Religion and declare it had to be kept a secret all these years till the New World Order was complete. Anyone who knocks this antichrist or the new World Religion will be targeted for termination and will be blamed for attempting to stop the conclusion of "paradise on earth.".

Double Speak.

The Illuminati often use "doublespeak" to conceal their genuine agenda and present effective propaganda to the masses who typically blindly accept it as the reality without a doubt. The public has been so dumbed down; they will think anything their preferred political celebration tells them and are quickly misguided by language and rhetoric indicated to camouflage the speaker's real intents. The Department of Defense is the Department of War, and that's what it used to be called up until the government altered its name in 1949.

The Patriot Act, the expense signed into law soon after the September 11th attacks on the World Trade Center in 2001, was an assault on the Bill of Rights and anything, however patriotic. Still, the term Patriot Act was developed to make the brand-new laws sound American as the Fourth of July. President Bush started a "War on Terror" when it was a "War of Terror." President Obama said that raising the debt ceiling wouldn't increase our country's debt when that's precisely what it does; however, since the masses have become zombies who respond to keywords or neuro-linguistic programs language patterns, many people accept statements from presidents as reality without hesitating.

The Hegelian Dialectic

Because the elite Illuminati are social Darwinist Satanists, they typically use the Hegelian Dialectic, which enables them to present their wicked plans with little opposition. What this requires is developing a problem on purpose through concealed ways so the federal government can then provide their option, which is a strategy they had waiting in the wings but were not able to carry out without the correct crisis, which was needed to justify their wanted actions.

The Hegelian Dialectic includes a thesis, an antithesis, and a synthesis, or an issue, a response, and a solution. This is the standard structure of a false flag operation, which is a military strategy where a federal government commits a terrorist act while making it appear as if it came from their political enemy or they allow a terrorist attack to take place when they might have quickly stopped it, since the success of the occasion works as a pretext (a reason) to bring out actions that formerly would have been widely inappropriate by the public. Still, after the attack occurs, much of the general public needs that a response occurs, all the while unaware that behind the scenes, the entire operation was prepared to get that specific support that was doing not have before the attack occurred.

Just three days after the 9/11 attacks, the co-chair of the Council on Foreign Relations specified, "There is a chance for the President of the United States to use the catastrophe to perform an expression his father used. I

This attack was the "New Pearl Harbor" event talked about in the Project for the New American Century think tank's own Rebuilding America's Defenses report released in September of 2000. From this Illuminati front group came the very plan explaining their need for a "catalyzing event, new Pearl Harbor," which would be used to set the phase for America to bring out the Illuminati's plan by invading the Middle East to finish the New World Order.

In 1962, a false flag attack strategy was drawn up by top U.S. military officials. They desired to dedicate numerous acts of fear in Washington D.Cand in Miami that would be made to appear as if Cuba had done them, to generate public support for an invasion of Cuba. Operation Northwoods, as it was called, clearly specified, "We could establish a Communist Cuban horror campaign in the Miami location, in other Florida cities, and even in Washington. The terror project might be pointed at Cuban refugees seeking haven in the United States.

Hijacking attempts against civil aircraft surface area craft ought to appear to continue as harassing procedures condoned by the federal government of Cuba.".

When confronted with such damning evidence, most people instantly dismiss it as a "**conspiracy theory**" however the Operation Northwoods documents have been declassified and are 100% authentic. The plan was even reported on ABC News in 2001 on their site where the short article checks out, "In the early 1960s, America's leading military leaders supposedly prepared strategies to kill innocent individuals and dedicate acts of terrorism in U.S. cities to create public assistance for a war versus Cuba."

For people still skeptical about the September 11th inside job, all they need is to read the Northwoods documents and understand that plans like this have been put on paper and approved by the Joint Chiefs of Staff (the heads of all U.S. military branches). Similar attacks have been performed by federal governments throughout history, such as Operation Gladio throughout Europe, the Gleiwitz occurrence and the Reichstag fire in Germany, the Gulf of Tonkin event in Vietnam, and others.

Henry Kissinger has been intimately included with almost every significant organization or front group that lags the push for a New World Order and was initially named the Chairman of the 9/11 Commission by President Bush, which was established to (pretend to) investigate the terrorist attacks on September 11th,

2001. Kissinger resigned from the commission after the relative of 9/11 victims found his company ties with the Bin Ladens.234 In an interview on CNBC in February 2009, Kissinger was inquired about the problems the Obama administration was facing relating to the ongoing "War on Terror" and the economic crisis, where he reacted that Obama "can give new impetus to American foreign policy partly because the reception of him is so remarkable worldwide. His task will be to develop a total technique for America in this period when a New World Order can be created. It's a great opportunity; it isn't simply a crisis.".

President Obama's Chief of Staff Rahm Emanual made a surprising statement after the economic crash of 2008, when he stated, "You never let a severe crisis go to waste. And what I mean by that it's an opportunity to do things you believe you could not do previously."

Because we're talking about power-mad megalomaniac Satanists here, it should not come as a surprise that these men would orchestrate fear attacks to acquire more power and further their political programs. And it's not a surprise that many of these males have ties to occult cabals like Skull & Bones, Freemasonry, or the Bohemian Grove, all of which are incubators for corruption and keepers of the fantastic "trick of tricks.".

Sex Magic.

Sex magick (with a "k" on end) is the belief that through secret sexual intercourse rituals, one can accomplish transformed states of consciousness which trigger dormant esoteric powers locked inside the mind, apparently allowing the practitioners to harness God-like symptom abilities in what has been described as a conscious, living lucid dream. As strange as this concept might be, it isn't necessarily a criminal offense for two consenting adults to participate in bizarre sex acts. Still, regrettably some horrific and very disgusting kinds of sex magic are beyond evil, and I caution you, what you are about to check out is very troubling.

In parts of Africa, many men believe if they rape an albino lady, it will provide great power. "There is a belief that if you have [intercourse] relations with a woman with albinism, you will treat AIDS. So there are many girls with albinism who are being raped in [Africa] because of this belief," stated Peter Ash, creator of human rights group Under The Same Sun.

In 2013 the vocalist of a famous heavy metal band in the United Kingdom called Lost Prophets was sentenced to thirty-five years in jail for thirteen child sex offenses consisting of sexually abusing children in black magic rituals. Several women were likewise sent to prison for willingly giving him their kids to use them for this exact purpose.

In 2014 it was exposed that a group of Aleister Crowley fans were abusing children in an England suburban area by doing

Satanic sex rituals. Jacqueline Marling even turned her child over to the cult and required her to get involved in sex magic rituals starting when she was simply seven years of age.

Such insane and evil sex magic practices aren't just consisted of primitive tribes in Africa or twisted rock stars or Aleister Crowley fans. It seems among the inmost and darkest tricks of the Illuminati also. Obviously in some sects within the Illuminati starts to think this sort of kid abuse can "supercharge" their "metaphysical powers," allowing them to conjure into their life whatever they want, in a perverted variation of the "Law of Attraction," the viewpoint popularized by the DVD The Secret in 2006.

In the 1990s, a Republican Nebraska State Senator named John DeCamp released a book entitled The Franklin Cover-Up. He declared kids were taken into the Bohemian Grove and ritualistically raped and murdered in black magic routines at the hands of some of the members in the1980s. DeCamp, an attorney, stated he interviewed several children from orphanages who supposedly determined the Bohemian Grove as the location of this supposed abuse.

Former CIA director Bill Colby is stated to have cautioned DeCamp that he was looking into something so dark he must leave and "Get as far away from this thing as you can. Forget you ever saw it or know it, heard it, or anything else." Colby later died in a canoeing accident, but many suspect he was murdered because of the strange circumstances surrounding his death and his conversations with DeCamp about sex magic. There were no witnesses to his death, and he drowns after mysteriously going canoeing by himself.

In 1989 the Washington Times printed a front-page headline reading, "Homosexual Prostitution InTuiry Ensnares VIPs with Reagan and Bush," after discovering a high-powered lobbyist named Craig Spence was operating a pedophile prostitution ring in the Washington D.C. area that catered to elite clients. Spence turned up dead a few months after the article was published from an alleged suicide. Whispers of select pedophile rings have alleged for decades that high-powered politicians and business people engage in child abuse for fun or part of secret society rituals.

This same dark cloud has hung over the heads of Catholic priests for many decades.

A major star at the BBC in England (the British Broadcasting Corporation) named Jimmy Savile reportedly abused hundreds of children, some as young as two-years-old, and even had sex with dead bodies, according to the Washington Post and other mainstream media outlets. Such news leads many to believe this kind of activity is part of an organized network of powerful perpetrators, not just separate incidences.

It's unknown how common these kinds of sex magic rituals are within the Illuminati or other Aleister Crowley-inspired groups. When one tries to understand why anyone would even consider doing such a thing, it challenges the mind to answer. These perpetrators aren't just sick psychopaths living in an abandoned cabin in the woods. These are successful men (and possibly women) who are addicted to power and wealth and fuel their ego with all of the most refined pleasures of this world, often becoming desensitize. So jade died, they are eventually unable to find excitement or joy in anything usual.

Since these acts of sexual abuse are the worst thing anyone could do to another human being, these acts of ultimate evil are believed to cause some kind of hormones to be released into the blood, which gives the perpetrators a kind of satanic adrenaline rush that magnifies their supposed ability to alter reality metaphysically by their thoughts, thus being the most potent "supernatural steroid" in the world. There is no doubt why sex magic is considered the deepest and darkest secret of the Illuminati. Any human being with a soul can agree that sex offenders of all kinds must be eradicated from the earth.

CHAPTER FOURTEEN

Transhumanism

Among the ultimate goals of the Illuminati is to become Gods themselves in what they think is the final stage of their development or "transcendence." This branch of science is called Transhumanism, indicating supporters want to shift from a human into a brand-new species or go beyond into a "God." 249 This isn't just a lofty sci-fi pipe dream of a couple of megalomaniacs with God complexes; this is a genuine strategy pursued by some powerful and extremely wealthy people. Billionaire Peter Thiel, the co-founder of PayPal and early financier on Facebook, thinks scientists will quickly "cure death," enabling him and other billionaires to live forever. "You can accept (death), you can deny it, or you can fight it. I believe our society is dominated by individuals who are into rejection or approval, and I choose to combat it."

The most famous "guru" of Transhumanism (often symbolized as H+) is Google engineer Ray Kurz Weil who believes by the year 2045, he and other elite will attain immortality through cybernetic improvements that transform them into actual supercomputing cyborgs who are physically wired into the Internet at all times, and even changing their biological brains and bodies completely with "more effective" silicone computer systems and mechanical bodies to "transcend." Kurzweil predicts, "As you head out to the 2040s, now the bulk of our thinking is out in the cloud. The biological portion of our brain didn't disappear; however, the nonbiological part will be far more effective. And it will be submitted automatically the way we support whatever now that's digital."

In 2013 Google produced Calico, a life extension and anti-aging biotech company, to help them pursue Kurz Weil's imagine beating death, and many other business are putting billions of dollars into transhumanist innovation and working non-stop, wishing to open immortality soon.

Transhumanist philosopher Zoltan Istvan, who thinks that mentor kids about the Bible ought to be prohibited which the federal government must manage who is enabled to have children, writes, "The transhumanist age, where revolutionary science and technology will revolutionize the person and experience will ultimately bring us indefinite life-spans,cyborgization, cloning, and even ectogenesis, where people use synthetic wombs outside of their bodies to raise fetuses. Breeding controls and procedures make more sense when you think about that some leading life extensionist scientists think we will conquer human death in the next20 years."

These "reproducing controls" likewise seem to align with the Georgia Guidestones, the 19-foot-tall granite monument requiring a world population decrease to 500 million people to protect the earth's natural resources. The idea is, if the life-extension technology extends individuals' lives by centuries or more, the elite feel they require to save the world's resources for themselves, because as CNN founder Ted Turner states, "There are lots of people using too many things, if there were fewer individuals, they'd be using less stuff."

The strange man behind the odd structure recommended transhumanism in a little recognized book he published quickly after the stones were put up in 1980. "We recommend that scholars throughout the world begin now to develop new bases upon which later on generations can establish a new universal language for men and devices. It will be adapted to our speaker system and the language professors and patterns impressed in our nerve systems. Its spoken and printed types will be capable of accurate interchange by electromechanical means," wrote R.C. Christian, a confessed pseudonym.

On the within cover of the book, titled Common Sense Renewed, it states the very first two writings were sent to several thousand politicians and "shapers of public viewpoint" around the world. Aside from confessing he represented the unnamed group responsible for creating the Georgia Guidestones, the author says part of their function is that, "The hearts of our human household need to be touched and warmed to invite an international guideline by reason."

Several of the "guides," or commandments as many individuals call them, aside from decreasing to human population down to500 million (which is more than a 90% decrease from 2014 levels), suggest producing a worldwide government, a worldwide universal language, and the last of the 10 "guides," engraved in 8 various languages on the faces of the stones, warns people to not be a "cancer on the earth.".

The elite's insane dreams of ending up being God get even more terrible the better you look into them. Richard Seed, a leading geneticist and transhumanist promoter, stated, "God made man in his image. God meant for man to end up being one with God. We are going to end up being one with God. We are going to have nearly as much knowledge and almost as much power as God. Cloning and the reprogramming of DNA is the first severe action in turning into one with God."

Regarding the resistance to such strategies, he ominously stated, "We are going to end up being Gods. Get off if you do not like it. You do not have to contribute, you don't need to take part, but if you are going to disrupt me becoming a God, you will have difficulty. There'll be warfare."

Illuminati Transhumanists think what Satan informed Adam and Eve in the Garden of Eden will quickly occur, that they will become all-knowing, all-powerful, immortal Gods. They will rule the world earth permanently and ever.

This New Age philosophy falls in line with their Social Darwinist "survival of the fittest" psychologically. While history is filled with a long list of males who have thought they were Gods from the ancient pharaohs in Ancient Egypt to Adolf Hitlertoday, the elite, and much of the public, anxiously await the Singularity and think they will soon achieve their Luciferian transition into a God, simply as Satan promised humanity so long back.

CHAPTER FIFTEEN

Economic Control

The majority of people do not have the faintest clue about what money is, how it is created, and how it functions in a society. The monetary system is so complex, lots of people chose not to learn how it works. The Dow Jones Industrial Average, Stocks, Bonds, Treasury Bills, put choices, 401k, IRAs, CDs, interest rates, inflation, the Department of the Treasury, the Federal Reserve, and so on etc. It's a lot to absorb.

You will typically hear individuals say, "the middle class is shrinking" or "the middle class is going to disappear," and the question is how that might happen. When you comprehend that the Illuminati's central means of power is by controlling money, and when you learn more about the systems they use to do this, a clearer understanding of personal and international finances will happen.

The Illuminati learned as far back as the twelfth century that they could lend money to people and governments, and after that, charge them interest on the cash that they had loaned them, thus making cash without working. Many people at that time, and even today, need to offer a service or product to show it to somebody else than thinking about that product or service, and that way, earn a profit. People worked to construct things, grow food, or offer various services consisting of preparing cleansing, food, or feeding and tending to animals.

When civilization was developing, if someone grew corn, they might trade a bushel of corn for a cow to a farmer who raised cows. They could likewise trade that bushel of corn to a man who assembled clothing in exchange for a brand-new set of trousers and some shoes. This is referred to as the barter system. There would be a problem if the man who grew corn desired to trade the corn for a cow; however, the farmer with the cow didn't desire any corn, but rather wanted some wheat, which the corn grower didn't have. For this factor, people settled on a medium of exchange. This medium of exchange, we'll use gold coins, for example, was something that they could trade their corn for, and after that, take the gold coins and trade those coins for a cow, or for whatever else they wanted that was for sale at the marketplace. The better the item or service was that they provided, the more gold coins they would exchange for that item or service. Throughout history, several items have been used as money, such as seashells, stones, and gold coins. This item would have to be rare enough so that people could create more of it, hence producing complimentary money for themselves. For thousands of years, gold and silver coins have been a primary circulating medium since their rarity and trouble counterfeit.

Metal coins were typically a problem to bring, so a system was designed where people would kip down their gold or silver to a bank. In return, they would get paper currency, which represented the amount of gold and silver they deposited. At any time, people might return to the bank and trade in their fiat money for its comparable in gold and silver. The paper currency was a receipt for the real cash that they had transferred to the bank. In the market place, people would accept these invoices as payment for items and services instead of gold and silver coins. Bankers would likewise loan out the cash (gold and silver coins) people had transferred in their vaults, and collect interest on those loans. These lenders again recognized that they could loan out cash to individuals they didn't have, and then gather the interest on those loans. Lending out cash they do not have does not seem possible; however, all they needed to do to accomplish this was to compose up a receipt and loan that out to somebody, and the person would be able to utilize that invoice in the market. Nobody would understand that it didn't represent any silver or gold that someone had transferred to the bank. It seems hard to believe, but when you comprehend how fiat currencies work, it is a genius idea on the part of the lenders. It's the supreme con, and a couple of individuals are aware of it.

This same system remains in place today and has progressed into a complex global economy, but it still runs in the same way. Hundreds of years ago, the Illuminati discovered how powerful of a system this is, which the ones who control the creation and loaning of money can have an unlimited supply of it without actually working. This is the big banking trick of the Federal Reserve System, and the factor the Illuminati have ended up being understood as international lenders.

Their supreme financial goal is to develop a socialist system where the government will manage all market, society, health care, realty, and financial resources. By building a New World Order where everybody should count on the government for tasks, health care, education, and standard services, the Illuminati will easily determine to individuals what they can and can not do. Their objective is to permanently establish a two-class society where a small portion of individuals (the Illuminati and their supporters) will own and manage all infrastructure, wealth, and realty. The rest of the world will be decreased to servants without any real possessions or power. This is similar to the caste system in ancient India where the children of a laborer was destined to be a worker, therefore would his children, and so on. Simultaneously, the upper-class caste maintains an elite and elegant way of life that their kids will enjoy, therefore will their kids' children and so on.

The New World Order will be a self-sufficient structure, and intelligent individuals wanting to prevent financial and social slavery will find it nearly impossible unless they wish to perpetuate the system. The majority of the general public will voluntarily accept their present status and economic enslavement, considering that they are entertained with telecasted home entertainment and sedated with various recommended pharmaceuticals that relieve their anxieties, distress, or desire to improve their situation. Any additional cash they have at the end of the month is generally misused away on alcohol or other products of no real value, which keeps them from accumulating any substantial assets. Interest paid on charge card debt likewise continues to siphon off cash that might be used to improve their living conditions. Many of the items acquired with those charge card were not required; however, the user's inability to resist their urge to mindlessly take in and buy exceedingly expensive items which have no purpose other than to try to communicate a social status that the individual does not have triggered them to invest compulsively.

The Illuminati's development and control of money, rates of interest, and inflation allow them to sustain economic booms, which they know will ultimately end as they hemorrhage into bubbles that break and leave a course of financial destruction behind for the average person. Because the Illuminati own genuine tangible assets, they are immune from the destructive impacts of economic bubbles rupturing or stock exchange crashing.

In 2007 and 2008, Peter Schiff, the president of Euro Pacific Capital, a brokerage firm, had been alerting that the mortgage bubble was soon to burst and the stock market would throw the nation and crash into an economic crisis or even worse. He was a relatively frequent guest on cable news programs, and his projection was always 180 degrees from the host and other visitors. At times other visitors on the sections chuckled aloud at Schiff's predictions. Schiff was selected by Congressman Ron Paul to be his financial advisor when he ran for President in2008. Schiff likewise anticipated the collapse in his 2007 Book Crash Proof: How to Profit from the Coming Economic Collapse.

One of the most respected pattern forecasters, Gerald Celente, the CEO of the Trends Research Institute, made news late in 2008 by saying that the American economy would collapse which there would be run-away inflation triggering costs for food and other goods to skyrocket, causing shortages, long lines, and federal government rate controls to prevent increasing rates on needs. Regardless of these cautions, nothing altered, and the American economy started collapsing and triggered a domino effect around the globe.

Right after the fall began, in October 2008, an unprecedented 700 billion dollar bailout for failing and having a hard time banks was proposed. Seven hundred billion is a 7 with eleven absolutely nos after it. $700,000,000,000 represented $2,300 for each male-female and child in America. Henry Paulson, the

378

Treasurer Secretary at the time, Ben Bernanke, the Chairman of the Federal Reserve, and others were saying that if the bailout didn't pass a vote which permitted it to take place, that within weeks the stock exchange would crash, and the nation would suffer inconceivable consequences.

Some members of Congress were privately told that if the bailout didn't pass a vote, America would completely break down and martial law would need to be enforced to prevent massive crime and civil unrest. Congressman Brad Sherman blew the whistle on such risks and called them unjustified fear-mongering.

California Senator Diane Feinstein publicly admitted that her workplace got 91,000 phone calls and emails about the bailout, and that 85,000 of them were opposed to it. Still, she chose the bailout anyhow because individuals were "confused" and "didn't understand it," and she did what she said was in the very best interest of the country.

After the bailout was gone by Congress, Ben Bernanke, Henry Paulson, and others decided to allot the cash to other areas instead of buying imperfect home mortgage financial obligations that they had initially proposed. The coin was currently approved by Congress, and no steps were required to hold these males to their initial pledge of where the money would go. They simply chose to spend the cash differently after the "financial stimulus" was passed, and the cash was theirs. Months later, the Fed declined to disclose the receivers of two

trillion dollars in loans, which originated from taxpayer cash, and many CEOs of stopped working banks, which received billions of taxpayer cash, were still enabled to collect their Christmas perks of millions, and sometimes 10s of millions of dollars.

In November of 2008, Barack Obama was chosen to be the next president of the United States. After being sworn into office on January 20th 2009, he quickly proposed a 2nd "economic stimulus" package, which exceeded the size of the first one, just months earlier. Contrary to good sense, president Obama and his financial advisors insisted on the American individuals that the only thing that would prevent America from entering into a depression as if the federal government would invest nearly 800 billion more dollars.

On February 13th, 2009, the 787 billion dollar "stimulus strategy" was gone by Congress without a single member, even reading it. Seriously, not a single member of Congress read the bill, however, passed it anyhow. The bill was over 1100 pages long, and from the time it was released to the time of the vote was less than 12 hours. The Obama administration had used fear-mongering to terrify Congress into passing it instantly and said if they didn't approve it, the nation and the economy would collapse. Even after the costs were passed by Congress and after that signed into law a couple of days later on by President Obama, the stock exchange kept dropping numerous points a day, and by the end of February, the Dow Jones Industrial Average had dropped more than 50% from its high a year previously to under 7000.

As an outcome of these "bailouts" and "stimulus bundles," the United States federal government has become the biggest investor in various financial organizations, thus nationalizing them. These as soon as failed banks used to be entirely independently owned and run, but can now be controlled by the government. The automobile market likewise received billions of dollars in "bailout" money and now should respond to the federal government regarding what type of automobiles and trucks to produce. The free market system and Capitalism itself have been changed with socialism as a result. The majority of the ignorant public was eased that the government was trying to "conserve the economy" from this unforeseen catastrophe, which happened due to the mortgage bubble breaking; however, in reality, the entire experience was orchestrated by the Illuminati. Lots of professionals alerted that the "stimulus" plans would only make the economy even worse. Still, the Obama administration rammed their strategies through as rapidly as they could with no oversight.

In her 1934 book, A Treatise on White Magic, Illuminati author Alice Bailey blogged about the financial control of the Illuminati, not to expose their methods, however, to educate members of the organization. She discusses," [the] group controls and orders the ways whereby he [humanity] exists, controlling all that can be transformed into energy, and constituting a dictatorship over all modes of exchange, commerce and sexual intercourse. They control the diversity of form-objects which modern male concerns as necessary to his mode of life. Cash, as I have before said, is just crystallized energy or vigor, what the Asian trainee calls pranic energy. It is a concretization of etheric force. It is; therefore, crucial energy externalized, and this form of energy is under the instructions of the monetary group. They are the most current group in point of information, and the Hierarchy most absolutely plans their work (it should be kept in mind). They are causing results upon the earth, which are most far-reaching."

Going back to the days of the Knights Templars, the Illuminati had found out how powerful they could be if they were to end up being the masters of cash and banking. War has continuously been a massive business for the Illuminati. The weapons manufacturers make a constant stream of earnings by providing the increased need, and private professionals such as Halliburton earn massive quantities of money. They are paid by the government to do tasks that can frequently be finished by the military at a portion of the cost. An effective film entitled

Iraq for Sale reveals just how much money the personal contractors are making with no-bid contracts.

Anton LaVey, the founder of the Church of Satan, had his grandson Stanton Zaharoff LaVey named after Sir Basil Zaharoff, an arms dealership. In LaVey's licensed biography, it discusses just how much he appreciated this arms dealership for his cunningness because he would sell weapons to governments of both sides of a dispute to generate income.

Such a practice has been used for decades, if not centuries. Personal banks have provided cash to governments to fund wars and conflicts. Interest is then made on these loans, making the banks a significant profit. But their plan does not end there. Throughout history, these private banks have loaned cash to both sides of a dispute, hence not just extending the dispute, however making interest from both governments that are combating each other.

The well-known stating "the love of cash is the root of all evil" can be comprehended with a deeper level of comprehending when the principles of money and loans are fully comprehended. Considering that cash is essential for today's society to operate, it ought to come as not a surprise that the Illuminati has covered its tentacles around organizations required for money to be produced and controlled.

CHAPTER SIXTEEN

TheEradicationofChristianity

Unlike theologian Martin Luther who notoriously nailed his ninety-five complaints on the door of the Castle Church of Wittenberg, Germany in 1517, thus beginning the Protestant Reformation with the hopes of ending the Catholic Church's hold on power and their corrupt un-Christian practices and perversion of Jesus' message-- Adam Weishaupt didn't value Christianity at all, and instead wanted it completely ruined.

Regardless of his strong distinctions with the Church, Martin Luther still appreciated Jesus and his teachings and merely desired to reform the Church. Still, Weishaupt wanted the Church and Christianity entirely eradicated.

According to John Robison, It requires little argument to prove that the Order of Illuminati had the abolishing of Christianity, for its immediate things, with the sole view of reversing the civil government, by introducing universal dissoluteness and profligacy [careless] manners, and then getting the help of the corrupted subjects to oversee the throne. The entire conduct in the preparation and instruction of the Presbyter and Regens [degrees] is directed to this point.

Another letter written by Baron von Knigge said, "I have been at unwearied pains to remove the fears of some who think that our

Superiors want to eliminate Christianity, but by and by their prejudices will disappear, and they will be more at their ease." He goes on to write that he made sure not to let them understand that "our General [Weishaupt] holds all Religion to be a lie, and uses even Deism, just to lead people by the nose."

Weishaupt states, "But I assure you this is no little affair; a new religion, and a new government, which so happily discuss one and all of these signs, and combines them in one degree.

The plan to destroy Christianity can be seen today with the liberal media and the gay mafia pushing homosexuality in everyone's face and then implicating Christians of "hate speech" and "bigotry" if they just disagree with gay marriage homosexual couples adopting kids.

There is a double standard in the mainstream media regarding what is considered "hate speech". When popular artists or liberal political analysts spew despiteful anti-Christian rhetoric continuously, such different attacks are touted as "understandable payback" for Tuition centuries ago. Imagine if significant media figures were to make the same vicious statements about Jews as they do Christians. Their professions would be over before the end of the day, and they would be forever branded an "anti-Semite" and never work again.

A popular reverend called Jedediah Morse preached a series of preachings between 1798 and 1799 in New England where he warned about the Illuminati's attack on Christianity in Boston and the surrounding location, saying, "Practically all of the civil and ecclesiastical establishments of Europe have already been shaken to their foundations by this awful organization; the French Revolution itself is doubtless to be traced to its machinations; the successes of the French armies are to be described on the same ground. The Jacobins are nothing more nor less than the open symptom of the covert system of the Illuminati. The Order has its branches developed and its emissaries at work in America. The Jacobin Societies affiliated in America have had as the objective of their establishment the propagation of the principles of the lit-up mother club located in France

Despite your personal spiritual beliefs, you need to admit that Christians have been (and continue to be) the primary opposition to the Illuminati and the New World Order (not to point out the coming Mark of the Beast), and are the last barrier standing in between the Illuminati and their remaining goals. Christians have long alerted about the "satanic conspiracy" being perpetrated by the Illuminati and have been on the cutting edge of the culture war being waged by Hollywood, which aims to destroy what little bit morality is left in the society.

CHAPTER SEVENTEEN

1000 Years of peace

The Millennium Begins

This is the age of which poets have dreamed. Men have labored; they have attempted many plans and developed many panaceas in their hope of constructing a utopian world. They have stopped continuously working. Repetitive efforts have been put forth by statesmen to develop a world government. It was the League of Nations; at its death, the United Nations took its location. The U. N. disappears effective than the very first attempt.

Today an awful peril faces the world. Nuclear warfare, with its horrible power to eliminate whole cities in a matter of seconds, hangs over civilization like the sword of Damocles. Huge amounts of hydrogen bombs with deadly power determined in megatons, or countless loads of TNT, have been prepared, all set at the push of a button to damage entire countries. These perils have been considered in previous volumes.

Nonetheless, man will not be allowed to ruin the world. After the fears of Armageddon are over and judgment has cleaned the earth of its iniquities, the Lord of heaven will come forth and establish His kingdom, which shall withstand permanently. We are informed that Christ and His saints shall reign and rule for 1000 years on this earth, after which time will merge into the brand-new paradises and the brand-new world of eternity. To the occasions of this thousand years, the golden era, we will now resolve ourselves.

All signs indicate the truth that this 20th century will wind up the age. Without recommendation to Bible prophecy, noted ecologists, scientists and authors, inform us that this present civilization can not endure beyond the year 2001 A.D. The population surge has become a grim factor that we can not disregard. Even in the last decade, the population increased from three billion to 3,600,000,000. This increase of 600,000,000 is more than the total population of the earth after 57 centuries from Adam. Pollution has ended up being another scenario that is quickly making the earth unviable. The atomic bomb danger is the most fearful of all because countries now have ways of destroying the entire population of the world (Matt. 24:21 -22).

Additionally, according to Bible chronology, the year 2001 A.D. will complete 6000 years of man's week. Four thousand years from Adam to Christ and the subsequent 2,000 years include up to 6,000 years. The Millennium, the earth's Sabbath of a thousand years, finishes the 7,000 years of male's span. Seemingly the years between 2001 and 3001 A.D. will mark the Millennium.

Earth's Population Greatly Reduced

The number of individuals remaining on the earth at the start of the Millennium will be considerably minimized in number. According to Revelation 6:8, the "pale horse," death, during the Great Tribulation, will cut off one-fourth of the world's population. According to Revelation 9:18, one of the excellent Trumpet Judgments will take away a third of those left. But there are lots of other judgments. The righteous who survived the Tribulation have been gotten rid of from the earth at the coming of Christ (Matt. 24:29 -31; Luke 21:36).

There might be no Millennium were it not that Satan, the old snake who has deceived humanity for so long, will be cast into the endless pit to remain there for the entire thousand years. The Scriptures reveal that this pit has been a place of confinement of devils and wicked angels. Revelation 9 speaks of devils' being released from the pit at the time of the apocalyptic judgments. Now angelic forces suppress Satan and his fans and confine them in this endless jail. There is no possibility of escape. Satan is not just chained; however, the upper egress of the void is sealed. Satan, ejected from heaven in the eons past, was at the beginning of the Great Tribulation erupted of the heavenly. Now merely before the beginning of the Millennium, he will be cast down into this dark pit, no doubt to lash about in a fury, however impotent to do anything. He will brood and strategy brand-new plans of deception for the time that he will be launched for that little season at the close of the Millennium.

It is not directly specified that the satanic force spirits will be incarcerated with him. There is little doubt about this. The wicked spirits that talked with Jesus in the country of the Gadarenes comprehended that the time was coming when they too would be cast into the pit (Luke 8:31).

There is a teaching abroad that the Millennium has currently been going on for the previous thousand years. This is indeed a naughty teaching. The devil will be bound throughout the 1,000 year Millennium as the Scripture specifies. How could any sane individual reason that the devil is bound at present? Evil spirits still possess bodies; witchcraft, including sorcery, is being practiced today, consisting of devil praise.

The imprisonment of Satan will have a salutary and remarkable impact on the world. He will be enabled to deceive the countries no more during the thousand years. Individuals of the world will, therefore, be devoid of his pernicious influence. The misconceptions and incorrect teachings of our present-day will have no place during the thousand years of Christ's reign.

The Period of Reconstruction

The prevalent destruction throughout the Great and Terrible Day of the Lord will need a considerable length of time for cleansing and repair. Wherever war has touched a place, the majority of its excellent cities will depend on ruins. The wreckage will be everywhere. For example, in Israel, after the Battle of Armageddon, seven months will be needed to remove and bury the dead who lost their lives in the terrific battle (Ezek. 39:11 -16). When it comes to the particles resulting from the conflict, it will require seven years to eliminate it and bring back the land to its original condition (verse 9). No doubt cleansing away the remains of the destruction and the restoring of the cities will occupy several years as held in devastated nations after the late war.

The new cities which will spring up no doubt will be constructed on a plan appropriate to the new social order. Those corrupt institutions which today are dedicated to breaking the laws of God will be evident by their absence.

Science and Invention

Some may envision that numerous inventions and scientific achievements will be gotten rid of during the Millennium. We do not think this will hold. God developed these laws in nature and meant that they must be used for the advantage of humanity. We may expect science and creation to reach its zenith during the Millennial age. The laws of the physical universe will no longer be prostituted for wicked uses. The television screen, which can connect the world no longer will be a medium for those wicked and disgusting programs which deteriorate the audiences that view them. It shall have many worthy uses for the advantage of the generations of the new period.

We may assume that the progress of science will continue during the Millennium. A substantial declaration regarding this is made in Zechariah 14:16:

"And it shall happen, that every one that is left of all the nations which came versus Jerusalem shall even go up from year to year to worship the King, the Lord of hosts, and to keep the feast of tabernacles."

The yearly banquet is analogous to the Lord's Supper of the church. It is both memorial and prophetic. It points forward to the kingdom-rest of Israel. As a memorial, it will be observed not just by Israel, however by all countries. They will increase to Jerusalem from year to year to worship the Lord. It will represent yearly conventions that are held by different Christian societies. The point here is that such a world convention would have been challenging in Bible days with transport then offered.

There are a half-million individuals each year that now go to Israel during the tourist season! The giant 747, now in service with nearly 400 individuals, can carry travelers from New York to Tel Aviv in 11 hours. Such centers were never dreamed of at the Millenium. Today we see how the prediction of Zechariah can quickly be satisfied. We require not to translate the Scripture to suggest that everybody will go to Israel each year. Just delegates or agents representing the families of the earth will make the journey.

Atomic energy quotes to supplant the nonrenewable fuel sources in time. The atomic energy in a pound of uranium surpasses by millions of times the energy released by burning a pound of coal. No doubt, the practical means of removing power from the aspect hydrogen, a trick at present held by the sun, will be learned during the Millennium. Since hydrogen is abundantly offered, such an approach, when perfected, will supply an unrestricted supply of energy. Something is particular; the power of the atom will be used for peaceful purposes and not for the production of atomic bombs for damaging functions.

This brings us to the wonderful promise that there will be no wars in the Millennium, for throughout that time, the Prince of Peace will reign. Isaiah states, "They shall beat their swords into plowshares, and their spears into pruning hooks: nation will not raise sword versus nation, neither will they learn war any more" (Isa. 2:4).

Although the earth may undergo severe depopulation throughout the Great and Terrible Day of the Lord, it is most likely that it will be renewed rapidly throughout the Millennium. This is because of two causes: First, there will be no wars to ravage the nations; second, as we have seen, longevity will be significantly extended.

CHAPTER EIGHTEEN

The Qanon Stronghold

Trying to write about Q as the plan is still ongoing every day. It's like attempting to build a submarine far below the sea level while sliding along to some undisclosed secret location. The task is quite daunting, with dizzying conditions and a completely alien landscape - however, Q reassures us that we are headed towards a very good place. It is, however, no surprise that following Q often leaves one feeling like she or he needs to come up for air at regular periods.

Many individuals love President Trump and the GOP; a lot more than the Legacy Media would prefer the world to believe. They will be happy to learn for the first time about the systematic and highly imaginative disclosure of long-suppressed intel by the Trump administration. They will be amazed as they find out about the military accuracy of this operation, carried out for their advantage. For them, the information about to be provided will unquestionably feel more like a missing puzzle piece eventually discovered after years of searching; a crucial foundation in their mental framework, and one which empowers them to build a more precise and meaningful worldview-- something that is going to have a profound effect on society when done en masse. And you'll note here that this is my hope: that after reading this book, both the people at first hostile to Q and those who willingly embrace Q from the beginning will end up at the very same spot- with a significantly increased understanding of reality, and that they will have the ability to come together as people or citizens of the same Republic, and develop a stunning future together. I hope that this increased understanding will assist people on both sides of the aisle to shake off the mass deception committed against everyone for so long and finally realize that this isn't a Right versus Left battle any longer. It never was.

No matter your reaction, the problem faced in attempting to discuss Q is more intensified by the inherent complexity of Q- from the numerous encoding methods he utilizes to the broad series of topics covered, to the key list of players involved. Even the misinformation intentionally positioned in the drops by Q himself, to mislead any evil person following along, to press them into making errors, tipping their hands too early, and using up important resources at a time when they really can't afford to lose anything. This is even further intensified by the sheer amount of Q's posts. Since this writing, Q has been posting for over a year and a half now, and has collected over 3,300 posts throughout this time. Who understands the number of posts there will be in the end, or for how long this operation will go on! Distilling that amount of information-- information that's been spread out over these numerous months and heavily supplemented by a research study from Anons throughout that whole time, is no small task.

Who is QAnon that the Legacy Media should malign him so? Why has his movement taken the world by storm, in a method that other "conspiracy theories" before him haven't? Is it merely the grand mack daddy of them all, rolling bits and pieces of all types of theories into one big tin foil mish-mash? Is the QAnon movement just conspiracy theory on "bath salts," as one reporter put it?

We need to step back and set the stage a little at this point, because a great deal of events were unfolding so quickly during this time that to understand QAnon genuinely, you have to understand everything that came before QAnon. You need to get a real feel for the landscape at the time, the whole context of these events, and not the Mockingbird Media's retelling of such events, but the true version they helped conceal from you, because that's the setting into which QAnon emerged. If you desire to understand QAnon, you need to first become an Anon by seeing the world and the events leading up to it, as an Anon would see them. This formidable look at history will not be very easy, but it will be needed if you wish to stand any chance of understanding what's taking place now, about Trump, Q, and the Great Awakening. It's time to strap on your Nightmare Vision safety glasses and see the world through the eyes of an Anon.

So, on June 16, 2015, Donald Trump formally announced his presidential campaign in Trump Tower. Many took it as a joke and dismissed it outrightly initially, but the man quickly gained the needed traction. By 2016, the Trump Train outshined the competition, beating out eleven other prospects.

Within weeks, on June 27, Anons created /r/The _ Donald on Reddit as a "/ pol/ colony," to help facilitate this effort by bringing in the "normies." The site became the single largest source of Trump's online support and triggered a multitude of continuous memes, which just served to drive his popularity and his message home to numerous people by directly bypassing the Legacy Media, much to the shame of Leftists all over

The campaign continued to grow, and quite quickly, the raucous fun was spreading like wildfire across social networks. Centipedes (that is, the label provided to Trump advocates on /r/The _ Donald- which was a reference to the tune "Centipede" by the drum and bass band, Knife Party) took over Reddit so efficiently, the Reddit admins quickly decided to censor the subreddit and pull it from the front page-- a relocation that had never been done before in the history of Reddit and which has considering that never been duplicated. The movement is a sensational one for those acquainted with the site, which had formerly prided itself on operating with FOSS principles in mind-- liberty, openness, totally free speech, democratic sharing, and so on. The admins would then obfuscate the real customer count, initially capping it around 600,000 (when in reality, the marketer tools on the web site's back end showed the count to be closer to six million users-- a far more precise count, considering the company would be devoting scams if they ever messed with those numbers).

Far too huge to delete straight-out (the users would revolt and ruin the site if they did), the Reddit admins (consisting of Steve Huffman, who is believed to be the mediator of/ r/Cannibals, where he discusses his very first time eating human flesh using a sockpuppet account) effectively turn/ r/The _ Donald into a "containment" subreddit, guaranteeing Trump's message and his supporters are cut off from the more comprehensive website, with the paid-off admins of other subs like/ r/Politics routinely censoring pro-Trump content at the "ground level."

On February 13, 2016, Supreme Court Justice Antonin Scalia would be discovered dead at Cibolo Creek Ranch Vineyard in Texas, leaving a vacancy on the greatest court in the land throughout the last year of Obama's presidency. Obama would nominate Merrick Garland as his replacement. Still, Republicans would block the verification by invoking, ironically, "the Biden guideline," named after the then vice president Joe

Biden, which mentioned that the Senate was under no responsibility to validate the Supreme Court choice of an outbound administration.

During the campaign, Trump dealt with a troubling quantity of disruption from the extreme left. On March 11, he would be forced to cancel a rally in Chicago as countless violent protesters came down upon the University of Illinois place, where brawls would break out on the rally floor. At least five arrests would be made, and two law enforcement officers injured as an outcome of the violent mob. In March, George Papadopoulos would sign up with the Trump project as a foreign policy adviser, after leaving the Ben Carson project.

Julian Assange, creator and editor of Wikileaks, would, later on, reject any involvement with Russian intelligence and these leakages.

However, after this, control of the Wikileaks Twitter account would be wrested from Assange and taken control of by the Deep State. The date when this transpired isn't clear, but in the wake of these drops, Assange remained in for a world of hurt, holed up in the Ecuadorian Embassy. Later on, in November of 2016, Russia Today would publish an "interview" in-between Assange and John Pilger. Still, several weird artifacts in the video, including what can best be explained as digital morphs (such as the kind used in Hollywood special impacts to change one subject into another, as in the movie Willow), were seen by Anons. At particular points in the video, his collar would snap in an unorthodox method, or he would have his eyeball shift position on his head, mixing into another picture of his eye, but focused in a completely various direction. It's something somebody needs to see in motion to genuinely value. The footage has been controlled in some startling methods.

On July 31, the FBI would formally open its "Crossfire Hurricane" counterintelligence examination into the Trump campaign, led by FBI representative Peter Strzok.

On August 1, Strzok and others would fly to England to meet numerous members of the intelligence community there and to interview one Alexander Downer, the same Alexander Downer, who had spoken with George Papadopoulos back in May.

On August 15, Strzok would message the Department of Justice legal representative Lisa Page, talking about their "insurance coverage" in case of a Trump win in November.

The story Strzok and Page had been given is that they were secret fans, admirers, but I do not believe that this is the case. The "enthusiasts" story is, in truth, one of the earliest cover stories the Deep State has at its disposal. I don't think they were ever enthusiasts. I believe they had actually both been tasked by the most significant levels of the Obama administration to assist spy on and take down Trump, a civilian. I do not have evidence of this assertion right now, but Q has told us that Lisa Page is working together witness now so that the fact will come out in time.

Q would later release a series of monitoring photos drawn from traffic webcams in London, tracking Strzok, Page, and several others as they worked their way through the city, to the CIA field office ... where one Gina Haspel (who Trump would designate as CIA director after the election) just occurred to be operating at the time.

On August 16, in the wake of the Seth Rich murder, the Washington, DC, chief of cops, Cathy Lanier, would step down to work as head of security for the NFL.

On August 19, Manafort would resign from the Trump campaign, amidst questions about his ties to Russian operatives.

On September 9, Hillary would stumble with her now-notorious "Basket of Deplorables" speech, which we discussed in the previous chapter.

And then, on September 11, Hillary would be shot collapsing outside of a 9/11 memorial occasion in lower Manhattan, losing not only her awareness, but a shoe while doing so. This, and several other episodes throughout the year (such as her duplicated coughing fits and the time when she spat up mucous plugs into a glass of water while giving a speech in front of cams and a crowd) would give rise to a variety of questions about the state of her health (and thus, her physical fitness for the workplace of the presidency). She would later begin Jimmy Kimmel and prove her vigor by ... opening a jar of pickles.

Sidenote: Kimmel would be explained as an "Activist" by Barack Hussein Obama in a promotion video he helped cut to support U2s straw man Bono with his RED initiative. Obama would go on in the same video to label Bono, a "Ringmaster." Q would clue us in that both were concealed titles/roles provided and acknowledged within the Cabal hierarchy, which Obama was sending out a message, hidden in plain sight, to interested parties who were focusing

In reality, Q would confirm that the surprise message Obama was sending at the time was, in reality, a response to this concern, sent out by Bono (or his handlers), through his RED website:

Obama was ready to meet whoever was asking the question, and Kimmel was intentionally assisting in transmitting the message. And that's simply a little a foretaste for the sort of mind-bending stuff the Cabal finishes with consistency, to keep their efforts hidden from the rest people. We'll be looking at a lot more of that example in the coming chapters.

On September 13, Halper would meet with George Papadopoulos in London, where his female "assistant," alias Azra Turk, would be designated by the FBI to accompany Halper and help in targeting Papadopoulos. Turk would try to seduce Papadopoulos, with Papadopoulos later calling her a honeypot-- in the hopes of extracting more details from him relating to Russian Collusion within the Trump campaign.

On October 7, 2016, Wikileaks would start posting what they would entitle "The Podesta E-mails." John Podesta, you may remember, was Hillary's campaign supervisor at the time. Discussions consisted of within the archive would cause discoveries about "Spirit Cooking" and "performance artist" Marina Abramovic, along with a "Pizza Code," all of which would form the basis of "Pizzagate;" a hypothesis that dark, even Satanic practices were commonplace amongst elites, and that human trafficking and pedophilia was happening with frightening regularity, right under typical individuals's noses. Searching for "Spirit Cooking" online would cause a video on YouTube which featured a routine where Abramovic would blend blood, semen, and breast milk in a vat, and then use that mix to compose inscriptions on the walls of the structure she was carrying out the ritual in, before putting the clotted sludge over child-sized effigies (such as the one pictured on the bottom right corner in the photo listed below, which is taken directly from that video):.

John Podesta would eagerly welcome his sibling (and one of the largest lobbyists in Washington, DC, at the time, Tony Podesta) to the "supper."

The revelation that Washington elites were going to bloody routines would set the web on fire, which was simply the start. When the "Pizza code" was found, all bets were off. The hypothesis here was that the code itself referred to kids and women and specific sexual show thinly-veiled food referrals, the most notorious example probably being this e-mail, here:

" Do you believe I'll do better playing dominos on cheese than on pasta?" Not precisely common English phraseology, is it?

And that is far from the only example. Others would include descriptions of a "walnut sauce" in a back and forth with Democrat mega-donor, financing, and billionaire source behind the continuous "Need to Impeach" project against Trump, Tom Steyer, in addition to an e-mail explaining the discovery of a "pizza-related" handkerchief, leading some to question if that was, in and of itself, a recommendation to the handkerchief code frequently employed within the homosexual neighborhood. Horrified by their initial findings, Anons, in dogged pursuit of the truth, combed through all of the e-mails and quickly found a striking relationship between the Hillary Clinton project and James Alefantis' DC-based pizza store, Comet Ping Pong.

The first thing that was right away obvious about Alefantis himself is that he was noticeably well-connected, being the ex-homosexuals partner of David Brock, creator of Media Matters for America and friend of the.

Rothschilds. (Full disclosure, Media Matters for America would, on their website in 2018, go on to attack me as a "right-wing amplifier" of Q. It's likewise believed that the Deep State attempted to assassinate David Brock at one point, causing a cardiovascular disease that put him in the hospital, but which eventually failed to kill him). GQ would even name Alefantis among the fifty most influential people in Washington, DC, which is very odd for a little restaurateur. It was heavily speculated at the time that Alefantis was a Rothschild himself, though no definitive proof of this was ever discovered one method or the other (at least to my understanding-- however, I find some of the theories out there rather engaging).

Anons instantly started scouring his social media accounts, which exposed, well ... lots of, lots of unfortunate images similar to the one you see here:

As you can picture, that didn't precisely assist Alefantis' case in the eyes of Anons. And it should be kept in mind that this was far from the only example, not even the worst image exposed. It also needs to be kept in mind that Alefantis' avatar on Instagram at the time was a statue of Antinous, the boy-lover of Roman Emperor Hadrian, even more fueling wild web speculation.

At any rate, the point I want to convey here is that the Cabal was so desperate for you not to take note of the Wikileaks, they needed to hunt up some secret recording from a year before and blast it out for weeks to incense the quickly manipulated, and distract them from the genuine scandal being discovered by volunteer researchers every day.

Another significant discovery consisted of among the Wikileaks was a record of a personal speech Hillary had offered to the National Multi-Family Housing Council in 2013, where she explained how you needed both a "public and private position" when it concerned the similarity Wall Street reform in essence, advocating lying and pandering to whoever occurred to be in the room at the time to gain impact and votes, while always understanding to whom you owed your allegiances. She would, later on, dismiss objections to this by referencing, of all things, the Spielberg film Lincoln, at a later governmental debate.

On October 20, Trump would offer his now-famous speech at the Al Smith charity dinner (what I've because taken to calling "The Red Dinner"), hurling some of his most vicious criticism of Clinton to date, to her face, with her cackling along with distinctly required laughter the entire time. To say it was savage would be an enormous understatement. It was clear from Trump's tone (and by the shocked expressions of the guests, who were by now profusely sweating in their seats and dying to get out of that space) that there was much more truth to these "jokes" than many in the space cared to acknowledge.

Parallel to the Pizzagate investigations, there was also a chain of query triggered by yet another Wikileaks email contained within the Podesta Archives, where a thinly veiled plot to assassinate Supreme Court Justice Scalia was discovered.

In essence, a "screenwriter" had pitched John Podesta a motion picture concept, complete with characters, plot, setting, and cost. Why is it practically looked like he was trying to get approval for an agreement? One big issue: John Podesta isn't a movie manufacturer. Add that to a few of the inconsistencies observed in Scalia's death: that he was initially reported to have been discovered with a pillow over his head, and then, all of a sudden, there was no pillow. There was likewise the reality that no autopsy was ever performed, which Scalia was cremated, regardless of being a devout traditionalist Catholic, who even rejected the rulings of Vatican II, and thus, would have rejected cremation on profoundly spiritual grounds. Things just didn't build up when it comes to Scalia's death, and Anons took notice.

On November 6, Donald Trump would lastly win the presidency, to the shock of many around the nation. And the shock was for a good reason. For weeks, the people had been becoming aware of how Trump had practically no chance of winning. A day before the election, the Princeton Election Consortium had offered Hillary a ninety-nine percent possibility of winning. The Huffington Post, a ninety-eight percent opportunity.

Daily Kos, ninety-two percent. CNN, ninety-one percent. The New York Times, eighty-five percent. FiveThirtyEight, seventy-two percent. All the polls were tilted in her favor, and yet, in a stunning upset, Trump had flown in from behind and trounced her like some kind of maniac dark horse.

Hillary would refuse to concede at first, instead, sending out her campaign manager, John Podesta, around 2:00 a.m. to speak with the crowd that had collected for her "crowning" as the presumptive winner. He would inform everyone to come back tomorrow after they had found out more, leaving several Hillary's upset and weeping fans mystified regarding what had simply occurred, unwilling to accept reality. And as a side-note, there's a popular story out there that Trump won the electoral college, while Hillary won the popular vote (therefore, we must do away with the electoral college; that old guideline that was developed by all those founders who happened to be "white males," and subsequently utilized each election to keep "white guys" in power-- when in reality the explicit function of this is to keep a balance of power between populated regions and, for instance, less populated regions where all the FOOD is grown). Lunatic Leftists-- particularly the kind that congregate in cities-- tend to forget that there's a whole world outside their metropolitan bubble. If the electoral college were gone, all somebody would have to do to rule as a despot from here on out is convince these populations to keep choosing them, frequently by promising all sorts of "advantages" they have no intention of ever genuinely delivering. But this misconception about Hillary winning the popular vote isn't genuine either, at least, not when you understand the full extent of the voter fraud that took place that night ... and who owns the ballot machines ... and the efforts patriots and White Hats went through to strategically secure the election

The country is FAR more Red and far more Conservative than anybody has been led to believe by the Legacy Media. You could even call it overwhelmingly conservative, but again, the extent and duration of the established citizen scams that have occurred every year have distorted our perceptions. And as of this writing, the Department of Homeland Security (DHS) has till the end of December 2018 to launch a report on the scope of election fraud throughout the 2018 midterm elections. We're visiting that come back around and bite lots of "chosen" officials in short order.

We would, later on, discover from Q that White Hats (that is, heroes included in intelligence, working to hinder the efforts of Black Hats) had tactically placed sufficient pressure on locations where scams were generally widespread and had guaranteed enough election stability to counteract and reduce all the citizen scams going on elsewhere. It sufficed to tip the electoral scales, however not the popular scales. It belonged to why none of the networks would call the election till really, too late (because, again, the media works with the Mono-party, and the election wasn't expected to have this outcome because it was rigged in Hillary's favor). This is likewise why all the polling outlets could offer us such exceptionally inaccurate ballot data right up until the day of the election. Even the surveys were deceptive, leveraged to establish an established narrative. As Q likes to advise us, "They never believed she would lose," and thus, didn't have a plan for that scenario when it finally happened.

Hillary would, however, be required to yield the next day eventually. And practically immediately, the motion that would become referred to as "The Resistance" got underway. Conjuring up all sorts of fiction, from Harry Potter to Star Wars, to A Handmaiden's Tale, the motion's acolytes saw themselves as some sort of brave army, rebelling versus a Darth Vader or a Voldemort (when in truth, they were unsuspectingly serving the most wicked character of them all). It was simply an amalgamation of anti-Trump rage without any real instructions, no unifying concepts, however a great deal of financing (thanks to George Soros) and lots of stars backing it.

On November 9, David Wilcox would be pulled from his car in Chicago by anti-Trump protesters and badly beaten by numerous foes while bystanders looked on and motivated the violence, yelling out expressions like, "He voted Trump! Beat his ass!"

On November 10, 2016, Besta Pizza would alter its logo design, getting rid of the interior decoration, distancing itself from the boy-lover symbol association.

On November 17, 2016, NSA director, Admiral Mike Rogers, unbeknownst to other members of the intelligence neighborhood, would privately travel to Trump Tower and, in an excellent act of heroism, divulge to Trump the presence of the unlawful spying operation against him and his campaign. Trump Tower itself had been jeopardized by the Deep State. However, instead of leaving then and there the day Admiral Rogers came to visit, Trump would have his individuals wait a day before lastly relocating the campaign headquarters the following day to Bedminster, New Jersey. And there was an excellent reason for this ...

Q would later disclose that the Trump project, upon knowing of the unlawful spying, would reverse and almost instantly utilize this to their advantage by utilizing it to feed bad intel to the Obama administration and Clinton project. In one particularly hilarious exchange, Q would verify that Trump had used a Twitter post to bait the Obama administration into spying in on all their "upcoming" project plans.

On May 20, Trump would show up in Saudi Arabia, where he would take part in a ritual called an "ardah" or "sword dance." It's a routine one does before going to war. Before leaving Saudi Arabia, Trump would broker an offer with the Saudis to wean them off their dependence on oil exports, allow them to join the United States stock exchange, and, at the brand-new Saudi counter-terrorism center, he would place his hands, along with Saudi King Salman bin Abdulaziz and Egyptian President Abdel Fattah al-Sisi, on a radiant globe that drew lots of contrasts to a Palantir from the Lord of the Rings novels.

On May 23, 2017, "MegaAnon" would appear for the first time. Much like FBIAnon before him, and QAnon after him, MegaAnon concerned drop all sorts of intel about, a minimum of to begin, Seth Rich. Most of MegaAnon's initial claims were that because there was a lot of data that needed to be moved around safely, the likes of Julian Assange were leveraging the server power of Kim Dotcom's MegaUpload service (and later, Mega.nz) to achieve their "White Hat" goals. He would validate Rich as "Panda" (Rich always used "panda" permutations in his different screen names, with a packed panda even making a look later on in a video recorded by his moms and dads). MegaAnon would continue for numerous months, publishing into January 2018, and speaking about various topics, practically all related to different facets of the Trump administration-- consisting of inside some of QAnon's own/ CBTS/ threads. In other words, Q and MegaAnon were publishing at the same time, typically along the same lines, about the same subjects, at the same time informing Anons' point of views:

I know it sounds absurd; however, that's merely since I'm trying to convey the broadness and scope of what will be publicly disclosed. My only point is that after it's all over, nobody will have the ability to turn away from the truth. The masses will never again be able to declare with 100% certainty that 9/11 DIDN'T have within, US-sponsored and moneyed, department/agency coordination, designated resources, and help. Nobody will ever have the ability NOT to think that our fucking firms and departments and previous admins didn't play a major function in shit like JFK, OKC, 9/11, ISIS, Pizza, Vegas, and so on. They won't be able to turn a blind eye to what they consider "conspiracy theories," today just since the MSM told them to.

The only thing that everybody will be able to agree on when it's all stated and done is that we've all been horrifically lied to on incomprehensible levels. Absolutely nothing we've been led to perceive as our "truth" for generations because the fucking day GHB was sworn into the admin as Director of the CIA has been the entire reality and nothing. Nobody will have the ability to use lack of knowledge as a reason anymore. Do individuals think they're in charge?! Haha, well, now Trump is going to offer it to them. He's going to give us all the fucking openness we can manage, and when he does ?! That's when you'll genuinely see what "we, individuals" are made from. You'll have individuals who can't manage it, pleading to give the reality BACK to the admin. I wish to ensure I'm clear here, too ... when I use terms like "reveal," "truth," and so on. I am in NO WAY IMPLYING Trump is revealing any of that things you all raise like "aliens," "Antarctica," etc. not saying I do not personally believe in some of it; however, that's not the "storm" that's coming. Simply to clarify.

While I can't state that MegaAnon was always one hundred percent precise (nor, like so a number of these "insiders" can we verify if it was all the same individual), I will say archives of MegaAnon's posts make for some of the fascinating reading you can discover out there, to date.

Even as experts, we're shedding light on years of corruption, the Deep State was at work, combating back, and on July 27, George Papadopoulos would be arrested for accepting cash from a foreign national while in Greece; $10,000, exactly. The pretense for this was that this was a "retainer" while Papadopoulos exercised an energy offer for Charles Tawil, an Israeli American business person. Except, Papadopoulos' "spy-der sense" was tingling. He attempted to give the cashback on one celebration; however, the man declined. Before leaving the island to return to the US, Papadopoulos left the cash in the care of a local lawyer in Greece, feeling agitated by the whole affair-- and it's an advantage he did, too, because upon landing and deplaning at Dulles Airport, he was instantly jailed by officers who went trying to find the $10,000. See, there's a guideline that you have to state quantities of cash over 10 thousand dollars when flying back into the United States (so our pal George would have been in huge difficulty if he had just packed that wad of money in his suitcase). Papadopoulos would, later on, tell federal private investigators that he believed Tawil was working for a foreign government. When the officers discovered out that Papadopoulos didn't have the money on him, that he left it in Greece, they were furious. Papadopoulos had seemingly dodged an entrapment scheme, and it appeared like he was about to get away completely untouched when the Special Counsel was able to catch him on a "process criminal offense" " lying" to the FBI. Papadopoulos said he thought he initially spoke to Joseph Mifsud before starting work for the Trump project, when in truth, it wanted.

Papadopoulos would become sentenced to fourteen days in jail, after which point he was complimentary to do and talk as he pleased.

And as summer season was warming up, so too was the political divide in the country. The "Unite the Right" rally was slated in Charlottesville on August 11 and 12, 2017. The goal of the rally was to have anyone even remotely on the Right reserved their differences and march against the forces of Marxism that were attempting to enforce Leftist ideology on all aspects of society, through things like the policing of speech; doing opponents online; deport forming major figures in the movement; and rioting at the similarity Jordan Peterson and Ben Shapiro rallies, on top of doing things like taking down Confederate monuments (and some not-so-Confederate monoliths; simply old monuments of historical figures who just took place to be white). The mostly-male group was made up of routine MAGA conservatives, groups like Identity Evropa, those associated with Richard Spencer's National Policy Institute, and more extreme groups like American Vanguard, the Traditionalist Worker Party, and different neo-Nazi/National Socialist groups (through intense study of the essential principles undergirding these latter groups would expose their ideology to be profoundly Left-wing in origin).

And state what you want about those groups, however, they were protesting peacefully—a minimum of, at the start. The rally would start with the individuals making their existence understood, marching with tiki torches in hand, much to the horror of Leftists across the country, who instantly drew parallels to the Ku Klux Klan. Then, due to some choices made by the mayor's workplace and the local authorities, decisions which went versus normal policy, these authorities decided to permit Antifa into the mix. Now, if you understand anything about Antifa, you know they're Communist foot soldiers. We're discussing the real dregs of society here—drug-using, gender-confused, violent anarchists, with a despicable nihilistic streak. Numerous like to consider themselves as "anti-fascist" revolutionaries, drawing comparisons to themselves and the D-Day soldiers of the Greatest Generation, when really, their actual ideological forebears were the ones developing the gulags in the USSR. Needless to state, when the two groups met (and were encouraged to meet, through the strategic opening and closing of streets, and redirecting of traffic by the cops, upon orders from greater ups), dispute erupted throughout the city.

Absolutely nothing is more emblematic of that dispute than the occurrence involving James A. Fields and Heather Heyer. Fields was with American Vanguard, and Heyer with Antifa. While attempting to leave the city in his Dodge Challenger, Fields' automobile was swarmed and attacked by Antifa, who had been poorly funneled into the street by the regional police. One Antifa member first struck the back of Fields' automobile with a bat, scaring Fields. Another struck a window. Finally, another tossed a bottle of frozen urine (tossing bottles of urine-- frozen or otherwise, is a favorite Antifa) at the windshield, breaking it and lodging itself there before the mob came down around the car. One Antifa member is even caught on an electronic camera pointing a pistol at Fields' vehicle.

In a panic, Fields sped up to twenty-eight miles per hour, charging the crowd, hoping it would distribute. It didn't, and he had to knock on the brakes simple split seconds later. He managed to slow it to twenty-three miles per hour before striking another vehicle, likewise stopped by the crowd in front of him, at seventeen miles per hour.

In a large panic, Fields reversed out of the crowd and backed up the one-way street, driving backward as quickly as he could, desperate to leave the mob.

When the cops discover him, he can't stop asking forgiveness. When he hears someone struck by his cars and truck has died, he weeps. He is jailed and charged with very first-degree murder in the death of Heather Heyer-- a morbidly overweight female who had been marching with Antifa for hours that day. The media does its best to prevent discussing her weight, which is seen in the video as at least SEVEN guys, firefighters, and lifesaver-- carrying her to an ambulance, stomach exposed and, honestly, undulating with each collective action of the emergency workers. Instead, they transmit photos of her face, painting her as an unfortunate martyr, instead of one of the mob who attacked Fields' car.

And while I apologize for the image, I include it, so you realize I am not overemphasizing one iota. The coroner would state she died of a cardiac arrest. He never said it resulted from being struck by a car going about twenty-three miles per hour and trying to decrease.

However, the story doesn't end there. Not able to manage representation, Fields was eventually assigned an attorney by the state-- but the attorney has a good record, and wishing to make an example out of Fields, the judge combs through the lawyer's records and finds that he, too, was opposed to the removal of Confederate statues. The judge frames this as, somehow, an ethical dispute, and now gets to change Fields' representation.

He subs in a social justice warrior-type, complete with pink hair (and who, previously, was also associated with a sex scandal); however, to her credit, she makes a demand that the case is vacated Charlottesville, where the regional press would continue to rail against Fields' the entire time. The judge rejects the motion. At the end of the case, Judge Moore would say to the jury, "I do not know what intent he had aside from to eliminate. We understand what we saw."

In December 2018, Fields would get sentenced to life in jail, plus FOUR HUNDRED AND NINETEEN years, for the criminal offense of first-degree murder, which requires intent. To call this, a miscarriage of justice is an understatement. And while I disagree with Fields' ideology, I do think the fact is important. This was a morbidly overweight lady marching with a mob on a hot summer day-- a mob who was intentionally funneled into locations where they must not have been permitted, stopping up traffic while swarming and attacking automobiles with weapons. The Leftists in charge of the government there sent in their infantryman to violently threaten and intimidate anyone they disagreed with; in this case, the Unite, the Right protesters. They wished to make an example out of Fields.

The rally had licenses to be there. Antifa did not. The rally had been serene till Antifa began attacking them. And completion result of all of it was a terrible and entirely preventable loss of life.

It would not be until a month later on when an Anon would ask United States Senate Anon a concern:

If conservative death squads became genuine and start massacring Antifa advocates left and right, will Trump intervene to stop us or let us cleanse the nation for him?

Is Trump simply as happy to put down a right-wing uprising as he is a left-wing one?

Can we count on him as a pal or enemy on the Day of the Rope?

SENATE Anon would have this to state on the matter: Soros desires you to form right-wing death teams and combat Antifa, so you don't combat him. I'm unsure there's ever been a clearer photo of that reality placed on display than in the disaster that occurred in Charlottesville that summer season day. At any rate, I didn't wish to be Soros' beneficial moron. As much as I may have sympathized with a few of the ideas being upheld by a few of the groups there (I've never disliked anybody by their race, or the color of their skin, even though I do tend to be pro-Western Civ), I wasn't about to be anyone's unwitting pawn-- not to mention some Hungarian Billionaire understood for sowing discord and strife throughout the world. Oh, but we'll be addressing George Soros later in this book. In the meantime, it's enough to understand that the man uses the Hegelian Dialectic to his benefit: synthesis, thesis, and reverse. In essence, Soros establishes opposed groups to eliminate with each other, which results in the weakening of the basic population, developing disunity, and promoting hatred amongst individuals, all to press everyone along to some established end.

So while the "directly, white males" at the Unite the Right rally were absolutely all reacting to the same, extremely genuine phenomenon of anti-white hatred (cultivated and moneyed by the likes of Soros), the reality is, they were all being used in the very same way as the Antifa foot-soldiers they claimed to be fighting. Everybody present at the rally that day was a helpful moron, driving the wedge of division deeper into the American soul.

Trump understood this, and would later on state of the catastrophe: What about the 'alt-left' that came charging at, as you say, the 'alt-right,' do they have any semblance of regret?

What about the reality they came charging with clubs in hands, swinging clubs? Do they have any issues? I think they do.

And:

You had a group on one side that was bad, and you had a group on the other side that was also extremely violent. No one desires to say it, but I will state it right now. See, Trump understood the reality of the situation on the ground that day, so many did not. And while his challengers in the Mockingbird Media were eager to make some type of racist association between Trump and the "Alt-Right," Trump's main concern was keeping the nation together and not permitting the media to exploit the occasion to develop more division-- division which had been intentionally and purposefully planted and fostered throughout Obama's tenure in office, both by governmental firms and NGOs, through the similarity lots of, numerous Soros-backed groups.

The strategy was to design their tactics on what had taken place overseas, in locations like Europe and different Baltic states, with numerous "color revolutions." Even a brief search online these days will reveal the manifold connections to Soros-backed groups to even the most dubious of skeptics. Soros poured billions over several years into whatever from Black Lives Matter marches, to the so-called Women'sMarch, and well beyond.

Top-level Insider Anon would say, of Soros, when asked by an Anon:

Why is Soros pushing all these opportunities of degeneracy such as Feminism?

• Strategies of stress.

He isn't an anti-white man for some inexplicable reason. He is pro-division and pro-tension, to get the masses concentrated on each other rather than the regime that is fucking them.

Crafty challengers need careful strategies to get rid of. It's very appealing for some to think, "Why not just crush our enemies?" The Right had essentially forced Trump into the workplace, and was now appearing in force worldwide. And let's face it; they might probably just run over the Left underfoot, if they were just enabled. That would inevitably lead to something like a civil war. If the objective of the likes of Soros and the Cabal is to plant division to trigger damage, and an overall weakening of the nation, doing so would only even more advance the program of evil. The effective action to counter solve is to announce and show unity instead. Understanding that those on the Left and the Right had been successfully brainwashed and demoralized through years of conditioning, Trump picked the most efficient path, announcing that there were terrible stars on both sides, refusing to blame just one side, which would serve to give aside from the "moral high ground," in effect, perpetuating the department and endorsing.

Again, this becomes part of why I wrote this book to help bridge the gap, bring people into the light, and help them see our common enemies who are so great at setting us at each other's throats.

However, the Cabal was refrained from doing combating, not by a long-shot. On August 30, bystanders would capture footage of a driver losing control of their lorry at the very minute President Trump's motorcade pass by on its way to a rally in Springfield, Missouri. The car emerged from the woods and careened down a hill, directed right at the motorcade. The vehicle stopped when it bottomed out on a drainage ditch before stalling out at the side of the roadway.

Q would, some months later, verify that the CIA has classified innovation that enables it to take control of specific kinds of automobiles remotely, and yes, this was an effort on the president's life (among many).

Yes, we are now in the remote-controlled assassination zone. And if that sounds like sci-fi conspiracy theory territory, just keep in mind that in 1975, the presence of the CIA's "Heart Attack Gun," which fired frozen darts of undetectable poison (and which mimicked a heart attack in its target) was disclosed openly before the Senate. And you much better think that the approaches and technologies at the disposal of the Deep State have considerably advanced in the intervening forty-plus years since that initially, unintentional disclosure.

But as soon as again, we need to continue with our timeline. On September 18, Donald Trump Jr. would drop his Secret Service detail.

Q would later describe why: On September 25, Trump Jr. would restore his Secret Service security. The issue, whatever it specifically had been, was now resolved, and it was safe for him to regain his security information. But then came the first big public crisis of the Trump administration.

The official story is that of a person called Stephen Paddock, raised fourteen AR-15s, eight AR-10s, a bolt action rifle, a revolver, and cases upon cases of ammunition to his space for six days before finally snapping, breaking out two windows made from hurricane-resistant glass with a hammer, and dumping over 1,100 rounds down into the performance crowd, around four-hundred. Fifty meters listed below, ultimately eliminating fifty-eight people and hurting over four hundred, while likewise trying to spark a jet fuel tank some 2,000 feet away. Images of Paddock, dead on the ground, would quickly leak on the internet.

And this is where the questions began for Anons!

Named the "most dangerous mass shooting in America," the occasion simply didn't entirely build-up to this day; there's been no official motive listed regarding why Paddock would do what he had done. Add that to the truth that the footage of the shooting plainly showed muzzle flare in both broken windows (regardless of the police report saying there was no second shooter), the bizarre interview provided by his brother the following day, the existence of black vans on the ground, and the bizarre interview offered by one Jesus Campos, security personnel at the Mandalay Bay who had been shot as soon as, when probably Paddock had fired thirty-five bullets through the door when he check on the commotion.

Campos would go on Ellen later on, together with someone who can just be explained as a handler, and give among the strangest interviews I've ever seen on TV. So weird was the interview, and so different-looking was "Campos" on TV from pictures we had been seen with earlier, there was speculation as to whether this was even the same Jesus Campos being presented to us, or some kind of Deep State body-double being used to shill a central narrative.

And there was, of course, the caution Anons had gotten about Las Vegas just a couple of weeks prior that had motivated them to keep digging. Then, on October 25, Stephen Paddock's sibling would be detained for belongings of kid porn and the sexual exploitation of a minor, leading some Anons to dig even more challenging and show up familial connections to the Bohemian Grove. The Paddocks owned an estate just outside the Grove, a fact revealed by independent private investigator Jake Morphonios at Blackstone Intelligence, leading some to question if the relations were Cabal possessions, leveraged to get, ship, and transport "resources" for all sorts of illicit deeds. Morphonios would, in the week of his investigations, have his channel eliminated from YouTube, censored after I started enhancing his videos beyond the YouTube community. This kind of censorship has become nearly associated with the extreme Left in Silicon Valley; the basic method they perform their affairs to silence dissent, functioning as publishers instead of open platforms (regardless of all congressional testament to the contrary).

Not only that, but MGM officers had discarded two-hundred and fifty million dollars worth of stock thirty days before the shooting, as had Soros, who had purchased up 1.35 million dollars worth of puts against MGM stock some sixty days before the strike.

But the story didn't end there. Survivors began passing away, with one death coming over a year later, when a Las Vegas survivor was captured in yet another mass shooting, this time in Thousand Oaks, California, one of thirteen who would end up perishing that evening. And then Anons discovered video footage of a VIP being escorted out of the Tropicana by SWAT operators.

I can just start to sum up the weirdness, and the depth of examination Anons did during that time, but the except it is this: Paddock was no the only shooter. Numerous Anons quickly concluded that he was an arms dealer working for the FBI. He was brokering a handle, well, the majority of Anons who checked out the subject figured it was some type of Saudi counter-coup terror/assassination operation.

Remember how Trump had traveled to Saudi Arabia and brokered an offer with the new king there? This was the action of the faction opposed to that new king. Yes, there were factions within our government supporting this operation, particularly by supplying weapons and ammo to terrorists.

And see how the VIP remains in the Tropicana?

Yeah, that was the massive problem with these prospective assassins. That guy, obviously a member of the Saudi Royal family, was the target. He was supposed to be in the Mandalay Bay gambling establishment; however, he had gone, on an impulse, to the Tropicana. However, by that point, the assassins' cover had been blown by ... many think it was Mandalay Bay security personnel, Jesus Campos.

The terrorists would fire upon Campos, mistaking him for a police officer, discharging some 200 rounds through the thirty-second flooring hotel room door, lodging one bullet in Campos' leg.

Campos would pull away and radio for help, suggesting word was out now, and the clock was ticking. The terrorists are required to produce an interruption to leave. They broke the windows, and numerous shooters opened fire at the crowd listed below. One spotted a jet fuel tank in the range and began firing at it, hoping to develop a gigantic fireball to sidetrack from their place. They also eliminated Paddock, making it appear like a suicide so that he might take the fall.

A similar story is distributed throughout/ pol/ by somebody claiming to be Q in a series of really engaging posts (but who most likely isn't Q). Still, the information set out in the drops is very thought-provoking and worth noting, even if the source is dubious.

One can only hope the true story about Las Vegas will eventually pertain to the surface area; however, all the proof I have seen indicates the official narrative is a carefully crafted fiction.

On October 5, 2017, George Papadopoulos would plead "guilty" to lying to the Feds about his communications with other foreign nationals, to enter into a plea deal, and serve all of fourteen days in prison. However, since this writing, he is presently thinking about recanting his plea offer, considering that it's now coming out that certain exculpatory proof might have been deliberately kept from him by the FBI.

On October 6, Trump would ask his "famous" (at least in Q-circles) "Calm Before the Storm." Surrounded by military leaders and their better halves, who were all present for dinner later on that evening, Trump asked the professional press photographers that existed:

" You guys understand what this represents? Maybe it's the calm before the storm.".

" What's the storm?" asked one bewildered reporter. " Could it be the calm before the storm," he responded, with a characteristic sly smirk on his face.

Really few people in the space, if any other than Trump, knew what he implied at the time. However, there in that room, surrounded by the top military minds in the nation, Trump gave the order for the 'Q' operation to go active. And this was far from the only Q-reference Trump would drop during the next year and a half, for those paying attention. Trump would even take to trolling the media utilizing Twitter, tweeting out the phrase

"Scott Free," which likewise occurs to be the name of Ridley Scott's production company, which had produced White Squall. In this movie, Q had ripped his preferred catch-phrase from, "Where we go one, we go all." It was one in a long line of winks and-nods to Anons, over a year after their cumulative undertakings had started.

Naturally, the media's only response was to play dumb and wax pedantic, after months and months of declining to ask anybody in the Trump administration about the integrity of Q.

Had the media done its job and even tried to approach the issue truthfully, they would have made the connection themselves. Heck, they make the connection; however, they just refused to tell you about it, choosing to keep you in the dark, rather. And this wasn't the very first time something like this occurred, not by a long shot. There are dozens, if not numerous circumstances like this, I could reveal you. No, the media wished to keep you in the dark, not just because they were Mockingbirds charged by the CIA with opposing Trump at every turn, but likewise since numerous of them already had the unredacted FISA warrants from so long ago, demonstrating that they were complicit in the treasonous cover-up. You're discussing journalist after journalist guilty of devoting sedition, if not outright treason. And so, they lied to you. They actively kept you in the dark so you wouldn't revolt. They lied to you to conserve their sorry hides and spun a web of lies, wishing to avert the inevitable, hoping that the truth would never see the light of day.

And yet, here we are.

The product of years of collective effort and planning, the Q operation would go live twenty-three days later, when Q would make his first post on/ pol/. On October 28, 2017, Q's very first main post read:

This has been mostly misconstrued by many critics, that I've frequently questioned if it was intentionally "misconstrued" to lead individuals astray and away from Q. On the other area, to the uninitiated, it appears like Q is predicting that Hillary Clinton would be apprehended on October 30, 2017. That never took place, so how could anybody trouble with QAnon all these years later on?

See, this is how silly many so-called "reporters" are. They don't comprehend how a Chan-based forum works, and the answer is straightforward: Q didn't compose that part. A random Anon wrote that entire upper section on/ pol/, just barfing out whatever rubbish he desired to publish that day. The text listed below that false prediction? The part about the passport being flagged, and the extradition order in effect in case of HRC making a run for it? That's Q's real post. Q was reacting to the initial Anon, fixing him.

Q started by authoritatively informing the board that Hillary was under constant surveillance and wasn't going to have the ability to run anywhere. She was being tracked, and there was no escape for her. (In fact, comprehending that none of these individuals will getaway is among the most important pillars to include your understanding of Q.

Depending on where we are in the timeline when you read this, and how far along Q's plan has advanced, there might still be exceptional or even continuous arrests. Nobody included is escaping, and by a specific point in history, all traitors will either remain in jail.)

For the record, Q also forecasted riots if a cross-border run was attempted, and that, when the arrest lastly takes place, it will be the military managing the details of that operation.

Q would also go on to add, in that very same thread:

And this was the start of Q.

Over the coming months and weeks, Q would regularly publish intel drops similar to the ones above, beckoning Anons to follow him more profound and much deeper into the rabbit hole, crafting eighty-three posts in the first week alone. And you may likewise be picking up on Q's unique design of writing, which can practically be described as Socratic and sporadic. The truth is, even this stylistic option was deliberate. Think back to the Trump Jr./ Secret Service drop. What did Q state?

" These questions and keywords are framed to reduce sniffer programs that constantly absorb and examine data, then pushed to z terminals for eval. Think keys on steroids.".

Not to get too technical here, but the Deep State had supercomputers at their disposal that were constantly trawling the internet, publishing in online forums, and disrupting communications to mold and form the story of the nation. Several strategies were utilized to achieve this, but yes, these supercomputers could imitate natural speech and engage with people on some topics, basically passing the Turing test, fooling users into thinking they were talking to real individuals. Not only would these computer systems do this, but they would do it with multiple accounts to participate in something called "consensus cracking." It's one thing to have a web argument with someone. It's another to have five or 10 "individuals" screaming you down, saying you and your only viewpoint are wrong/radical/stupid/ and so on. When the "right" consensus was established, the bots would proceed to the next target (after all, CPU cycles are still a minimal resource-- even for leading secret supercomputers).

And "keys" here refers to XKeyScore, which was an NSA application that generally allowed the NSA to draw down all the information crossing the internet, anywhere in the world, and shop it in their huge archive in Utah.

All classified and indexed. The program was disclosed by Edward Snowden in 2013, which resulted in, according to Q, the NSA being seriously paralyzed in its ability to perform SIGINT operations. Before you go thinking Snowden is a hero, let me tell you, that guy is a traitor. His factors for disclosing the program before running away to "Russia" (he left to Hong Kong) were to give the CIA and the Cabal an edge when it came to OpSec. Keep in mind Hillary's private, unlawful e-mail server? The one filled with blackmail? The one she was offering Special Access Programs to other countries with? Oh, did I mention that little factoid yet? One of the significant factors Hillary set up an insecure server was to enable foreign nationals access to our SAPs and other classified intelligence.

So, somebody may contribute to the Clinton Foundation, and in return, they would be informed how to access files on the server. It was a fiendishly devilish pay-to-play arrangement (and believe me when I state this is just the idea of the iceberg when it concerns Hillary's treasonous activities).

Hillary wasn't the only game in town. Obama had his e-mail servers too. Eric Schmidt, co-founder of Google, went to North Korea to assist establish one of these private e-mail servers (because North Korea is nothing like what you've most likely been told it is. Don't worry, we'll go over that in detail later, too). And at first, the NSA was using their xkeyscore program to spy on the illegal activities of these Cabal-affiliated politicians, and strategy ahead.

It would be pretty funny if it weren't so ill; to avoid surveillance, Q would inform us, these different Cabal actors would resort to utilizing Gmail drafts (because, once again, Eric Schmidt had set up a personal Gmail server for them all) to interact with each other. They'd compose up a draft, conserve it, never send it, and after that, give the signal for the next individual to log in and check out the draft. That was one method they attempted to navigate the NSA's monitoring programs. They even attempted to use "game comms," as Q has informed us. They utilized the likes of XBOX Live, Playstation Network, and different mobile game chat spaces to attempt and go incognito with their communications. (Thankfully, it didn't work.).

So when Q states "believe keys on steroids," it implies there was a program on Cabal supercomputers that was even more powerful than what the NSA had formerly had access to, before Snowden occurred and paralyzed them with a little bit of publicity. Q had to skirt around that through bland, Socratic phraseology, lest the Cabal computer systems detect what was going on and overwhelm the boards with a flood of spam and sound.

Oh, and if you were paying attention at the time, you'd recognize Eric Schmidt stepped down from Alphabet (the parent corporation of Google) the very same day (December 21, 2017)

President Trump would sign the executive order entitled "Blocking the Property of Persons Involved in Serious Human Rights Abuse or Corruption," mandating overall property seizure for anyone associated with such criminal activities.

Schmidt resigned that really day to safeguard the company he had helped develop (with the assistance of the CIA, through its devoted tech incubator, In-Q-Tel). Schmidt would, later on, make an appearance in June 2018 during Inspector General Horowitz's testament before your home and Senate Judiciary committees. He would be sitting on the edge of his seat the entire time.

CHAPTER FOURTEEN

The Regeneration of the Earth

During the creation week, God prepared the world for habitation; he observed after His work was ended up that "it was extremely great." There were no destructive storms as we understand them today, but the earth was watered by a mist that increased from the ground.

Each day in Eden was best and fair from early morning till sunset. The sky was a deep blue, uncontaminated with man'sways. The earth was warmed under the rays of a warm sun. There was no rainfall until the time of the Flood. Noah's warning of a deluge fell on deaf ears as the antediluvian race had never seen rain. It appears that at the time of the Flood, a negative change occurred in the earth's meteorological conditions, which significantly changed its weather condition. In the Psalms, we read, "all the earth's structures are out of course" (Psalm 82:5). We also notice in comparing the sequential statements discovered in Genesis 7 and 8, which refer to the Flood, that the pre-flood year was composed of 12 months of 30 days. Thus the antediluvians had a perfect calendar. This remains in sharp contrast to our present calendar, which has a year that is around 365 1/4 days. According to Kepler's laws concerning planetary bodies, the earth should have receded from the sun about a million miles. In such cases, the world would receive on an average of 2 percent less heat, which unquestionably would adversely impact the weather condition.

These significant changes in the environment, which have brought suffering and disaster to countless millions, will be corrected at the beginning of the Millennium.

According to Ezekiel 47:1 -12, the waters will issue from under your home of the Lord. The quantity of the water which drains from a river so deep that they rise over a male's head. On its banks, Ezekiel saw multitudes of trees growing.

The Dead Sea Healed

These new waters will be to alter the aspect of the desert on the east slopes of the mountains of Israel. Down listed below on the plains of Jericho are lots of acres of fertile land; however, only a little portion of it is efficient, mainly because of the absence of water.

The waters of the river will plunge on down towards the Dead Sea. At present, this lonely body of water is a fantastic saline sea with a concentration of various salts to the quantity of 26 percent. No fish nor living thing can reside in this deadly brine.

When a periodic fish in the Jordan River swims too far south and is captured in the lethal waters of the sea, it quickly dies. No plant can grow on its shores and even near the ocean. When this revitalizing gush of living waters from Jerusalem flows into the sea, all this will be changed. It will become fresh, and astounding numbers of fish will populate its waters. The banks will be lined with gorgeous plants and trees. Anglers will also ply their sell its waters:

Man naturally will continue to cultivate the land, even as Adam, before the fall, was commissioned "to dress" the garden and "keep it." Even in the New Heavens and New Earth, men will continue to be active and engaged in profitable pursuits. No longer will man make his living by the sweat of his brow. Because the curse will be removed, the race will not need to have a hard time making it through, but the residents will have an opportunity to "long take pleasure in the work of their hands" (Isa. 65:22).

Every man will own his own home and "sit under his fig tree." No home mortgage or lien will endanger it. The wealth of the earth will be equitably dispersed, so that all may share in its blessings. The most terrific part of it will be that people will, with their success, worship the Lord and serve Him with all their hearts, and He, in turn, "will answer while they are yet speaking."

The Millennial Government

We are now to think about the government, which will rule the countries throughout the Millennium. The above Scriptures reveal that the capital of the world will be at Jerusalem, which agents from all the nations will go up to that city to learn the law of the Lord, which will be the constitution of the kingdom age. The very first job of the Great King, as we have seen, will be to evaluate the countries after that will come the destruction and elimination of the armaments of the countries. Numerous disarmament conferences have been kept in the past by the excellent powers of the world. They all have been failures; outlaw nations have used them merely as a cover to increase their weaponry covertly, while the democracies disarm. The genuine disarmament conference will be at Jerusalem after Christ comes!

The material used in the armaments, the weapons, the tanks, and the war aircraft will all be junked, and the metals will be melted down for peaceful usages. Much of the wealth of the nations has gone into the manufacture of the weapons of war. This terrible waste of earth's resources will be ended forever, and the energies of humanity will be directed to end poverty.

The seriousness of the need resulted in the development of the League of Nations, now defunct, and the United Nations, which in turn has become more or less an impotent assembly, not able to apply any real impact in the time of crisis. Both global organizations have signally failed, with the result that the countries are now hurrying pell-mell toward a showdown at Armageddon. Communism, boldly intent on making the world atheist and communist, will not rest till it has plunged the world in the most horrible bloodletting in the history of the countries.

The Illuminati Protocols Explained And The Arrival Of A New World

Simon Smith

447

The information herein is provided for educational purposes exclusively and is universal. The presentation of the data is without contractual agreement or any kind of warranty assurance.

All trademarks inside this book are for clarifying purposes only and are possessed by the owners themselves, not allied with this document.

Disclaimer

All erudition supplied in this book is specified for educational and academic purposes only. The author is not in any way responsible for any outcomes that emerge from utilizing this book. Constructive efforts have been made to render information that is both precise and effective. Still, the author is not to be held answerable for the accuracy or use/misuse of this information.

Foreword

I will like to thank you for taking the very first step of trusting me and deciding to purchase/read this life-transforming book. Thanks for investing your time and resources on this product.

I can assure you of precise outcomes if you will diligently follow the specific blueprint I lay bare in the information handbook you are currently checking out. It has transformed lives, and I firmly believe it will equally change your own life too.

All the information I provided in this Do It Yourself piece is easy to absorb and practice.

INTRODUCTION

The Illuminati is either a "conspiracy theory" or a "conspiracy fact," depending on who you talk to. Those acquainted with the Illuminati society may tell you that it is a wicked and criminal network of some of the world's most educated, wealthy,elite leaders, business people, and political leaders, who work behind the scenes to gain and maintain high levels of power, enormous wealth, and wield control over the world. The list of claims that occurred with this monstrous conspiracy is extensive, and also range from the Illuminati being an elite good-old-boy network watching out for their interests (often in unethical ways) to claims that they are alien beings from another galaxy who masquerade as people, drink the blood of people to make it through, and are working to prepare the earth for the arrival of the Antichrist who will rule and control the New World Order as a god, using those who praise him "immortality" through transhumanist technology merging machine with a man.

This book is written to assist you in getting to the core of the conspiracy by providing you with some of the initial evidence proving the existence and activities of this infamous group, going back to the late 1700s in the state of Bavaria, Germany, and as a growing number of evidence is stacked up, we will slowly move into the recent times, showing beyond reasonable doubt that the Illuminati is still completely functional, and a lot of the "conspiracy theories" are in fact, very true.

This analysis will investigate and analyze the numerous accusations and conspiracy theories related to the Illuminati. Because the subject is so large, this second volume was required to continue my analysis of the extensive claims and evidence linked to the "Illuminati conspiracy." I am dedicated to separating the realities from the fiction, showing that facts within the hill of "conspiracy theories" are well distributed on this subject, there is a considerable quantity of irrefutable evidence that there is undoubtedly a powerful "Illuminati" secret society that is running today in America and worldwide.

There is also a large amount of wild speculation, lies, and half-truths about what the Illuminati is doing, who is involved with them, and what evidence is offered. Some individuals dismiss the idea that there is a "conspiracy" and do not even think such a thing exists, because when an informed. Rational person stumbles upon a few of the more outrageous allegations originating from the Illuminati conspiracy; they shake their head in disbelief and conclude that all the claims and "conspiracy theories" have to be incorrect as well; thinking such requests must have come from mentally psychopathic people who claim a few of the more far-fetched and made-up information as "proof" and "evidence.".

In this book, I will offer you a rational approach to the concept of an "Illuminati conspiracy," I will discuss the historical evidence of the genuine Bavarian Illuminati and the roots of this secret society spawned countless tales of its power and reach.

I will likewise cover many affiliated secret societies and will continue to investigate different individuals who claim to be real previous members. The book will also take a look at some elite political insiders and see what they have to say about the Illuminati and the belief that a secret society of men is posing a risk to the world and our flexibilities.

Doubters of an Illuminati conspiracy will be very shocked to see the names of some popular individuals throughout history who have made stunning statements plainly showing their conviction that the Illuminati is genuine and creates a threat to all of us.

I do not like to use the word "conspiracy" because it has a negative connotation that it is simply a "conspiracy theory. The terms "conspiracy theory" and "conspiracy theorist" have ended up being pejorative, which indicates they have a negative connotation and are used to insult people and shut down the discussion, comparable to someone shrieking "racist" at someone in efforts to bypass important thinking and cause a knee jerk reaction to paint them as such, when in reality they merely have an opposing ideology on a specific issue.

Much to some people's surprise, lots of "conspiracies" are true, and the dictionary meaning of a conspiracy is "an agreement by two or more individuals to perpetrate a criminal offense, scams, or other wrongful act." Individuals are charged with "conspiracy" in criminal courts every day for merely "conspiring" or planning to engage in a criminal activity.

Conspiracies do happen on a small scale, such as when two individuals conspire to steal or rob a bank, and on a large scale when a country's leader creates a reason to go to war.

Conspiracies are a fact of life. When researchers point out real and irrefutable evidence that exposes a conspiracy, they are often attacked or labeled as "hat-wearing conspiracy theorists," because the term causes people to dismiss the claims as a paranoid deception imagined by someone on the Internet who resides in their mother's apartment. The reality is that genuine conspiracy theorists can be found in high positions of power, and well-read individuals put forth conspiracy theories. Let's not forget that Hillary Clinton openly declared that a "right-wing conspiracy" was fabricating claims that President Bill Clinton had a sexual affair with intern Monica Lewinski. Hillary Clinton was just being a conspiracy theorist, when in reality, her other half Bill was having sexual relations with the intern, and there was no conspiracy attempting to bring him down-- it was only individuals reporting on the truth.

The Bush administration came up with a conspiracy theory that Iraq had weapons of mass destruction and were getting set to use them on America and allies, thereby attacking the country based upon this conspiracy theory, which was later shown to be

100% false. Not just was it incorrect; it was a lie cooked up to justify the invasion and war. As everybody now understands, there were no weapons of mass destruction at all, and Americans had been fooled into fighting based upon a conspiracy theory made up by the United States government.

Until the twenty-first century, a lot of Americans had never heard of the Illuminati. Dan Brown's novel Angels & Demons somehow introduced people to the group in 2003 (although his version was more like a purposeful disinformation campaign). And with the advancement of the information age, social media such as YouTube videos and many websites becoming committed to the subject, more individuals have started to learn about it.

The 2004 election in America brought John Kerry and George W. Bush together to compete for the presidency, both of whom are members of the Skull & Bones secret society headquartered at Yale University, which somehow added fuel to this growing fire.

This was how two Skull & Bones members were able to secure the nominations for both the Democrat and Republican parties in the same election, so no matter which one of them won (George W. Bush or John Kerry), it would be a success for Skull & Bones.

It was around this same time that "9/11 conspiracy theories" were growing, and the cover story for the War in Iraq continued to fall apart. The official report of the September 11th attacks and the increasing "war on terror" just wasn't adding up. For the first few years after the World Trade Center was destroyed, so-called "9/11 conspiracy theories" were limited to the Internet. Still, around 2005 and 2006, they proceeded into the mainstream and found many high-profile advocates whose comments about 9/11 being an "inside job" couldn't be overlooked by the mainstream media.

When individuals thinking about examining the huge disparities in the main story attempted piecing together what happened that day, it inevitably took many people "down the rabbit hole" to find the various secret societies that all led back to the Illuminati. 9/11 would lead to Skull & Bones, which would lead to the Bilderberg Group, which would cause the Bohemian Grove, which would result in the Illuminati and a whole lot of evils that raised much more questions about what the shadowy elite of the world are engaging in behind the scenes was opened.

When people take their minds off mainstream media and popular culture, step back from their self-absorbed way of life, and look deeper into world events and the power structure-directing society, they start to see the world in a very different way.

When someone starts to comprehend that there is more than meets the eye in our world and finds the different branches of elite networks that all assemble under one umbrella, their life is often never the same. People explain it as their awakening to what's occurring on the earth or "decreasing the bunny hole," or having their eyes lastly opened.

If one truly wants to learn about the world's history and the driving force behind major world events, the economy, and even our very culture, then one should check out the Illuminati. At one point in history, in the late 1700s, when the Illuminati was first exposed, many people learned about them and the threats they posed, but as time went on and generations have passed, the majority of people had ignored them. Celebrity News andSports entertainment had controlled the majority of people's minds, and a lot of people had fallen asleep, believing everything was simply outstanding.

Many people used to doubt and deny that the Italian Mafia even existed, the same holds of the modern Illuminati. Ancient secret societies are admitted by mainstream historians to have existed and were not just social clubs for men looking to keep themselves amused after work. They had a useful function, even at that time. Manly P. Hall, a respected secret society expert, explains, "The esoteric organizations of ancient times were, for the most part, philosophical and spiritual. In the medieval world, they were political and philosophical. In the modern-day world, political and social."

He goes on to explain more clearly, "It is beyond doubt that the secret societies of all ages have worked out a significant degree of political impact," which "a second purpose for secret societies was to develop a mechanism for the perpetuation from generation to generation of policies, concepts, or systems of learning, confined to a minimal group of initiated persons."

For many years, FBI director J. Edgar Hoover rejected that the La Cosa Nostra or Italian Mafia even existed. Some had the belief that the mob was blackmailing Hoover with some compromising photos of him and his partner Clyde Tolson. Still, for whatever reason, even the head of the FBI openly denied there was any such thing as an organized criminal network that had judges, lawyers, police, and other public authorities on their payroll. All the denial changed in 1957 after a crucial mafia meeting held on a farm in Apalachin, New York (about 200 miles northwest of New York City), was discovered, now understood as the Apalachin Meeting.

What are the realities, and what is fiction? How did it all begin? What is the evidence for the Illuminati's existence? What are its objectives? Are they communicating with alien beings from another galaxy that covertly work with them and guide them in their evil methods? Are they alien beings disguised as people? You will discover as you dive headfirst Inside the Illuminati.

CHAPTER ONE

Qanon Conspiracy Theory and The New World Order

QAnon might best be understood as an instance of what historian Richard Hofstadter in 1964 called "The Paranoid Style in American Politics," associated with spiritual millenarianism and apocalypticism. The vocabulary of QAnon mirrors Christian tropes--" The Storm" (the Genesis flooding narrative or Judgement Day) and "The Great Awakening," which evokes the historic spiritual Great Awakenings from the very early 18th century to the late 20th century. According to one QAnon video, the fight between Trump and also "the cabal" is of "scriptural percents," a "fight for the planet, of wicked versus outstanding." Some QAnon states the forthcoming numeration supports a "reverse rapture," which is not merely the end of the world as it is currently understood, yet a clean slate also, with redemption and a paradise on earth for the survivors. Within less than a year of existence, QAnon came to be significantly identified by the whole populace. According to an August 2018 Qualtrics survey for The Washington Post, 58% of Floridians recognize QAnon to have a viewpoint regarding it. Of those who had a point of view, many were unwanted. Positive feelings towards QAnon were uncovered to be significantly associated with being at risk of conspiracy theory thinking. According to a March 2020 Pew study, 76% of Americans claimed they had never heard of

QAnon, 20% had listened to "a little concerning it," and 3% stated they had heard "a great a lot."

Some QAnon followers have inevitably begun to acknowledge that they have been divided from family and liked ones and experience isolation due to it. For some, this is a path to beginning the process of divesting themselves of their cultish ideas. In contrast, for others, the isolation reinforces the advantages they obtain from originating from the cult.

People in the QAnon community usually mention alienation from friends and family members. Though they typically speak regarding just how Q tore their connections on private Facebook groups. Yet they think these problems are temporary and also primarily the mistake of others. They frequently comfort themselves by visualizing that there will be a time of retribution at some point in the future, which will show their beliefs. After this occurs, they think that not just will their relationships be brought back, but individuals will depend on them as leaders who understand what's taking place better than the remaining of us.

There are many systemic conspiracy theories where the concept of a New World Order is seen. The following is a checklist of the major ones in roughly sequential order:

Freemasonry Masonic Conspiracy Theory

Freemasonry is just one of the globe's earliest nonreligious fraternal business and developed during the late 16th and early 17th century Britain. Over the years, several cases and conspiracy theories have been routed towards Freemasonry, including the claims that Freemasons have a concealed political agenda and are conspiring to cause a New World Order, a world government organized according to Masonic concepts or governed just by Freemasons. The mystical nature of Masonic importance and ceremonies resulted in Freemasons initially implicated in secretly practicing Satanism in the late 18th century. The original claims of a conspiracy theory within Freemasonry to overturn religion and governments to take control of the world traces back to Scottish writer John Robison, whose reactionary conspiracy theory concepts went across the Atlantic and influenced breakouts of Protestant anti-Masonry in the United States throughout the 19th century. In the 1890s, French writer LéoTaxil composed a series of pamphlets and books disparaging Freemasonry and billing their lodges with venerating Lucifer as the Supreme Being and Great Architect the universe. Even with the fact that Taxil confessed that his claims were all a rip-off, they were and still are believed and also repeated by many conspiracy theory philosophers and had a significant effect on succeeding anti-Masonic claims regarding Freemasonry.

Some conspiracy theory philosophers eventually assumed that some Founding Fathers of the United States, such as George Washington and Benjamin Franklin, were having Masonic spiritual geometric layouts interwoven right into American culture, particularly in the Great Seal of the United States, the United States one-dollar bill, the design of National Mall sites and the roads and highways of Washington, D.C., as a component of a master method to create the first "Masonic federal government" as a design for the coming New World Order.

A Masonic Lodge area

Freemasons rebut these claims of a Masonic conspiracy theory. Freemasonry, which advertises rationalism, places no power in occult symbols. It is not a part of its principle to see the illustration of symbols, regardless of how large, as an act of managing or consolidating power. Additionally, no published details establish the Masonic membership of the men accountable for the Great Seal design. While conspiracy philosophers assert that there are aspects of Masonic impact on the Great Seal of the United States, these components were purposefully or accidentally used, considering that the developers knew the symbols. The many Grand Lodges are independent and sovereign, recommending they act independently and do not have a common agenda. The points of belief of the numerous lodges regularly differ.

End time

In the 19th century, a lot of apocalyptic millennial Christian eschatologists, starting with John Nelson Darby, have forecasted a globalist conspiracy to impose a tyrannical New World Order, controlling structure as the fulfillment of prophecies concerning the "end time" in the Bible, specifically in the Book of Ezekiel, Daniel, the Olivet discovered in the Synoptic Gospels and the Book of Revelation. They claim that individuals who have dealt with the Devil to obtain riches and also power have become pawns in a supernatural chess game have moved humanity right into approving a utopian globe government that hinges on the spiritual frameworks of syncretic-messianic world faiths, which will in the future subject itself to be a dystopian globe empire that imposes the imperial cult of an "Unholy Trinity" of Satan, the Antichrist and also the False Prophet.

Dynamic Christians, such as preacher-theologian Peter J. Gomes, caution Christian fundamentalists that a "spirit of fear" can batter scripture and history with precariously incorporating scriptural literalism, apocalyptic timetables, demonization, and overbearing bias. In contrast, Camp cautions the danger that Christians could pick up some added spiritual baggage" by credulously accepting conspiracy concepts. They seek Christians that enjoy conspiracism to repent.

Illuminati

The Order of the Illuminati was an Enlightenment-age secret society established by Adam Weishaupt on 1 May 1776, a university professor, in Upper Bavaria, Germany. The movement include advocates of freethought, secularism, sex, liberalism, and also republicanism equal rights, hired from the German Masonic Lodges, that looked for to educate rationalism through enigma schools. In 1785, the order was penetrated, separated, and reduced by the government reps of Charles Theodore, Elector of Bavaria, in his preemptive campaign to neutralize the risk of secret societies before winding up being dens of conspiracies to topple the Bavarian monarchy and its state religious beliefs, Roman Catholicism. There is no evidence that the Bavarian Illuminati survived its reductions in 1785. In the late 18th century, reactionary conspiracy philosophers, such as Scottish physicist John Robison and French Jesuit clergyman Augustin Barruel, started hypothesizing that the Illuminati had withstood their reductions come to be the masterminds behind the French Revolution and the Reign of Terror. Throughout the 19th century, fear of an Illuminati conspiracy was a real concern of the European gentility. Their oppressive reactions to this unproven fear provoked in 1848 the changes they sought to prevent.

The Protocols of the Elders of Zion

The Protocols of the Elders of Zion is an antisemitic canard, at first released in Russian in 1903, proclaiming a Judeo-Masonic conspiracy thcory to obtain globe prominence. The message proclaims to be the minutes of the secret meetings of a cabal of Jewish masterminds, which has co-opted Freemasonry and is plotting to rule the world on all Jews because they think themselves to be the chosen people of God. The Protocols integrate many of the core conspiracist themes outlined in the Robison and Barruel assaults on the Freemasons and overlay them with antisemitic allegations about anti-Tsarist movements in Russia.

The Open Conspiracy

The Open Conspiracy British author and futurist H. G. Wells promoted cosmopolitanism and prepare blueprints for a world to establish a technocratic world state and also ready economic situation. Wells warned, nonetheless, in his 1940 book The New World Order that: when the battle seems drifting in the direction of a world social democracy, there might still be great delays and disappointments before it winds up being an efficient and beneficent world system.

Countless individuals will indeed despise the brand-new world order, be rendered disgruntled by the frustration of their enthusiasm and aspirations with its growth, and will die protesting against it. When we attempt to assess its promise, we have to bear in mind the distress of a generation or more of malcontents, countless of them graceful-looking and mostly gallant individuals. Wells's books were significant in offering the 2nd meaning to the term "new world order," which would just be used by state socialist supporters and anti-communist oppositions for generations to come.

Despite his ideas' appeal and prestige, Wells failed to work deeper because he could not concentrate his energies on a direct request to intelligentsias who would, inevitably, have to collaborate the Wellsian brand-new world order.

CHAPTER TWO

The Illuminati World

The infamous Illuminati secret society has remained the focus of so-called "conspiracy theorists" for centuries. They have been called the puppet masters who secretly pull the strings of the world's events from elections to revolutions, and from business monopolies to stock exchange crashes. A substantial variety of researchers and ordinary citizens have differing degrees of suspicion that, in some way, someplace, a secret program is continuously hiding behind the scenes.

When unexpected occurrences happen on the planet, these individuals don't see them as a random incident, but as the work of a hidden hand that has managed or encouraged these occurrences to take place for the personal, professional, or monetary gain of particular individuals. Usually, such speculation is referred to as a "conspiracy theory" and dismissed as creative thinking. Many of the world's events don't make total sense, even to the so-called specialists who study them. Something is missing out from a strong explanation. More to the story than meets the eye, but these supposed professionals are often afraid to hypothesize on what that missing piece of the puzzle is.

Individuals look at disastrous occurrences like the attacks on the World Trade Center on 9/11 and question how such a thing could happen without law enforcement and intelligence firms knowing about it. Individuals take a look at the home mortgage collapse of 2008 and the following financial consequences of bank failures and government bailouts and question how such a thing could occur. People see their standard of living going down and how they can hardly manage and question how can this be? People hear on the news that child molesters and rapists get out of jail after just a couple of years, but others are locked up for decades after getting busted with some marijuana.

So individuals turn to the television to keep their mind off such things. With the push of a button, their reason is made for relaxing with the relaxing images of seeing stunning candidates contend with being this season's American Idol, or they get an adrenaline rush as their preferred football team scores a winning touchdown with just seconds left on the clock. These things make good sense to them, and its what others will discuss the next day at work, and if they wish to feel connected with others, they have to participate in these pointless activities.

The reality of the matter is that when you step back and take a closer look at the world that we are living in and at what truly matters, at the sources of information we continuously rely on, and put together several pieces of this mysterious puzzle called life, a quite different image starts to emerge. What ought to be the top story on the news is mitigated to a little and unwary article in the back half of the paper and is entirely left out from broadcast news. What should ordinarily be in celebrity chatter publication is the top story on the significant television networks. Why does this occur?

One begins to see things much differently when discovering the concrete reality of secret societies and their influence and power. As in the last few years, when one discovers the growing trustworthy details about these secret societies, their subscription, objectives, and achievements, one sees a gaping hole in the legitimacy and precision of traditional media and general knowledge.

Any discussion of a "conspiracy" or secret agenda being performed by an organization of rich and powerful guys is generally countered with laughter by the average person who mindlessly follows the herd.

Is it that difficult to think an organization of powerful men has made a pact with each other to enhance their programs secretly? Is it that tough to design a self-perpetuating structure that would enable such an organization to continually function no matter who inhabits any one position at any time? Is it far-fetched to think that these people would buy and manage the mainstream media and utilize this useful tool to further their objectives?

One of the first truth shows ever produced was called Survivor, which began airing in May of 2000. The show featured sixteen individuals placed on a secluded island and contended for one million dollars every week; an entrant was voted off the program by their fellow castaways. As the show went on, some people on the island would secretly arrange to help each other out at the expense of others who were not part of their plan. The outsiders had no idea such an agreement was made, and when bad occurrences fell upon them, they didn't think anything aside from misfortune. However, unknown to them, they were a victim of a conspiracy—a victim of the workings of a secret society within the group of candidates.

As future seasons of Survivor were aired, the secret alliances would end up being a common theme of the show to viewers who had a watchful eye of the functions of all who were on the island. Devious contestants constantly found such an idea a reliable and practical way to get ahead.

If the development of a secret alliance among members on Survivor became a standard method of taking advantage over others and to "make it through," is it that far-fetched to believe that similar secret alliances take place in business or politics? It appears that the idea to form a secret alliance exclusively for the benefit of those involved is completely sensible, and the very best way to safeguard such an alliance and ensure its success is to prevent others who are not a part of it from becoming mindful that such a thing even exists.

We understand the fact that secret societies exist in politics, business, and faith. A lot of these associations have existed for centuries. The existence of such societies spawns speculation from outsiders, and often fear. With little information to work from to formulate a trusted theory as to what these individuals are doing and the repercussions of their actions might be, it is often hard to accurately comprehend the functions of a secret society or alliance. But just as the most careful criminal, secret societies often leave hints behind. No matter the number of preventative measures one takes to prevent any understanding of their actions, it is nearly difficult to carry out a plot flawlessly without leaving proof behind. Similar to some murder cases, the evidence might not be understood right away after the criminal offense, or it may not even be discovered as proof at all. As time passes, other hints from comparable criminal activities may emerge and shed new light on things that were initially neglected.

In regards to the Illuminati, hints have been discovered over the past several hundred years. Something is undoubtedly being kept secret by some powerful and influential individuals. A network, a plan, a source of wealth and power, a reason for the secrecy, and more. In more modern times, beginning in about the late 1970s, various people have stepped forward and claimed to be real members of this elusive group and said they had defected and turned to Christianity. These guys have stated stories declaring to expose some of the Illuminati secret society's history, beliefs, and objectives. A few of their claims appear reasonable, others stretch of the creativity, and others apparent lies. Their statement, together with any inconsistencies, will be addressed in this book.

Covered are collections of many pieces of proof about the Illuminati, consisting of initial works taken in 1786 from the homes of some of the members. These works are indeed genuine, and no scholar or historian will refute that. The only refutations are regarding whether the organization could continue its work in the years following its initial exposure to the general public, over about two hundred years earlier. When one checks out the words of creator Adam Weishaupt, it appears difficult that the organization didn't continue to exist and later prosper. Since its leadership was found, it seems somehow stupid to believe that their objectives would merely be abandoned.

Had Adam Weishaupt not created and documented such an organization's plans, it seems that another power starving diabolical would have done the same. If Thomas Edison had not invented the light bulb, surely you would not have the opportunity to read these words by candlelight. Another man would have used the power of electricity just as efficiently. Such an invention was inevitable, and other men who had no connection with Edison were working towards the same objective. Cultures worldwide throughout history that have had no contact with each other have made comparable and often similar developments and discoveries. Humanity's interests are equal worldwide, just as our ethical drawbacks are.

The very idea of a secret alliance among guys to include each other's goals at the expense of others and under a shroud of secrecy surely isn't a unique idea. Mafias and arranged criminal businesses have sprung up worldwide and have similar structures and approaches, but another has influenced few.

The idea of a secret group that has vowed allegiance to each other over all others need to be as significant to our lives as falling in love. And just as this human condition of interpersonal relationships has ended up being a classic theme in Hollywood motion pictures, we ought to think that a similar style would be found too, and it is. A deceptive group of bad people who outline greed, destruction, or harm.

While a range of traditional Hollywood stories continues to be produced, with a number of them involving secret criminal alliances, it is interesting that an uncommon variety of them will integrate plots very comparable to occurrences in reality associated with the functions of the Illuminati.

Even more unusual, the name "Illuminati" is used to explain the group that is behind the events in these films. After analyzing Illuminati themes, symbolism, and recommendations in popular Hollywood films, one can arrive at no other conclusion than the writers and producers of those movies have a detailed understanding of the Illuminati itself.

While they are not producing a documentary film attempting to expose the company like the different ones discussed in this book, one can't help but think that they are trying to get across to the audience in a similar method. After all, one can learn a lesson from reading the facts or hearing a story about such events in a fable or allegory.

Much like Aesop's fables include underlying ethical messages conveyed through made-up words. A few of these Hollywood films' themes consist of plotlines surrounding terrorism, mind control, Big Brother, secret societies, and occult mysticism and magic.

While some uninformed skeptics believe that when someone discusses the Illuminati, they got the idea from a Hollywood movie, the reverse is true. Many writers and producers have gotten their ideas from the accurate and historic Illuminati.

In October of 1963, a man named Joe Valachi testified before the McClellan Congressional Committee on organized criminal activity where he informed the authorities about the Italian Mafia's inner workings and how significant their organization was. He described how they controlled a market selection and had cops and judges in their pockets from either dangers or rewards. The story was too unique for the authorities when Valachi was first taken into custody and began informing the police about the Mafia. They could not comprehend how a secret criminal business could be useful and operate without notice in so many social sectors. Valachi was locked away in a mental medical facility and was believed to be outrageous. Just later, did authorities recognize he was telling the truth, and as La Cosa Nostra was uncovered, their criminal empire's level started to be comprehended.

The topic of "the Mafia" continues to fascinate people. If one didn't understand their history, they might think that well known Hollywood films such as Goodfellas and Casino are entirely fictional, but are based on true stories. The gangsters represented in these films did live lives of high-end and fantastic influence. They were also callous killers.

One can't help but discover the deafening and odd silence on specific issues by so-called experts in the mainstream media. How is it that Rush Limbaugh, Sean Hannity, Alan Colmes, Bill O'Reilly, and others disregard concerns surrounding the Illuminati every year? Problems with tangible, strong evidence that is undeniable. For instance, the annual Bilderberg conference or the Cremation of Care event at the Bohemian Grove or the Federal Reserve Bank's dedicated functions. Surely these are at least fascinating enough stories for a periodic section. Still, for years, these so-called political professionals and analysts inexplicably omit any mention of such problems and organizations from their shows.

The response is that the majority of these people know much about these concerns. A lot of them accomplices and individuals in such things.

These individuals are paid millions of dollars a year to captivate the general public with problems of little significance and to set the program of the public state of mind in a manner that excludes any genuine responses to what is at stake and what is occurring in Washington. These propagandists parrot talking points that are offered to them daily by the people who sign their paychecks and choose to act as gate-keepers whenever a delicate concern might be dealt with. These talking heads can't plead ignorance because they are often a part of the inner circle they protect. Even during call-in radio talk shows, when the format is relaxed, and the hosts inform the audience that "any subject is fair game," they do not mean what they say. Any pertinent concern that falls beyond the recommended paradigm they are perpetuating faces the call screener. If it makes it on the airwaves, the caller gets hung up immediately, and their question is either ridiculed or overlooked.

Some essential gamers in settings of power and influence might not be a participant, and even mindful that they are serving the Illuminati, or that the culture exists in all. These people perform an egotistical plan to benefit those who have guaranteed them rewards in return or progress for their participation.

While these gamers recognize that they are a component of a private or deceptive agreement pushing an agenda, many do not acknowledge that they are a pawn in a bigger conspiracy. Their only objectives are power, status, and money. A few of their activities are criminal, and some have been caught as well as imprisoned. The basic reason is that many prepared servants go along with Illuminati schemes while not seeing the underlying forces directing a larger operation.

Knowledge or Information is power, and the Illuminati know this. Having accessibility to accurate and reliable information is indeed power, and the capacity to dispense false and misleading information is additional power. As one reads words of the initial writings of the Illuminati, one finds that the beginning participants recognized this in the late 1700s, long before the communication age. By taking over the mainstream media in all forms as it created, television, print, and also radio, they have been able to contain information and also dispense deceptive or pointless stories to the public.

If the people did not see it on CNN or Fox News, they have not to be taking place, they assume. It has only been with publications released by small independent authors. In the later years of the Internet's arrival, it has allowed those that are hungry to find something substantial to please their wishes. Web sites like Infowars.com and, to a lower degree, DrudgeReport.com have let us bypass the monopoly control of information given by the mainstream media.

In compliance with web pages, this author has compiled both details from the original works of the Illuminati and a few of the first writers to create publications exposing them and their objectives, in addition to one of the most exact writers and researchers who have continued that tradition. You will find the testament of women and men who either asserted to have been Illuminati members or victims of some of its members. You will additionally find a compilation of the uncommon circumstances that Illuminati associated topics are discussed or alluded to in mainstream media sources.

Many suspected or confirmed Illuminati created and controlled class of organizations are rarely pointed out in the mainstream information. These one-of-a-kind occurrences have been put together in this book.

Finally, you will find a summary of several references, both indirect and direct, to the Illuminati and their activities that are found in prominent Hollywood movies, books, and television shows. Such rare mentions go undetected by visitors unaware of the deeper meanings that these storylines and personalities have.

With bits and items of dependable details regarding some fairly popular secret societies and organizations like the Skull and Bones society, the Bohemian Grove, and the Bilderberg team being launched to the public, we have concrete evidence those who are involved with such organizations. Authentic subscription lists have been taken or otherwise obtained from the Bohemian Grove, and visitor listings have been gotten incomparable fashion concerning Bilderberg guests. Sometimes, as with President George W. Bush and Senator John Kerry, men have publicly confessed being members of Skull and Bones, but rejected any comment beyond that. We have a clear suggestion of who is included in such an organization. We can see by their résumés that they have achieved personal, economic, and political success far beyond various other competitors. It would certainly be crazy not to see a clear pattern in all of this.

These secret societies, organizations, and meetings exist. This is beyond a doubt and with mountains of undeniable proof to sustain this type of conclusion. They live for an objective they have existed for centuries. Their existence and purpose exceed a plain social gathering, as alcohol, parties and dinners are for.

After reading all the evidence, one must reasonably conclude that they exist partially to improve each other's occupations using secret alliances. One has a better idea of just how the political landscape is created when this is realized. There is also a more extensive program that is being carried out and is directed by those at greater levels of power within the Illuminati. A satanic and occulticschedule is sustaining the New World Order's building and the organized slavery of the human race.

Suppose this level of understanding is gotten to by an outsider. In that case, it is just the outcome of their standard being tested after discovering the truth of mysticism and occult philosophies and rituals that are part of most of these organizations.

It is one thing to observe and understand secret alliances among the rich and powerful implied for their personal and professional enhancement. It is something entirely different to see these alliances in the context of fancy and unusual hellish routines, as in the initiation into the Skull and Bones society, or the yearly Cremation of Care ritual in the secluded redwood forest of the Bohemian Grove.

These are established men we are discussing about. One of the most innovative, informed, and wealthy men on the planet from famous households, but they take part in such things. Initially, it appears so improbable that it is reasonable to easily reject such accusations as extravagant rumors or the ramblings of a mentally insane individual. The closer one looks right into these points; the more irrefutable such claims come to be.

One who ponders these issues also inevitably comes to the question of the Illuminati's ultimate purpose? Why is there a need to create the New World Order global government? What then? What role do the occult rituals and necromancies play in all of this? The solutions are located both in Bible prophecy and also within the teachings of the occult as well as New Age organizations. They parallel each other entirely to their verdicts, at which point they substantially differ.

New Age and occult teachings predict that when the New World Order facilities and ideologies are complete, from within the hierarchy of the Illuminati will indeed arrive the long-expected and awaited messiah. They believe that he will undoubtedly unify all the world's religious beliefs into one compatible formula, and the fact that he will fulfill all predictions of the coming savior of the world. They also say that, at the moment, the secret hierarchy of well-informed masters will be able to appear from the shadows in what is called the externalization of the order, and afterward, finally reveal themselves to the world and disclose the surprising wisdom that they had kept protected for many generations.

The appearance of this New Age Christ will then eliminate all discomfort and struggle with the world. All poverty and sickness, all prejudice as well as criminal offense. All lacks as well as shortage, all worries, as well as stress and anxiety. It is at this point that the world and all that populate it will ultimately have the ability to stay in perfect peace and consistency with each other, many thanks to the revelations of this Illuminati messiah and the hierarchy.

They needed to work in secret and deny their presence for hundreds of years, to secure themselves from their opponents. It is only now that their very great work is completed that they may lastly expose themselves with no anxiety of consequences. This is all, according to the teachings in New Age enlightenment circles and occultic hierarchy. These teachings report that this Illuminati Christ will be a super-human demigod or perhaps a being from one more planet or dimension.

On the other hand, according to Christianity, Islam, and various other religions, the New World Order global realm will be taken control of by the Antichrist and his followers. In this sight, a man will additionally claim to be the world's messiah and hold the trick to fixing humankind's problems. Only in this view, the core of humanity's troubles include those who disagree that he is the messiah. The freedom from prejudice that he promises is impeded by Christians and others that see him as a fake Christ and the Antichrist. The perversions and immorality that he is preaching are resisted and denounced by faithful Christians that see such habits as sinful and socially and spiritually destructive.

Equally, As Adolf Hitler guaranteed tranquility and financial success in Germany once the Jews were gotten rid of, the Antichrist will use the same remedy and single out the resistant Christians and others as the challenge to peace and prosperity. These old made Christians with their outdated customs and beliefs hold back the unity of humanity; the Antichrist will inform the world. Individuals who still believe in personal property, individual privacy, and the concepts set out in the United States' initial Constitution are the ones who are disrupting the new system. Those that will decline implantable integrated circuits and tracking tools or neural interfaces wired directly into their minds. Those who talk out against such things are the individuals who need to be eliminated for there to be peace. This, obviously, according to the Illuminati messiah and his advocates.

At some point throughout this challenge, Christians think that Jesus will go back to the planet, and the Apocalypse will take place, exposing the fake Christ and also casting him right into Hell. God is stated to ultimately introduce the enigmas of existence and life's struggles and damage or punish those who did not follow his rules. Those faithful to God's ideas will then be permanently awarded for their nonpartisanship and guts

Pre Illuminati Organizations.

Many of the information dispersed about the Illuminati comes from the Knights Templar, the Freemasons, and the Bavarian Illuminati established in Germany in 1776. It's crucial to keep in mind that nearly the same kind of organization had existed previously, for hundreds of years. The Knights Templar date back to the 1100s and the Freemasons to the late 1500s, but before these organizations had developed, secret cultures which possessed supposed underground expertise had existed much previously. It would later turn into these newer and much more advanced groups.

Expertise has usually provided power, and dating back to old Egypt as well as Greece, groups of men had maintained expertise to themselves and only exposed it to others in incremental degrees within what was called the Mysteries, or the Mystery institutions. As medicine, art, and research were progressing and new explorations were being made, the adepts or beginning of these Mystery schools were the ones on the cutting side. These organizations were often comprised of the brightest guys.

The Mystery schools served as a strategy for spiritual enlightenment as well. Mystical and spiritual theories were shown and acted out in routines and events to communicate symbolic significance to the initiates. While these Mystery colleges might not have helped in any bad intentions or plotted any wicked plans against non-members and society all at once, one can comprehend how launches in the Mysteries might establish a superiority complex and use the cover of the organizations to assist them in performing their professional and political programs. Some believe that the Mystery schools once had the highest possible standards relating to the personality and stability of the members, and they were slowly damaged, and such virtues were replaced with selfishness as well as wickedness.

CHAPTER THREE

The Luciferian Doctrine and the Dark Agenda

It is obvious from the works of famous Freemasons and Illuminati authors that the elite members' religious beliefs and approach are that of Satanism or Luciferianism. Whether this is a literal belief or a symbolic or a metaphoric belief is of little difference. It would then be metaphoric as well if it were literal. If it were metaphoric, it additionally increases into a literal style as the participants' activities materialize themselves.

To sum up, Satanism or Luciferianismone must comprehend the distinction between theistic Satanism and atheistic Satanism.

Atheistic Satanism was popularized in the late 1960s by Anton LaVey, the creator of the Church of Satan, and also the writer of The Satanic Bible. While misleading and complicated, he and his followers profess that they are atheists and don't believe in a literal Devil, and even God. They don't rely on an afterlife or a Heaven or Hell, either. These individuals prefer to call themselves Satanists and use the symbol of Satan for its rebellious and nonconformist undertones.

Theistic Satanism, on the other hand, is the belief in a God and a Devil, as well as superordinary beings. These Satanists take the opposite side of the Christian perception concerning the Garden of Eden and the Fall of Man. In Christianity and Judaism, the book of Genesis defines how God created Adam and Eve as well as how they lived in the Garden of Eden. God was claimed to have informed them that they were not to eat the forbidden fruit from a specified tree of knowledge of good and evil, for if they did, they would certainly pass away.

As the story goes, Satan showed up to Eve as a serpent and attracted her to eat the fruit. Genesis 3:1 -7 states; "The woman started to the snake, "we might eat fruit from the trees in the garden, yet God said, 'You shall not eat fruit from the tree that is in the middle of the garden, and you shall not touch it, or you will die.'".

" You will certainly not die," the serpent stated to the woman. "For God knows the fact that when you eat of the fruit, your eyes will be opened, and you will certainly be like God, understanding evil and good.".

" When the woman saw that the fruit of the said tree was great for food as well as pleasing to the eye, and additionally desirable for gaining knowledge, she eventually took some and ate it. She later offered some to her husband, who was actually with her, and he also consumed it. The eyes of both of them were opened, and they found out they were naked, so they went ahead to sew fig leaves together and made coverings for themselves.".

Theistic Satanists and Luciferians believe that Satan came to the Garden of Eden to save Adam and Eve and humankind from ignorance, and that God didn't want them to have the understanding since, then they would not be his slaves. In this way, God is viewed as the oppressor and the bad one, while Satan is viewed as the hero and savior. This is why in such publications as The Secret Doctrine, author Helena Blavatsky refers to Satan as the holy spirit.

She wrote in the book, "Thus "SATAN," once he ceases to be viewed in the dogmatic, superstitious, unphilosophical spirit of the Churches, grows into the glorious image of someone who made from terrestrial a divine MAN; who offered him, throughout the long cycle of Maha-Kalpa the law of the Spirit of Life, as well as made him free from the Sin of Ignorance.".

"The real meaning is even more philosophical, as well as the legend of the first "Fall" (of the angels) takes a scientific coloring when adequately understood."

This is among the reasons the Illuminati has a hierarchical structure, and only gives knowledge gradually as members climb the ranks. Indeed, knowledge is power, and they have taken the fruit from the tree of knowledge of good and evil. They have hidden it away, making use of it as a carrot to attract lower degree initiates to do the organization's bidding so that they may be well awarded with not just their social and financial assistance, but with the prohibited occult knowledge of Man's past and of the nature of truth itself. Such prohibited knowledge, they think, holds the potential for a man to come to be god-like.

The term Lucifer, being synonymous with Satan, is Latin for "light-bearer," which is the reason Satanists and Luciferians believe that the Devil is the source of wisdom and knowledge. Thus he is excellent. While in Christianity, Jesus is claimed to be the light of the world, the Illuminati direct this quality to Satan or Lucifer. Satan's name implies "opponent" or accuser and is, for that reason, the enemy of God. Satan is given the title of Lucifer simply because he brings the forbidden wisdom or knowledge that God did not want humanity to have, In Christianity and Luciferianism and various other religions, the term "light" stands for love, wisdom, and knowledge. One primary difference between a lot of faiths and Luciferianism is that Christianity and most religions freely educate their message and welcome everyone to discover it and comprehend it, where occultism keeps its message hidden from the majority of people and doesn't share its expertise with others.

The word occult implies "concealed." The primary distinction between Luciferianism and Christianity is that traditional Christianity teaches that salvation comes just by believing in Jesus, where sorcerers believe that one is saved by learning the secret understanding. While this idea of salvation by knowledge is not overtly wicked and sinister, it is what the Illuminati have done with this concept that shows they are a cabal of hypocrites, liars, and tyrants.

The term Illuminati is Latin for Illuminated ones and is additionally a reference to light, brilliance, and Lucifer.

Inside the Mindset of the Illuminati.

When one completely comprehends the religion of the Illuminati and its subsidiary branches such as high-level Freemasons, Skull and Bones members, as well as attendees of Bohemian Grove, one can battle it out with the reality of this Luciferian doctrine. While several openly known organizations such as the Freemason pride themselves on getting their members instilled with moral character, how come these elite members can be Satan adorers? Do they know the truth? Is

Satan truly the good god, and the God of the Bible is the wicked one holding knowledge, wisdom, and blessings back from the human race?

If the Illuminati possess the truth about the history of our creation, existence, and God's nature, then are they betraying their own god by keeping that truth, wisdom, and knowledge from others? What about not just keeping that said truth from people, but actually lying to them, or ruthlessly taking advantage of other people or stealing what belongs to them? Whatever they believe the truth is, they are keeping it to themselves and putting out a continuous stream of propaganda, out-right lies, and disinformation, just to protect against others discovering that truth.

While almost every religion on earth from Christianity, to Islam, to Buddhism and Hinduism, wants every person to understand what they consider to be the truth, it is the Illuminati that do not comply with these ideals. Elite members do not adhere to the principle of life, treating others the way you intend to be treated. Instead, they violate virtually every significant values found in faiths or religions around the globe. Please do not lie, do not swipe, do not murder, do not fancy; these rules mean nothing to the Illuminati and its subsidiary organizations' elite members.

These revelations commonly result in whether these people count on an afterlife or a judgment from God after they pass away. Many religious beliefs think that they will undoubtedly stand before God and face sentences for their transgressions when one passes away. Under this form of belief system, even if a person survives life without being caught for their transgressions, they will one day pay the afterlife price in a purgatory for short-lived punishment or burning in Hell forever.

As a result, one wonders what the Illuminati believe will happen to them when they die. Just how will they escape Divine justice for all of their misdeeds?

There are two explanations for this. One is that they do not believe in an afterlife, that we are just sophisticated animals having no soul, and when we are dead, there is no afterlife, nor judgment. This explains their social Darwinist world view and their unreasonable parasitic techniques, which eventually robs others of their sanity, money, health, and freedom. Another necessary explanation is that the Illuminati believe that God does not judge us personally, but in an impersonal fashion based on a scale of good deeds versus evil acts. In this sight, one is thought to be able to cancel their Karma, in a manner of speaking, as well as stay clear of any type of undesirable effects for their indiscretions.

Both of these explanations bring about other questions. Is the Illuminati, right? Are we merely animals without soul or afterlife? If we are religious, are we the ones living a lie? For argument's purpose, they are right that there is no immortality and no judgment from God after one dies. Even if it holds, if most of us were to obey their philosophy, then our society would undoubtedly be a dangerous place, meaningless and unfulfilling. Life would be Hell on earth if every man were out for himself, and we all would break the necessary moral code of the civilized world. If there is no immortality or judgment from God, no Heaven or Hell, then the short life that we live on this world would still be more pleasurable, fulfilling, as well as safe if we were to live by Biblical principles than if we were to obey the Illuminati's code of do what thou wants.

The Illuminati might have the whole truth, or they may have just a piece of it and assume they have it all as a whole, like a blind guy who gets hold of an elephant's tail and thinks that it is an elephant, not recognizing he is only holding a tiny part of an elephant and can not begin to picture what an elephant is, based upon the small part that he is holding in his hand.

Regardless of their supposed exceptional wisdom and knowledge, the Illuminati have been wrong in the past. They have been blinded by their pride and intoxicated from their power. Adolf Hitler, together with his elite inner circle of Nazis, thought that they would rule the world and build a new race of enlightened super-men. They thought that magical powers were on their side, and their destiny was to build a thousand-year empire with Adolf Hitler as its high priest. Instead, their strategies fell apart as Hitler and his closest allies were compelled to commit suicide in defeat.

In philosophy, a concept called Pascal's wager suggests that if one were to live as though there was no God or final judgment, and they were incorrect, they would have a significant loss. But if somebody were to live as though there is a God, and God has established rules for us to comply with, which each individual will be rewarded or punished for their acts, then if they turn out to be wrong, they would have lost nothing and would have had a much safer and more fulfilling life anyway. Pascal suggested that even though we can not prove God's true existence through scientific inquiry or reason, people should wager as though he exists because one has potentially everything to gain and nothing to lose by doing so.

While learning the details of occult philosophy can cause one to wrestle with their faith, one must know there are real consequences to how we chose to live our lives.

Whatever one's faith is, a universal code of conductin the world exists. It is clear that the Illuminati consistently breaks that code while providing the society with a false face that they abide by the same rules everyone else is required to follow.

CHAPTER FOUR

The Edicts

The1stEdictAgainsttheIlluminati

A mandate can be referred to as an act of law made by a monarchy (just like an executive order made by a president today). On June 22, 1784, Duke Karl Theodore, the Elector of Bavaria, made the first order against the Illuminati after his sister-in-law Duchess Dowager Maria Anna was given some documents an early defector called Joseph Schneider, and then passed them onto the Duke.

The proclamation reads, in part, "Whereas all communities, societies, and associations without approval from a public authority and the confirmation of the Monarch are illegal, prohibited by law, suspect and dangerous things in [and] of themselves. His Electoral Highness [the Duke] has decided not to tolerate them in his State, whatever their designation and interior constitutions, ordering categorically ... one and all subjects to withdraw from any association or secret assembly of this kind ... those societies [have] drawn the attention of the public and awakened its fears ..."

The 2nd Edict Against the Illuminati.

In 1785, Duke Karl Theodore issued a second proclamation, which was a lot more threatening and particularly named the Illuminati and Freemasonry as the wrongdoers with a conspiracy against the government. In this order, the Duke also revealed that if anyone were to come forward and reveal who was included or specifically which masonic lodges had been infiltrated and were being used in this conspiracy-- that informant might remain confidential and even keep half the cash that was seized as a result of their confession. The other half [of the money], the proclamation stated, would be offered to the poor.

It reads in part, "We [the government] ... have been deeply impacted and displeased to learn that the different Lodges of so-called Freemasons and Illuminati, who are still in our States, have taken so little hearken of our General Prohibition released on June 22nd of last year against all fraternal societies clandestine and unapproved, as not only to continue to convene in secret, but to raise funds, and to recruit new members, seeking to boost the currently large numbers of adepts further."

The proclamation continues, "We had deemed this society, very much degenerated and of primitive organization, too suspect, both as regards to spiritual issues and from a social and political point of view, so that we could no longer tolerate it in our States ... we command that all authorities should execute our orders exactly and privately notify us of any disobedience. We state that all cash and any funds collected illegally [by the lodges] will be seized [and] half will be provided to the poor. In contrast, the other half will go to the denunciator [informant], even if he is a member of one of those societies, with a guarantee to keep his name confidential."

It concludes, "We hope that each of our subjects value enough of our favor and his honor and happiness so that all over we can count on due obedience to our orders and be excused from needing to take more serious steps."

The 3rd Edict Against the Illuminati.

On August 16, 1787, not long after the castle of Baron de Bassus was searched, where more documents were discovered, the 3rd edict against the Illuminati was made by the Duke of Bavaria saying the penalty would be death for any Illuminati member found meeting or hiring anybody to join them. "Any so charged and condemned are to be denied of their lives by the sword, while those thus hired are to have their items confiscated and themselves to be condemned to continuous banishment from the areas of the Duke. Under the same penalties of confiscation and banishment, the members of the order, no matter under what name or circumstances, irregular or regular, they should gather, are forbidden to assemble as lodges."

" As more time passes, it is further realized how harmful and dangerous the Order of the Illuminati will be for the State and religion is allowed to flourish here and beyond. It is difficult to predict the deplorable effects of posterity if we stand back, if not dealt with very seriously. At the same time, there is still time to forcefully get rid of a disease, which is far more daunting than the plague itself.".

" ... for the recruiter, he is to be deprived of life by the sword, and for the hired, he will be sentenced to have his property seized and eliminated for life from all States of His Electoral Highness, with a guarantee of never being allowed to return. Under the same penalties of forfeiture and expulsion, the prohibited Lodges of the Illuminati, under whatever name they might conceal and carefully present themselves, in all locations, must be subject to strenuous security. Those in lodge clothes will be held and dealt with as if they had attended meetings secretly, in suspect places such as hotels or specific homes. We will not permit the baseless excuses usually offered-- an open society of good friends-- specifically when those present have now been suspected of impiety and Illuminism."

The 4th Edict Against the Illuminati.

Many mainstream sources (including the frequently incorrect and unreliable Wikipedia) declare that shortly after the 3rd order was issued in 1787, the Illuminati was entirely irradiated and wasn't much of a concern after that. The issue is-- the Duke of Bavaria issued a 4th edict a couple of years later in 1790 saying that the Illuminati was not only still active but were continuing to hire new members!

On November 15, 1790, the following announcement against the Illuminati was issued by the Duke, stating, "The Elector has learned, partly by the spontaneous confession of some members, partly by sound intelligence, that despite the Edicts of July 14, 1784 and August 16th 1785 (and in the very same month in 1787), the Illuminati still hold, albeit in smaller numbers, secret meetings through the Electorate, but particularly in Munich and the surrounding area; they continue to attract boys to the cause and have maintained a correspondence with [secret] societies and with members in other countries.".

It goes on, "They continue to assault the State and especially religion, either verbally or through handouts ... Every speech, every printed book or manuscript against religion and the state need to be reported to the authorities or the Elector [Duke] himself, as well as any secret meetings. Those who have remained quiet on these problems, having undoubtedly been shown to have possessed information, will be severely punished.

The denunciator, even if he was an accessory to the crime, will receive a cash reward, and his identity will be kept confidential.".

The 4th order cautions, "Any member who has assisted in a secret meeting, has hired new members or referred [secret] societies or brothers in other countries, will be mercilessly punished by death. Any civil servant or [those in the] military, any holder of a beneficial workplace, a parish priest, and so on, must swear that he has not and will never be a part of the sector they'll be convicted of perjury and shall be penalized accordingly.".

Taking Over the Government.

One of the original Illuminati defectors called Joseph von Utschneider, who provided a deposition to the court about the Illuminati strategies, alerted that they prepared to "present an around the world ethical regime which would be under their control in every nation. This council would decide on all matters concerning promotions, appointments, and pardons, in addition to rejections ... This would give it the limitless right to pronounce last judgment over the sincerity and effectiveness of an individual.".

The confiscated correspondence between members of the group confirms this accusation. One of the letters reads, "The Order needs to have the power of life and death in consequence of our oath; and with propriety, for the same reason, and by the same right, that any government in the world possesses it.

-- for the Order comes in their place, making them unnecessary. When things can not be otherwise, and ruin would occur if the association did not use this means, the Order must, as well as public rulers, employ it for the good of humanity; therefore, for its preservation."

Several letters revealed their intent to deceive people to "guarantee their happiness."Weishaupt's megalomaniacal objectives of world domination became very clear with such declarations as, "the Order will, for its own sake, and therefore certainly, place every man in that circumstance in which he can be most efficient. The pupils are convinced that the Order will rule the world. Every member therefore becomes a ruler.".

"The great strength of our Order lies in its concealment; let it never appear in any location in its name, but constantly covered by another name, and another profession." This has successfully occurred with private organizations like the Council on Foreign Relations, the Bilderberg Group, and the Federal Reserve, taking over society's key power centers. It must be pointed out that the Founding Fathers of America documented their grievances with the Monarch in the Declaration of Independence, and 56 men signed their names to it and sent it off to the king of England. They didn't hide their objectives or trick people hoping to further their objectives. Unlike Weishaupt and the Illuminati, they were honest and open about their beliefs, strategies, and goals, who used deception and fraud as a standard practice.

Similarly, when theologian Martin Luther opposed the Catholic Church's oppressive control over 250 years before Weishaupt, he made a note of his complaints. He nailed them on the front door of his regional church in 1517. He didn't deceive or lie to anybody about his hopes of breaking the Catholic Church's stranglehold on society. Still, fellow German, Adam Weishaupt, was power-hungry himself. Rather than wanting to free society from the tyranny of the Jesuits and the Catholic Church, he wanted to be the tyrant himself.

CHAPTER FIVE

The Thirteen Bloodlines Theory

In some cases, people refer to the "Illuminati families" or the "leading thirteen bloodlines of the Illuminati" as the ruling elite within the pyramid of power that regulates our world. A few names are thrown around and claimed to be Illuminati families that interbreed to retain their broad range power amongst the little group of the ruling elite. Some of the most common affirmed thirteen families are: Astor, Bundy, Collins, DuPont, Freeman, Kennedy, Li, Onassis, Rockefeller, Rothschild, Russell, Van Duyn, and the Merovingian bloodline.

Among the much more popular promoters of this theory is FritSpringmeier, that in 1999 released Bloodlines of the Illuminati, where he wrote, "The goal of this publication is to lay out the historic truths concerning these elite families ... as soon as one recognizes these families, the battle between kings no longer look like battles between elite intrigues, but often can be recognized as contrived battles created to control the masses of both sides by their hoggish Machiavellian masters."

Springmeier continues, "The Illuminati themselves decided to boost thirteen bloodlines. The number 13 is very crucial amazingly, and these 13 occult individuals mock the 13 tribes of Israel (remember the 13th people, the Tribe of Joseph was split right into Ephraim & Manasseh). This does not imply that just

13 Illuminati families are influential. Various other families have risen to prominence.

Further, worldwide there are other families of excellent oligarchical power that have allied themselves to the Illuminati in the financial and political realms without needing to intermarry right into the Illuminati."

While Frit]'s publication shows up externally to be an excellent evaluation of the intended thirteen bloodlines, it is clear that he bought right into some known scams and reprinted them as truth, such as the commonly unmasked claims of John Todd, a man who in the 1970s claimed to be an Illuminati "defector" coming from among the "Illuminati families."Springmeier also declares that the Illuminati have been running a spaceport station on Mars, which he claims they started colonizing in the late 1990s.

A lot more reliable scientist, Antony Sutton, who was given a Skull & Bones membership listing in the early 1980s by the daughter of a member, has a far more sensible and precise strategy. In his exceptional evaluation, America's Secret Establishment, Sutton has specified that twenty to thirty families have controlled the Skull & Bones society since its creation in 1832. His publication offers a scholarly overview of their tasks.

The thirteen family theory is a more contemporary variation of the old "divine right of kings theory, which was bolstered for thousands of years, declaring that God ordained households of kings and majesties to rule. Frequently, as with Egyptian Pharaohs, the Caesars of Rome, and the Chinese Dynasties, kings believed (or at the very least asserted to believe) that they were Gods or literal descendants of the Gods, which consequently, they thought, offered them the divine right to rule. This is not just an old idea. The Nazi's thought that white individuals were the offspring from the (supposed) God-like inhabitants of the Lost City of Atlantis.

Adolf Hitler and his internal circle of Nazi officers, consisting of Heinrich Himmler, Rudolph Hess, and Joseph Goebbels, literally believed that white people (the Aryan race, as they usually call them) were descendants of Gods that once lived in the Earth, that lived in the City of Atlantis. The Nazis assumed the misconception of the "Lost City" was a literal background. According to their ideas, when the city supposedly sunk into the sea, many of the demigods got away to the Himalayas of Tibet, where they were said to have started the Aryan and nordic races.

According to the Nazi view, the Jews, claiming to be "God's chosen people," were preventing the Aryans from their "divine right" to rule the earth, and race-mixing was weakening the enchanting power of the Aryan race. Hitler was influenced mainly by Helena Blavatsky's 1888 publication, The Secret

Doctrine, which asserts that Satan helped to free Man in the Garden of Eden, allowing human beings to "develop" right into gods themselves. "Satan will now be revealed, in the teaching of the Secret Doctrine, allegorized as Good, and Sacrifice, a God of Wisdom," the book reads, "Blessed and sanctified is the name of the Angel of Havas-- Satan," Blavatsky wrote.

Mainstream historians concentrate on the racial facets of the Nazis Test for power. However, they usually ignore the root of their ideological background, which was a twisted occult doctrine and essentially based upon Satanism and the idea that they had divine blood in their blood vessels and were descendants of gods. A German secret society called the Thule Society offered birth to the Nazi event. It ran just like the Skull & Bones society does in America, working on grooming the nation's future leaders. The Thule Society's logo was a swastika with a blade before it.

The "most imperial candidate" theory is the idea that every presidential election in the United States has been won by the candidate with the most royal blood, thus having the closest connections to the kingship bloodline of Europe.

Proponents of the theory claim that every U.S. president since George Washington can have their family traced back to European royals, and claim that thirty-three head of states are offspring of Alfred the Great and Charlemagne.

However, this pleads the Question of why a small group of families would certainly consider themselves to have "imperial blood." What does "imperial blood" mean? Well, it implies that they think they are straight offspring of the Gods. Individuals who agree with this theory usually point to a passage in the Book of Genesis in the Bible as proof. (Genesis 6:1-2) "And it came to pass, when men began to multiply on the face of the earth, and daughters were birthed unto them, That the children of God saw the daughters of man, that they were fair; and they made them wives of all which they selected." Genesis 6:4 proceeds, "There were giants in the earth in those days; and additionally after that, when the sons of God came in unto the daughters of man, and they bare children to them, the same ended up being magnificent men which were of old, men of renown.".

Some Christians and Biblical scholars believe that the "Sons of God," which came and took the children of men and had children with them, were an alien race called the Annunaki. Some versions of the Bible claim that the Sons of God were "superordinary beings" and clearly describes some type of unusual creatures that involved the planet and mated with human females, creating some sort of alien/human crossbreed called the Nephilim.

Some believe that God caused the flood wishing to destroy these Nephilim creatures and afterward have Noah, his sons. Their wives later repopulate the earth after they arise securely from

511

the Ark. According to some beliefs, those intended crossbreed creatures went and endured on to become the very first kings and queens, and later on developed into what we describe as the Illuminati today.

The misconception that Jesus Christ covertly had a child with Mary Magdalene was brought into the mainstream with Dan Brown's 2003 publication The Da Vinci Code, which was influenced by the commonly unmasked Holy Blood, HolyGrail (1982). Dan Brown's book was made right into a movie in 2006 starring Tom Hanks, which lugged the suggestion to a much bigger target market that believed the scam of the "Jesus family.".

According to the myth, the Knights Templar and Freemasons are the Holy Grail's guardians, which according to this theory, the Grail describes the descendants of Jesus and Mary Magdalene. Thus the "Holy Grail" is the divine family. Their supposed members have to stay in secret to shield themselves from being eliminated by the Catholic Church, which presumably will do anything to avoid this "secret reality" from being understood because it would undoubtedly undermine their power.

This Jesus bloodline misconception may very well be introduced eventually in time as "evidence" of the Illuminati's supposed "divine right to rule" by claiming they are the actual offspring of Jesus. It might effectively end with the look of the antichrist, who will declare to be the long-awaited messiah of the world and cite his supposed genetic connection to Jesus as evidence that he is the return of Christ.

When exploring the supposed "families of the Illuminati," you will commonly come across people speaking regarding "the Reptilians" that believe the Illuminati are essentially a group of "form moving extraterrestrials" or demonic inter-dimensional entities masquerading as humans to work towards confining the human race. The "Reptilian" concept is extensively ridiculed, although a sizable portion of the population does not doubt that renowned political leaders and stars are "impostors," only acting to be human.

Many of the Reptilian claims are straight out of the X- Files, the popular paranormal thriller from the 1990s. They are practically similar to the plot of a 1980s mini collection titled V (for visitors).

A British conspiracy philosopher named David Icke is mainly responsible for spreading this concept and claims these "Reptillian Illuminati" need to consume human blood, "since they are consuming the person's life-force and since they require it to exist in this dimension in a human form."

More lately, Icke seems to have distanced himself from "Reptlillians" and started concentrating on the Archons, which refer to supernatural representatives of the wicked Gnostic maker God, the Demiurge. Icke is also a big proponent that these "Reptillian Illuminati" families have interbred with each other throughout history to keep their unique family and conceal their trick from outsiders.

It was relatively easy to regulate who would marry whom and maintain imperial family members reproducing with other royal families in old times. The majority of people married others in the same socioeconomic level because they run in the same circles, go to the same prestigious colleges, and grow up in the same affluent areas. While the ancient alien/Nephilim bloodline theory is interesting on its surface area, there is little to no proof that people from these supposed royal or divine/alien/reptilian families have any kind of significant difference in their DNA from "normal" people or "citizens" as we are called.

In more modern times, the law of who marries whom through arranged marital relationships has become nearly impossible to control, so if this concept were real, then the "alien" DNA would undoubtedly be so commonly spread that we would see it turn up in clinical reports worldwide.

One likely reason for a handful of households rising to power in the old past is that they simply so occurred to be surviving on fertile land, allowing them to have reliable and healthy and balanced spawns because of a wealth of food and easily accessible water.

I would not eliminate the possibility that some kind of extraterrestrial (or demonic) race is privately functioning with the Illuminati leadership and directing them in their affairs, but the subject of aliens is past the scope of this book. For the most part, the "evidence" of such beings is impossible to verify or limited to interpretations of old art or "video clip evidence" of strange flying things-- a lot of which are top secret speculative aircraft or scams. Aliens (or demons) dealing with the Illuminati is one thing-- a handful of households interbreeding with each other to maintain their "unusual ancestral tree" a secret amongst themselves is something entirely different.

CHAPTER SIX

Affiliated Secret Societies

Secret societies got into pop culture in the 21st century, thanks partly to Dan Brown's novels and Hollywood films such as The Skulls (2000) and National Treasure (2004). As the 2004 US election approached, it was well reported in the mainstream news that George W. Bush and his rival John Kerry were Skull & Bones, the now-famous secret society based at Yale University. The correct terminology is really that they "are" members, not that they "were" members, given that it is a life-time membership beginning their senior year of college.

While many people have become aware of Skull & Bones, many wrongly believe it's just an elite fraternity for rich kids, but Skull & Bones differs from a fraternity in several essential ways. First off, nobody "promises to join" the club hoping to get accepted. Instead, they recruit individuals who are seen as deserving to be members. The club does not do any charity work, which is quite familiar with a lot of fraternities, and their whole focus is tailored for members' postgraduate life, which is why somebody doesn't become an official member up until their senior year, rather than rushing a fraternity freshman year like many other college clubs.

While there are several secret societies in colleges worldwide, Skull & Bones is in a league of their own regarding their power and impact. While they are possibly one of the more well-known secret societies, there are other effective lesser-known ones.

There are secret societies of politicians, businessmen, media moguls; there is a secret society of scientists (the Jasons); there's even a secret society of secretaries, who deal with men in other secret societies. Few individuals know that there is a secret society of women designed after the Bohemian Grove, who call themselves the Belizean Grove. Much of these strange groups comprise overlapping members, and at the higher levels, work together with each other in one giant compartmentalized pyramid-shaped structure of power.

Mystery Schools

The first or initial secret societies were called the Mystery Schools, which implied that they taught the Ancient Mysteries of life and death. The word "mystic" suggests one who studied the secrets, and ancient inquisitive men formed groups or "schools" to research and consider life's most important questions. Specific expected responses were found, or misconceptions developed, intended to help man understand his presence here on this earth.

Some see the secret occult understanding originating from these Mystery Schools not as evil, but as a tool that can be utilized for either wicked or good, comparable to "the Force" in Star Wars.

Simply as guys get into relationships based upon specific interests like model airplane clubs, car meets, and many other types of clubs, men in ancient times who discovered they had a common intriguing contemplating the mysteries of life found themselves coming together in these Mystery Schools.

Numerous Mystery Schools turned up in the ancient world, claiming to, or looking for to, find the powerful secrets of life, and aim to get in harmony with the divine to receive the blessings deep space uses or describe the human condition. While these groups appear to have at one time had the sufficient intentions, many people think they were eventually destroyed and taken over by sinister men who turned the once honorable schools into a mafia of madmen who use their remarkable intellect and social media networks to shackle society. Illuminati expert Manly P. Hall discusses, "The masses, deprived of their birthright of understanding and groveling in lack of knowledge, eventually became the abject slaves of the spiritual impostors. Superstitious notion widely prevailed, and the black magicians entirely dominated national affairs, with the result that humanity still suffers from the sophistries [fallacious arguments, particularly with the intention of deceiving] of the priestcrafts of Atlantis and Egypt.".

The mystical custom, as it is in some cases referred to, appears to have begun in Mesopotamia, the oldest human civilization and the first to develop a written language. It can be traced to ancient Egypt and the Isis cults (3100 B.C.) and then over to Greece in the Eleusinian Mysteries (1500 BC), including the Demeter and Persephone cults. Throughout this time, the Dionysian Mysteries were practiced in ancient Greece and Rome and included making use of intoxicants and other trance-inducing methods to come into a higher understanding of the Mysteries.

The Dionysian mysteries were mostly based upon Dionysus, who happens to be one of the Twelve Olympians in Greek mythology, as well as the God ecstasy and wine

If you follow the chain consistently, you progress to the Pythagoreans and onto other Greek secret cults like Mithrasim (100 A.D.), then to the Gnostics (1-300 A.D.), to the Knights Templar (1118), and on to the Cathars in the 13th Century, and then to the Jesuits (founded in 1540), continuing to the Rosicrucians (1614), then to Freemasonry (1717) and continuing to the Illuminati (1776). If you keep moving ahead, when you get to more contemporary times, you'll see organizations like Skull & Bones (1832), Bohemian Grove (1872), the Federal Reserve Bank (1913), the Council on Foreign Relations (1921), the Bilderberg Group (1954), and so on.

While you may be used to some of these major Illuminati organizations, each piece of the puzzle contains numerous details. When carefully assembled, you develop a mosaic that shows a specific and typical theme. They are all hierarchical fraternities who use various routines and pageants to impart in their members that they are a select elite group of masters who know "the truth" that will enable them to become gods among men. To protect their secrets to a selected few, initiates free swear blood oaths to never reveal their understanding to outsiders or those in the lower hierarchy levels.

The Knights Templar

At this moment in time, lots of people have become aware of the Knights Templar. They might be familiar with a bit of the story surrounding them and their allegations against them by the Catholic Church. Still, a couple of individuals have taken a comprehensive look into the organization and its activities. While most people think the Catholic Church made up the allegations of devil worshiping and blasphemous rituals as an excuse to seize the Templar's wealth and put them out of commission, you might be shocked to discover who confesses the accusations were real.

The Knights Templar name indicates they were the knights of Solomon's Temple, and were a group of Christian knights who offered to safeguard Jerusalem from the Muslims who were trying to capture the land. The Templars were founded in 1118 in France by a man named Hugues de Payens, who hired around nine others, mostly members of his own family, who then offered to secure pilgrims traveling from the coast of the Mediterranean to the Holy Land.

While they were committed "warrior monks" who desired to 'protect' the Holy Land, it appears the creators had an ulterior intention. While most of the growing Templar organization might have been completely committed to securing the Holy Land, the inner circle were hectic covertly excavating Solomon's Temple site for treasure and rare artifacts.

Amongst the most damning accusations made against the Templars was that their inner circle performed devilish homosexual rituals, including a Baphomet demonic idol. While most people believe these accusations were made by the Catholic Church to demonize the Templars, others have a different view. Eliphas Levi, a popular occultist in the 19th century, explains, "Did the Templars adore Baphomet? Did they provide a disgraceful salutation to the buttocks of the goat of Mendes? What was this secret and powerful association which threatened Church and State, and was hence damaged unheard? Judge nothing lightly; they are guilty of a terrific criminal activity; they have exposed to profane eyes the sanctuary of antique initiation. They have gathered once more and have shared the fruits of the tree of knowledge so that they may become masters of the world."

He continues, "Yes, in our profane conviction, the Grand Masters of the Order of the Templars worshipped the Baphomet, and triggered it to be worshipped by their starts." In the notorious Satanic Bible, published in 1966 by Anton LaVey (real name Howard Levy), Baphomet is noted as the demon the Knights Templar worshiped. So even the Church of Satan's founder accepts the allegations made against the Templars as real.

Manly P. Hall, a 33rd-degree mason, best recognized for his revealing book The Secret Teachings of All Ages, wrote, "The well-known hermaphroditic Goat of Mendes was a composite creature formulated to symbolize this astral light. It is similar to Baphomet, the mystic pantheons of those disciples of ritualistic magic, the Templars, who most likely got it from the Arabians.".

According to Hall and others, it is believed the Templars not just found physical treasure like gold and silver in their executions, but informational treasure also in the type of ancient scrolls where they discovered their unusual secret doctrine.

Researchers Knight and Lomas, who are not considered "conspiracy theorists," discussed that according to their findings, "Hence it follows that the mysteries of the craft are the secrets of faith. The Knights were, however, mindful not to entrust this important secret to anyone whose fidelity and discretion had not been completely proved. For that reason, they developed various degrees to test their prospects. They offered them just symbolical secrets without any explanation, to avoid betrayal and exclusively to allow them to make themselves well know to each other. For this reason, it was resolved to use different indications, words, and tokens in each degree, by which they would be protected against the Saracens, cowans, or trespassers."

In The History of Magic (released in 1860), Eliphas Levi reveals, "The Templars had two teachings; one was hidden and reserved to the leaders, being that of Johannes [Gnosticism]; the other was public, being Roman Catholic doctrine. They deceived in this way the enemies that they wanted to supplant. The Johannes of the adepts was the Kabalah of the Gnostics. Still, it degenerated quickly into a mystic pantheism brought even to idolatry of Nature and hatred of all revealed dogma ... They went as far as recognising the pantheistic importance of the grandmasters of Black Magic. The better to isolate themselves from obedience to a religion by which they were condemned before, they rendered magnificent honors to the monstrous idol Baphomet."

Lynn Picknett and Clive Prince also confirm the secret teaching accusations in their book The Templar Revelation, stating, "It is most likely that the bulk of the Knights Templar were no more than easy Christian solders they appeared to be, but the inner circle was different. The Templars' inner circle appears to have existed to further active research into esoteric and religious matters. Probably one reason for their secrecy was that they dealt with the arcane elements of the Jewish and Islamic worlds.

They sought, literally, the secrets of deep space anywhere they presumed they might be discovered, and in the course of their intellectual and geographical wanderings came to tolerate-- even to embrace, some unconventional beliefs."

These "unconventional beliefs" appear to have included what's called sex magic (typically spelled sex magick with a "k" at the end), which is the practice of including different sex acts into secret rituals in the belief that the sexual energy produced is changed into spiritual power, supposedly allowing participants to activate dormant supernatural capabilities. Theodore Reuss [co-founder of the Ordo TempliOrientis] exposed that sex magic was the best trick of occult fraternities, stating, "Our order possesses the secret which opens up all Masonic and Hermetic tricks, namely, the mentors of sexual magic, and this mentor describes, without exception, all the tricks of Freemasonry and all systems of faith." He also stated that sex magic was the big trick of the Knights Templar.

In his book to The Secret Teachings of All Ages, titled Lectures on Ancient Philosophy, Manly P. Hall again reveals some amazing occultic secrets few individuals have found about the Templars. He wrote, "It was not the physical power of the Templars, but the understanding which they had brought with them from the East, that the church feared. The Templars had discovered part of the terrific Arcanum; they had become smart in those secrets which had been celebrated in Mecca thousands of years before the development of Mohammed; they had read a few pages from the dread book of the Anthropos, and for this knowledge, they were destined to die.".

Eliphas Levi writes in agreement, "It was the memory of this religious and scientific absolute, of this teaching summarised in a word, of this word alternately lost and recovered, which was transmitted to the elect of all antique initiations ... it was this same memory handed on to secret associations of Rosicrucians, Illuminati and Freemasons which provided a significance to their unusual rites, to their less or more standard signs, and a validation above all to their commitment in common, as well as a hint to their power."

This "occult power" wasn't the only thing that resulted in their downfall. With the assistance of other secrets, the Templars likely learned from the unusual scrolls they acquired, ultimately prospered bankers who issued loans, not just to individuals, but to emperors and governments. The Catholic Church would not allow people to charge interest on money they lent to someone else because it was considered a sin (called usury). Still, the church looked the other way when the Templars did it, likely because they needed their protective services in the Holy Land.

Through giving money with interest, the Templars had exploited one of the most mysterious and compelling principles on the planet today. The Illuminati banking cartel utilizes the same method through its front groups like the Federal Reserve, the World Bank, and the International Monetary Fund.

The Jesuits

Moving forward to some hundred years later and we can see the Catholic Church following the same pattern of the Templars hoarding knowledge, wealth, and power, so insiders can live like kings by benefiting from the ignorant masses. Ignatius of Loyola established the Society of Jesus (aka the Jesuits) in the year 1540. Their members are likewise known as the "Pope's Marines" because of their militant support of the Catholic Church. The Jesuits were founded to battle against the Protestant Reformation to keep the Catholic Church in power by any means necessary. While supposedly being a Christian group, the Jesuits' activities have been anything but it.

Some think that Illuminati founder Adam Weishaupt was discreetly working for the Jesuits. Still, his correspondences reveal he deeply disliked the Jesuits, although he did embrace their "ends justifies the means" strategies in hopes of replacing them with his comparable type of tyranny.

A document entitled The Secret Instructions of the Jesuits, was published in the 1600s, allegedly written by a general in the society, and exposed the techniques and "ends validates the means" code of the Jesuits. The Church declares the documents are a forgery created to libel the Jesuits, obviously, but when one becomes mindful of the criminal and callous activities Church experts have taken part in to gain and keep their power, it doesn't truly matter if they're a forgery or not, because the tactics of the Jesuits and the Vatican have ended up being commonly known.

The Catholic Church's crimes are legendary, from imprisoning Galileo for declaring the earth revolved around the sun, to the Spanish Inquisition, where officials tortured and killed anybody who dared disagree with them. And everybody is familiar with their institutional pedophile issue and the generations of cover-ups they have taken part in to secure the criminals.

These actions continue to give Christians a bad name with the majority of anti- Christian bigots obviously uninformed (or willfully overlooking) the many non-Catholic Christians (like Protestants, Methodists, Lutherans, Baptists, non-denominational groups, and so on) which were (and still are) horrified by the actions of the Catholic Church who, for centuries, held a monopoly on Christianity, albeit their twisted and un-Biblical brand of it.

Jesuits were basically to be blamed for the 1605 Gunpowder Plot in England, an assassination effort where the criminals, including Guy Fawkes, attempted to blow up the house of Parliament to eliminate King James and the Protestant aristocracy. Every November 5th, bonfires and fireworks are used to commemorate the plot's failure, an event that has come to be known as Guy Fawkes Night.

In Rome, Vatican City is not just a city, but a sovereign country owned and run by the Catholic Church that was created in 1929 by the Lateran treaty. It is only 110 acres and has a population under a thousand people and has over 8 billion dollars in assets. The Pope is the head, and is secured by his army, the Swiss Guard.

The Popes, Bishops, and Priests of the Catholic Church are essentially the very same as the Pharisees who Jesus criticized about 2000 years ago for their hypocrisy and pride due to their spiritual knowledge. One needs to look no further than the Inquisition or the enormous institutional cover-up of several pedophile priests to see the Catholic Church is corrupt to the core. The Catholic Church also diverts and perverts the many teachings of Jesus in several ways, such as having individuals admit their sins to a priest instead of to God himself, along with having a indulgences, which, if you don't know, implies that people used to pay cash to the church and in return a priest would forgive that person's sins and inform them they could then enter Heaven. Some indulgences were even sold for sins people would commit in the future. Such a practice was a disgraceful abuse of power and contradictory to the teachings of Jesus.

The Catholic Church generally took the releasing messages of Jesus and packaged them up and then offered them to the public, when Jesus had intended them to be available to all free of charge. This is the same thing the Jewish Pharisees did with Judaism, causing Jesus to denounce them openly. For these reasons and more that the Vatican, specifically the Pope, is taken a look at with suspicion regarding the New World Order and is thought by some to one day be the false prophet spoken about in the Bible.

According to Biblical prediction, the fake Christ (the Antichrist) will be a political figure and the world leader, who will be accompanied by the false prophet. This global spiritual leader will (wrongfully) confirm to the world that the messiah has gotten here when the Antichrist announces he is God. Given that the Catholic Church is attempting to reinstate itself as the only Christian authority on the planet, many people see the Pope as a prime prospect for this false prophet.

In 2007 Pope Benedict declared that the Catholic Church was the only place to provide redemption and held the only secret to Heaven. He didn't mean Christianity is the only course to salvation, a primary renter of the faith. He implied specifically that the Catholic Church was the only way to God, which all other Christian denominations were leading the people astray and were not "real" churches.

This is the same Pope who, when he was still a Cardinal (then named Cardinal Ratzinger), was in charge of covering the extensive pedophile priest network which has been operating within the Catholic Church for generations.

A 69-page document typed in Latin and drawn from the Vatican's Secret Archives bearing the seal of Pope John XXIII, was sent out to every Bishop in the world in 1962 and comprised of comprehensive guidelines and policies about keeping allegations or claims of sexual abuse a secret.

The title of the documents in Latin, Criminesolicitationies, translates to "Instruction on proceedings in cases of solicitation" and was generally similar to an earlier set of instructions issued in 1922. The documents were confirmed genuine by the Roman Catholic Church in England and Wales.

Bishops were instructed to handle child abuse allegations "in the most secret method" and were reminded of their commitment to "perpetual silence" for what the documents called the "secret of the Holy Office."

They further state, "The oath of keeping the secret needs to be given in these cases likewise by the accusers or those denouncing the priest and the witnesses." Anyone who talks about the "secret of the Holy Office" or admits openly that any victims have stepped forward were threatened with ex-communication.

All complaints or claims about sexual assault were saved in the Secret Archives of the Vatican. Daniel Shea, a lawyer for abused kids, stated, "It shows there was a worldwide conspiracy by the Church to hush up sexual abuse issues. It is a devious effort to hide criminal conduct and is a plan for deception and concealment."

Another attorney for abused children, Richard Scorer, stated, "We always believed that the Catholic Church systematically concealed abuse and tried to silence victims. This document appears to show it. Threatening ex-communication to anyone who speaks up reveals the lengths the most senior figures in the Vatican were prepared to go to avoid the details getting out to the general public.".

This results in the dark road of sex magic, which is the most sinister secret of Satanism. The leader of the Jesuits is officially called the "Superior General," often nicknamed the "Black Pope," and is thought by lots of people to be the actual leader of the Catholic Church who wields his power from behind the scenes.

The Rosicrucians

The Rosicrucians are an intriguing secret society-type of group because the "group" started as a hoax that influenced people to form such a group (or factions) based on the strange teachings Rosicrucian Manifestos, the first of which was published in Germany in 1614. Two other manifestos appeared later, one the following year in 1615, and another the year after that, stated to have come from a secret brotherhood that comprised an Invisible College preparing to expose themselves to the world.

There are various theories regarding who the author or authors of these mysterious books were. Many people believe they were written by Johann Valentin Andrea, a German Lutheran theologian who was supposedly hoping they would help break the Catholic Church's stranglehold on power.

Whoever wrote the manifestos chose to launch them under the pseudonym Christian Rosencreut. Since the name translates to Rosy Cross-- a rose having been an alchemical sign of incredible perfection and paradise, as a sign for the work. The first manifesto states a story of how "Christian Rosencreut went on a journey to the Middle East to study the occult and the ancient secrets. The books consist of covert meanings and mystical understanding, which could only be exposed to a select couple of people.

In the texts, "Christian Rosencreut] blogged about a future utopia where people of different religions would all worship the same God in their style while having tolerance for all other views. The Catholic Church condemned the manifestos and anyone who supported them.

The books also anticipated a coming age of enlightenment arising from the discovery of ancient Hermetic secrets. Some think making it through Knights Templars were behind the mysterious manifestos, and some also credit Rosicrucianism for altering stonemason guilds into the philosophical Freemasonry we are familiar with today.

Rosicrucian researcher Christopher McIntosh wrote, "It has often been recommended that the Hiramic legend in Masonry may be related to the legend of Christian Rosenkreu] and his burial place ... It is not impossible.

That an impulse of a Rosicrucian nature (using the word "Rosicrucian" in its best sense) was entirely responsible for the improvement of operation into speculative Masonry." The transformation from "operative" masonry to "speculative masonry" implies altering from a simple stonemason trade union to the philosophical and spiritual type of Freemasonry that exists today. The 18th degree of Scottish Rite Freemasonry is called the Knight of the Rose-Croix (Rose Cross), plainly revealing a connection between the two groups.

The Mormon Church, or the Church of Latter-Day Saints, includes several parallels with Rosicrucianism as they prefer to be called. First, both stem from books said to have been "discovered" or inexplicably appeared, which cleverly blend occult misconceptions and routines with Christian philosophy. Mormonism founder Joseph Smith Jr. most likely knew of the Christian Rosencreut] legend when he planned his tale of "finding" a supposed ancient text himself. Considering that Joseph Smith was a Freemason, he would have identified with the Legend of Enoch, which declares that the true name of God was carved into a golden delta (triangle) and hidden before the terrific flood so that it would be protected (and found) by a future generation.

These misconceptions of ancient "lost and discovered" magnificent texts mentioning past cultures and mystical secrets were the motivation for 'The Book of Mormon' which Joseph Smith claimed to have "discovered" written on a stack of Golden Plates in the 1820s, which naturally aren't in a museum someplace because he said an angel took them back to paradise for safekeeping! Smith was a Freemason who combined Masonic folklore with Christianity to develop Mormonism, which declared "brought back" the lost secrets from the ancient past with his "discovery" (fabrication) of the Book of Mormon, again, which he amazingly "equated" from "Golden Plates" that are no place to be found.

The name "R. C. Christian" appeared in 1980 surrounding the creation of an enormous and mystical occult monolith in Elberton, Georgia-- a structure known as the Georgia Guidestones. The name was selected as a pseudonym by the individual who paid and created for this bizarre monument. "R.C. Christian," obviously standing for Rose Cross Christian, and the Brotherhood of the Rosy Cross, which was a popular calling card of early Rosicrucians. The Georgia Guidestones monument stands nineteen feet tall and displays ten commandments in 8 different languages as the New World Order's ten commandments. The very first of which is to maintain the human population under 500 million individuals. The monolith is stated to be the "Guidestones to an age of reason" and has several astrological markings in style, including a hole in line with the North Star.

It wasn't merely Mormonism creator Joseph Smith and the man behind the Georgia Guidestones who got motivation from the Rosicrucians, but likewise the early creators of Freemasonry and even the dad of the Illuminati, Adam Weishaupt. Lots of Rosicrucians in his time, in fact, denounced Weishaupt and the Illuminati for taking what they thought about to be a worthy principle of an informed brotherhood, and turned it into a system to exercise his own tyrannical goals.

Skull & Bones Society

Even if you're familiar with Skull & Bones and a few of the claims about them (numerous of which are real, by the way), the much deeper you look into this group, the more apparent it ends up being that they are anything but a common college fraternity. Since it has already been discussed earlier in this book, I won't repeat many of what has currently been covered. However, I will add a couple of more pieces to the pu]] le that many people are not acquainted with so you can get a full photo of them.

Skull & Bones was the FIRST secret society at Yale and the first senior society-- meaning somebody does not end up being a member until their senior year at Yale. There were fraternities at Yale. However, Skull & Bones started a new chapter in the school's history in 1832 when they developed the first secret society, quickly to be followed by Scroll & Key and then later Wolf's Head, the leading three senior (and hidden) societies. The three clubs even hold regular "inter-council conferences" numerous times a year to coordinate their activities.

Each year fifteen new members are recruited (or "tapped," as they say) to sign up with. They are chosen during the last few weeks of the term their Junior year to prepare them to replace the outbound seniors who lead them through the fancy and hellish initiation event where they are given a new name (Long Devil, Machiavelli, Baal, Beel] but are just a few examples). During part of the initiation, they lay in a coffin and provide an in-depth history of their sexual experiences up to that point in a routine called Connubial Bliss.

Members consider the world "their realm" and call outsiders "Barbarians." When initiated, the men (and now some women) are considered "Bonesmen" or Knights of Eulogia, which is Greek for "Knights of the Blessing." They even hold an impressive Skull & Bones wedding when some of their members get married to initiate the brand-new wife into the "Bones Family." Behind every corrupt man, there's usually a woman going to look the other way. They also own a 40-acre island situated on the St. Lawrence River in Alexandria Bay, called Dear Island, used as a personal getaway for "Bonesmen" and their households.

After the summertime, when the new school year starts, and the new beginners are then elders, they meet every Thursday and Sunday night for an expensive dinner (typically steak and lobster) followed up with "sessions" that include various lectures and arguments. It is believed that they eat their food using Adolf Hitler's spoon that a "Bonesmen" in some way obtained. Skull & Bones has its collection of books in its library located in the Tomb [headquarters] to help new members find out the world's ways. There is even a "Bones Bible" and other black books kept in the clubhouse library. They operate as a 5013c organization under the Russell Trust Association (or RTA Incorporated).

Their 2012 filings with the IRS show they invested 469,000 dollars on "individual advancement" for their members.

No form of alcohol is allowed inside the Skull & Bones Tomb clubhouse; that's how serious they are. This is not a party. Taking control of the world is a significant business.

Another difference between Skull & Bones and traditional fraternities is that fraternities usually do neighborhood or community service and assist with regional fundraisers. Still, this weird group only looks out on their own. The men (and now ladies) recruited into Skull & Bones are never engineers or mathematicians because these professions hold little power compared to those in business, banking, media, politics, and law, which are the dominant careers of the members.

You are probably, familiar with the fact that the most famous member is President George W. Bush, but many people don't know that his family has a long history with the group. Aside from his father, George Herbert Walker Bush, being a member, Prescott Bush, George W's grandfather, and his uncles John Walker, Jonathan Bush, and his other uncle George Herbert Walker III. So also was his cousin Ray Walker and his great-uncle George Herbert Walker Junior.

After George W. Bush ended up being president in January 2001, he selected several of his fellow Bonesmen to numerous high-level positions within the government. For instance, he chose William H. Donaldson as chairman of the Securities and Exchange Commission; Edward McNally was offered a job in the Department of Homeland Security. Robert D. McCallum was selected to be Assistant Attorney General; Roy Austin was offered the ambassadorship to Trinidad and Tobago; Victor Ashe was given a spot on the board of directors of Fannie Mae (the Federal National Mortgage Association), America's biggest house mortgage investor, and so on.

The list of Skull & Bones members who have got to the peaks of power is long. Co-founder Alfonso Taft became the head of the Department of War, which was the Department of Defense's name up until the government altered the name in real Orwellian double-speak style. Alfonso Taft's son, William Taft, ended up being President of the United States. Pierre Jay was the first chairman of the New York Federal Reserve Bank; Winston Lord became chairman of the Council on Foreign Relations. Percy Rockefeller was on the board of Brown Brothers Harriman & Company, which had its assets seized in 1942 under the Trading with the Enemy Act after finding the firm was helping fund Adolf Hitler.

Later on, John Kerry, who ran for president against George W. Bush in the 2004 election, ended up being Secretary of State under President Obama.

The list of significant power gamers in government simply goes on and on. Raymond Price (1951) was a speechwriter for Presidents Nixon, Ford, and Bush. When he was the Vice President, Christopher Taylor Buckley was the chief speechwriter for George H. W. Bush. Austan Goolsbee became President Barack Obama's primary economic consultant, etc., and so on. It's fascinating to mention that the father of American football, Walter Camp, was a Bonesman. As you may understand, football serves as a contemporary bread and circus distraction for most Americans, transporting their energy and aggression into viewing a lot of men chasing after a ball instead of focusing on crucial social issues. This is all part of the plan because it keeps the majority of people out of the way so the elite can perform their program.

Skull & Bones members produced the American Historical Association, the American Chemical Society, the American Psychological Association, and the American Economic Association. The atomic bomb was essentially a Skull & Bones work involving William Averell Harriman, Governor of New York, Henry Stimson, Secretary of War, McGeorge Bundy, U.S. Intelligence Officer, Robert Lovett, Secretary of Defense, and

George L. Harrison, consultant to the Secretary of War and President of the New York Federal Reserve Bank.

It shouldn't be surprising that an organization whose symbols and styles revolve around death would ultimately be responsible for developing the most deadly weapon in the history of humanity. The group's obsession with death is incredibly disturbing. All the death symbolism is meant to work as a constant reminder of their own demise. Given that they do not believe in an afterlife, they are prompted to become gods on earth during their short time here.

We often think about the society "ruling the world" in terms of political leaders and organizations, but they have also dominated the faculty of Yale University. Some reports declare that four out of five professors between 1865 and 1916 were Bonesmen.

In 1873, a students paper called The Iconoclast published a short article denouncing Skull & Bones control of Yale. "Out of every class Skull and Bones takes its men ... They have got control of Yale. They carry out their business. Cash paid to the college must pass into their hands, and go through their will ... It is Yale College versus Skull and Bones!".

Aside from being accused of controlling the professors at Yale and power positions in politics and business, they are also accused of worshiping Satan and performing disturbing rituals.

The group's favorite number, 322, possibly holds a secret satanic meaning. Many individuals think the number 322 is a referral to the Book of Genesis chapter 3, verse 22, which discusses Adam and Eve eating the Forbidden Fruit from the Tree of Knowledge of Good and Evil and using this number is seen as a recommendation to the Luciferian teaching or the satanic secret.

In 2001, a press reporter called Ron Rosenbaum from the New York Observer used a night vision camera to video the initiation routine from the edge of a nearby structure that ignored the yard of the Skull & Bones clubhouse. The footage reveals it initiates kneeling and kissing a skull, and after that appearing to take a knife and slit the throat of a naked woman who was being held down by other members.

People were also heard shouting a strange mantra, "The hangman equals death, the Devil equals death, death equals death!" The hangman most likely describes Jesus holding on the cross, and the mantra appears to convey the same significance as the riddle of the four human skulls when they are asked which one is the wise man, the beggar, the king, and the fool. The response given is that it does not matter to the fact that "all is the same in death.".

Rosenbaum was not exactly sure what to make of this behavior and asked, "Is that the trick they've been concealing since the society was established in 1832, the spin-off of a German secret society: devil worship? A satisfaction of the paranoid fantasies of the fundamentalist right, who believe the Eastern establishment is a front for hellish conspiracy."

Scroll and Key Society

The Scroll & Key society is another secret society at Yale University, created in 1842, ten years after Skull & Bones, and was the second secret society composed of seniors. Just like Skull & Bones, Scroll & Key hires fifteen new students at the end of their junior year, which they see as having the possible and determination to advance the organization's objectives. Scroll & Key is considered one of the "Big Three" senior societies at Yale-- the other two being, Skull & Bones, in addition to Wolf's Head.

Fareed Zakaria, a CNN commentator on foreign affairs, was initiated as a Scroll & Key member when he attended the university in 1986. Fareed went on to attend Bilderberg conferences (in 1993 and 2009) and became a member of the Council on Foreign Relations. He didn't simply join the CFR; he was the handling editor of their Foreign Affairs publication, which dishes out their political propaganda on a platter for the members.

Fareed once argued that the Constitution is dated and must be "fixed" to get rid of the Second Amendment to "modernize the Constitution for the 21st Century."

Other significant members include Ari Shapiro, who ended up being the White House Correspondent for National Public Radio (NPR); Cornelius Vanderbilt III of the rich Vanderbilt dynasty; James Stillman Rockefeller (class of 1924), who was the President and Chairman of the First National City Bank of New York; and Huntington D. Sheldon worked for the CIA as the Director of the Office of Current Intelligence.

The Scroll & Key society run under the legal entity called the Kingsley Trust Association, which creates a guard of privacy to secure them from individuals looking for information utilizing the name "Scroll & Key" and according to their 2012 IRS filings, which should be offered for public assessment, they have over 9 million dollars in assets and invested 650,000 dollars that year.

Wolfs Head

Wolf's Head is the 3rd of the "Big Three" senior secret societies at Yale and was established in 1884, partly to counter the supremacy of Skull & Bones over student affairs. They, too, recruit fifteen brand-new upcoming seniors for subscription and are now part of the bigger network, including Skull & Bones and Scroll & Key.

The club's logo is a wolf's head on an inverted Egyptian hieroglyph called an ankh, often called the Egyptian Cross and stated to symboli] e "the secret of life." Wolf's Head developed its own Egyptian themed "tomb" headquarters in 1924 thanks to a contribution from one of their members, Edward Harkness, who became John D. Rockefeller's right-hand man. Harkness himself was listed by Forbes magazine as the 6th wealthiest man worldwide throughout his life.

The club convenes every Thursday and Sunday night, where the men prepare themselves for life after college, when their real work starts. Among their most widely known members was Erastus Corning, who went on to be the Mayor of Albany, New York, for more than 40 years! Another prominent member was Paul Moore Jr., who later became a bishop of the New York Episcopal Church and one of the best-known clergy. After his death, his daughter revealed that Moore was bisexual and had a history of homosexual affairs. She detailed her father's double life in her book, The Bishop's Daughter: A Memoir. While the Bush crime family has been active in Skull & Bones for generations, they are also involved with Wolf's Head. President George H. W. Bush's younger brother William Henry Trotter "Bucky" Bush was inducted in 1960.

The service name of Wolf's Head is the Phelps Association, and according to their 2013 IRS filings, which need to be revealed since they are registered as a 501c3 tax-exempt foundation, the organization holds over $6 million in assets and spent over $373,000 on their members that year alone. The members of Wolf's Head were responsible for developing the Yale Political

Union, which is the center for politically minded students at the
University.

Communism

Communism is usually promoted as a political philosophy to presumably help the typical worker fight against the "overbearing" business owners. Still, it's a conspiracy controlled by the elite who have utilized Communism as a system to encourage the development of an all-powerful state that they are in control of.

As Gary Allen puts it, author of None Dare Call it Conspiracy, "Communism isn't a movement of the downtrodden masses, but it's a movement formed, controlled and utilized by power-seeking billionaires to get control of the world... first by developing socialist governments in the numerous nations and then consolidating them all through a 'Great Merger,' into an all-powerful world, socialist super-state probably under the auspices of the United Nations.".

The Communist Manifesto, composed by Karl Marx and his mostly ignored coauthorFrederichEngles, was first published in 1848, and is commonly believed to have stimulated the Communist Revolution in Russia in 1917 and infecting other countries such as North Korea in 1948, China in 1949, and a few years later, moving to Cuba in 1953-- but what most individuals neglect is that Karl Marx was just a secretary who wrote the book laying out the Communist views for a secret society called the Communist League.

The manifesto itself goes thus; "The Communist League (previously called the League of Just Men) ... which could of course, only be a secret one ... commissioned the undersigned [Karl Marx and Friedrich Engels], at the Congress held in London in November 1847, to draw up for publication a comprehensive theoretical and practical program of the Party. Such was the origin of the following Manifesto, the manuscript of which traveled to London to be printed a few weeks before the February Revolution.".

In 1953, the California Senate Investigating Committee on Education stated thus, "So-called modern-day Communism is the same hypocritical and deadly world conspiracy to destroy the civilization that was founded by the secret order of the Illuminati in Bavaria on May 1, 1776, and that raised its hoary head in our colonies here at important periods before the adoption of our Federal Constitution."

The report goes on to say, "The acknowledgment of May 1, 1776, as the starting date of this world revolution conspiracy is easy to understand when it is realized that May Day is frequently commemorated, even in recent times, by rioting and bloodshed on a world-wide scale.".

"It was not until 1847 or 1848, that the Communist conspirators, who had previously operated in secret, came out in the open with the Manifesto of the Communist Party, by Karl Marx and Friedrich Engels, boldly pronouncing against almost everything upon which civilization is based -- God, religion, the family, individual liberty, etc.-- the concluding paragraph of the manifesto explaining: 'Communists refuse to conceal their views and objectives. They honestly state that their purpose can only be accomplished by the forcible overthrow of the entire social order. Let the ruling classes tremble at the possibility of a Communist revolution. Proletarians have nothing to lose but their chains. They have a world to win.'".

"In issuing this manifesto, the Communist conspirators think the time had arrived when, with the help of oblivious victims, a worldwide take-over could be achieved; there were not enough oblivious victims then, and the anticipated coup failed."

"The Communist conspirators thereupon developed the strategy, for the future, of supplementing the long-established secret conspiracy, around since May 1, 1776, with a constant public campaign for victims amongst the oblivious of all countries. And, in an attempt to conceal from view the underlying hypocritical conspiracy existing since May 1, 1776, it was decided that, in such a public project, the manifesto of 1848 ought to be heralded as the founding date of communism, and Karl Marx incorrectly declared as its author.".

New Age guru Benjamin Crème, who is looking forward to the arrival of the Antichrist, thinking he will turn earth into an incredible paradise, confessed, "Marx was undoubtedly a member of the Hierarchy, of a certain degree. Taking a look at the effect of his work over the years-- that could just have been the work of a disciple of some degree, an initiate of some level-- very first to have the vision, and second of all to have the capability to embody that vision so that the work might spread out."

While Christians are often stated to have eliminated the most variety of people in the name of God, the truth is that Communists have been responsible for the best genocides in the world, stopping in the name of the State (their government), in countries like China and North Korea. Over 30 million were eliminated in the Chinese Communist Revolution lead by Mao Zedong, and Joseph Stalin eliminated over 3 million in Russia in the name of Communism.161 Massive numbers have also been killed in Vietnam and North Korea by Communist revolutionaries. Belief in any God besides the government is forbidden because it lowers individuals' obligation to the State. The government is God in Communist nations.

At the heart of Communism is a huge all-powerful government that controls every aspect of an individual's lives-- from the schools to their jobs to healthcare and banking, with a little group of elite bureaucrats living luxurious lives expense of the working class. Naturally, this is one of the Illuminati's main objectives, who are promoting the idea as a romantic paradise.

CHAPTER SEVEN

Symbolism and Protocol of Illuminati

It is often said that a picture is worth a thousand words. Just because pictures contain lots of information, someone could speak for hours attempting to describe every information but still couldn't convey whatever one encapsulated. Symbols reach deep into the soul and the psyche, as it purposefully and unconsciously convey meanings and stimulate emotional reactions. We live in a world loaded with symbols. A traffic sign at an intersection implies you stop; a wedding ring symbolizes a man and woman's dedication to each other. The American flag represents the values, principles, and hard work that America is built upon. The true power of symbols originates from their ability to evoke specific thoughts and feelings.

A souvenir you purchased on a trip reminds you of all the fun you had there, and just the sight of the object promotes memories and feelings about the journey. A framed image of your favorite car hanging on the wall in your office unconsciously reminds you of the flexibility you feel on the weekends driving down the road, briefly leaving your concerns or worries behind. Family images conjure up feelings of delight and fond memories simply from glancing at them for a minute as they rest on our desk or hang on our fridge.

While we can all articulate and agree on what many symbols imply, what makes them so unique is that the same sign might have completely different meanings to different people. Let us now translate some popular Illuminati symbols and uncover their occult "hidden" meanings and see why they are used and what they imply to insiders. Most of these symbols themselves aren't "wicked" in and of themselves; they've simply been adopted by people or groups who are wicked, so different symbols have taken on negative undertones. The swastika was a popular Hindu sign of health and well-being before the Nazis included it as the Nazi party's logo; therefore, now we negatively associate what was originally a positive symbol. The symbol itself is certainly not evil, but we had come to associate it with evil when in reality, it was pirated and perverted, so for many people, its meaning has been tainted from what it originally meant to communicate.

The Sun

To the ancient Mystery Schools in the past, and several contemporary magical or knowledge groups (including the Illuminati), the sun is their main sign. It is often incorporated into their logo designs and artwork. The sun represents power and light. The word Illuminati means enlightened ones, and the word enlighten contains the name light, which originates from the sun. Someone is said to be bright if they are smart and are likewise called fantastic, which, if you look that word up in the dictionary, you will discover that it suggests "shining vibrantly."

The sun increases and brings life to the world by repelling the cold and frightening darkness of the night. It is an amazing, massive, and strange power that affects all life on planet earth. We tell the time based on the sun, it affects the seasons, and it even has an immense impact on our psyche and health. The 28th degree in Freemasonry is called the Knight of the Sun, and is simply one example of how Masons admire this enormous star at the center of our solar system.

The Pyramid

The pyramid represents society's social hierarchy, symbolically illustrating a little enlightened few at the top, and the masses of oblivious "worker bees" on the bottom. A sun on top of a pyramid symbolically represents the little number of Illuminati "enlightened leaders" at the top of the social hierarchy judging over the masses of oblivious slaves below who make up the pyramid's base.

The Dictionary of Symbols discusses, "The base is square and represents the earth. The pinnacle is the starting-point and the finishing-point of all things -- the mystic 'center.' Joined with the pinnacle to the base are the pyramid's triangular-shaped faces, symbolizing fire, magnificent revelation, and the threefold principle of development. Consequently, the pyramid is viewed as a sign revealing the whole of the work of growth in its three vital elements."

The ancient Egyptian pyramids, constructed over four thousand years ago, are still among the seven wonders of the world and have been an endless secret source even to this day. While mainstream historians think the pyramids were constructed as burial places for the Pharaohs, the Illuminati believed that they were temples where the Mystery Schools taught their essential secrets.

The 33rd degree Freemason Manly P. Hall describes, "The Great Pyramid was not a lighthouse, an observatory, or a tomb, but the first temple of the Mysteries, the very first structure put up as a repository for those secret facts which are the specific foundation of all the sciences and arts ... Through the mystic passages and chambers of the Great Pyramid passed the illumined of antiquity. They entered its websites as guys; they came forth as gods. It was the place of the 'second birth,' the womb of the Mysteries, and knowledge dwelt in it as God dwells in the hearts of guys.".

As you may be aware, a pyramid with an all-seeing eye can be found on the back of the one-dollar bill, which many people believe is generally a stamp of ownership by the Illuminati. The man who developed this Great Seal was a Freemason named Charles Thomson, validating many peoples' suspicions that a concealed hand strategically placed the sign on the currency as a secret indication of their power.

The expression Novus Ordo Seclorum (Latin for New Order for the Ages) has appeared on the bottom of the pyramid on the dollar's back since the year 1935. At the opening of the 110th Congress on January 4th 2007, Speaker of the House Nancy Pelosi made a puzzling referral to the Great Seal, announcing, "Our Founders visualized a new America driven by optimism, opportunity, and courage. So confident were they in the new America they were advancing, that they place on the Great Seal of the United States, 'Novus ordo seclorum'-- a new order for the ages ... This vision has sustained us for more than 200 years. It accounts for what is best in our great nation: chance, liberty, and justice. Now we must bring forth that vision of a new America.".

The All-Seeing Eye

The symbol of one eye, usually with rays of light emanating from it, represents God's omniscient power and dates back to ancient Egypt, where it represented the sun God Horus who could see all. In some cases, it's called the Eye of Providence, and as you are aware, it sits on top of the pyramid on the back of the one-dollar note. This all-seeing eye sign also represents Big Brother and the Orwellian power of the intelligence companies seeing what everyone does, what they purchase, and cataloging their online activities.

Not only are there all-seeing eyes watching people in the shopping center and walking down the streets of significant cities, but the majority of people have voluntarily installed an all-seeing eye in their living-room-- and even their bedrooms--. With the click of a couple of keys, these eyes can be activated by crafty hackers or government institutions. I'm speaking about webcams that are built into televisions, tablets, and laptop computers, not to mention, possibly a lot more disturbing, listening to people too through the microphones that accompany them.

While much of this has become fairly popular by now, one interesting point, a couple of individuals contemplate is that the all-seeing eye, aside from representing the Illuminati-- may end up being a sign of the Antichrist himself. One Bible prophecy about the Antichrist is that an attempt will be made on his life to secure or damage one of his eyes. Since the symbol often represents a "God," it's possible that the coming fake Christ might embody this sign as a technique to encourage the masses that he is God. In Islam, Muslims have a similar prediction saying that the Antichrist, who they call the Dajjal, will be symbolized by one eye.

Serpents and Snakes

The serpent's sign is maybe best understood as the animal in the Garden of Eden who lured Adam and Eve into disobeying God by eating from the Tree of Knowledge of Good and Evil. The word snake has negative connotations, implying someone is a liar or deceptive. While the usual sense of a snake is negative, and the Biblical story of Adam and Eve illustrates Satan as the opponent of God and humanity, the occult analysis is quite different. Occultists and Satanists praise the snake and think it brought wisdom to Mankind, allowing human beings to become gods.

Again we seek the revelations of 33rd degree Freemason Manly P. Hall who explains, "The serpent is real to the concept of wisdom, for it tempts men to the knowledge of himself. Therefore the understanding of self resulted from man's disobedience to the Demiurges, Jehovah [God]" Hall continues; "The serpent is the symbol and prototype of the Universal hero, who redeems the worlds by giving development the understanding of itself and the realization of good and evil."

The Secret Doctrine states, "The Serpent of Eternity and all Knowledge that Manasic spirit [the logical faculty of the mind], that made him find out the secret of creation on the Kriyasaktic, and of procreation on the earthly planes-- led him as naturally to find his way to immortality, notwithstanding the jealously of the Gods."

The evil scumbag Aleister Crowley had this to state: "This serpent, Satan, is not the enemy of Man, [because it is he] who made Gods of our race, knowing Good and Evil." 264.

Like Satanists and occultists, Freemasons adore the serpent as a hero and worship its wisdom. Here is a quote from Albert Pike's Morals and Dogma about the snake, reading, "It is the body of the Holy Spirit, the Universal Agent, the Serpent devouring its tail."

Complicating the meaning of the snake symbol are several cryptic declarations in the Bible, the first of which is when Jesus advised people to be as smart as snakes but as mild as doves in Mathew 10:16. This declaration appears to acknowledge that serpents consist of knowledge or represent a power that might be used for either good or evil. Another hard and intriguing to reconcile story about serpents is when Moses made a bold (brass) snake and attached it to the top of his personnel to recover the Israelites who had been bitten by snakes in the desert. The American Medical Association's logo design is a snake coiled around a person, and the same symbol is often found on ambulances as a symbol of health and healing. When somebody reaches the 25th degree of Freemasonry, they are called a Knight of the Brazen Serpent.

One of the reasons snakes have to symbolize knowledge and enlightenment is since their eyes are always open, given that they don't have eyelids. Snakes are unique animals because they have no legs but walk around, shooting across the ground like a bolt of lightning. To early Man, they might have seemed magical since they can appear out of no place and then disappear into the turf or into the earth itself. The shedding of their skin has symbolized a renewal or immortality, perhaps since primitive man believed that snakes were never-ceasing and would bring to life a new self, when a snake "dies" it would rise once again, leaving behind its old "carcass" in the form of its shed skin and continue to live on.

It's possible that the serpent does not necessarily represent evil in and of itself, but might represent a force that might be used for either good or evil.

The Phoenix.

A phoenix is a large mythical bird that symbolizes cyclical renewal, immortality, or resurrection. The animal is portrayed similar to an eagle and is usually linked to the sun. Several myths speak about the phoenix passing away, breaking down, and then rising once again out of its ashes. Some think that many of the eagle symbols we see today are covertly symbols of a phoenix, including the double-headed "eagle" that is a symbol of Freemasonry's 33rd degree.

The eagle that has come to be a popular sign of America, and discovered on the back of the dollar, is also thought to represent a phoenix occultly. The Secret Teachings of All Ages mentions that "The hand of the secrets managed in the facility of the new government for the signature of the mysteries might still be seen on the Great Seal of the United States of America. A cautious analysis of the seal reveals a mass of occult and Masonic symbols chief among them, the so-called American Eagle ... only the student of symbolism can see through the deception and realize that the American eagle on the Great Seal is but a conventionalized phoenix."

The book, released in 1928, also mentions that, "Not only were many of the founders of the United States government Masons, but they received aid from an august and secret body existing in Europe which helped them to develop this country for a specific and peculiar purpose known only to the initiated few. The Great Seal is the signature of this exalted body-- hidden and for the many part unidentified-- and the unfinished pyramid upon its reverse side is a teeterboard setting forth symbolically the task to the achievement of which the United States Government was dedicated from the day of its in conception."

The phoenix has been suggested to be the name of the new unified international currency that global banksters have long-awaited. The cover of the January 1988 edition of The Economist magazine reads "Are you ready for a world currency" and had a short article that explained, "Thirty years from now, Americans, Japanese, Europeans, and individuals in lots of other rich nations, and some fairly poor ones will probably be paying for their shopping with the same currency. Prices will be quoted not in dollars, yen, or D-marks but in, let's say, the phoenix. Because it will be more practical than today's national currencies, the phoenix will be preferred by shoppers and business."

The metaphor of "rising from the ashes like a phoenix" describes a rebirth or something being eliminated or destroyed to bring to life something new, and so by eliminating the U.S. Dollar and other currencies around the world through inflation, the banksters are symbolically bringing to life their new currency, which many are planning to call the "phoenix."

The Owl

When discussing Illuminati significance, the owl is most known for its connections to the Bohemian Grove, the Illuminati's summertime retreat in northern California. Esoterically, the owl represents wisdom because it sees in the dark, and Adam Weishaupt picked the Owl of Athena as one of the Bavarian Illuminati symbols. Early civilizations saw the owl as mystical because it is just seen at night, considering that they are nocturnal animals.

The Dictionary of Symbols describes, "In the Egyptian system of hieroglyphs, the owl symbolizes death, night, cold and passivity. It also relates to the world of the dead sun, that is, it is of the sun which has set below the horizon and which is crossing the lake or sea of darkness."

A tiny owl can also be found hidden on the one-dollar bill, perched on the upper left corner of the frame surrounding the "1" located in the upper right-hand corner of the bill. Many individuals see an owl made into the street design of Washington D.C., right on top of the U.S. Capitol building when viewing the area from overheard or taking a look at it on a map.

Images of owls are often seen in classrooms based on a small stack of books to symbolize knowledge. The National Press Club's logo design also consists of an owl standing on a book. Owls are also viewed as guardians, and typically owl statues are put on the top of structures to frighten other birds.

The Skull and Crossbones.

The skull and crossbones symbol has a sinister appearance, which is why dubious groups have been utilized for centuries--from pirates and bicycle rider gangs to the Nazis. It represents death, or the power over life and death, which is why it interest megalomaniacs and psychopaths. The Nazi officers in charge of concentration camps where over six million people were eradicated wore a skull and crossbones sign on their uniforms, the same emblem utilized by the Skull & Bones secret society as their logo. The Nazis called it the Totenkopf (German for skull or dead man's head), and it was a blatant declaration of their objective. Hitler personally handed out a Death's Head ring to elite SS soldiers.

Since they were dedicated to battle or fight to the death and promised never to be taken alive as a detainee, the Knights Templar incorporated the symbol into their lives. Some Freemasons have a human skull sitting on their desk to remind them of their death and the fact that their life is ticking away quickly. It is meant to prompt them to work towards achieving their objectives before it's too late.

As earlier discussed, both the Bavarian Illuminati and Skull & Bones society at Yale use the object in their induction ceremony with their four different skulls. The question about which one is the fool, the wise guy, the beggar, or the king. The answer to this induction riddle, "Whether rich or poor, all's the same in death," is implied to enhance their mortality to them and remind them that the clock of life is ticking, so they had better do all they can to end up being kings here in this life because when you're dead-- to them-- absolutely nothing matters. The riddle is indicated to convey that they do not believe in an afterlife or a last judgment from God.

Baphomet

Baphomet is an occult idol that is illustrated as an androgynous man with female breasts with the head of a goat. Prometheus's torch is often protruding of its head and linking serpents is rising from its crotch. It's a strange and ugly looking figure that dates back to the 1300s when the inner circle of Knights Templar integrated it into their rituals and secret doctrine,

An early depiction of the figure comes from an 1854 book entitled Transcendental Magic written by a French occultist Eliphas. Giving support to his illustration, Eliphas Levi stated, "According to some, the Baphomet was a monstrous head, but according to others, a demon in the kind of a goat. A sculptured coffer was dug up recently in the ruins of an old Commandery of the Temple, and antiquaries impressed upon it a Baphometic figure, corresponding by its credit to the goat of Mendes and the androgyne of Khunrath."

Several Satanists have proudly integrated the Baphomet figure into their signs and routines. Aleister Crowley wrote that the snake or the "devil's emblem" was Baphomet, who he also called the "hieroglyph of arcane perfection."

One variation of the figure is the Church of Satan's logo, printed on the cover of The Satanic Bible. While many people claim that the Catholic Church made the claims that the Knights Templar were utilizing it in secret routines as an excuse to detain them and seize their wealth throughout the Inquisition, most Satanists and occults hold the belief that the Catholic Church's claims were true.

Again, Eliphas Levi boldly declared in his book Transcendental Magic, "Yes, in our profane conviction, the Grand Masters of the Order of the Templars worshipped the Baphomet, and caused it to be worshipped by their initiates."

The Pentagram

An upside-down pentagram drawn within a circle is among the most apparent and familiar symbols utilized by occult organizations, defiant teens, and rock stars today. It is a lower level occult symbol typically utilized to represent dark powers or sinister forces. Because it's so extensively understood, it's never truly utilized by high-level occultists or the Illuminati, who instead use much less familiar symbols like all-seeing eyes, pyramids, black and white checkerboards, owls, and other less polarising images.

A pentagram differs from a regular five-pointed star in a couple of methods. A pentagram is drawn using five straight lines to make up the points and form a pentagon in the middle. The Satanic pentagram is drawn upside down and often incorporated by a circle. Satanists use it because Christians originally utilized the five points of a pentagram (called the pentalpha) to symbolize the five wounds of Jesus (the two spikes through his hands, two through his feet, and the spear that pierced his side). Satanists like to pervert things and turn Christian signs upside down or backward to signify their opposing views and beliefs, and this is how their use of upside-down pentagrams came into existence.

The Dictionary of Symbols entry on the star reads, "As far back as in the days of Egyptian hieroglyphics a star pointing upwards represented 'increasing upwards towards the point of origin' and formed part of such words as 'to raise,' 'to educate,' and 'the teacher.' The inverted five-pointed star is a sign of the infernal and utilized in black magic."

In Freemasonry, the pentagram is called the Blazing Star and represents the sun, Lucifer, carnal understanding, and power. To Wiccans and Pagans, the star's five points represent air, fire, water, earth, and spirit. The female branch of Freemasonry, called Eastern Star, uses an upside-down pentagram as their emblem.

Square and Compass.

A square (the tool utilized by carpenters to layout an ideal angle or a "square" angle) overlaid on top of a compass (the tool used for drawing arches and circles-- not the navigation tool for recognizing directions) is a popular sign in Freemasonry and is frequently seen with the letter G in the middle. The square and compass symbolize the alchemical teaching of "as above, so below" or the joining of earth and heaven by forming two opposite facing pyramids with one pointing up and the other pointing downward. The letter G in the center means God or Gnosis (the Greek word for knowledge). It is also usually stated to represent the "Great Architect of deep space," a term many masons utilize to describe God.

The Statue of Liberty.

If you asked the typical American what the Statue of Liberty represented, they'd most likely inform you it involves "America," "liberty," or "democracy." Some may understand that it was provided to America by the French. Still, few know its very design and development was managed by Freemasons, the secret society, not France's government, who then gave it to America as a "present" and placed it in New York Harbor.

Frederic Bartholdi, the designer of the Statue of Liberty, was, of course, a Freemason, and knowledgeable about occult and Illuminati importance and philosophies. The three significant figures included with the Statue-- Frederic Bartholdi, who developed the statue itself; Gustave Eiffel, who created the inner assistance structure; and Richard Hunt, who created the pedestal-- were all Freemasons.

Bartholdi's original plan for a huge statue of this type was put in a harbor in Egypt. After the Egyptian government rejected his proposal, he changed his style slightly and approached America to see if he could erect his recently created statue in the United States. The point is, he initially wanted to construct a bizarre "God-like" figure and have it stand somewhere other than America. Bartholdi's first choice for his mystical statue was Egypt, not the United States.

The initial name of the statue was "Liberty Enlightening the World," not the "Statue of Liberty." Once again, the word Enlightening fits in with the Illuminati style-- Enlightening, knowledge, light, the sun, intelligence, bright, brilliance, Lucifer.

A near mirror image of the Statue of Liberty stands in France, also on an island, in the Seine River in Paris, set up in 1889, just three years after the one in America was completed. If it's an "American" symbol, why is there an almost similar one in France? There are, in fact, numerous almost identical "Statue of Liberty" figures all around the world, including Leicester, England; Lviv, Ukraine; Carinthia, Austria; Cenicero, Spain; Arraba in Israel, and lots of other places.

The Statue of Liberty is a modern-day variation of the Colossus of Rhodes, a 100-foot-tall statue portraying the Greek sun god, Helios (Helios being Greek for sun) in ancient Greece. The Colossus was created in the third century B.C. and depicted Helios (the Sun God) holding a torch high in one hand and stood on the island of Rhodes dealing with the water. "This massive gilded figure, with its crown of solar rays and its upraised torch, signified occultly the wonderful Sun Man of the Mysteries, the Universal Savior," states The Secret Teachings of All Ages.

A poem is printed on a plaque that sits prominently near the base of the Statue of Liberty entitled The New Colossus, plainly signaling that it was imitating the Greek sun god. A Masonic cornerstone ceremony was carried out when construction began.

A Masonic plaque was positioned on the site—the statue is a composite of a range of ancient goddesses who represent the womanly concept.

The torch that the Statue of Liberty is holding represents Prometheus's torch, who occultly symbolizes Lucifer. The Greek mythological story of Prometheus is the same allegory of taking fire (i.e., knowledge) from God or the Gods, and giving it to people, therefore outraging God.

Here is Manly P. Hall again, one of Freemasonry's greatest thinkers, explaining in Lectures on Ancient Philosophy, that, "Man wandered hopelessly in the gloom of mortality, dying and living without light or understanding in his thrall to the Demiurgus [the developer God] and his host of spirits. At last, the spirit of disobedience entered the creation in Lucifer's form, who, in the guise of a snake, tempted man to revolt against the demands of Jehovah (the Demiurgus). In Greece, this character was called Prometheus, who brought from the gods the impregnating flame that would launch the life latent in this wide range of germlike potentialities."

The seven horn-looking spikes coming out of the Statue of Liberty's head represent rays of the sun, and symbolically represents the spirit radiating from the mind as enlightenment or "knowledge." There are seven of them because the rays represent the seven liberal arts and sciences, therefore consisting of a necessary knowledge base. The statue is also holding a book, symbolic of information and knowledge-- once again fitting in with the style of enlightenment and knowledge, because knowledge is power, which the Illuminati has.

Rockefeller Center's Prometheus.

In New York City, Rockefeller Center is a substantial 22-acre complex made up of nineteen different buildings and the home of Bank of America, NBC, General Electric, and other major international Illuminati-controlled corporations. Standing plainly within the property is a big gold-colored statue of Prometheus holding a ball of fire in one hand as he flies through the air. The mythological Greek story of Prometheus stealing fire from the Gods and offering it to humanity regardless of the punishment he will deal with is seen by occultists as identical to Lucifer's story providing humanity the knowledge of good and evil that God had forbid us to have.

This statue that stands outside of Rockefeller Center is a homage to Lucifer, which goes undetected by the average individual not acquainted with Illuminati symbolism. Many people are most likely not even know about the Prometheus myth, or have long forgotten it since studying Greek mythology in high school and just believe the statue is just another random piece of art with little or no significance.

Helena Blavatsky describes in her traditional occult work, The Secret Doctrine, that, "The allegory of Prometheus, who takes the magnificent fire as to enable men to proceed consciously on the path of spiritual advancement, hence transforming the best of animals on Earth into a prospective god, and making him free to take the kingdom of heaven by violence. Hence, Zeus's curse is pronounced against Prometheus, and by Jehovah [God] against his 'defiant son,' Satan."

So as you can see, it's not just me making the connection between Prometheus and Lucifer-- It's occultist experts themselves. It's no coincidence this stands on a Rockefeller home, a family with generational ties to the Illuminati establishment.

The Washington Monument

The Washington Monument, which lies straight west of the United States Capitol structure in Washington DC, standing around 555 feet high, controls the sky throughout the city and can be seen from miles everywhere, particularly at night with the traffic signal shining from the top appearing like the evil Eye of Sauron in the Lord of the Rings motion pictures. The monolith is an Egyptian obelisk with a pyramid capstone on the top and was completed in 1884.

The structure is among the most important symbols in America to the Illuminati, although most people are uninformed of its covert meaning. Occultists see the monument as a massive phallic symbol-- a big penis-- representing manly energy and supremacy. One would anticipate the "Washington" Monument to be a statue of George Washington himself, similar to the Lincoln Memorial's substantial figure of Abraham Lincoln. Rather it's a giant erect penis of the Egyptian god Baal. Naturally, it was developed and built by Freemasons, who even had a ceremony to lay the foundation when building started.

FritzSpringmeier, author of Bloodlines of the Illuminati, explained, "Every early morning when the United States President awakens, he can watch out the window, see the Masonic obelisk and be reminded of who controls America. If the president has any training in the Mystery Religion of Egypt, he will also understand what body part is symbolically set up in the Washington Memorial."

Springmeier goes further to state, "If the U.S. were ever to go back to serving God, that monument would be a great one to destroy. God asked the Israelites not just merely to avoid worshiping such abominations. He asked His people to ruin them, for their very creation was an abomination."

Cleopatra's Needle.

While the Washington Monument might be the most well-known Egyptian obelisk in America, it isn't the only one. Another one stands in Central Park in New York City-- called Cleopatra's Needle, and this one is an authentic Egyptian obelisk that dates back to around 1500 B.C. and is transported to New York in 1881.

Comparable "Cleopatra's Needles" actually stand in London and Paris, symbolizing the Illuminati's guideline in those nations as well. Not surprising, there is also one in Vatican City. The one in New York's Central Park stands 70-feet tall and weighs 220 tons. Why and how it was brought to America from Egypt is an intriguing story.

For some reason, Henry G. Stebbins, the Commissioner of the Department of Public Parks in New York in the 1880s, revealed he was looking for assistance financing a strategy to bring the statue to America. William H. Vanderbilt, who was one of the wealthiest guys worldwide, was asked to help make it occur and contributed over $100,000 (over $2 million in 2014 dollars) to assist. Remarkably, the shipping expenses for the one sent out to London were spent for by Dr. Erasmus Wilson, a Freemason.

When the obelisk arrived in America, thousands of Freemasons took part in a parade as it was rolled up Fifth Avenue from 14th Street to 82nd Street. The Grand Master of Masons in New York performed a foundation-laying ritual as a celebration when it was put up at its last destination in the park. When it initially got here in New York in 1881, Cleopatra's Needle was covered with plainly noticeable hieroglyphics about the sun god Horus, but most of the carvings have since been alert far from acid rain. While they endured 3000 years in Egypt, it seems the ancient relic was no match for the contamination of New York City.

Music and Movies

For hundreds of years, knowledge of the Illuminati and their symbols was mostly contained within the Mystery Schools that taught the esoteric custom. Outsiders didn't even hesitate about most occult signs because they were viewed as common art, and a couple of individuals paid much attention to them. With the birth of the information age, things started to change. In the 1990s and early 2000s, a growing variety of online forums and sites were dedicated to examining secret societies and exposing these little known issues to a wider variety of individuals.

For years, those interested in such things were thought about a fringe minority of patriots and "conspiracy theorists." Still, with the emergence of social networks becoming a standard feature in many people's lives, and with video sharing websites like YouTube altering the nature of media and information exchange, a fascinating phenomenon started to occur early in the twenty-first century. Illuminati and occult significance overflowed from what was mainly the topic of fringe websites, and "computer system geeks" on Internet forums, to end up being part of popular culture, finding its way into various traditional video and blockbuster motion pictures.

While a sizable portion of the population has become acquainted with using Illuminati symbols in rap videos and supposed "Illuminati hand indications" being flashed by celebrities, many people who notice this element of the symbolism hardly have a fundamental understanding of the history of the signs or their significances. Many individuals who have heard the frequently farfetched claims about "Illuminati stars" have dismissed the presence of the Illuminati all together as a conspiracy theory or think it's merely a secret society in Hollywood that leading celebs are part of.

While there certainly have been countless allegations made against a variety of celebrities like Jay-Z, Lady Gaga, Beyoncé, Kanye West, and several others, when you take a good analysis of stars as a whole and the power their music and personas have over the culture, it becomes obvious that music is not always "just entertainment.".

As the Illuminati prepare to announce the "royal secret," as they call it, by declaring that Satan is the King of the Earth and the "hero of humanity," hoping to finally topple the "inferior" and "evil" Creator God to finish the New World Order "utopia," celebrities have just recently played a major part in paving the path to the apocalypse.

The large majority of the public praise celebrities who operate as contemporary Gods that form our cultural attitudes and beliefs because their every action is imitated. Every opinion they voice is viewed as profound.

The public is growing to see the Illuminati-- not as a hazard to their freedoms or a corrupt mafia of bankers, political leaders, and entrepreneurs--. Still, as a "cool" group of great men, they wish they might be a part of it. The ethical or moral decay and disintegration of the work ethic have resulted in the typical person being happy to do almost anything for just a taste of the Illuminati's "success." Popular culture has begun representing the Illuminati as holding the secret to success or a secret society of the abundant and famous.

Occasionally movies have portrayed the Illuminati or an affiliated group as the villain in a plot to communicate a warning to the audience. Some celebs have publicly knocked them as the shadowy puppet masters pulling strings in worldwide affairs, but the overwhelming bulk of mainstream media content and celeb idols paint the Illuminati as holding the master key to success. As an outcome, many individuals would almost kill their mother to join them to have a bigger piece of the pie.

CHAPTER EIGHT

"Ex-Illuminati Members"

Similar to government whistleblowers or career criminals developed into informants who reveal the closely concealed of their organization, a handful of people have stepped forward throughout the years declaring to have been included with the Illuminati in one way or another, and offer up what they declare to be insider information about the activities and goals of the network. Most of these individuals are total scams and are merely con artists attempting to sell books and lectures or simply delight in the conspiracy community's attention, considering that numerous people believe their stories, sinker, hook, and line.

There is a detailed analysis of John Todd and William Schnoebelen, who are 2 of the most popular men who have made such claims; however, there are likewise others whose stories have spread out everywhere on the Internet like urban legends, so in this book, we'll determine and take a close appearance whether there is an authenticity to them.

Far none of the declared "defectors" have used up any evidence to back up their claims; however, they have just told tales based on the openly understood info about the Illuminati's history, beliefs, and activities. None of the "former members" has ever revealed any brand-new info that wasn't currently published in literature widely available in the conspiracy culture. However, review some of the of the YouTube videos featuring their claims. You will see that a too sizable percentage of the audience ultimately believes these individuals and see them as brave whistleblowers who "left" their dark past and are now on a mission to "expose" the Illuminati.

An astute student is committed to reality and doesn't approach these people's stories with confirmation predisposition. If one has diligently done their research of the errors and fabrications, stick out like aching thumbs. For those who are new to examining the Illuminati, or to Tuite gullible, these "former Illuminati members" just serve to confirm their greatest fears. The majority of these "defectors" are just gifted writers providing publicly known details from a first-person perspective as if they witnessed it or took part in it.

Some of these people are psychologically ill and may believe what they are stating, but the evidence proves one after the other to be phony.

Let's take a close appearance at some of these individuals' stories so we can avoid them and future hoaxers from tricking people who are searching for responses and precise details concerning the Illuminati and the New World Order.

Doc Martius

Joseph "Doc" MarTuis (born upon October 26th 1956) is allegedly a previous U.S. Army medic, which is how he says he got his label "Doc," and is one of numerous self-proclaimed "previous Illuminati members" who says he was born into an Illuminati household now is dedicated to "exposing" them.

" Doc," who claims to have been raised as a seventh-generation witch, says when he was three-years-old, his household brought him to an occasion and committed him to Lucifer in a satanic baptism. For the next ten years, he says, he remained in the "external court" of the Illuminati, which he referred to as a hellish seminary school where he found out about the approaches and secret signs, and what he declares are the "eight nights of human sacrifice" that Illuminati members allegedly commemorate.

According to his story, when he was thirteen-years-old, he was "a new member of the Illuminati" after signing his name in his blood in a book made from lambskin, which he called the Book of the Dead, which so happens to be the name of an ancient Egyptian scroll containing information on how to navigate through the afterlife to participate in Heaven.

Four years later, when he was seventeen, "Doc" says he underwent another initiation ceremony and became what he called a Master Witch, or a High Druid Priest, which granted him "automated authority over a region of the United States" where he supervised over 1000 other Illuminati members. This all happened before he even finished high school! He says his superiors then bought him to join the United States Army to assist the Illuminati infiltrate the militaries. Within two weeks of being stationed at Fort Lewis in Washington, he states he had twenty individuals recruited for the Illuminati. A couple of months later on says he had more than a hundred more! In reality, the real Illuminati more likely includes nothing more significant than a couple of hundred men; however, when "Doc" MarTuis was simply seventeen-years-old, he states he was "in charge" of over 1000 of them!

Throughout an online lecture produced by Prophecy Club, he says he practiced human sacrifices eight times a year and had "continuous interaction with Demons." Marcus claims to have personally seen dozens of human sacrifices before he "went out." Still, no police have ever shown any interest in him and have never considered him to be a suspect or a witness to any murders whatsoever. On the other hand, Garbage television provided him a platform to spread his rubbish in the late 1980s. He was as soon as a guest on The Oprah Winfrey Show, where he was discussing all these expected murders and stated, "The thing is, we didn't get body bag these individuals later on. We'd simply take them [and], throw them in the woods, on the side of the roadway on a highway. Somebody's going to find them." Of course, nobody ever has because these "victims" do not exist.

The "8 nights of human sacrifice" that MarTuis claims to have commemorated was cooked up from the eight celebrations that Pagans celebrate (or Sabbats as Wiccans call them), which are commemorated throughout the year on solstices, equinoxes, and the four mid-points in between, none of which involve human sacrifices. I'm not stating that Satanists don't dedicate human sacrifices still to this day, because such events have been well recorded, but the closest MarTuis has come to one was enjoying a scary motion picture.

Regional authorities would have taken him into custody to question if there was even a shred of evidence to support his claims and no one involved with such crimes would attempt to speak about them out of fear of being apprehended. Indeed, in the 1980s, before the Internet, an average person might not easily verify or negate most claims made about the Illuminati and the occult. Very few people understood much about the topic at all. This led to the "hellish panic" in the 1980s when stories like MarTuis' were spread through tabloids and garbage TV talk shows, triggering individuals who didn't know any better to believe Satanists were abusing children and sacrificing individuals in neighborhoods throughout the country.

" Doc" states that in between dedicating his evil deeds, he was repeatedly asked by Christians if he wished to go to church or if he knew Jesus. For whatever reason, despite being a "high-level Illuminati master," he decided to go to church on Easter Sunday in 1979, where he realized he was "offered out as a slave of Satan," ended up being a Christian, and "left the Illuminati."

In among his video lectures' entitled Arrival of the Antichrist, he can be seen giving the typical history lesson about Adam Weishaupt and the formation of the Bavarian Illuminati, their structure and goals, and reveals the all-seeing eye on the back of the dollar while informing the audience to take out their wallets to look at the dollar themselves as if this was some major revelation. The eye on the back of the one-dollar expense has become so primary and Illuminati 101 that most middle school trainees are now familiar with it, but back in the 1980s and 90s, when MarTuis started providing his lectures, things were Tuite various.

After his discussion on the dollar symbology, he goes on to cover the famous quotes from Pike's book, Morals and Dogma, and then shows the fascinating designs in the street layout of Washington D.C. and then grumbles about the federal government, the dumbing down of America, the Constitution, the demonization of Christians, and so on, etc. He concludes that the Illuminati will state martial law and is establishing a New World Order for the antichrist's reception.

When performing my research study into the Illuminati and encountering Doc MarTuis' claims of being a former Illuminati member, I carefully listened to his lectures online, which, like almost every other self- proclaimed "previous Illuminati member," didn't expose a single shred of info that wasn't currently extensively understood. Not only that, however, a number of his claims are ludicrous to anybody who has standard knowledge about the Illuminati conspiracy.

For instance, he states that they place a $10,000 bounty on anyone's head who tries to leave. After he "left the Illuminati," he says they attempted to kill him six times! The Illuminati can assassinate world leaders and other presidents, but they've stopped working over twenty times to eliminate this man? Absurd.

Of course, there are no authorities reports or news stories about any of these alleged murder efforts against him. Because the Illuminati is the most effective secret society globally, they would have no problem killing anyone, mainly no-name losers like "Doc" Martius.

He sells a DVD called Frontmen of the Illuminati, which includes nothing more than a badly produced home video of him sitting at a table showing different pictures of signs and people while discussing the Illuminati. The information on a website selling his DVDs checks out, "Doc MarTuis is a former Satanist who was trained in the Illuminati Plan before he came out of the coven to become a Christian. In 1992, Doc was worked with by the Boston Police Department to train their homicide detectives on how to find evidence in a criminal offense scene that the criminal was a practicing occultist. Doc likewise has appeared on the following TELEVISION programs: Oprah Winfrey, Geraldo Rivera, Hard Copy, and Inside Edition. He is the author of numerous books, videotapes, and audio cassette series and has appeared as a skilled witness in several documentaries.".

His claim of having worked with the Boston Police department has not been validated, and to believe that this guy would be hired to "train" murder detectives is absurd, particularly after having declared to have killed a lot of individuals in hellish rituals! I think the police simply decided to forgive him for all those supposed murders!

Marcus has also claimed to have degrees in sociology and history, and once claimed he would quickly be getting his doctorate in psychiatry from Baptist Christian University in Shreveport, Louisiana. Still, it was later on revealed he wasn't even participating in the school. He then said the school would be accepting a book he was composing on the occult as his doctoral argumentation!

Martius wrote several books (as does every supposed "Illuminati defector") to make a couple of bucks off the conspiracy community. Martius and other "Christians" who claim to be "previous Illuminati" members like Bill Schnoebelen and John Todd, while being total phonies might, in their mind, really believe that they are assisting people in finding out about the

Illuminati conspiracy. After all, there is a massive conspiracy, and these people do expose a few of them. Still, their produced pasts and long lists of lies about being personally included with the Illuminati when they don't even have some of their standard truths directly reveal that men like Doc MarTuis are not just scams, however quite shameful and useless too.

Leo Zagami

Another man claiming to be an Illuminati defector who went on to give interviews and lectures about the wicked plans he learned while supposedly "inside" the secret society is Leo Zagami (born in Rome on March 5th, 1970). While other alleged defectors declare to have ended up being born again Christians after "leaving the Illuminati" and state that Jesus assisted them reali] e they were on the wrong path and discovered support from Christian audiences, Leo Zagami instead has taken the New Age angle. He firmly insists the Illuminati hold "the reality" but are a corrupt group of enlightened ones who have pirated the Mystery School teachings, so he decided to leave the Illuminati to preach their philosophy to the masses.

To assist spread the "enlightening truth" kept suppressed by the Illuminati, Leo Zagami claims to have started a brand-new "faith" called Matrixism based on the popular Matrix movies! He says he began this new "faith" in 2004 to celebrate the 100th anniversary of the "deliverance" of Aleister Crowley's Book of the Law, the brief bloodthirsty book Crowley claimed was dictated to him by a devil while he was going to Egypt in 1904. Yes, Zagami is a fan of dirtbag Aleister Crowley, whose philosophies he thinks about "the truth."

His website described his brand-new "faith" as, actually having been inspired by the Matrix movement pictures, however, insists it was "conceived by a confidential group in the summer of 2004 and has brought in over 16,000 followers."

The explanation goes on to state, "The Matrix trilogy, together with associated mass media equipment such as computer game, is usually considered to be the 'spiritual text' of the movement." He says The Matrix films and computer games are "sacred texts" of his "religion." He also says the "faith" can be traced back to a book called The Promulgation of Universal Peace, published in 1922 that includes a series of speeches provided by Abdu' l-Baha, the creator of the Bahá' í Faith. All of these details, he states, comes from his knowledge of being an "Illuminati Grand Master" himself.

Zagami's site declares that he is "a high-ranking Illuminati Grand Master, who got considerable attention in the conspiracy research neighborhood between 2006 and 2008 as a defector and whistle-blower." He went by the name Khaled Saifullah Khan after having allegedly converted to Islam, but later changed his name back to Leo. He claims that his goal is to organize now "the Knights Templars of the Apocalypse" to combat the Illuminati, and says this "group" has hired 12,000 soldiers from the U.S. Military, CIA, FBI, etc., who are going to stop the "Dark Illuminati plans."

In Leo's mind, the primary enemies of humanity are: The Jesuits, which he calls "the head of the snake"; Zionists, who he states are "the financial arms of the Vatican New World Order"; the United Nations, which is "a corrupt organization in the hands of the Jesuits and their Zionist allies devoted to enslave mankind"; and "all spiritual fundamentalist because organized religious beliefs in all types and shapes is a legal mafia manipulated by the Vatican and Jerusalem in the hands of corrupt individuals who work for the elite families and their intelligence services to keep our race in ignorance and superstition in the end of times.".

Despite Leo's rambling and weird history and his new "faith" that he produced based on The Matrix movies, and his claim to still be involved with the "good" Illuminati and the "Knights Templars of the Apocalypse" and other undercover "Illuminati Resistance" members in the CIA, FBI, military, and authorities; and regardless of revealing no new details about the operations of the Illuminati-- some completely gullible fools think that he really was, or still is included with the secret society.

Leo Zigami's claims never acquired anywhere near the traction of other supposed "defectors" before him, such as John Todd or

Bill Schnoebelen, because he's not a gifted writer like some other hoaxers. And we were into the info age by the time Leo decided to step on the scene (in 2006), whereas John Todd began his talks in the 1970s, and Bill Schnoebelen in the early 1990s before the Internet was entirely used by many people who can now quickly check claims online. Even with this resource at people's fingertips, nevertheless, a stunning variety of people still think the stories from "ex-members" like "Doc" MarTuis, Leo Zagami, John Todd, and others.

Many individuals delight in conspiracy home entertainment or conspiratainment as I call it, and have little or no issue about real facts or the truth. They simply love the cleverly cooked up tales by individuals who are influenced by real events or conspiracies. After that, they manufacture an often amusing conspiracy folklore based upon grains of truth. It's sort of like a great sci-fi story that's based in part on real technology and then extrapolates into a dream created to captivate the audience.

Supreme Rockefeller.

A man calling himself "Supreme Rockefeller" and claiming to be a member of the popular Rockefeller family developed a little a stir on the Internet in 2010 after announcing that the Rockefellers were launching a strategy to fund the structure of the Third Temple in Jerusalem in what was called the "Temple

Now Project." The Third Temple describes the restoring (again) of Solomon's Temple in Israel, which was initially destroyed in 586 BC by the Babylonians, and later restored to be also destroyed by the Romans in 70 AD. Christians believe that when the temple is reconstructed for the third time, it will signify the satisfaction of one of the final predictions worrying about the increase of the Antichrist and the return of Jesus.

Presently, a Muslim mosque called the Dome of the Rock stands on the ruins of the temple, and the only way Solomon's Temple can be restored on that area is if Israel inhabits and ruins the mosque that part of the land. This is why the "Rockefeller" announcement of supposed strategies to construct the Third Temple captured many individuals' attention.

A couple of official websites released a press release about the "Supreme Rockefeller" plan without verifying his identity or the supposed plan's authenticity. With websites like CNNMoney. Com and MarketWatch having the press launched posted, that was all the evidence numerous conspiracy blogs needed to keep up the story that a person of the last Biblical prophecies will be fulfilled thanks to the Rockefellers.

None of this was real, nevertheless, and "Supreme Rockefeller" didn't exist. The scam guy was determined as a high school dropout called Kris from Louisiana, born in 1975. While living with his mother, he worked as a cashier at a quick food dining establishment and attempted to earn money by betting and selling ringtones on different websites.

After he was fired from his job for apparently stealing, the thirty-four-year-old then began passing "Supriem Rockefeller" online and saying he was the secret kid of David Rockefeller Jr. "Supreme" posted online about how he was authorized to finalize the New World Order and "exposed" that the Rockefeller household had come down from the Annunaki, the supposed ancient race of aliens, who are thought by some to be accountable for the production of humans.

It appears his "Temple Now Project" hoax was an effort to receive donations from individuals who wished to support the plan, wanting to meet Bible prediction. One news release claimed he would be "raising funds to go towards developing the Third Temple in Jerusalem in stringent coordinance with The Temple Institute, Rabbi Hiam Richman and The Palestinian National Interest Committee (PNIC)," and his mission was to "build the Temple and to produce a One Israel-Palestine state.".

What made this hoax credible for some, aside from the Christian prophecy of the Third Temple, was the straightforward Jewish plan to accomplish this same task one day. Ever since 1987, a non-profit Jewish group called the Temple Institute has been working to do just this. In 2008 they revealed they had the High Priest's garments currently made along with do] ens of other products they intend on utilizing in "sacred routines" once it is rebuilt. Naturally, the Temple Institute had nothing to do with "Supreium Rockefeller," however, he skillfully included their name in his press release to include an aura of trustworthiness to his claims, given that they are an open group working to accomplish this objective.

This hoax didn't last too long, and his Facebook page was soon deleted. Still, many Jews and Christians continue to await the actual rebuilding of the Temple, an event that will be seen by Christians as one of the Bible's final prophecies being satisfied because, in this Temple, it is thought the Antichrist will announce himself to be "God" and order individuals of earth to praise him as such.

In the 1970s, 80s, and 90s, Illuminati phonies managed their frauds with a remarkable amount of success. While the Internet can put an end to the majority of these frauds rather quickly today, countless people are simply lost in the sea of info readily available on the internet and continue to spread out Illuminati scams far and wide, thinking every word. These are the same kinds of people who believe that whenever a famous celeb dies from a drug overdose, vehicle mishap, or health issue-- they believe they were actually "killed" by the Illuminati or fabricated their death. If you browse YouTube for keywords like "Paul Walker Illuminati Sacrifice," "Michael Jackson Murdered by Illuminati," or "Tupac eliminated by Illuminati," you will find hundreds of videos with millions of views literally and countless comments from people who are 100% convinced the Illuminati lags every celeb death.

The "Supreme Rockefeller" Third Temple hoax is not the very first time that somebody has impersonated a member of the well-known Rockefeller household. A man who called himself Clark Rockefeller (genuine name Christian Karl Gerhartsreiter) was sentenced to 27 years in jail for murdering his proprietor's kid, which put an immediate end to his elaborate scam.

Gerhartsreiter even asked his spouse into believing he was a Rockefeller for several years by taking extreme steps to hide his genuine identity. To accomplish this, he had his better half file her earnings taxes as a specific instead of jointly as many married couples do, so his real name would not need to be on the couple's income tax return, which she more than likely would have noticed. He even created their marriage license to avoid having her see his real name.

Another guy calling himself Christian Rockefeller (genuine name Christopher Rocancourt) scammed tens of countless dollars from rich people in New York in the 1990s through phony investment rip-offs after they believed he might increase their wealth because they thought he was a Rockefeller.

Saly

The list of people who have stepped forward claiming to be previous members of the Illuminati are primarily men, however in 2006, a female calling herself "Svali" turned up on the Internet declaring to come from an Illuminati family in Germany who then transferred to America when she was too young. "Svali" stated when she was a kid; she was informed that she was "special," which the Illuminati had big plans for her. At 12-years-old she underwent her "initiation" at the Vatican, as she declared all the Illuminati management's management do. By the time she was twenty-two, she was the youngest person in the "Illuminati leadership council" in Southern California.

" Svali" stated that secret Illuminati meetings were held three times a week in Escondido, California, which is a lower-income location inland where no wealthy or influential members of the Illuminati would ever go, let alone select to live. I have lived near this area for over 15 years and have buddies who have lived in Escondido, and I've seen the city with my own eyes many times. It's mostly a Mexican ghetto and would be the last place in the world the Illuminati would ever think of going.

The security for these "Illuminati" conferences, she said, was a "spy" who had actually climbed into a tree with a walkie talkie to find unwanted visitors and would then radio ahead to the group so they could "leave within five minutes." I guess the group would just run off into the woods if the individual in the tree saw anybody unforeseen rolling up to your home! You'd believe the Illuminati's security information would be a bit more sophisticated than somebody climbing up into a tree with a walkie talkie! Her claims get dumber by the second the more she informs her story.

The source of information coming from Svali appears to lead back to Greg Szymanski, who wrote (or might continue to write) for a little known site called ArcticBacon. Com, among many amateur websites, includes posts about the Illuminati, the Jesuits, and other conspiracy problems. "Svali" supposedly connected and contacted him with her claims, so he then interviewed her in January of 2006 on his practically new Internet radio show. Audio of the interview can be discovered if you can require yourself to listen to more than 30 seconds of her incoherent rambling, YouTube.

In the interview, she stated her adult co-conspirators would "get up in the middle of the night to attend conferences," and while the adults were doing their thing, the kids were "finding out how to march and shoot guns and were being trained in martial arts." She declares her initiation at the Vatican included child sacrifice. Throughout the interview, she was extraordinarily forgetful and had a tough time describing her story, which isn't even remotely convincing. However, Greg, the interviewer, ate it up and appeared to think every word she was stating, as did a measurable variety of individuals on the Internet who took place to come across her story.

When she was socializing with the Illuminati, she claimed to be a "head programmer" associated with mind control programs but never provided any details about her supposed duties and could not even articulate the fundamental ideas or history of mind control.

Svali isn't even a creative hoaxer like some others before her, and appears to be a psychologically deranged person just looking for somebody to pay attention to her. It's likewise possible that Greg Szymanski, the man who initially interviewed her, crafted the Svali hoax himself by dealing with a female friend to concoct the whole story so he could be the person to have the "unique" interview and permanently be linked to her as the person who initially "broke her story."

His site is just among countless virtually unidentified sites in the sea of conspiracy theories online, so it makes no sense why a "former Illuminati member" would connect to him since there is a great deal of relatively well-known conspiracy sites that cover such topics. She did attempt to have an e-book entitled " Breaking the Chain: Breaking Free of Cult Programming; however, it's not even listed in any of the significant e-book shops and appears like an unsuccessful attempt to attempt to make a couple of bucks by offering a PDF file from a site.

I can confirm to the reality that I have received several e-mails from different individuals making exceptionally bizarre claims such as being stalked or pestered by cults, and the incoherent and rambling nature of their emails reveal that they are from psychologically disturbed and crazy people sounding much like this female.

Actual Illuminati members are educated, smart, and well-spoken individuals. They are persuading and very convincing, none of which can be attributed to Svali, whose stories are so convoluted they're hard to follow as she jumps from faith to belief. How did she eventually "get away" the clutches of the Illuminati? Well, she said she left the organization because she started to realize, "what I was doing was wrong." Now that she is a "former member," she is a born once again Christian and has repented of the activities she claims to have taken part in. Today, the lady says she's a "diabetic educator" living in Texas with her hubby and two children.

The bio on the site of the man responsible for performing the interview checks out, "Greg is primary and first a satirist, an author and a reporter," so he was most likely merely trying and playing a function to have a good time with conspiracy theories by producing a new Internet urban myth of conspiracy theory fiction about the "lady who left the Illuminati."

Brice Taylor

A female calling herself Brice Taylor (a pseudonym) published a book in 1999 entitled Thanks For The Memories: The Truth Has Set Me Free! The Memoirs of Bob Hope's and Henry Kissinger's Mind-Controlled Slave, where she details what she states is her account of being a CIA mind control victim who was utilized as a sex servant Illuminati.

David Icke, a famous conspiracy author, best known for his theories that the Illuminati are an alien race of shape-shifting reptilians, is listed as a recommendation on Amazon. Com's listing of the book, in addition to Ted Gunderson, a previous FBI Agent from Los Angeles who stated, the book "verifies truths provided by lots of other witnesses."

With recommendations by such massive players in the conspiracy world as David Icke and Ted Gunderson, many individuals are inclined to believe her claims; however, upon even a quick analysis of the book, the female's story Quickly goes from being hard to think to be impossible and ridiculous by any stretch of the creativity.

This story's first wobbly leg comes when we discover Brice Taylor is simply a pseudonym and the authors' real name is Susan Lynne Eckhart Ford, who admits that she suffered from numerous character conditions from a young age. "But as I started to recover and remember more of my hidden past, I realized that routine abuse was simply the mind control injury base my ritually mistreated, set pedophile father, Calvin Charles Eckhart, and others used to condition me for involvement in the still-active supersecret Project Monarch, the Central Intelligence Agency's white slavery operation that belongs to MKULTRA and its various sub-projects," she writes.

"The outcome of several years of trauma, deliberately caused on me by my father and others to produce within me split personalities, was that I was transformed into a programmed, totally robotically slave that might not remember to tell or think what took place to me, due to the mind control and sophisticated programming I was under. I was frequently used in child and teen prostitution and pornography. By my pre-teen years, I had many characters particularly configured to be the best sex servant with government mind files and a photographic memory equipped to deliver (most often through sexual encounters) messages, some puzzling, to leading federal government authorities, performers, and other world figures."

She writes that when her memories began returning to her at the age of thirty-five she, "began having vivid, in-depth memories of being used both as a sex servant and human mind file computer system to some of our nation's highest level federal government officials in and out of the White House." She then lists Presidents John F. Kennedy, Lyndon Johnson, Gerald Ford, Ronald Reagan, George Bush, Jimmy Carter, Henry Kissinger,

Nelson Rockefeller, Bob Hope (the popular entertainer), and lots of others as men she says all abused her.

When she was four months old, Taylor states that while meditating, she began to keep in mind things all the method back to! (Not four years of age, four months old.) She states her dad worked as a welder who owned a welding shop in Los Angeles; however was also secretly working for the CIA as a mind control developer. "My father started the strenuous training and deliberate abuse needed to shatter my base character to produce lots of different private personalities for training and usage by others as I aged."

Her mother too, she says, was under mind control and "was listening to music she was told to listen to keep her memory of our life locked deep within her subconscious mind, while the programmed reality of herself and our 'perfect delighted household' was kept alive through configured expressions in the music."

Most of the book consists of rambling and prolonged tales of supposed abuse by such a long list of individuals, both popular and regular individuals in her neighborhood, that reads like a parody of a poorly written horror story. Individuals included in the conspiracy include her ballet instructor, her medical professional, her dental professional, her choir teacher, her next-door neighbor, individuals at her local church (who she says all had tunnels under their homes connecting them and likewise resulting in the church); the owners of the local bowling street were also in on it, and naturally the Freemason Shriners, and even the owners of a regional gas station! They were all sacrificing kids and shooting snuff films or involved with the "CIA's mind control program," she states.

The list of her alleged abusers and human-sacrificing CIA Satanists she was included with simply goes on and on. Prince Philip, Prince Charles, and even Sylvester Stallone are on her seemingly endless list of abusers. She declares that Sylvester Stallone directed several bestiality films where she says she made love with dolphins and other sea creatures! Other stars such as Jane Fonda and Barbara Streisand were likewise under mind control, she states, and Elton John was aware of such things and attempted to help the victims with the lyrics in his music.

Aside from noting half the people in her neighborhood as being "in on it," and a dozen celebrities and presidents, she likewise names some odd places where she states everyone sexually abused her or "programmed" her with mind control. Among these expected places as Disneyland, where she says her father presented her to Walt Disney himself when she was five years old, she made her appearance into a View-Master box, including dead individuals and dead felines.

" Brice Taylor" stated she would also fulfill Henry Kissinger at Disneyland, where he would "program" her using CIA mind control techniques. One of these "shows sessions," she stated, required to be carried out in front of a carrousel for some unknown factor. "I also continued to be taken to Disneyland for base shows for my new global mind file system," she composed. Who would have believed the CIA was using Disneyland as a secret mind control? Like I stated, her book reads like a bad parody of a horror story written by a teen.

She goes on to claim she was likewise asked to about McDonald's around the nation and "programmed there too." And naturally, she says she was also taken inside the National Archives, the State Department, NASA, the Pentagon, the Federal Reserve, the World Health Organization, and other military bases around the country, and insists she was "set" at each. Her handlers would require to take her to the Federal Reserve Bank to "program" her using mind control techniques. These claims are outrageous and the outcome of another over-active imagination of a crazy person or by a horrible writer fabricating such tales wanting to sell many books to the conspiracy neighborhood.

She wrote that she was even told that she would be killed in a couple of years and her services would not be needed any longer. Why would her handlers notify her that they would kill her at some point in the future? Wouldn't they keep this to themselves and lead her on? After all, if she understood she would be killed soon, would not this offer her even more reason to betray them and leave before this occurred? The more of Brice Taylor's story you read, the more unreasonable it gets, well beyond the point of rubbish.

The question remains ... why would this lady comprise all these dreadful things that she says taken place to her? What would force a female to compose such a book? I speculate that the only truthful part of the book is that perhaps she was sexually abused as a kid, but not by any of the political figures or celebs she pointed out, but at the hands of a relative or maybe even her dad. She might feel justified and achieve some healing degree by venting her anger and betrayal in a fictionali] ed book. She has projected that the perpetrators of her abuse are guys in high positions of power within society. It's likewise likely that she wrote the book only as "conspiracy fiction," wanting to pass it off as accurate to the frequently gullible conspiracy neighborhood.

Some individuals believe her claims are because there are grains of fact (albeit small little grains) considering that the CIA did do horrific mind control experiments in their MK Ultra program. They did drug, hypnoti] e, and torture people in those experiments attempting to develop mind-controlled servants. In 1994 the United States federal government awarded 77 individuals $100,000 each in monetary payment to explore them,374. Still, Brice Taylor (whose real name is potentially Sue Ford) never even went to court over her claims and was not one of the receivers.

A couple of years before Brice Taylor's book was published, another lady named Cathy O'Brien released a book entitled The Transformation of America, where she had claimed to be a test subject for the CIA's MK Ultra program and a "sex slave" of the Illuminati's top political leaders. O'Brien even claims to have been taken inside Bohemian Grove. It's most likely Brice Taylor was influenced by Cathy O'Brien's book and hoped she could make money by making similar claims. While Brice Taylor is a fraud, Cathy O'Brien's claims are a bit more believable (however perhaps fabricated) and analyzed.

"Jess LaVey"

A guy calling himself "Jess LaVey" stating he was the boy of Anton LaVey, the infamous founder of the Church of Satan and the author of The Satanic Bible, threw his hat into the conspiracy home entertainment ring around the year 2000 and got himself a small quantity of attention on a couple of Internet radio shows who eagerly took the bait and offered him a platform to spread his rubbish.

" Jess LaVey" not only claimed to have been the kid of Anton LaVey (whose real name was Howard Levey by the method), however also said he climbed up the ranks of Satanism all the way approximately the Illuminati. In one interview "Jess" claims, "I never could forget the counsel of thirteen, they were very wicked looking guys. When I reached the age of twelve, my father told me I needed to go before them. They cautioned me of what could happen to me if I did not do as they suggested. George H.W. Bush Senior was among these men. I stood before them and told them I was not going to follow their ways, and I was not going to take my papa's location, and that there was nothing they could do to me. I told them I think in a higher power which greater power said in His Word that no damage could concern me.

After he refused this "invitation" to the Illuminati, he says they castrated him as his penalty. He also talked about the Kimball-Cherokee Castle in Sedalia, Colorado, a 1450s design castle developed in the 1950s on a 3,100-acre cattle ranch in Colorado. He claimed the Illuminati fulfill every year to make human sacrifices. "Satanists come together and do offensive things. To think that Bush and his entire household belongs to this example is tough for some people to believe. The entire Bush family is Satanists. He is a cool guy for Satan. Like a lethal weapon. Other "expert" hellish "leaders" have stepped forward throughout the years, generally in the 1980s and 90s such as Mike Warnke and Stephen Dollins, attempting to use their expected "satanic credentials" to enhance their new career as Christian evangelists; however, most were never included in any organized cults or groups and wildly exaggerated the expected activities they declared to have gotten involved in.

In 2002 John W. Morehead of the Watchman Fellowship, a group that monitors the activities of cults, was given a copy of what "Jess LaVey" claimed to be his social security card, which was fake and when the number was run for a background check it was shown to be void.

" Sadly, lots of have declared to be LaVey's child to acquire financial backing from churches and to provide credibility to their ministries supposedly resolving Satanism and the occult," Morehead informed Charisma Magazine in 2002.

Anton LeVay, Aleister Crowley, Helena Blavatsky, Manly P. Hall, and other real occult insiders have revealed a lot of information to see exactly what is going on in numerous Satanic groups and secret societies; however, conspiracy bilker appear to keep developing the idea that they can make some cash by claiming to have been an "insider" who is offering a "first-hand account" of what they have supposedly seen and done.

The interviews "Jess LaVey" can be discovered on YouTube. After listening to one for about 5 seconds, any sane adult ought to be able to tell he is making up his story practically as he goes along and does not even have the faintest tip of authenticity. Anton LaVey (again whose genuine name was Howard Levey) had two children and only one son; a boy called Satan Xerxes, born in 1993.

George Green.

An expected previous investment banker named George Green declares to have once attended secret Illuminati conferences where men were making "god-like choices as to who lives and who dies" and pondered "dropping neutron bombs" on major American cities to reduce the population following the Georgia Guidestones.

In his interview, which can be seen on YouTube, Green speaks about the World War Three looming in the Middle East, a coming one-world currency, FEMA concentration camps, the coming economic collapse of America, the prepared extermination of the majority of the world's population to save the earth's natural deposits for the elite, and rattles off a list of popular plans of the Illuminati. Green doesn't reveal an ounce of brand-new details whatsoever. Like numerous others, it discusses the same old widely available claims while presenting them from an expected expert who says he sat in on the meetings. He, too, is attempting to offer a book entitled Chaos in America, which never gained much traction.

If George Green did participate in any of the Illuminati meetings, he would have the ability to expose some formerly unidentified details about their plans; however, instead, he simply recycles the same old material that has been drifting around the Internet and patriot circles for lots of years. A fascinating phenomenon in the info age is that if you claim to have some sort of Illuminati "scoop" and toss the video online, individuals are going to find it, and individuals will believe it.

Aside from the common Illuminati talking points about the Georgia Guidestones, FEMA camps, and the collapse of America, George Green goes directly into crazy town and states the Illuminati have been making " synthetic individuals." He's not speaking about secret cloning programs, which most likely exist; he claims that most presidents have been "replaced" by these synthetic clones! That's right. He states our significant world leaders are all grown in an Illuminati lab and are simply pretending to be real individuals.

To "prove" this is occurring, he points to the movie Boys from Brazil, a 1978 movie about Nazi researchers producing Hitler's clones to reconstruct the Third Reich. This cloning technology, he states, was provided to us by the "greys" (aliens). He says he knows this.due to the fact that while operating in the Air Force, he claimed to have "supersecret" clearance, which offered him access to some dead Nordic-type aliens called the Pleiadians who concerned earth from the Pleiades star cluster.

While aliens may be directing the Illuminati, and leading secret human cloning programs more than likely do exist, George Green's discussion is so poorly carried out and unconvincing, it reeks of a scam from the very moment he opens his mouth. And again, he hasn't supplied a single piece of new "proof" that wasn't already widely understood by most conspiracy researchers.

Not to discuss, no one has been able to validate any part of his expected background as an "investment lender" or having any kind of "super-secret" security clearance in the armed force. Once again, we're living in a world where numerous individuals think Tupac faked his death, which simply shows that some people will think practically anything, no matter how crazy it is, despite zero evidence, and defying all reasoning and good sense.

CHAPTER NINE

The Structure of Power

Now in the U.S, the Middle East region was to be organized along the lines established by late British imperialism, which World War I acknowledged that direct colonial rule was no longer feasible. Regional management, therefore, would be entrusted to an "Arab.

Exterior" of weak and pliable rulers, with "absorption" of the colonies "veiled by constitutional fictions as a protectorate, a sphere of impact, a buffer State, and so on," a gadget more economical than direct rule (Lord Curzon and the Eastern Committee, 1917-18). We must never run the risk of "losing control," John Foster Dulles warned. The Facade would consist of family dictatorships that do what they are informed and guarantee profits to the United States, its British customer, and their energy corporations. They are to be secured by regional enforcers, preferably non-Arab (Turkey, Israel, Iran under the shah, Pakistan). British and U.S. muscle stand in reserve, with military bases from the Azores through North Africa to the Indian Ocean and the Pacific. The system has operated with sensible effectiveness over a substantial duration, and has new potential customers today.

Successes have been dramatic. Inexpensive oil fueled the "golden age" of postwar development. "Profits beyond the imagine avarice" enriched Western corporations,13 also assists in keeping the ailing British economy afloat, later on, the U.S. economy as well. The postwar settlement perpetuated the separation of the big population concentrations of the region from the oil wealth, retained in the hands of the Facade with sparse populations to share it. Apart from its unfairness, this "insanely manipulated ownership of home worldwide's most greatly armed region, with a long history of volatility and violence, is a continuous recipe for destabilization and violent upheavals," Dilip Hiro warns. "An increasing variety of Arab intellectuals and spiritual leaders," he composes, are coming to share the perspective articulated by Saddam Hussein on August 10, 1990; nevertheless, they may dislike the author of the sentiment. In Saddam's words: Through its partitioning of the [Arab] lands, western imperialism founded weak mini-states and set up the households who rendered it services that facilitated its [exploitative] objective. Hence it avoided most of the kids of the individuals and the [Arab] country from benefiting from their wealth. As a result of the brand-new wealth entering the hands of the minority of the [Arab] country to be made use of for the advantage of the immigrant and the few new rulers, social and financial corruption spread in these mini-states and from there to numerous quarters of the bulk of the Arab nations.

The United States opposes democracy in the region, Hiro writes, since "it is much simpler to manipulate a few ruling families to secure fat orders for arms and guarantee that oil price remains low than a wide range of policies and personalities bound to be thrown up by a democratic system," with chosen governments that may show popular require "self-reliance and Islamic fellowship." Hence the determination of Washington's policy of "supporting dictatorships to maintain stability" (Ahmad Chalabi), and the admitted preference for the "iron fist."

Hiro's analysis is persuasive. The roots of policy lie deep in firmly established institutional structures of power, with results that have long been evident worldwide. The fundamental policy thrust is periodically acknowledged with some regret by world leaders. Reflecting on British policy in the Middle East, Prime Minister Harold Macmillan found it "rather sad that circumstances oblige us to support reactionary and truly rather outmoded routines because we understand that the brand-new forces, even if they start with moderate opinions, constantly appear to wander into violent revolutionary and highly anti-Western positions." We require only add the usual gloss: a "violent advanced position" might be nothing more than one that seeks an independent course, becoming " strongly anti-Western" when that course is disallowed by Western power, a disaster that has been enacted over and over once again.

Rights accrue to regional actors by their position within the three-tiered tactical conception. At the regional level, the Facade of supervisors has rights, as long as they do their task; otherwise, they will be squashed. For internal "stability," the "iron fist" has often been preferred, precisely as the State Department presently discusses through the medium of the Times chief diplomatic correspondent. The local guardians likewise have rights, as does the British assistant. And the United States naturally has rights without credentials. Kurds, Palestinians, slum-dwellers in Cairo, and others who contribute absolutely nothing to the standard structure of power have no rights, by the most primary concepts of statecraft. Perhaps they can periodically be used in one or another power play, but that is where their rights end. Much of the modern history of the Kurds show these realities, as when they were supported in their revolt versus Iraq in the early 1970s in the interests of Washington's Iranian client, then delegated be butchered when that episode was effectively terminated, leading Henry Kissinger to comment acidly, in action to criticism, that diplomacy is not to be confused with missionary work. Current events, evaluated previously, include another awful chapter to the story.

Today, it is not hard to comprehend Eisenhower's lament that "the problem is that we have a project of hatred versus us, not by the federal governments; however, by the people." One may ask, however, why that should have currently held in July 1958, when the words were spoken, not long after the United States had expelled Britain, France, and Israel from the Egyptian area they had actually conquered in their 1956 intrusion, and well before the "special relationship" with Israel was in location. It is easy to discuss the hatred in Iran five years after the repair of the shah. Washington's rejection of attempts to carry out independent advancement was also unlikely to have elicited warm sensations. A year of CIA operations in Syria might shed further light on the matter.

Syria had typically been pro-American, but private U.S. intervention "assisted reverse a century of relationship," Douglas Little observes in a review of these operations. In 1948, the CIA approached Chief of Staff HusniZaim to discuss the "possibility of an army supported dictatorship," a result attained when Zaim toppled the government a few months later. Zaim authorized the Aramco oil pipeline (TOPLINE) concession according to U.S. wishes, and required peace talks with Israel, providing to transplant 250,000 Palestinian refugees, a diplomatic opening that Israel chose not to pursue. Zaim was toppled a few months later on. In 1951, Col. AdibShishakli toppled the federal government and set up a military dictatorship, with private U.S. assistance. Matters drifted out of control again. In March 1956, Eisenhower authorized Project OMEGA, which intended to overthrow the progressively pro-

Nasser program in Syria as part of a more basic strategy weaken Nasser. Operation Straggle, arranged jointly with British intelligence to topple the government of Syria, was timed (obviously, at British initiative) for the day of Egypt's invasion, which France and Britain had concealed from Washington. Perhaps Britain's objective was to keep the United States preoccupied elsewhere. In any occasion, Syrian counterintelligence had uncovered the plot, and it quickly deciphered. Several further clandestine operations looked to subvert Syria's government, leading lastly to a bungled CIA effort again permeated by Syrian intelligence.

The "Eisenhower Doctrine," authorized by Congress in March 1957, licensed the president to supply help, including U.S. troops, "to secure and secure the territorial stability and political independence of such Middle Easter nations, requesting such aid, against overt armed aggressiveness from any country controlled by global communism." While Egypt was the publicly designated offender, U.S. authorities thought that Syria was more "almost under the control of international communism," Douglas Little concludes. Completion result of years of such machinations was hostility to the United States, close Syrian relations with the USSR, and much hysteria in Washington about "losing the whole Middle East to Communism."

The resemblance to Cold War history in Latin America, Southeast Asia, and Africa is apparent, and its sources in U.S. policy are easy enough to discover.

CHAPTER TEN

From Demons To World   Rulers

There are levels of demonic forces that are attacking the world. These vary from demonic attacks on individuals, to principalities that look for dominion over countries or regions, to "world rulers" that look for dominion over the entire earth.

When the terrorist leader Osama bin Laden prophesied that America would fear from north to south and east to west, he issued a demonic prediction that was a clear indicator of the opponent's strategy against America. Since the opponent is always looking to counter God's work, we can understand for sure that it is God's preparation for faith to be launched in America from north to south, east to west. We are, in truth, close to another Great Awakening sweeping over America.

As the opponent steps up his assault across the world to dominate diplomacy with worry and terror, we can be ensured that it is the biggest chance for faith to be launched in every position the opponent attacks. Faith is much more powerful than worry, and faith will ultimately prevail.

The governments need to combat the war against terror on natural weapons; however, only the Church can attain the ultimate victory over this opponent. As we are told in Ephesians 6:12, "For our struggle is not versus flesh and blood, however versus the rulers, against the powers, versus the world forces of this darkness, against the spiritual forces of wickedness in the heavenly locations." This is not a war against flesh and blood; it is a spiritual battle that must be fought with spiritual weapons if we will have a true and lasting triumph.

Satanic forces assault individuals in the very same way that a principality attacks a city or area. They both start merely by looking to gain influence. They increase their influence up until they have control over the actions of those they are seeking to dominate. When this happens to a private, it is called being "possessed" by devils. Lesser levels of control by them are normally referred to as demonic injustice. Cities, regions, and even nations can be possessed by the more powerful forces of evil.

Christians are provided authority over satanic forces. No Christian who has come to understand our Lord Jesus Christ's authority must worry about being had by satanic forces. It releases God's authority to cause satanic forces to fear us and run away from us if a Christian is strolling in faith. Recognizing, facing, and erupting devils is regular, scriptural Christianity.

The next level of wicked authorities resolved in Scripture is called "principalities and powers." As specified, these are more effective than devils, and they look for rule over regions or countries, not simply individuals. Every Christian has the authority to cast out satanic forces; we do not cast out principalities and powers; rather, we must "wrestle" with them to displace them. This level of warfare is addressed in other books I have written, such as Epic Battles of the Last Days, Mobilizing the Army of God, and A Prophetic Vision for the 21st Century.

There is another, greater realm of evil called "world rulers." These do not simply affect individuals or areas; however, they can control much of the earth. This level of wicked I attend to in my book Shadows of Things to Come. Above this level is the wicked lord, Satan himself. Christians have contacted us to battle evil on all these levels. We just have true spiritual authority to the degree that the King lives within us or the degree to which we abide in the Lord. As we grow in authority, which is evidenced by our increased faith, we will be called to battle battles on greater levels.

Normally, only demons will have people, and the fight that many Christians deal with is personal. This is mainly with the evil that attempts to gain entryway to our own life. As we are victorious on this level and are trusted with more spiritual authority, we may be gotten in touch with to challenge evil on a high- er level, seeking the liberation of an area or perhaps a country from the enemy's domain. As my good friend Francis Frangipane likes to say, "With brand-new levels come new devils." This might not be too motivating, but among the ways that we understand, we have been promoted in spiritual authority is by the larger satanic forces that we need to combat.

Francis has written what numerous think about to be the greatest book ever on spiritual warfare, The Three Battlegrounds. He describes how our battle against evil starts with the fight in our minds in this timeless message. As we get victory there, we should then fight for the success of the Church. When the Church is triumphant in an area, will it displace the principalities over it, only?

If we are provided national or global spiritual authority, we can depend on attacks from principalities and powers. If we have been offered authority that will impact the whole earth, we will have to face a world ruler eventually. Paul, the apostle, was such a man, which is why he needed to face Caesar. Since Jesus is the highest authority in the Kingdom, He needed to be challenged by satan himself and prevail.

Since Caesar's scope of authority, he was not being manipulated by a simple satanic force, however, by a world ruler. Satan has to use males to do his will just as the Lord works through His individuals. As one grows in spiritual authority, they will be buffeted by those managed by more powerful demonic forces. This is not something that we ought to fear, as the one in us is much greater than all of the evil one's power. To be assaulted on a higher level should be an encouragement to us.

There are watershed events that cause sweeping changes over the entire earth. You can count on a world ruler being behind them if these occasions are evil. We saw such an occasion on September 11, 2001. This was the start of another tactical assault of worry on the level of a world ruler. This did not simply impact the United States; the entire world was shaken that day. The civilized governments of the world should now make terrorism the world's primary enemy it is. This is a spiritual opponent that can not be defeated by simple bombs and bullets. Christians must get rid of the fears that control their own lives, and then the Church needs to overcome the same. Then we should rise to the place of faith and authority where we confront the world ruler that is assaulting the entire world.

The Two Mandates

To understand that the genuine war is not natural and spiritual is not to negate the righteousness of the war in which our earthly governments are now engaged. As we are informed concerning them in Romans 13:1 -4,.

Every person is to be in subjection to the governing authorities. For there is no authority except from God, and God establishes those which exist. For that reason, whoever withstands authority has opposed God's ordinance; and they who have opposed will get condemnation upon themselves.

For rulers are not a cause of worry for excellent habits, however, for evil. Do you want to not worry about authority? Do what is good, and you will have praise from the same; for it is a minister of God to you for good. But if you do what is wicked, hesitate, for it does not bear the sword for absolutely nothing, for it is a minister of God, an avenger who brings rage on the one who practices evil.

As this passage states, civil governments have a mandate from God to avenge evil and bring rage on those who practice evil on the earth. For this factor, civil governments have been given the sword or military power. We must always wish our governments and for their success in bringing the rage of God on those who practice evil. Throughout the Bible, we see that many of the time when the Lord satisfied His Word by bringing judgment upon a country or individuals, it was done by using the military power of other nations.

Civil government is necessary for keeping order to the degree that it is possible until the Kingdom of God pertains to restore righteousness and justice on the earth. It will never be worked out entirely because fallen men exercise this authority. It does at least restrain the forces that would bring about a complete meltdown of order and authority. God ordains civil authority; however, we should not error it for the Kingdom of God's authority.

A Different Spirit

As Christians, we have a different requirement of authority. We are not here to avenge evil in this age, but in reality, we are required to like our opponents and hope for them. Our warfare is not against people, but against whatever has people in chains. The greatest triumph of all would be the repentance and salvation of our enemies. Many Christians have a tough time understanding the two various mandates offered to federal civil governments and the Church. However, this is something crucial that we should settle in our hearts if we will be efficient in our task of taking apart the spiritual fortress that keeps males in bondage.

Our civil governments are battling a righteous war versus evil as they fight terrorism or governments that promote terrorism. However, the Church has contacted us to a much various battle. We are called to battle the hidden war that is being waged in the heavenly places. Ours is a spiritual war.

This does not suggest that Christians can not join the military forces of countries to fight the war on the level of civil authority. They need to comprehend that while marching under civil governments' orders, their authority will be worked out through their physical weapons, not their spiritual ones. This does not suggest that Christian soldiers must not hope and try to use their spiritual authority, too, however when you're in battle, don't drop your gun to do so! You must not think twice to use the weapons that the federal government has given to you for battling if you are under orders from a civil government.

Also, if we are operating under the required provided to the Church, we do not have the authority to utilize the weapons utilized for battling flesh and blood for our fight. This is why "Christian militias" that arm themselves with weapons or other physical weapons will always be inspired by worry and paranoia. They are managed by the wicked since they are not correctly under either of the mandates of authority God has offered to men.

Fight the Good Fight

Spiritual authority is something that we grow into. We are offered more authority as we grow spiritually and are given higher commissions by the Lord. This will be evidenced by an increase of faith to brand-new levels. We see in the Book of Acts that Paul the apostle was called as an apostle lots of years before he was commissioned to that ministry. With that commissioning came authority on a greater level. However, "... many are called, but few of are chosen" (Mt. 22:14). One interpretation of this is that numerous are called; however, few persevere through all that is needed to receive their commission.

Being called to a high position does not immediately give one authority. Maturity and the loyalty that goes on to possess the promises will launch true authority. How - ever, we should comprehend that spiritual authority is not offered so that we get more regard from individuals, however, so we can combat effectively against the powers that are destroying people.

Our first objective should be to face and conquer our demons and our worries, so that we can grow in authority to handle larger satanic forces and set other people free. Because there is a faith that gets rid of the world, nothing less than this can be our goal to conquer the evil that is now controlling the world. We may not see wicked fully displaced up until the King Himself returns to earth, but there is a scriptural mandate for us to do all we can to prepare the method for His coming Kingdom by getting rid of evil in every manner in which we can now.

I have heard lots of reveal fear that this can be brought too far. I am rather sure that if we get brought away with excessive faith and take down some fortress of evil that we were not contacted us to tear down, saving more souls than we were contacted us to set free, I believe the Lord will forgive us!

Among the ways the enemy has kept much of Evangelical.

Pentecostal and Charismatic Christianity in chains has been to impart a belief that since it is unavoidable, the entire world will be up to the antichrist, it is ineffective to eliminate the evil worldwide, and therefore we must just attempt to be devoted ourselves and wait on the Rapture. Some Scriptures challenge this deceptiveness, such as the one we priced estimate in an earlier chapter, Daniel 11:31 -32.

We understand from the Scriptures that there are specific methods that evil will increase, which will prevail over the earth for a time; however, hasn't that been continuously the case? In the first century, the apostle John wrote that "the entire world depends on the power of the wicked one" (1 Jn. 5:19). It might depend on the power of the wicked one now. However, it does not come from him! It is a usurped rule that will be restored to its rightful owner-- the Lord, who paid the supreme rate with His own life to redeem it. As Psalm 24:1 declares, "The earth is the Lord's, and all it consists of, the world, and those who dwell in it." That is the truth that we need to identify to live by.

The main inroad that the opponent has into our lives, our households, our schools, and our world, is through worry. We must take a stand versus the worry that the opponent is looking for to increase over the whole world to enhance his control. We need to identify that we will not let fear dictate the course of our lives or our present actions. We are at war with fear.

As President Roosevelt said, "We have nothing to fear, however, fear itself." If we grow in faith, we can win this war. Real faith is not an uncertain confidence in ourselves; it results from a living relationship with the God who enjoys us, has called us, and will empower us to do all that He created us to do.

The Lord Jesus said that completion of the age is the harvest (see Mt. 13:39). The world is currently experiencing the excellent- est ingathering of souls into the Kingdom in history. Nevertheless, as we likewise comprehend, the harvest is likewise the time when everything that has been sown in man will come to complete maturity, both the excellent and the evil. This is why we see in such Scripture passages as Isaiah 60:1 -5 that the light and splendor are appearing upon the Lord's individuals at the very time when "darkness" and even "deep darkness" will cover the earth. At the end of this age, we can expect to see the ultimate yoke of chains of fear coming to its complete maturity at the same time the Lord's people are experiencing the most significant levels of faith and peace.

We are about to experience the best fear and the most significant faith ever launched on the earth. These will be happening at the very same time. If we are not growing in faith also evidenced by growing in the peace of God, we will be growing in fear and the stress and anxiety that will eventually even trigger males' hearts to stop working. The ultimate response to combating fear is growing in faith, and God's peace that goes beyond understanding.

We must first brighten the evil nature of fear and how it is used to position a wide variety of shackles on our life. This illumination alone will start to break that fear off of our lives. The opponent dwells in darkness, and whenever the light exposes him, it rapidly starts unraveling his power. We desire to change every worry in our life with a biblical, step-by-step method for growing in the faith, love, and peace of God.

CHAPTER ELEVEN

Seeking Peace: The Recent Phase

Going Back To Middle East diplomacy in the post-1967 period, together with UN efforts, those of the Arab states, the PLO, the USSR, and the European allies were frequently rebuffed. These initiatives shared two vital features that were inappropriate to Washington. They made at least some gesture towards Palestinian national rights; 2nd, they called for meaningful international involvement in a settlement. The reason for the U.S. rejection of such proposals has already been sorted out. The Palestinians perform no services for the United States, certainly are an irritant because their predicament stirs up Arab nationalist sentiments; therefore, they lack rights. And the United States is reluctant to accept disturbance outdoors in a region successfully drawn under the Monroe Doctrine, much as Kissinger had explained.

By 1988 it was challenging for the U.S. federal government and the media to hide PLO and other Arab initiatives for a political settlement. By December, the U.S. federal government had become something of an international laughing-stock with its increasingly desperate efforts to reject the apparent.

Washington grudgingly accepted "declare victory," claiming that at last, the PLO had been obliged to utter George Shultz's "magic words." The function of the exercise, Shultz discussed to Reagan, was to make sure optimum humiliation. In his knowledge on apologia, Turmoil and Triumph, Shultz reports that he informed Reagan in December 1988 that Arafat was stating in one location "' Unc, unc, unc,' and in another he was stating, 'cle, cle, cle,' but he never bring himself to say 'Uncle,'" in style anticipated of the lesser breeds. Likewise, Shultz needed that the PLO not just condemn terrorism but "renounce" it, therefore yielding that it had taken part in terrorism. However, at a level hardly noticeable in comparison to the record put together by Shultz and his predecessors, another unmentionable truth. Once again, the function was to grind a helpless and weak adversary underfoot, which frequently gives terrific enjoyment to the effective and makes them much regard. PLO requires renouncing violence "on a shared basis" have constantly been dismissed out of hand, as ludicrous.

It is, by the way, beside inconceivable that U.S. news reporting or commentary may keep in mind of the major UN resolution on terrorism, which mentions "that nothing in the present resolution could in any method prejudice the right to self-determination, independence, and liberty, as stemmed from the Charter of the United Nations, of individuals forcibly deprived of that right, particularly peoples under colonial and racist regimes and foreign occupation or other forms of colonial domination, nor the right of these individuals to have a hard time to this end and to receive and seek support [following the Charter and other principles of worldwide law]" The resolution passed 153-2, U.S. and Israel opposed, Honduras alone abstaining. It is therefore banned, and banned from history.

Naturally, Washington rejects any ideal to withstand the terror and injustice enforced by its customers. Since Washington's stand is undoubtedly legitimate by U.S. commentators, undoubtedly axiomatic, there is no requirement to report the truths, or what they suggest about the occupied territories or southern Lebanon, which is apparent enough. On these matters, silence has been overall, apart from margins of the usual margins, and the most elementary conclusions would by now be essentially unintelligible to a U.S. (undoubtedly, Western) audience.

It is only reasonable to keep in mind, in this connection, that Israeli practice is even more truthful. After four hundred Hamas activists were deported in December 1992, a leadership post in the Israeli press observed that "we can not accuse [Hamas] of practicing random horror which hits innocent females and kids, because they don't"; "we should attend to the fact that ... all Hamas guerrilla operations before the expulsion were targeted at soldiers." The same point was made about Hezbollah by Uzi Mahanaimi, a respected hawkish commentator on Intelligence and Arab Affairs. Talking about Israel's attack on Lebanon in July 1993, he asserted that "Hezbollah is not a terror organization," considering that it avoids striking civilians except in retaliation for Israeli attacks on Lebanese civilians. Moreover, "Hezbollah separates in between the Israeli conquest of Southern Lebanon and the presence of the State of Israel," taking its task to be just that of reversing the conquest, that is, legitimate resistance against an army inhabiting foreign area in offense of Security Council orders. Other commentators mock the U.S. State Department, "which knows no better than to provide Hezbollah higher status by declaring it 'the most obvious horror company in the world.'" American commentary, in contrast, keeps strictly to State Department doctrine.

Mahanaimi's analysis, undoubtedly right, simultaneously raises the concern of why Israel has demanded occupying southern Lebanon. Not for security factors, as both the history and his precise observations make clear. A widespread suspicion is that this needs to do, when again, with long-term strategies for control over the region's water resources, much as in the case of the "little trick" about Labor Party settlement programs from the 1970s exposed by Haim Gvirtzman. However, in the absence of any closer query, the questions stay open.

Returning to the shenanigans of December 1988, the record reveals clearly that the gap between the U.S. and PLO positions stayed about as before on every major issue. The farce continued smoothly in the public arena. Having stated victory, the United

States could then impose its analysis of what had taken place and proceed on course, without worry of contradiction.

As a benefit for saying "uncle" inappropriately modest tones, the PLO was offered the right to participate in a "dialogue" with the U.S. ambassador in Tunis. Publishing leaked procedures of the very first meeting; the Jerusalem Post could hardly contain its satisfaction over the fact that "the American representative adopted the Israeli positions." Ambassador Robert Pelletreau stated two crucial conditions that the PLO should accept: it must abandon the idea of a worldwide conference, and call off the "riots" in the occupied territories (the Intifada), "which we view as terrorist acts versus Israel." Simply put, the PLO must guarantee that the previous status quo is restored, so that Israel's repression and expansion in the territories with firm U.S. assistance could once again continue unhindered. The ban on an international conference follows that the world is out of action. Participation of outside celebrations beyond the United States and its clients would lead to undesirable pressure for a non rejectionist political settlement. Britain might be permitted, later on, Russia, however, no voice that might prove too independent. The characterization of the Intifada as "terrorism" (for example, tax resistance in Beit Sahour, efficiently stated invalid by the United States at the Security Council a year later) follows from the U.S.-Israeli rejection of the otherwise consentaneous worldwide consensus on the right of resistance to military occupation, already gone over. The "large accumulation of unlimited humiliations and casually committed cruelties" that close Israeli observers consider the "important factor" generating resistance has been removed from the record together with the global agreement on "fear.".

A couple of weeks later, in February 1989, Rabin had a conference with 5 Peace Now leaders in which he expressed his satisfaction with the U.S.-PLO discussion. He described it as an "effective operation," reporter Nahum Barnea reported, including just "low-level conversations" that avoid any serious issue. The Americans are "now satisfied, and do not look for any [political] option, and they will give us a year, at least a year," to deal with the scenario in our method. By doing this is force. "The inhabitants of the territories go through severe military and economic pressure," Rabin discussed. "In the end, they will be broken," and will accept Israel's terms.

Backing the essentials of this view, a top-level U.S. official urged Israel to put an end to its public objections to the dialogue, which "just add significance" to it, hence hindering its designated objective: to displace attention from the strong repression of the Intifada. In early March, Bush administration proposals, using "ideas" to Israel and the PLO, highlighted the point. Israel was advised to restrict the repressive procedures set up to suppress the Intifada, and the PLO to end the "violent demonstrations" and the circulation of "inflammatory leaflets."

The proposal, then, is that the PLO cooperate with Israel in developing a somewhat harsher, but not too severe differences of the former status quo.

The methods embraced in December 1988 worked like a charm. News protection of the occupied areas declined further, thus granting Israel the chance to turn to still harsher steps so that "they will be broken" as ultimately, they were; there is a limitation to what flesh and blood can endure, when any hope of assistance from the outside is gone. Attention was concentrated on the U.S.-managed "peace process," not the repression heightening with U.S. backing. Nonviolent resistance was lastly displaced by violence, much to the relief of U.S. and Israeli authorities, who have constantly been particularly concerned about the risk of small amounts, as Israeli analysts have long acknowledged.

The violence of the Israeli response to the Intifada got some general notice; however, neither these reports, nor the periodic accounts in earlier years when atrocities passed beyond the norm, offer a precise photo of the "large accumulation of limitless humiliations and delicately committed cruelties" that lastly led to the uprising. More illuminating are the innumerable cases thought about too insignificant to report, for example, an occasion in Gaza a couple of weeks before the Intifada broke out there. A Palestinian girl, Intissar al-Atar, was shot and killed in a schoolyard by a resident of a neighboring Jewish settlement.

The murderer, Shimon Yifrah, was apprehended a month later on and launched on bail because the courts determined that "the offense is not severe adequate" to require detention. In September 1989, he was acquitted of all charges other than triggering death by carelessness. The judge concluded that he only meant to shock the girl by firing his weapon at her in a schoolyard, not to kill her, so "this is not a case of a criminal individual who needs to be punished, deterred, and taught a lesson by imprisoning him." Yifrah was given a seven-month suspended sentence, while inhabitants in the courtroom broke out in tune and dance.

Below the limit of attention in the United States, these events left some memories amongst Israelis. As inhabitant violence against Arabs installed in the months after the Oslo Agreement together with the "need that the Israeli-Jewish public, and especially the government, ought to understand the spiritual inhabitants in these tough times they are going through," OlekNetzer recommended another appearance at a photo of the settlers "who danced in a circle of happiness with Uzi [rifles] on their shoulders" after Yifrah's release, and who now "fear that they will no longer be able to kill individuals, especially children, and be immune from penalty." Such cases and their reaction in the United States provide a bargain more understanding than the periodic massacre that is too violent to ignore. They also supply insight into the values that inspire U.S. leaders to decline

637

the right of resistance and declare it to be terrorism against U.S. clients, standing alone versus the world.

While Rabin's "extreme military and financial pressure" had the intended impacts on the subject population, Washington monitored a version of the "peace procedure" that would satisfy the two basic requirements: no meaningful outside interference, and no Palestinian rights. On May 14, 1989, Israel's coalition Labor-Likud (Peres-Shamir) government adopted an in-depth "peace plan," with three basic concepts:

1) There can be no "additional Palestinian state in the Gaza district and the area between Israel and Jordan" (Jordan currently being a "Palestinian state");

2)" There will be no change in the status of Judea, Samaria and Gaza other than following the standard guidelines of the [Israeli] Government," which rejects an "extra Palestinian state."

3)" Israel will not conduct settlements with the PLO," though it might concur to speak to certain Palestinians other than their picked political agents.

On these conditions, "complimentary elections" were held under Israeli military control, with much of the Palestinian leadership in jail without charge or expelled.

The United States backed the Israeli proposal while keeping its essential content under wraps. There appears to have been no main reference to the May 14 plan, nor any report in journalism. However, it was the operative policy statement, and this was comprehended in Washington, where the May initiative was lauded for its "terrific guarantee and potential." 70 Secretary of State James Baker revealed in October that "our goal the whole time has been to attempt to help in applying the Shamir effort. There is no other proposition or effort that we are working with." A different "Shamir initiative" had been proposed in April, then superseded by the May 14 Shamir-Peres Election Plan, which was the only "proposal or effort" that Israel had presented formally, and was for that reason, the only "Shamir effort" that Baker or anyone else was working with.

In December 1989, the Department of State released the five-point Baker Plan, which stated that Israel would attend a "dialogue" in Cairo with Egypt and Palestinians acceptable to the United States and Israel. These Palestinians would be permitted to talk about execution of the Israeli propositions, however nothing else: "The Palestinians will come to the discussion prepared to go over elections and the negotiating procedure following Israel's effort and would be free to raise issues that associated to their viewpoints on how to make elections and the negotiating procedure succeed."

In brief, the Palestinian delegation would be permitted to express viewpoints on the technical features of Israel's proposition to disallow any significant type of Palestinian self-determination, and even this right was accorded just to Palestinians who encourage Israel and its patron that they are complimentary from any taint of association with the PLO. The purpose of the latter condition was again a little bit more than humiliation. It has been comprehended on all sides that these associations exist, in which the PLO was directing the negotiating process.

The Bush-Baker plan, then, was to have the Intifada squashed by force while attention was diverted to a "peace procedure" that bars Palestinian rights. While pursuing this two-part program to deal with the Israel-Palestinian issue, the Bush-Baker team pushed forward with their policies in the Gulf, extending still even more their support for Saddam Hussein, relatively unconcerned to his appalling record of atrocities. In October 1989, as the Baker Plan was being offered its final type, the White House intervened in an extremely secret meeting to ensure that Iraq would get another $1 billion in loan warranties, eliminating Treasury and Commerce department objections that Iraq was not creditworthy. The reason the State Department discussed, was that Iraq was "essential to U.S. interests in the Middle East"; it was "influential in the peace process" and was "a secret to maintaining stability in the area, using terrific trade opportunities for US business." A few weeks later on, as U.S. invasion forces were bombarding slums in Panama, the White House revealed plans to lift a ban on loans to Saddam, executed quickly after-- to attain the "objective of increasing U.S. exports and put us in a better position to handle Iraq regarding its human rights record, the State Department explained with a straight face.

Once once again, to comprehend the performance of American democracy, it is worth noting that practically absolutely nothing that has simply been examined worrying the Bush-Baker programs reached the general public, apart from the dissident margins, where a record of the ongoing events was readily available to a tiny portion of the population.

Bush administration aid to Saddam Hussein continued until the day of his intrusion of Kuwait in August 1990. At that point, policy moved in the way currently discussed, as the administration seized the opportunity to establish much more firmly U.S. control of the oil-producing areas by a force program.

The war's consequences offered both a chance and a need to rejuvenate the "peace process." The requirement arose from the Gulf's sordid spectacle: huge damage and casualties, the human rights disaster intensifying under the effect of sanctions; the Gulf tyrannies secured from democratic pressures; Saddam Hussein securely in power, having demolished popular rebellions with indirect U.S. support. All in all, hardly a scene that might be left in public memory, especially after the craze of jingoist hysteria and wonder for the Grand Leader that had been worked up by the doctrinal organizations.

The chance emerged from the international context. At last, Europe had completely conceded the Middle East to the United States; Europeans would henceforth avoid independent initiatives, restricting themselves to implementation of U.S. rejectionist teaching, as Norway certainly did in 1993. The Soviet Union was gone, its remnants now faithful customers of Washington. The UN had ended up being virtually a U.S. company. Whatever space the superpower dispute used for independent nonalignment was gone, and the catastrophe of commercialism that swept the standard colonial domains of the West in the 1980s left the Third World mired in general misery, disciplined by forces of the Western-managed "market." With Arab nationalism dealt yet another squashing blow by Saddam's aggression and terror and PLO techniques of more than the normal ineptitude, the Arab rulers had less require than before to react to popular pressures with pro-Palestinian gestures. The United States was, for that reason, in an excellent position to advance its rejectionist program without interference, moving towards the option laid out by James Baker well before the Gulf crisis while satisfying the fundamental conditions stressed by Henry Kissinger years previously, now change by changed conditions. Europe, having deserted any independent function, was less of a threat. Russia could now be welcomed rather than history's "Greatest Prize" excluded, loyal, and powerless. The PLO approached the same status, for similar reasons, by mid-1993.

The "peace process" was restored with terrific excitement at Madrid in the fall of 1991. The "exceptional tableau" in Madrid exposed "that a very good deal had changed," Times diplomatic correspondent R. W. Apple observed, as "George Bush and the United States today plucked the fruits of victory in the Persian Gulf war." The reason Bush might now "dream such great dreams" about Middle East peace, Apple discussed, is that his "vision of the future" can be implemented without any fear that "regional tensions" may cause superpower confrontation, and "no longer should the United States contend with countries whose cantankerousness was reinforced by Moscow's interest in continuing discontent"-- the basic referral to Soviet adherence to the worldwide consensus that the United States declines, in magnificent isolation.

U.S. diplomats naturally agreed. As the Madrid negotiations opened, Alfred Leroy Atherton, in charge of Near East affairs in the State Department under Ford and Carter and a participant in the Camp David settlements, observed that "no significant Arab-Israeli arrangement, a minimum of since 1967, has actually been reached without an active U.S. function, and this need still exists." Now, he continued, "the U.S. task will certainly be much easier in the absence of a Soviet spoiling role." That an active U.S. function has been essential is correct. Simply as in the Caribbean affairs, absolutely nothing else is allowed by the ruling superpower; that, after all, is the standard significance of the Monroe Doctrine, understood for Latin America in 1945 and reached the Middle East. It is also true that the previous Soviet Union had played a "spoiling function," signing up with the rest of the world (consisting of Europe) in challenging U.S. rejectionist styles.

Experts found "fantastic inspiration" in Bush's statement that "the time has come to put an end to the Arab-Israeli dispute," words "talked with commitment by an American president at the height of his powers" and forming part of his "broad vision of Middle East peace-building" (Helena Cobban). Even critics were impressed. Anthony Lewis composed that the president is "at the height of his powers" and "has made very clear that he wishes to breathe light into that theoretical creature, the Middle East peace process." The reasons that the animal remained theoretical are unarticulated, unthinkable. Palestinian Middle East scholar WalidKijalidi, an adviser to the Jordanian-Palestinian delegation, hailed "the personal dedication of the U.S. president to a simple and extensive settlement." In the occupied territories, educated Palestinians reported, there were fantastic expectations and hope.

Something else that "had altered," the press exulted, was "the birth of a brand-new pragmatism among the Palestinians," now raised "another important notch" through Baker's benign influence at Madrid (Thomas Friedman). Until Madrid, Friedman continued, "both sides have hidden behind the argument that there is nobody on the other side with whom to work out" the official variation of the fact that the PLO called on Israel to negotiate; however, the United States and Israel refused. The Palestinian delegation at Madrid called "clearly for a two-state service," Friedman wrote admiringly, so different from the abhorred PLO, which supported (or maybe "prepared") the Security Council resolution calling for a two-state solution fifteen years earlier. Madrid's excellent accomplishment was "the Palestinian self-adjustment to the real-life," Palestinian acceptance of "a duration of autonomy under continued Israeli supremacy," throughout which Israel can build the realities of its irreversible dominance with U.S. help, as it proceeded to do after Madrid. This determination to follow U.S. orders-- the real world-- has "tossed the negative stereotypes out the window," Times reporter Clyde Haberman observed approvingly. With their "brand-new pragmatism."

Palestinians are at last prepared "to talk with Israel, to set aside all-or-nothing needs, to accept half a loaf in the kind of interim self-rule under Israeli dominance." The Madrid conference was organized under unilateral U.S. management, an obsequious

Russian partner providing a fig-leaf of internationalism. The Palestinian delegation, after passing U.S.-Israeli tests of legitimacy, was informed by James Baker that the negotiations would be based exclusively on UN 242, which uses absolutely nothing to the Palestinians: "Anything else, the president kept in mind, would fail the twin tests of fairness and security." The adjustments in the global agreement through the 1970s, as reflected in the vetoed Security Council resolutions and other obstructed initiatives, were completely off the program. However, Baker did unwind the need in his December 1989 five-point plan that Palestinians should strictly keep the technical information of Israel's program for integration of the territories.

As was fairly clear from the outset, the objective of the most current stage of the "peace process" has been to develop a peace settlement among the states of the region, with Palestinian national rights left out. The best result from Washington's perspective would be a settlement that entrenches the conventional strategic conception and offers it a public type, raising implied understandings to an official treaty. Well and good if some version of regional autonomy can remove the Palestinian concern. Meanwhile, security arrangements amongst Israel, Turkey, Egypt, and the United States can be extended, perhaps bringing others in to accept the customer role. There need be no more concern over independent European or Third

World efforts, or Soviet support for attempts within the region to hinder such styles.

While the settlements were continuing without problem, Israel stepped up the harsh repression in the areas, following the believing detailed by then-Defense Minister Yitzhak Rabin in February 1989. These U.S.-Israeli measures achieved much success, extended with Rabin's "closure" of the areas, which administered a crushing blow to the staggering Palestinian economy and also took an essential step towards the meant "canonization" by effectively barring West Bank Palestinians from their organizations (health centers, etc.) in East Jerusalem, and avoiding travel from the northern to the southern part of the West Bank, considering that the main roadway connections pass through East Jerusalem.

The current circumstance is evaluated plausibly, in my opinion, by General (res.) Shlomo Gazit, previously head of Israeli military intelligence, a senior authorities of the military administration of the occupied territories, and a leading individual in the secret meetings that developed the Oslo Agreement's security arrangements. With the collapse of the Soviet Union, he composed, Israel's primary job has not altered at all, and it stays of essential value. Its area at the center of the Arab Muslim Middle East Moira is Israel to be a dedicated guardian of stability in all the nations surrounding it. It's [role] is to safeguard the existing routines: to prevent or stop the processes of radicalization and block the expansion of fundamentalist spiritual zealotry or any other form of "radical nationalism" that comes along. In this job, it is to be joined by U.S. allies, maybe more freely than in the past. These are generally the conclusions that had been articulated by American coordinators thirty-five years earlier. What has changed is that they no longer have to contend with a possible "ruining function" of outsiders who may assist in indigenous efforts to cause modifications undesirable to the rulers.

Subsequent shifts in U.S. policy add trustworthiness to Gazit's assessment.

Israeli analysts rapidly recognized the Clinton administration to be much more severe in the rejection of Palestinian rights than Israel's government. Political reporter AmnonBarzilai observed that the new Clinton administration's proposals to Israel and the Palestinians broke brand-new ground in rejectionism. For the very first time, they specified that "all the alternatives will be left open," consisting of even "the demand for full addition of the territories" under "Israeli sovereignty." In this regard, he notes, Clinton went well beyond the governing Labor Party, "which never demanded that all the choices be kept open," only "territorial compromise." The U.S. effort will, for that reason, "strengthen the suspicion amongst the Palestinians that there is a factor to fear an Israeli conspiracy with American assistance," he writes; though in truth, neither the United States nor the

Israeli political blocs would consider the addition of the territories, for reasons already pointed out.

Reporting from Washington, Ron Ben-Yishai established the point further. He described the Clinton administration's new Middle East policy as "innovative," "a various diplomatic position from those of preceding Administrations," and one that is "entirely positive" from Israel's perspective. Senior U.S. government officials have made it clear that Arabs "will not be able to get concessions from Israel through American pressure, diplomatic or financial." Similarly, Ben-Yishai continued, security relations were boosted, consisting of arrangements kept secret. "Never have we had such great relations with an American administration," a senior Israeli authorities observed. According to Washington, thinking, the disappearance of the Soviet Union, removing any alternative choices for the Arab states, is one of numerous factors leading American policy in this instructions. Clinton experts "see the [increased] support for Israel as part of a much broader international conception that includes a brand-new view of the Middle East in the era after the Cold War and the Gulf war," now that U.S. dominance of the region is more firmly established than before. The new technique to "Israel and its next-door neighbors," "the western part of the region," is matched by the new technique to "the eastern part": the policy of "dual containment" intended at both Iraq and Iran, formerly played one versus the other. "It is necessary to stress that there is no political leader in Israel, and likewise not in Riyadh or Kuwait, who would take any exception to this global conception."

The same may be true of Cairo and other capitals, which have reasons to pin the blame on malign outsiders (Iran, Sudan, and others) for violence and disturbance that lead to large measures from their own social and financial policies.

Ben-Yishai pointed out the significance of Clinton's appointments for the Middle East, notably his choice as chief Middle East adviser and "one of the peace team's main figures, Martin Indyk, up until [January 1993] the head of the Washington Institute for Near East Policy." Before Clinton's inauguration, "Indyk and the deputy director of the Institute, Robert Satloff, had presented to Clinton's transition group a policy memorandum on a brand-new Middle East policy," now being implemented under Indyk's instructions. Indyk, an Australian who was approved citizenship a couple of days before his visit, was a worker of the Israeli lobby (AIPAC), mainly representing the policy spectrum's hawkish right-wing. Indyk left AIPAC to found the Institute to counter the impact of Washington think tanks that the lobby considered pro-Arab and anti-Israel. Some even have recommended that the United States consider joining the international agreement on a peaceful diplomatic settlement. The Institute has played an interesting function in American cultural life. It makes it possible for press reporters to present U.S.-Israeli propaganda while maintaining their fabled neutrality, "merely reporting the realities" while citing some "professional" offered by the Institute to provide the opinions they want propagate.

Clinton policies conformed to the picture presented by Israeli experts. Among the administration's very first jobs was to deal with the embarrassment brought on by Israel's deportation of four hundred Palestinians in December 1992. The deportees were accused of responsibility for "terrorist acts," particularly attacks versus the inhabiting Israeli army that can not be called "terrorist," as acknowledged in the Israeli press. Danny Rubinstein observed that about half the declared "Hamas activists" operated in Islamic spiritual organizations, including preachers, instructors, "a huge number of youths who function as missionaries for increasing religious practice," and specialists who "assisted establish the Islamic motion's network of academic and well-being organizations that includes clinics, kindergartens, kitchens for the clingy, and companies providing aid to detainees' households, orphans, and invalids." "Members of the military wing of Hamas and the Islamic Jihad organization are not among those deported," he included. The analysis was verified in a study by Middle East Watch, which found that half the deportees were imams, spiritual scholars, or shari'a (Islamic law) judges, consisting of the head of the

Palestine Religious Scholars Association, an imam at Al-Aqsa Mosque. In contrast, others are university teachers, medical professionals (sixteen on the UNRWA personnel), school teachers, entrepreneurs, students, and manual employees. Courts had actually convicted four, and eight others had been in administrative detention (imprisoning without charge or trial). A "significant percentage of the deportees had never been convicted of offenses," something of an understatement. Middle East Watch described conditions in the "snake-pit" where they had been transferred in Lebanon as harmful and disgraceful, and when again hired Israel to end this "serious breach of the Fourth Geneva Convention." Israeli intelligence concurred with these evaluations. Ha'aretz priced estimate a "senior government official" who stated that the intelligence services (Shabak) provided Prime Minister Yitzhak Rabin with six names of Hamas activists, including one more when they were asked "to increase the number." Israeli intelligence was "astonished" to discover that more than four hundred had been expelled-- with no appropriate intelligence info.

The American press had no usage for any of this, choosing the New York Times' variation by Israeli Arabist Ehud Yaari, a partner of Indyk's Washington Institute. According to Yaari, who ignores the intelligence reports and other Israeli sources, "About 300 of the 413 deportees made up Hamas's command network in the West Bank and Gaza Strip." His account makes some sense on the assumptions expressed by Cabinet Legal Advisor Yosef Harish, arguing for the expulsion before Israel's High Court: asked the number of homeowners of the occupied areas are members of terrorist organizations, he responded, "I think all of them."

The Security Council passed a resolution demanding that the deportees be returned forthwith. Israel declined, stating that it would permit them to return as it chose. The Clinton administration then determined that Israel was honoring the Security Council resolution by flagrantly breaching it. The problem was stated closed, and without delay, disappeared from press protection, which returned to the "peace procedure." The Washington Institute's much-quoted professional Robert Satloff discussed that Palestinians need to be heartened by the administration's decision to back Israel's defiance of the UN: "It's to the Palestinians' negotiating benefit that the U.S. and the Israelis have the relationship they have now."

While not as revolutionary as Ben-Yishai indicates, the policy modifications are instructional and fascinating nonetheless. The conventional tactical conceptions and objectives are not being abandoned with the Soviet Union; rather, as General Gazit observed, they are being pursued more vigorously, the deterrent having disappeared and the Third World becoming much more unprotected for this and other reasons. The pattern is exactly what we have seen somewhere else in the world. It is significantly irregular with years of propaganda about the Cold War, but quite in accord with both preparation and history with the basic thinking that has supported the policy. The method events have unfolded.

Conclusion

Even skeptics and debunkers need to admit that often no matter how "crazy" the so-called "conspiracy theories" sound, there are undeniable facts at their structure. It's a full-time task to separate the fiction's realities when discussing conspiracy theories or the Illuminati given that there is so much disinformation, false information, half-truths, and hoaxes out there. I hope this book has helped you in your Pursuit understand the fact and revealed strong, verifiable details that have helped you increase your knowledge.

For over the years, I've been tirelessly investigating this topic and thoroughly putting together the puzzle pieces to develop an accurate picture of this huge secret.

Elitism has continuously been the dark side of illuminism; the innovative vanguard that seizes control since it knows what's great for individuals, the philosopher-king who knows the reality, the technocrat who knows how to run wars and societies, all try to hoard the light at the top of the pyramid. Factor, which can be used to rescue man from churches and kings, can likewise be used to enslave him with dogmas of its own. Knowledge is power that can be abused."

Elitists and Big Government New World Order promoters desire individuals to believe that rights originated from the government instead of God. The United States Declaration of Independence says, "Our Creator endows all men with particular unalienable rights," which suggests our rights can't be eliminated and are irreversible from the moment we are born. No society can vote to stop them; no government can offer you cash in exchange for approving them; they are fundamental, irreversible, and unchangeable. The State (the government) is God in the New World Order, so most bureaucrats and the mainstream media portray presidents as contemporary day. The Illuminati desire the government to be the supreme authority, not God. They desire your loyalty to be to them, not to your family, community, or spiritual belief. The law is thought about the Gospel. The government is your protector, instructor, and service provider.

Because of the 24-hour cable news and satellite networks, the Internet, and social media, numerous individuals are inclined to think that we can Quickly resolve all the world's issues because we are instantly informed about them; however, this info age appears to be a double-edged sword. On one level, this innovation notifies us about significant events or issues, but at the same time, it usually prevents people from acting to solve them. The term narcotizing dysfunction describes the theory that because modern-day media, when people are notified about a particular problem, they replace working to fix it, for just understanding it.

Cultural Marxism creates an unnoticeable pressure that prevents many people from breaking away from the crowd and keeps almost everybody following the herd and subscribing to society's norms and is scared to question the deeply ingrained patterns of their peers.

Many individuals who criticize "conspiracy theorists" claim that all of us have a "confirmation bias," which is the tendency for individuals to prefer info that supports their existing worldview or hypothesis, which in most cases is an accurate evaluation of conspiracy theorists. However, this isn't the case for me. For numerous years after the 9/11 attacks on the World Trade Center, I believed the official account of what occurred. I thought the conspiracy theory about Iraq having weapons of mass damage was prepared to use against us anytime.

We know that searching for the fact is unpleasant and challenging, not to discuss time-consuming; most people never even begin on the journey. Instead they turn their mind, body, and soul over to the mesmerizing traditional media or celebrity news or sports home entertainment, so I praise you on your decision to be different and for taking the roadway less taken a trip. I hope I've been able to supply you a few of the responses you've been seeking since I too have a burning desire to know the fact, and we are on the same course.

In this book, we've covered a variety of evidence, ranging from the Illuminati's original works, to how they were discovered, what their strategies are, and tracking them to their Skull & Bones, Bohemian Grove, and the Bilderberg Group offspring.

We've seen some obscure expert discoveries, checked out their approaches, signs, and more, which, when thoroughly assembled, an indisputable image proving the Illuminati is still alive.

CPSIA information can be obtained
at www.ICGtesting.com
Printed in the USA
LVHW020323230121
677173LV00001B/15

9 781801 254519